DATE DUE

TAKING SIDES

Clashing Views
on Controversial Issues
in American History
Volume I
The Colonial Period to Reconstruction

third edition

Edited, Selected, and with Introductions by

Larry Madaras
Howard Community College

James M. SoRelle
Baylor University

The Dushkin Publishing Group, Inc.

*To Eugene Kuzirian (1939–1987),
coeditor of the first two editions of*
Taking Sides: Clashing Views on
Controversial Issues in American
History, *whose devotion to good
teaching and critical thinking still
permeates this text*

Taking Sides ® is a registered trademark of
The Dushkin Publishing Group, Inc.

Library of Congress Catalog Card Number:
88-51456
Manufactured in the United States of America
Third Edition, Fourth Printing
ISBN: 0-87967-761-9

PREFACE

The success of the past two editions of *Taking Sides: Clashing Views on Controversial Issues in American History* has encouraged us to remain faithful to its original objectives, methods, and format. Our aim has been to create an effective instrument to enhance classroom learning and to foster critical thinking. Historical facts presented in a vacuum are of little value to the educational process. For students, whose search for historical truth has probably concentrated on *when* something happened rather than on *why*, and on specific events rather than on the *significance* of those events, *Taking Sides* is designed to offer an interesting and valuable departure. The understanding that the reader arrives at based on the evidence that emerges from the clash of views encourages the reader to view history as an *interpretive* discipline, not one of rote memorization.

As in previous editions, the issues are arranged in chronological order and can be easily incorporated into any American history survey course. Each issue has an issue *introduction*, which sets the stage for the debate that follows in the pro and con selections and provides historical and methodological background to the problem that the issue examines. Each issue concludes with a *postscript*, which ties the readings together, briefly mentions alternative interpretations, and supplies detailed *suggestions for further reading* for the student who wishes to pursue the topics raised in the issue.

Changes to this edition In this edition we have made an earnest effort to move beyond the traditionally ethnocentric and male-oriented focus of American history, both in terms of the issues and the authors selected to represent the clashing viewpoints. This edition depicts a society that benefited from the presence of Native Americans, African-Americans, and women of various racial and ethnic origins. Eight of the seventeen issues and twenty-two of the thirty-four historical essays are new to this edition and represent some of the most recent interpretive trends. Moreover, the introductions and postscripts for those issues which were retained from the previous edition have been revised to include important recent works in the relevant fields of historical inquiry. Part 1 (From Settlement to Revolution) has been revised significantly to present questions framed by the new social historians, whose investigations over the past twenty years have illuminated our understanding of the colonial era, especially the seventeenth century.

Supplements An Instructor's Manual with Test Questions (multiple-choice and essay) is available through the publisher for the instructor using *Taking Sides* in the classroom. And a general guidebook, which discusses methods and techniques for integrating the pro-con approach into any classroom setting, is also available.

i

Acknowledgments Many individuals have contributed to the successful completion of this edition. We appreciate the evaluations submitted to the Dushkin Publishing Group by those who have used *Taking Sides* in the classroom. In many instances their suggestions have been incorporated into this volume. We particularly are indebted to Maggie Cullen, Cindy SoRelle, Barry A. Crouch, Virginia Kirk, Helen Mitchell, and Jean Soto, who shared their ideas for changes, pointed us toward potentially useful historical works, and provided significant editorial assistance. Jeffrey Fultz, a student research assistant in the Baylor University Department of History, kept in shape by making frequent trips to the library to track down bibliographic citations. Finally, Lynnette Geary (Baylor University) and Marsha Madigan (Howard Community College) performed the indispensable typing duties connected with this project.

James M. SoRelle
Baylor University

Larry Madaras
Howard Community College

CONTENTS IN BRIEF

CONTENTS

Nash argues that colonial American culture developed from a convergence of three broad cultural traditions—European, Native American, and African—which produced a unique tri-racial society in the New World. Hayes views American society as a New World extension of the traditions of European or Western culture.

Vaughan presents the Native American as a victim of color symbolism, racial differences, and nonconformity to European cultural traditions. Johnson chronicles cooperative relations between settlers and natives in the New World.

Carr and Walsh identify several factors that coalesced in the seventeenth century to afford women in Maryland a higher status with fewer restraints on their social conduct than those experienced by women in England. Koehler contends that the division of labor that separated work into male and female spheres and Puritan attitudes towards rights of inheritance severely limited opportunities for upward mobility among New England women.

Kulikoff claims that Chesapeake slaves developed their own social institutions and a distinct indigenous culture in the half century between 1740 and 1790. Lee emphasizes the difficult and often unsuccessful efforts of slaves to create and maintain a stable family and community life in eighteenth-century Maryland.

McLoughlin claims that the Great Awakening, by promoting religious revitalization, intercolonial unity, and democracy, paved the way for the American Revolution. Butler challenges the validity of the term "the Great Awakening" and argues that a link between the eighteenth-century colonial religious revivals and the American Revolution was virtually nonexistent.

Historian Richard F. Morris argues that the American Revolution was both a
war of decolonization and a movement of wide-ranging political, social, and
economic changes. Pulitzer Prize-winning author Carl N. Degler believes
that, because of its unique conservative attempt to maintain the "status quo,"
the American Revolution is meaningless as a model for Third World nations
to imitate.

Political scientist Michael Parenti argues that the Constitution was framed by
financially successful planters, merchants, and creditors in order to protect
the rights of property ahead of the rights and liberties of persons. Well-
known essayist and historian Henry Steele Commager maintains the Constitution was essentially a political document designed to solve the problem of
the distribution of power between the national government *and* the state and
local governments.

Pulitzer Prize-winning historian Hofstadter argues that Thomas Jefferson
was a moderate, practical politician who followed a course of action which
eventually co-opted the major policies of the Federalists. Professor Forrest
McDonald believes that President Jefferson attempted to replace Hamiltonian Federalist principles with a Republican ideology and wanted to restore
America's agrarian heritage.

Woloch describes the exercise of autonomy and authority in the domestic life
of middle-class wives. Lerner considers a spectrum of women's roles, emphasizing the subservient position of female industrial workers.

war from which she never recovered. Diplomatic historian Robert Ferrell, however, believes that although the American government waged an aggressive war in Mexico, it remained the manifest destiny of the United States to possess Texas, New Mexico, and California.

Stampp contends that the master's absolute power prevented slaves from establishing and maintaining stable family units. Owens recognizes the threats to family stability among slaves but emphasizes the relentless efforts of fathers, mothers, and children to achieve family unity within the slave quarters.

Craven believes that the fanaticism of the abolitionist crusade created an atmosphere of crisis that resulted in the outbreak of the Civil War. Bartlett differentiates between agitation and fanaticism and claims that abolitionists like Wendell Phillips were deeply committed to improving the quality of life for all Americans, including those blacks held as slaves.

Marxist historian Eugene D. Genovese believes "that slavery gave the South a social system and a civilization with a distinct class structure, political community, economy, ideology, and set of psychological patterns." Social historian Edward Pessen argues that a comparison of Northern and Southern states in the three decades before the Civil War reveals common political, economic, and social practices.

Oates insists that Abraham Lincoln's greatness as president of the United States stemmed from a moral vision that had as its goal the protection and expansion of popular government. Bradford characterizes Lincoln as a cynical politician whose abuse of authority as president and commander-in-chief during the Civil War marked a serious departure from the republican goals of the Founding Fathers and established the prototype for the "imperial presidency" of the twentieth century.

Randall argues that Reconstruction failed because carpetbaggers and their "Negro" allies misgoverned the South and looted its treasuries. Foner believes that, although Reconstruction was nonrevolutionary and conservative, it was a splendid failure because it offered blacks a temporary vision of a free society.

INTRODUCTION

The Study of History
James M. SoRelle
Larry Madaras

In a pluralistic society such as ours, the study of history is bound to be a complex process. How an event is interpreted depends not only on the existing evidence but also on the perspective of the interpretor. Consequently, understanding history presupposes the evaluation of information, a task that often leads to conflicting conclusions. An understanding of history, then, requires the acceptance of the idea of historical relativism. Relativism means that redefinition of our past is always possible and desirable. History shifts, changes, and grows with new and different evidence and interpretations. As is the case with the law and even medicine, beliefs that were unquestioned a hundred or two hundred years ago have been discredited or discarded since.

Relativism, then, encourages revisionism. There is a maxim that "the past must remain useful to the present." Historian Carl Becker argued that every generation should examine history for itself, thus assuring constant scrutiny of our collective experience through the lens of new perspective. History, consequently, does not remain static, in part because historians cannot avoid being influenced by the times in which they live. Almost all historians commit themselves to revising the views of other historians, synthesizing theories into macro-interpretations, or revising the revisionists.

SCHOOLS OF THOUGHT

Four predominant schools of thought have emerged in American history since the first graduate seminars in history were given at The Johns Hopkins University in Baltimore in the 1870s. The *progressive* school dominated the professional field in the first half of the twentieth century. Influenced by the reform currents of Populism, Progressivism, and the New Deal, these historians explored the social and economic forces that energized America. The progressive scholars tended to view the past in terms of conflicts between groups, and they sympathized with the underdog.

The post–World War II period witnessed the emergence of a new group of historians who viewed the conflict thesis as overly simplistic. Writing against the backdrop of the Cold War, these *neo-conservative* or *consensus* historians argued that Americans possess a shared set of values and that the ares of agreement within our nation's basic democratic and capitalistic framework were more important than the areas of disagreement.

In the 1960s, however, the civil rights movement, women's liberation, and the student rebellion (with its condemnation of the war in Vietnam) fragmented the consensus of values upon which historians and social scientists of the 1950s had centered their interpretations. This turmoil set the stage for the emergence of another group of scholars. *New left* historians began to reinterpret the past once again. They emphasized the significance of conflict in American history and they resurrected interest in those groups ignored by the consensus school. In addition, new left scholars critiqued the expansionist policies of the United States and emphasized the difficulties confronted by Native Americans, blacks, women, and urban workers in gaining full citizenship status.

Progressive, consensus, and new left history is still being written. The most recent generation of scholars, however, has focused upon social history. Their primary concern is to discover what the lives of "ordinary Americans" were really like. These new social historians have employed previously overlooked court and church documents, house deeds and tax records, letters and diaries, photographs, and census data to reconstruct the everyday lives of average Americans. Some have employed new methodologies such as quantification (enhanced by advancing computer technology) and oral history, while others have borrowed from the disciplines of political science, economics, sociology, anthropology, and psychology for their historical investigations.

The proliferation of historical approaches, which are reflected in the issues debated in this book, has had mixed results. On the one hand, historians have become so specialized in their respective time periods and methodological styles that it is difficult to synthesize the recent scholarship into a comprehensive text for the general reader. On the other hand, historians know more about the American past than at any other time in our history. They have dared to ask new questions or ones which previously were considered to be germane only to scholars in other social sciences. Although there is little agreement about the answers to these questions, the methods employed and intriguing issues explored make the "new history" a very exciting field to study.

The topics that follow represent a variety of perspectives and approaches. Each of these controversial issues can be studied for its individual importance to our nation's history. Taken as a group, they interact with one another to illustrate larger historical themes. The issues, when grouped thematically, reveal continuing motifs in the development of American history.

NEW SOCIAL HISTORY: RED, WHITE, AND BLACK

Some of the most innovative historical research over the last twenty years has dealt with the colonial period (1607–1763) and reflects the interests of the new social historians. The work of several representatives of this group appear in this volume. For example, in Issue 1, Gary Nash sets the tone for the readings on early America when he suggests that colonial society must be studied from the perspective of the cultural convergence of three broad groups in North America—Native Americans, Europeans, and African-Americans. He takes issue with the European-centered focus of Carlton J. H. Hayes, who insisted that American culture belongs within the pattern of Western civilization stretching back to the ancient Greeks.

Issue 2 discusses the nature of the early conflicts between Native Americans and European colonizers. Alden T. Vaughan relies on the concept of historical change to explain how Europeans initially thought Native Americans were Caucasians like themselves but later assigned American Indians to an inferior racial status as "redskins." Richard R. Johnson, on the other hand, concludes that Indians were active participants, not passive victims, of colonial policy.

Issues 3 and 9 cover the field of women's history. One question frequently asked is whether or not the colonial period was a "golden age" for women in America. Lois Green Carr and Lorena S. Walsh argue that "the four characteristics of the seventeenth-century population—immigrant predominance, early death, late marriage and sexual imbalance" gave women in early Maryland power in the household which English women did not enjoy. Yet Lyle Koehler finds that members of the "weaker sex" in seventeenth-century New England were similar in status to their English counterparts and did not possess legal or political rights or control the affairs within the household.

Issue 9 explores a similar question for a later time period. In the early nineteenth century, society became more settled and the family's role was defined more clearly. The home took on a new significance, and women were in charge of preserving the moral climate of the family. Nancy Woloch believes that acceptance of the "cult of motherhood" enabled women to achieve greater power in the new nation. But the well-known feminist scholar Gerda Lerner challenges this interpretation.

Within the past three decades our perception of blacks in American history has changed drastically. More consideration has been given to African-Americans as active participants in American history, not simply as "victims" or "problems." In Issue 4, Allan Kulikoff concludes from his analysis of probate inventories, runaway advertisements, court depositions, and several diaries and account books kept by whites that slaves in late eighteenth-century Maryland and Virginia had begun to develop a distinct Afro-American culture. Jean Butenhoff Lee, however, thinks that Kulikoff overstates his case.

Issue 13 deals with a similar question in the context of the nineteenth century. Most scholars have offered generalizations about slavery based on an examination of the records of large plantation owners in the antebellum Deep South. Several have considered the impact of the slave system on black community institutions, such as the family. Did slavery destroy the black family? In one of the first revisionist treatments of slavery, Kenneth Stampp contended that the master's absolute power prevented slaves from establishing and maintaining stable family units. Leslie Howard Owens, however, disagrees. He recognizes the threat to family stability among slaves but emphasizes the relentless efforts of fathers, mothers, and children to achieve family unity within the slave quarters.

RELIGION, REVOLUTION, REFORM, RECONSTRUCTION

Beyond suggesting that much of the colonizing experiment in British North America was motivated by a search for religious freedom, many textbooks avoid extended discussions of religion as a force in history. In the last half century, however, professional historians have assumed that the religious revivals in the middle of the eighteenth century, known as the "Great Awakening," played a major role in the political and social evolution of colonial society. In Issue 5 the well-known religious historian William G. McLaughlin argues that the criticism of mainstream theology that many laymen and clergy made during the Great Awakening set the stage for later challenges to British political authority. Historian Jon Butler disputes the interpretation of McLaughlin and others who view the Great Awakening as the first "intercolonial movement." In fact, Butler denies that any great unified revival movement existed in the eighteenth century.

During the 1830s and 1840s, a wave of reformism swept across America. Various individuals and groups sought to strengthen the democratic experiment in the United States by ridding the society of its imperfections. There were health faddists and spiritualists, as well as advocates for peace, temperance, public education, special education for the deaf and blind, and communal living experiments. Issue 11 explores the motivations behind these antebellum reforms. In *Freedom's Ferment*, the classic treatment of this subject, Alice Felt Tyler insisted that humanitarian goals underlay antebellum reform impulses. Recent students of the antebellum reformers, however, offer a different explanation for this group's actions. Michael Katz has argued that public policy made no provision for the periodic unemployment which emerged under industrial capitalism in the early nineteenth century. By the 1850s, institutions such as schools, prisons, and hospitals for the mentally ill were established to control the behavior of the nation's citizens. Writing from a new left perspective, Katz sees the emerging poorhouses as an attempt by a middle- and upper-class elite to control the social behavior of the masses.

The major and most controversial reform effort in the pre-Civil War period was the movement to abolish slavery. Issue 14 also deals with the complexities of motivation. Avery Craven, a well-known Southern historian, believed that the Civil War had been caused unnecessarily by extremists in both the North and the South. In particular, Craven denounced the abolitionists as irresponsible fanatics who filled their propagandistic literature and speeches with lies about lazy, aristocratic plantation owners who constantly brutalized their slaves. By the early 1960s, the brutalities accorded civil rights workers in the South made Craven's pro-Southern interpretation of abolitionism unacceptable to most historians. Irving Bartlett reflected a new approach to abolitionists in his sympathetic portrayal of Wendell Phillips.

The debate over slavery worked to isolate the South from the rest of the nation, but just how different was Dixie? Issue 15 poses the question: Was the Antebellum South a Unique Section in American History? Marxist historian Eugene Genovese believes "that slavery gave the South a social system and a civilization with a distinct class structure, political community, economy, ideology, and set of psychological patterns." A more recent analysis by social historian Edward Pessen takes issue with Genovese. Summarizing much of the recent scholarship on the antebellum social and economic structure in the North and South, Pessen finds more similarities than differences between the two sections.

Perhaps no period of American history has been subjected to more myths than the Reconstruction era. It has been only within the past twenty-five years that the older, pro-Southern interpretation has been revised in high school and college texts. In Issue 17, the late James G. Randall, a noted biographer of Lincoln, presents the traditional treatment of the Reconstruction "debacle." Reconstruction failed, according to Randall, because the carpetbagger-"Negro" coalition of radical Republicans mismanaged the Southern state governments and looted their treasuries. This view began to change during the 1960s when, in the midst of the civil rights struggle, scholars significantly revised this negative portrayal of Reconstruction. What impressed the revisionists was the fact that Reconstruction brought to the South new, more democratic state constitutions, improved public services, and public education for both white and black children. Professor Eric Foner brilliantly summarizes this "new view." Searching for an interpretation which places the event within the context of an era of tremendous economic change, Foner concedes that Reconstruction was not very radical, much less revolutionary. Reconstruction was, nevertheless, a splendid failure because it offered blacks a vision of what a free society should look like.

POLITICS IN AMERICA

The American people gave legitimacy to their revolution through the establish-ment of a republican form of government. The nation has existed under two constitutions: the first established the short-lived confederation from 1781 to 1789; the second constitution was written in 1787 and remains in effect over two hundred years later. Ever since Charles Beard wrote *An Economic Interpretation of the Constitution of the United States* in 1913, historians have been debating the motivations of the "founding fathers." In Issue 7, Michael Parenti restates Beard's thesis by arguing that the Constitution is an elitist document framed by a group of financially successful planters, merchants, and creditors in order to protect the rights of property over the rights and liberties of persons. The well-known historian and essayist Henry Steele Commager sums up the concerns of most recent scholars who feel that Beard oversimplified the motivations of the drafters. Commager reminds us that the Constitution was essentially a political document designed to solve the problem of distributing power between the local and national governments.

According to the Constitution, an election is held every four years to choose our president. Political scientists have designated those elections which mark a significant change in the distribution of power as "key" or "realigning" elections. In Issue 10, Professor Robert V. Remini argues that the 1828 election both symbolized the people's arrival at political responsibility and began a genuine, nationally organized two-party system that came of age in the 1830s. In contrast, Richard P. McCormick employs a clever statistical analysis of voter participation in state and local, as well as presidential, elections from 1812 through 1840. Based on this analysis, McCormick claims that a genuine political revolution did not take place until the presidential election of 1840.

No discussion of American politics is complete without examining the lives of some of the key presidents. Two of the greatest (and among the most controversial) were Thomas Jefferson and Abraham Lincoln. Issue 8 explores the nature of Jefferson's presidency, Issue 9, Lincoln's.

THE UNITED STATES AND THE WORLD

The question raised in Issue 1 concerns the cultural relationship between America and Europe. As indicated above, Carlton Hayes insists we owe a large debt to Western civilization not only for our values but also for our experiences. Issue 6 reverses this question of cosmopolitanism and unique national identity by asking if the United States could serve as a model for today's emerging nations of the Third World. Richard Morris is convinced that, as the first great revolution of modern times, the American Revolution was both a war of national liberation and a movement of far-ranging political, social, and economic changes. Carl Degler, however, believes the American Revolution was too conservative to have any real meaning for Third World nations today.

A discussion of early nineteenth-century foreign policy in Issue 12 concerns both our diplomatic relations with the rest of the world and our self-perception within the world of nations. Did the United States government conceive of its power as continental, hemispheric, or worldwide? Ramon Eduardo Ruiz argues that the United States waged a racist and imperialistic war against Mexico for the purpose of conquering what became the American Southwest.

CONCLUSION

The process of historical study should rely more on thinking than on memorizing data. Once the basics (who, what, when, where) are determined, historical thinking shifts to a higher gear. Analysis, comparison and contrast, evaluation, and explanation take command. These skills not only increase our knowledge of the past but also they provide general tools for the comprehension of all the topics about which human beings think.

The diversity of a pluralistic society, however, creates some obstacles to comprehending the past. The spectrum of differing opinions on any particular subject eliminates the possibility of quick and easy answers. The variety of thought demands thorough comparison and contrast. In the final analysis, conclusions often are built through a synthesis of several different interpretations, but, even then, they may be partial and tentative.

The study of history in a pluralistic society allows each citizen the opportunity to reach independent conclusions about the past. Since most, if not all, historical issues affect the present and future, understanding the past becomes necessary if society is to progress. Many of today's problems have a direct connection with the past. Additionally, other contemporary issues may lack obvious direct antecedents, but historical investigation can provide illuminating analogies. At first, it may appear confusing to read and to think about opposing historical views. In the end, however, the survival of our democratic society will depend on such critical thinking by acute and discerning minds.

PART 1

From Settlement to Revolution

The settlement of the colonies took place in the context of conditions that were unique to that time and place. The ethnic identity of the colonists affected their relations with Native Americans and with each other and influenced the nature of the institutions that developed. Many of the institutions and ideals that grew out of the colonial experience served the early settlers well and are still emulated today. Others, such as slavery, have left a less positive legacy.

Was Colonial American Culture Unique?

Was Conflict Unavoidable Between Native Americans and Colonists?

Was the Colonial Period a "Golden Age" for Women in America?

Did American Slaves Develop a Distinct Afro-American Culture in the Eighteenth Century?

Was the Great Awakening a Key to the American Revolution?

1

ISSUE 1

Was Colonial American Culture Unique?

YES: Gary B. Nash, from *Race, Class, and Politics: Essays on American Colonial and Revolutionary Society* (University of Illinois Press, 1986)

NO: Carlton J. H. Hayes, from "The American Frontier—Frontier of What?" *American Historical Review* (January 1946)

ISSUE SUMMARY

YES: Nash argues that colonial American culture developed from a convergence of three broad cultural traditions—European, Native American, and African—which produced a unique tri-racial society in the New World.
NO: Hayes views American society as a New World extension of the traditions of European or Western culture.

Michel-Guillaume Jean de Crèvecoeur was a French immigrant who became a naturalized subject of the Colony of New York in 1764. He married an American woman, and the couple settled on a comfortable estate in New York. In 1782, Crèvecoeur published a volume entitled *Letters from an American Farmer* in which he attempted to analyze the culture and national character of his adopted land. In probing the unique quality of the American, Crèvecoeur wrote: "What then is the American, this new man? He is either an European, or the descendent of an European, hence that strange mixture of blood, which you will find in no other country. . . . *He* is an American who, leaving behind him all his ancient prejudices and manners, receives new ones from the new mode of life he has embraced, the new government he obeys, and the new rank he holds. He becomes an American by being received in the broad lap of our great *Alma Mater*. Here individuals of all nations are melted into a new race of men, whose labors and posterity will one day cause great changes in the world." A half century later another Frenchman, the aristocratic Alexis de Tocqueville, explored this uniqueness of America through the twin components of democracy and equality. But it was an American historian, Frederick Jackson Turner, who captured the attention of generations of scholars and students by emphasizing the unique qualities of life in America and by distinguishing that life from Old World culture. For Turnerians, it was the American frontier experience which was most responsible for Crèvecoeur's "new man."

Historians continue to express interest in the nature of American culture as they explore the Old World and New World roots of the American people and the society they created beginning in the seventeenth century. Just how new was that early American culture? How much did it depart from the cultural heritage of those tens of thousands of immigrants who arrived in England's North American colonies prior to the American Revolution? Although modern-day students may be unfamiliar with the writings of Crèvecoeur, Tocqueville, and Turner, it is nevertheless worthwhile to explore the basic components of the American culture that emerged in the colonial period. By understanding the nature of that culture, Americans can better grasp who they are.

For Gary Nash, the main problem in developing a clear picture of colonial American culture has been the tendency of past generations of scholars to operate from a male-dominated and highly ethnocentric framework. It is impossible under these circumstances, where scholars have ignored important segments of the population that played significant roles in colonial social development, to describe that development accurately. Nash's essay makes clear that while white male Europeans were prominent in carving a cultural base for the American people, they were assisted by their female counterparts, as well as Native Americans and Africans, male and female. That culture was unique, he suggests, primarily because it was a tri-racial composite, not one simply transferred intact from Europe.

Carlton J. H. Hayes's essay represents the scholarly point of view criticized by Nash. In his presidential address to the members of the American Historical Association, delivered in the wake of World War II, Hayes reminded his colleagues that Europe and the United States should not be viewed as estranged and alienated lands. With a critical eye focused on the Turner frontier thesis, Hayes scanned the history of early America and concluded that colonial culture developed out of the traditions of Western civilization. Although removed from European shores by several thousand miles of ocean, the American colonies (and, subsequently, the United States), Hayes claimed, were part of a broader Atlantic community by virtue of having embraced most of the same values and traditions of European society.

YES

Gary B. Nash

THE SOCIAL DEVELOPMENT OF COLONIAL AMERICA

The history of social development in colonial America—portrayed in this paper primarily as the history of social relations between groups of people defined by race, gender, and class—is in glorious disarray. Disarray because all of the old paradigms have collapsed under the weight of the last generation of scholarship. Glorious because a spectacular burst of innovative scholarship, the product of those who have crossed disciplinary boundaries, transcended filiopietism, and been inspired in the best sense by the social currents of their own times, has left us with vastly more knowledge of the first century and a half of American history than we ever had before. . . .

So much creative work has been done during the last generation that it may seem that the time has arrived to build new models of social development. Yet this still may be premature because in spite of their many virtues, the innovative studies of the past two decades are so male-centered and oblivious to the black and native American peoples of colonial society that any new synthesis would necessarily be constructed with materials that present a skewed and incomplete picture of the social process in the prerevolutionary period.

If social development is defined as changing social relations between different groups in society, then the foundation of any such study must be rigorous analysis of the structural arrangements that did not strictly govern most human interaction but set the boundaries for it in the preindustrial period, as between masters and slaves, men and women, parents and children, employers and employees. Those relationships, moreover, must be examined within the context of a triracial society. This marks a fundamental difference between social development in England and America or in France and America. Of course other differences existed as well, but perhaps none was so great as that produced by the convergence of three broad cultural groups on the North American coastal plain in the seventeenth and eighteenth centuries. Some of the best work in colonial social history has been unmindful of this, drawing conceptually on European historical studies as if

From *Colonial British America: Essays in the New History of the Early Modern Era*, ed. Jack P. Greene and J. R. Pole (Baltimore/London: The Johns Hopkins University Press, 1984). Reprinted by permission.

the colonies were pure offshoots of English society. . . . We must regard the social development of colonial America as *sui generis* because of the triracial environment in which most colonists lived their lives. This racial intermingling had profound effects on the social formation of the colonies. . . .

NATIVE AMERICANS

Ideally, a discussion of the role of native American societies in the social development of eastern North America should be regionally organized because there was no unified "Indian" experience and the various tribal histories that ethnohistorians have reconstructed are closely related to the histories of European colonizers in particular areas. But space limitations permit only some general remarks about the underdeveloped field of native American history and its connection to the history of the colonizers. It is important to differentiate between coastal and interior tribes: even though disease and warfare thoroughly ravaged the numerous seaboard tribes by the third generation of settlement in every colony, these small societies profoundly affected the shaping of settler communities.

The process of decimation, dispossession, and decline among the Indian societies of the coastal areas occurred in different ways during the first century of European colonization. Everywhere that Europeans settled, a massive depopulation occurred as the invaders' diseases swept through biologically defenseless native societies. Yet this rarely broke the resistance of the native peoples. In New England that occurred only after the stronger coastal tribes, such as the Wampanoags and Narragansetts, finally succumbed in a long war of attrition to an enemy who sought no genuine accommodation. In Virginia and Maryland the tidewater tribes genuinely strove for accommodation following their unsuccessful resistance movements of 1622 and 1644. But, as in New England, their inability to function in any way that served European society finally led to conflict initiated by whites. Even as friendly colonized people they were obstacles in the path of an acquisitive and expanding plantation society. In South Carolina it was not dead Indians but Indians alive and in chains that benefited the white settlers. The build-up of the colonizer population was slow enough, and the desire among the Indians for trade goods intense enough, that the white Carolinians, most of them transplanted from Barbados, where they had learned to trade in human flesh, could lure the coastal tribes into obliterating each other in the wars for slaves.

The result was roughly the same in all the colonies along the seaboard. By the 1680s in the older colonies and by the 1720s in the new ones the coastal tribes were shattered. Devastated by disease and warfare, the survivors either incorporated themselves as subjects of stronger inland groups or entered the white man's world as detribalized servile dependents. Their desire for European trade goods, which kept them in close contact with European colonizers, and the persistence of ancient intertribal hostilities, which thwarted pan-tribal resistance, sealed their fate once the growth of the settler population made it apparent that their value as trading partners was incidental in comparison with the value of the land that their destruction would convert to European possession.

Although they were defeated, the coastal cultures served a crucial function for tribes farther inland. Their prolonged resistance gave interior societies time to adapt to the European presence and to devise strategies of survival as the white societies grew in size and strength. "People like the Iroquois," T.J.C. Brasser has pointed out, "owed a great deal to the resistance of the coastal Algonkians, and both peoples were well aware of this." The coastal tribes provided a buffer between the interior Indians and the Europeans, and when the coastal tribes lost their political autonomy, their remnants were often incorporated into the larger inland tribes. This was important in the much stronger opposition that the Iroquois, Cherokees, and Creeks offered to European encroachment—a resistance so effective that for the first century and a half of European settlement the white newcomers were restricted to the coastal plain, unable to penetrate the Appalachians, where the interior tribes, often allied with the French, held sway.

During the first half of the eighteenth century the interior Indian societies demonstrated their capacity for adapting to the presence of Europeans and for turning economic and political interaction with them to their own advantage. Drawing selectively from European culture, they adopted through the medium of the fur, skin, and slave trade European articles of clothing, weapons, metal implements, and a variety of ornamental objects. To some extent this incorporation of material objects robbed the Indians of their native skills. But agriculture, fishing, and hunting, the mainstays of Indian subsistence before the Europeans came, remained so thereafter. European implements such as the hoe only made Indian agriculture more efficient. The knife and fishhook enabled the natives to fish and trap with greater intensity in order to obtain the commodities needed in the barter system. However, pottery making declined, and the hunter became more dependent upon the gun.

Yet, interaction with European societies over many generations sowed seeds of destruction within tribal villages. It is not necessary to turn Indians into acquisitive capitalists to explain their desire for trade goods. They did not seek guns, cloth, kettles, and fishhooks out of a desire to become part of bourgeois culture, accumulating material wealth from the fur trade, but because they recognized the advantages, within the matrix of their own culture, of goods fashioned by societies with a more complex technology. The utility of the Europeans' trade goods, not the opportunities for profit provided by the fur trade, drew native Americans into it, and from the Indian point of view, trade was carried on within the context of political and social alliance.

Nonetheless, the fur trade required native Americans to reallocate their human resources and reorder their internal economies. Subsistence hunting turned into commercial hunting, and consequently males spent more time away from the villages trapping and hunting. Women were also drawn into the new economic organization of villages, for the beaver, marten, or fox had to be skinned and the skins scraped, dressed, trimmed, and sewn into robes. Among some tribes the trapping, preparation, and transporting of skins became so time-consuming that food resources had to be procured in trade from other tribes. Ironically, the reorientation of tribal economies toward the fur trade dispersed villages and weakened the localized basis of clans and lineages. Breaking up in order to be nearer the widely dispersed trapping grounds, Indian villages moved closer to the nomadic woodland existence that Europeans had charged them with at the beginning of contact.

Involvement in the fur trade also altered the relationship of native Americans to their ecosystem. The tremendous destruction of animal life triggered by the advent of European trade undermined the spiritual framework within which hunting had traditionally been carried out and repudiated the ancient emphasis on living in balance with the natural environment. Trade also broadened vastly the scale of intertribal conflict. With Europeans competing for client tribes who would supply furs to be marketed throughout Europe, Indian societies were sucked into the rivalry of their patrons. As furs became depleted in the hunting grounds of one tribe, they could maintain the European trade connection only by conquering more remote tribes whose hunting grounds had not yet been exhausted or by forcibly intercepting the furs of other tribes as they were transported to trading posts. Thus, the Iroquis decimated the Hurons of the Great Lakes region in the mid-seventeenth century as part of their drive for beaver hegemony.

While the interior tribes were greatly affected by contact with the colonizers, they nonetheless rejected much of what the newcomers presented to them as a superior way of life. Tribes such as the Iroquois, Creeks, and Cherokees were singularly unimpressed with most of the institutions of European life and saw no reason to replace what they valued in their own culture with what they disdained in the culture of others. This ap-plied to the newcomers' political institutions and practices, system of law and justice, religion, education, family organization, and childrearing practices. Many aspects of Indian life were marked by cultural persistency in the long period of interaction with Europeans. Indian societies incorporated what served them well and rejected what made no sense within the framework of their own values and modes of existence.

Despite their maintenance of their traditional culture in many areas of life, the native Americans' involvement in the European trade network hastened the spread of epidemic diseases, raised the level of warfare, depleted ecozones of animal life, and drew Indians into a market economy that over a long period of time constricted their economic freedom. The interior tribes reorganized productive relations within their own communities to serve a trading partner who, through the side effects of trade, became a trading master.

Social development within the British mainland colonies proceeded in some unexpected ways because of the Indian presence. Unable to coordinate themselves militarily and politically in the first 150 years of settlement, English colonizers were unable to conquer or dislodge from their tribal homelands—as did their Spanish counterparts to the south—the powerful interior native American societies. Hence, the settler's societies, restricted to the coastal plain, developed differently than if they had been free to indulge their appetite for land and their westward yearning. Higher mortality rates associated with the spread of epidemic diseases in more densely settled areas, the rise of tenantry in rural areas, underemployment in the cities at the end of the colonial period, the decline of indentured servitude because of the growing pool of landless free laborers, and the rise of class tensions in older seaboard communities are some of the social phenomena that may be attributed in part to the limitations placed upon westward movement by the controlling hand of the major eastern tribes in the trans-Allegheny and even the Piedmont region. The native American was also of primary importance in forging an "American" identity among English, Scotch-Irish, German, and other European immigrants in North America. In their relations with the native people of the land the colonizers in British North American served a long apprenticeship in military affairs. Far more populous than the settlers of New France and therefore much more covetous of Indian land, they engaged in hundreds of military confrontations ranging from localized skirmishes to large-scale regional wars. The allegiance of the diverse immigrants to the land, the annealing of an American as distinct from an English identity, had much to do with the myriad ways in which the colonists interacted with a people who were culturally defined as "the others" but were inextricably a part of the human landscape of North America.

AFRO-AMERICANS

Unless we wish to continue picturing some one million Africans brought to or born in America before the Revolution as mindless and cultureless drones, it will be necessary to push forward recent work on the social development of black society and then to incorporate this new corpus of scholarship into an overall analysis of colonial social development. It bears noting that a large majority of the persons who crossed the Atlantic to take up life in the New World in the three hundred years before the American Revolution were Africans. Their history is still largely untold because so much attention has been paid to the kind of slave systems Europeans fashioned in the New World—the black codes they legislated, their treatment of slaves, the economic development they directed—that the slaves themselves, as active participants in a social process, are often forgotten.

In attempting to remedy this gap, historians have borrowed heavily from the work of anthropologists. The encounter model of Sidney Mintz and Richard Price, developed with reference to the Caribbean world, is especially useful because it explores how Africans who found themselves in the possession of white masters five thousand miles from their homeland created institutions and ways of life that allowed them to live as satisfactorily as possible under the slave regimen imposed upon them by the master class. In their New World encounter with European colonizers the problem was not one of merging a West African culture with a European culture, because the human cargoes aboard slave ships were not a single collective African people but rather a culturally heterogenous people from many tribes and regions. Hence, arriving slaves did not form "communities" of people at the outset but could only become communities through forging a new life out of the fragments of many old cultures combined with elements of the dominant European culture that now bounded their existence. "What the slaves undeniably shared at the outset," according to Mintz and Price, "was their enslavement; all—or nearly all—else had to be created by them."

Major strides have been taken in tracing this process of social adaptation in the Chesapeake region and along the rice coast of South Carolina and Georgia, though much remains to be done. Already, it is apparent that in this process of adaptation there was a premium on cultural innovations and creativity, both because slaves had to adjust rapidly to the power of the master class and because of the initial cultural heterogeneity of the Africans. Unlike the European colonizers, Africans were immediately obliged "to shift their primary cultural and social commitment from the Old World to the New." This required rapid adaptation, learning new ways of doing things that would ensure survival. It is not surprising, therefore, that Africans developed local slave cultures rather than a unified Afro-American culture. In adapting to North American slavery, they adopted "a general openness to ideas and usages from other cultural traditions, a special tolerance (within the West African context) of cultural differences." Of all the people converging in seventeenth- and eighteenth-century North America, the Africans, by the very conditions of their arrival, developed the greatest capacity for cultural change.

The complexity of black culture in America cannot be understood without considering the evolution of distinct, regional black societies as they developed over the long course of slavery. One of the accomplishments of the new social historians of the colonial South is to have broken much new ground on the life cycle, family formation, and cultural characteristics of the black population, which was increasingly creole, or American-born, as the eighteenth century progressed. This work makes it possible already to go beyond earlier studies of slave life in the colonies, which were based largely on studies of nineteenth-century sources, when discussing the development of Afro-American society in the eighteenth-century colonies.

How much of African culture survived under eighteenth-century slavery is an oft-debated question. There can be little doubt that slave masters were intent on obliterating every Africanism that reduced the effectiveness of slaves as laborers and that they had some success in this. It is also true that slavery eliminated many of the cultural differences among slaves, who came from a wide variety of African cultural groups—Fulanis, Ibos, Yorubas, Malagasies, Ashantis, Mandingos, and others. At the same time, it must be remembered that throughout the eighteenth century, unlike the nineteenth, large numbers of new Africans arrived each year. Slave importations grew rapidly in the eighteenth century, so that probably never more than half the adult slaves were American-born. This continuous infusion of African culture kept alive many of the elements that would later be transmuted almost beyond recognition. Through fashioning their own distinct culture within the limits established by the rigors of the slave system, blacks were able to forge their own religious forms, their own music and dance, their own family life, and their own beliefs and values. All of these proved indispensable to survival in a system of forced labor. All were part of the social development of black society. And all affected the social development of white society as well.

WOMEN

One final aspect of social development, occasionally alluded to in this essay but indispensable to the work that lies ahead, concerns social relations defined by gender. In the last ten years, and especially in the last four or five, a wave of new work has appeared, some of it defined as women's history and some as demographic or family history. This work shows how rich the possibilities are for those who wish to study the lives of women and female-male relationships. It is crucial to the construction of new paradigms of social development that these studies of women's productive and reproductive lives, which need to be studied with class, racial, and regional differences in mind, be pushed forward at an accelerated pace and then integrated with the studies of the much better understood male half of the population. It is out of the convergence of the already completed demographic and community studies and the studies of women, blacks, and native Americans still remaining to be done that a new understanding of the social development of colonial America will emerge.

NO

Carlton J. H. Hayes

THE AMERICAN FRONTIER—
FRONTIER OF WHAT?

We used to know that we were Europeans as well as Americans, that we were not Indians or a people miraculously sprung from virgin forests like the primitive Germans described by Tacitus, but modern Europeans living in America on a frontier of Europe. All our original white ancestors on this continent knew they came from Europe. They and their sons and grandsons knew they had ties with Englishmen, Spaniards, Portuguese, Hollanders, or Frenchmen, as the case might be, not only on this side of the ocean but on the other. And generation after generation of their descendants on this side, no matter on what segment of the frontier they chanced to be, and no matter how intent on clearing new lands, were concerned and found themselves participants in all the successive major wars of Europe from the sixteenth century to the twentieth: the English-Spanish wars, the English-Dutch wars, the War of the League of Augsburg, the War of the Spanish Succession, the War of the Austrian Succession, the Seven Years' War, the Revolutionary and Napoleonic Wars, the war of 1914, the war of 1939. From the first, moreover, it has been known or knowable, if latterly obscured, that our language, our religion, our culture are rooted in Europe, that our ideals of liberty and constitutional government are a heritage of Europe.

In paying tribute to the members of the Constitutional Convention of 1787, Charles A. Beard has remarked:

> It is not merely patriotic pride that compels one to assert that never in the history of assemblies has there been a convention of men richer in political experience and in practical knowledge, or endowed with a profounder insight into the springs of human action and the intimate essence of government. It is indeed an astounding fact that at one time so many men skilled in statecraft could be found on the very frontiers of civilization among a population numbering about four million whites.

It is not quite so astounding, I would add, if one bears in mind that those men "on the very frontiers of civilization" possessed lively contacts with, and solid knowledge of, the European civilization on whose frontiers they were.

From the *American Historical Review* 51 (January 1946). Reprinted by permission.

One has only to run through the numbers of the *Federalist* to recognize the sure and firm grasp of such men as Hamilton, Madison, and Jay on the history and political experience of ancient Greece and Rome and of the countries of medieval and modern Europe—Britain, Germany, France, Poland, the Netherlands, Switzerland. The founding fathers may have been frontiersmen and greatly influenced by economic conditions in the New World, but they could readily have passed a searching examination for the doctorate in European history and European comparative government, which, I dare say, is more than the majority of our senators or even of our Ph.D.'s in American history could now do.

That the United States could become an independent nation and enjoy the freedom and opportunity to extend its frontiers and greatly to increase its population and prosperity and strength during the perilous fifty years of Revolutionary and Napoleonic Wars and Metternichean reaction, from 1775 to 1825, is attributable less to American aloofness from Europe than to the informed statecraft of Americans who were then in familiar touch with Europe and equipped to treat it intelligently and realistically. Almost without exception, our presidents and secretaries of state and key diplomatists of that time had practical experience in European, as well as American, affairs—Franklin, Jefferson, Jay, Marshall, Madison, Monroe, John Adams, John Quincy Adams. Monroe, for example, served in diplomatic posts in France, England, and Spain for six years before he became Madison's Secretary of State, and his own Secretary of State, John Quincy Adams, had been a student at Paris and Leiden and had had twenty years' diplomatic experience in France, the Netherlands, Prussia, Russia, and Great Britain. The words which this qualified statesman put into Monroe's celebrated message of 1823 to the Congress expressed an enlightened realism in notable contrast with utterances and actions of certain American statesmen of a later date less in touch with the realities of Europe and more with ideological propaganda in America.

Said the message of 1823, without trace of a holier-than-thou attitude:

> Our policy in regard to Europe . . . remains the same, which is, not to interfere in the internal affairs of any of its powers; to consider the Government *de facto* as the legitimate Government for us; to cultivate friendly relations with it, and to preserve those relations by a frank, firm, and manly policy; meeting, in all instances, the just claims of every power; submitting to injuries from none.

It was not only our statesmen of that time who knew and appreciated the relationship between Europe and America. Our colleges and academies, with their classical curriculum, and our literary men and publicists, with their extensive reading of British and French philosophers of the seventeenth and eighteenth centuries, possessed like knowledge and appreciation. Our commercial classes, including our cotton planters, had it, too. To protect our commerce with Europe, Jefferson dispatched to the Mediterranean an American armed expeditionary force which made landings in North Africa nearly a century and a half before the recent repetition of American campaigning in the Mediterranean. And what a reading public there was in the United States for those literary historians in our "middle period"—Irving, Prescott, Motley, and Parkman—who dwelt on exploits of Spanish, Dutch, and French. It might well be envied by any historian of the American frontier or even by the Book-of-the-Month Club. The Mediterranean Sea was not then so far off, or the Atlantic Ocean so wide, as our developing isolationist nationalism later made them.

Our successive American generations of frontiersmen on the eastern seaboard, in the piedmont, across the Alleghenies, along the Ohio, the Great Lakes, and the Mississippi, over the prairies, and into and beyond the Rockies, may have thought of themselves as Americans first. They may have adopted Indian dress and Indian usages in hunting and fishing and scalping. They may have exerted, and doubtless did exert, a profound and lasting influence on the nationalist evolution of the United States. But all this did not make them Indians or immunize them against the superior and eventually mastering civilization which emanated from Europe and relentlessly followed them. They remained Europeans and retained at least the rudiments of European civilization. After all, the American frontier, as Professor Turner so ably and perhaps regretfully showed, was an evanescent phenomenon, ever passing from primitiveness toward the social and intellectual pattern of the area in back of it. In other words, the abiding heritage of traditional civilization outweighed, in a relatively brief period, the novelties acquired from Indians and wilderness. Continuity proved stronger than change. The transit of culture was not so much *from* as *to* the frontier.

Differences admittedly obtain between Americans in the United States and the peoples in Europe from whom they are descended, but the differences are not greater in kind, and hardly greater in degree, than those obtaining between Englishmen and Spaniards or between Germans and Italians, or between the people of the United States and the peoples of Central and South America. True, the nationalism which has progressively infected all peoples of Europe and America during the last hundred and fifty years has grossly exaggerated the differences and given wide currency to the notion of distinctive and self-contained national cultures—a French culture, a Norwegian culture, a Spanish culture, an American culture. The result has been an obscuring and neglect of what these several national cultures have in common, a European or "Western" culture, the community of heritage and outlook and interests in Europe and its whole American frontier.

Actual differences are differences of emphasis and detail, associated with political sovereignty and independence, and arising from variant geographical and historical circumstances. Back of them all, however, is a unifying fact and force, which is describable as "European" or "Western," and which, now more than ever before, needs to be appreciated and applied. Actually and fundamentally, just as the European remains a European while thinking of himself first as an Englishman, a Frenchman, a German, or a Spaniard, so the descendants of Europeans in America remain European even while insisting that they are Americans first.

The frontier has undoubtedly been a very important source of what is distinctive and peculiar in the national evolution of the United States. But few European nations have been without a frontier in the American sense at some time in their history and without significant lasting effects of that frontier. Contemporary peculiarities in the life and customs of Spain, for instance, cannot be dissociated from the slow advance, during several centuries, of a frontier of conquest of Moorish lands; nor Germany's, from an analogous frontier in barbarous regions of north central Europe. In a larger way, all America is a frontier: Latin America, of Spain and Portugal; Quebec, of France; the United States, of Great Britain and Holland, Spain and France, Germany and Ireland, Scandinavia and Italy and Poland. Our Negroes and Indians, as these have been civilized, have been Europeanized as well as Americanized. The "melting pot" is no novelty in the history of Western civilization; it has latterly been doing in America, on a large scale, the same sort of fusing which at earlier dates produced the chief nations of modern Europe. Comparative study of frontiers in Europe and America, together with comparative study of melting pots and nationalisms in both, might serve to demonstrate that obvious differences between nations of European tradition are fewer and relatively less significant than their similarities.

"European," as I here use the term, does not refer merely to a detached piece of geography or to a continent by itself, and not to another "hemisphere" or a hoary and pitiable "Old World." Rather, it refers to a great historic culture, the "Western" civilization, which, taking its rise around the Mediterranean, has long since embraced the Atlantic, creating what Mr. Walter Lippmann has appropriately designated the "Atlantic Community." As Professor Ross Hoffman says:

> Every state of the North and South American continents originated from Western European Christendom which

Voltaire, in the age before the independence movements, characterized so well as a "great republic." Englishmen, Frenchmen, Spaniards, Portuguese, Dutchmen and Danes in the early modern centuries made the Atlantic Ocean the inland sea of Western civilization; they made it an historical and geographical extension of the Mediterranean. . . . Many of these early-forged bonds still span the Atlantic, and the spread of British, French, and American ideals of liberty and constitutional government has made this oceanic region the citadel of what today is rather loosely called Democracy.

Of such an Atlantic community and the European civilization basic to it, we Americans are co-heirs and co-developers, and probably in the future the leaders. If we are successfully to discharge our heavy and difficult postwar responsibilities, we shall not further weaken, but rather strengthen, the consciousness and bonds of this cultural community.

Against it, militate two current trends of quite contradictory character. One, which I have already indicated, is the nationalistic tendency to view each nation as *sui generis,* and to attribute to it an independent and distinctive culture all its own. The second is the hypothesizing of a "world civilization." This has already passed from the fictional titles of high-school textbooks to the solemn pronouncements of statesmen. It represents a leap from myopic nationalism to starry-eyed universalism. I, for one, have not the faintest idea what world civilization is. I know there are enduring and respectable civilizations in Moslem areas, in India, in China, and presumably in Japan. I also know there are considerable influences of such civilizations upon ours, and, especially in the material domain, heavy impacts by ours upon them. But the many existing civilizations still do not constitute a single "world civilization," and for a long time to come, I hazard, the common denominator among them is likely to be low—as low, I should suppose, as unadorned "human nature."

Neither devotion to one's nation nor idealization of the world at large should obscure the important cultural entities which lie between. These are the power-houses of civilization for their constituent nationalities, and the units which must be brought into co-operation for any world order of the future. The one to which Americans belong is the "European" or "Western." It has conditioned our past. And whether we are aware of it, or not, it conditions our present and future.

Of what does it consist? First, in the Greco-Roman tradition, with its rich heritage of literature and language, of philosophy, of architecture and art, of law and political concepts. Second, in the Judeo-Christian tradition, with its fructifying ethos and ethics, its abiding and permeating influence on personal and social behavior, its constant distinctions between the individual and the race, between liberty and authority, between mercy and justice, between what is Caesar's and what is God's. Third, proceeding from joint effects of the first two, it comprises traditions of individualism, of limitations on the state, of social responsibility, of revolt and revolution. Fourth, likewise proceeding from the others, particularly from the Christian tradition, it includes a tradition of expansiveness, of missionary and crusading zeal, which has inspired not merely a spasmodic but a steady pushing outward of European frontiers—from the Mediter-

ranean to the Arctic and across the Atlantic, in turn over lands of Celts, Germans, Slavs, Magyars, and Scandinavians, over the full width of both American continents, and beyond to the Philippines and Australasia and into Africa.

In all these characteristics of European or Western civilization, every nationality of central and western Europe and of America shares. In measure as the frontier advances and is civilized, it is these characteristics which actuate and are embodied in the civilization. The United States is no exception.

One does not have to go to Athens and Rome to behold Greek and Roman architecture, or to Palestine and Europe to see Jewish synagogues and Christian churches. There are more churches and synagogues in the United States than in any other country in the world. There is more classical architecture in Leningrad or London than in Athens, and still more in Washington. It is indeed the practically official architecture of our American democracy from Jefferson to Hoover, and the favorite style for bank buildings, railway stations, and public schools, whether in Virginia or Illinois or the Far West. Our prevailing language continues to be transatlantic English, and distinctively American only in pronunciation and raciness of idiom. Shakespeare and Milton are as much ours as England's. Our juristic conceptions and legal usages are likewise transatlantic, and I know of no philosophical speculation on this continent, in the whole gamut from the pragmatic to the Thomistic, or on any subject from theological to scientific, including political and economic, which has not had its equivalent and usually its antecedent in Europe.

If we belonged to a Moslem or Confucian culture, or to a purely indigenous one, we would not have the mores which we have. We would not, for instance, be free on Sundays for church or golf or for surreptitious privacy in library or laboratory. Probably we would not use knives and forks, and we would wear different clothes. We might be more ceremonial and more externally polite. We might think, as well as behave, differently. Our sense of values and our frames of references could not be quite the same. We are what we are only in part because of biological heredity and physical environment. In larger part it is because we are stamped from infancy with a historic culture of singularly educative and perduring potency. . . .

There will doubtless be dissent from the thesis I have here advanced, and from its implications. May I suggest, however, that, among us, dissent be attended by informed thought rather than by nationalist emotion. In the past, American historians, by concentrating their thought and labor more and more on the United States and its western frontier, have contributed immeasurably to the conscious solidifying, in time and space, of the great independent Republic of the New World. Now, when the Republic's old frontier, completing its western march, has disappeared from the American continent and been superseded by new and quite different frontiers on distant isles of the Pacific, in the Azores, and on the Rhine and Danube, our historians, whether they agree or not with my particular views, might appropriately devote more attention to fields which have hitherto been relatively neglected and whose cultivation will be conducive to clearer appreciation in this country of its historic setting and current responsibilities.

It is no longer a question of creating a great American nation. It is now a question of preserving and securing this nation in a world of nations. Nor is it now a question of isolationism versus internationalism. This has finally been determined by the Senate's almost unanimous ratification of the Charter of the United Nations. The question now is whether as a nation we are going to be sufficiently informed and intelligent about foreign conditions, sufficiently freed from provincialism, to ensure the effective operation of the United Nations' organization in the best interest of ourselves and of world peace. Toward satisfactory solution of this question, American historians, if they will, can make major contributions.

One contribution would be to put much greater emphasis than in the past on cultural history—on the history of language and literature, of religion and church, of art and science, of intellectual currents, and of the transit of culture. Our national past and present, like the world's at large, are only partially explicable in terms of industrial and material development; and I would hope that the "economic interpretation," which has had such stimulating and valuable influence on historical research and writing during the past half century, might now be qualified and supplemented by a broader "cultural interpretation." There is doubtless already a trend in this direction. It is evidenced in a considerable number of recent monographs, and especially in the important co-operative *History of American Life* edited by Professor Schlesinger and the late President Fox. It requires, however, for its confirmation and proper fruitage much deepening and broadening and a much larger number of scholarly investigators and writers. It is cultural considerations, let me stress, which most profoundly affect American relationships with the world, not only of the past, but of the present and future.

I hope, too, that we shall not lose sight of the continuity of history. There is a pronounced tendency in the United States to dwell on the "newness" and "uniqueness" of the "New World" and our "new nation"—new freedom, new frontier, new deal, new knowledge, new thought—and to accept a cataclysmic view of history. Serious historical scholars know—or should know—that such striking events as the invention of gunpowder or of printing, the discovery of America, the Protestant Reformation, the French Revolution, the American Revolution, were not really cataclysmic, that they merely speeded some continuous process long previously under way and left untouched vastly more habits of human thought and action than they altered. With this knowledge well in mind, we should be very skeptical of contemporary popular notions concerning the cataclysmic character of the Russian Revolution, the second World War, or even the atomic bomb. We may confidently expect that the world of the future will continue to be mainly the world of the past. The principal threads of our historic Western culture, like those of the Chinese or Moslem cultures, have not suddenly been cut in A.D. 1945. Unconsciously if not consciously, whether we like it or not, we shall go right on in the Greco-Roman and Judeo-Christian traditions. It would be realistic to recognize the fact.

Of course, there is change, and what may properly be called progress, in America and in the world. But how are we to gauge it or to try intelligently to direct it without relating it to the constants and continuities in human experience? American history should, of course, be taught in our schools—more, rather than less—but it should not be taught as beginning with the political independence of a new nation in 1776 or even with the discovery of a New World in 1492. To understand what America really is, of what actually it is a frontier, its history should be studied continuously from at least the ancient Greeks and the first Christians.

Finally, I would earnestly urge that greater attention be paid to comparative history. The comparative method is the surest means of diminishing racial, political, religious, and national prejudices. As the distinguished Belgian historian Henri Pirenne has written:

> These prejudices ensnare him who, confined within the narrow limits of national history, is condemned to understand it badly becaue he is incapable of comprehending the bonds attaching it to the histories of other nations. It is not due to *parti pris* but because of insufficient information that so many historians lack impartiality. One who is lost in admiration of his own people will inevitably exaggerate their originality and give them the honor for discoveries which are in reality only borrowed. He is unjust to others because he fails to understand them, and the exclusiveness of his knowledge lays him open to the deceptions of the idols set up by sentiment. The comparative method permits history to appear in its true perspective. What was believed to be a mountain is razed to the size of a molehill, and the thing for which national genius was honored is often revealed as a simple manifestation of the imitative spirit.

The student of the history of the United States, whether dealing with its political, economic, or cultural development, would be the better historian and the more enlightening if he was a specialist also in the history of a foreign country from which comparisons and contrasts could be drawn. Similarly, the student of the history of a foreign country could profitably extend his study beyond that country. Most of all, the historian of a particular phenomenon, such as nationalism, slavery, democracy, the frontier, etc., however specific in time or space may be his immediate work, must needs possess, if his work is to be informed and judicious, a wide background of acquaintance with other and comparable examples of the phenomenon.

In summary, the American frontier is a frontier of European or "Western" culture. This culture, however modified by or adapted to peculiar geographical and social conditions in America or elsewhere, is still, in essential respects, the culture and hence a continuous bond of the regional community of nations on both sides of the Atlantic. Like its predecessor and inspirer, the Mediterranean community of ancient times, the Atlantic community has been an outstanding fact and a prime factor of modern history. Despite the growth in latter years of an anarchical nationalism and isolationism on one hand, and of a utopian universalism on the other, the Atlantic community has lost none of its potential importance for us and for the world. We must look anew to it and strengthen our ties with it, if we are to escape the tragedy of another world war and ensure the blessings of liberty and democracy to future generations. To this end the historical guild in America can immeasurably contribute by extending the use of the comparative method, by emphasizing the continuity of history, and by stressing cultural and social, equally with political and economic, history.

POSTSCRIPT

Was Colonial American Culture Unique?

Although both Hayes and Nash have developed theories pertaining to the cultural character of colonial America, their works clearly reflect divergent approaches to the study of history and reflect the distinctive climate of the times in which each wrote. Hayes's essay, presented as a refutation of Arthur Schlesinger, Sr.'s, 1942 presidential address to the American Historical Association, appeared at the end of World War II at a time when many people were attempting to emphasize the essential unity of a civilization—the Atlantic community—so recently threatened by Hitler's war machine. Gary Nash, on the other hand, has developed his views of American colonial society against the backdrop of the civil rights movement, the women's movement, the Indian rights movement, and efforts by numerous ethnic Americans to demonstrate their contributions to American culture. As a consequence, Hayes's Eurocentric cultural approach is challenged by Nash's appreciation of cultural pluralism, which is developed in greater detail in *Red, White and Black: The Peoples of Early America*, 2d ed. (Prentice-Hall, 1974).

Another significant issue in the study of our cultural origins is the question of their impact on the American character. Frederick Jackson Turner's "The Significance of the Frontier in American History," a paper read at the annual meeting of the American Historical Association in 1893, reflects the views of Crevecoeur and Tocqueville by asserting that a unique national character developed out of America's frontier experience. The Turner thesis remained a hot topic of historical debate for three quarters of a century as Turnerians and anti-Turnerians debated the fine details of the impact of the frontier on American national character. The staunchest disciple of Turner was Ray Allen Billington, whose *The Far Western Frontier, 1830–1860* (Harper & Row, 1956), *The Frontier Heritage* (Holt, Rinehart, 1966), and *Frederick Jackson Turner* (Oxford University Press, 1973) should be examined by interested students. An important extension of the Turner thesis is offered in David M. Potter, *People of Plenty: Economic Abundance and the American Character* (University of Chicago, 1954), which identifies another factor contributing to a distinctive American character. Michael Kammen's *People of Paradox: An Inquiry Concerning the Origins of American Civilization* (Knopf, 1972) argues that American distinctiveness derives from the contradiction produced by a culture created from an interaction of Old and New World patterns. Students interested in pursuing these questions of culture and character should examine Michael McGiffert, ed., *The Character of Americans: A Book of Readings*, rev. ed. (Dorsey Press, 1970) and David Stannard, "American Historians and the Idea of a National Character: Some Problems and Prospects," *American Quarterly* (May 1971).

ISSUE 2

Was Conflict Unavoidable Between Native Americans and Colonists?

YES: Alden T. Vaughan, from "White Man to Redskin: Changing Anglo-American Perceptions of the American Indians," *American Historical Review* (October 1982)

NO: Richard R. Johnson, from "The Search for a Usable Indian: An Aspect of the Defense of Colonial New England," *Journal of American History* (December 1977)

ISSUE SUMMARY

YES: Vaughan presents the native American as a victim of color symbolism, racial differences, and nonconformity to European culture.
NO: Johnson chronicles cooperative relations between settlers and natives in the New World.

Relations between Native Americans and Europeans were marred by the difficulties that arose from people of very different cultures encountering each other for the first time. These encounters led to inaccurate perceptions, misunderstandings, and failed expectations. While at first the American Indians deified the explorers, experience soon taught them to do otherwise. European opinion ran the gamut from admiration to contempt; for example, some European poets and painters expressed admiration for the Noble Savage while other Europeans accepted as a rationalization for genocide the sentiment that "the only good savage is a dead one."

Spanish, French, and English treatment of Native Americans differed and was based to a considerable extent on each nation's hopes about the New World and how it could be subordinated to the Old. The Spanish exploited the Indians most directly, taking their gold and silver, transforming their government, religion, and society, and even occasionally enslaving them. The French were less of a menace than the others because there were fewer of them and because many French immigrants were itinerant trappers and priests rather than settlers. In the long run, the emigration from England was the most threatening of all. Entire families came from England, and they were determined to establish a permanent home in the wilderness.

The juxtaposition of Native American and English from the Atlantic to the Appalachians resulted sometimes in coexistence, other times in enmity.

English settlers depended on the Indians' generosity in sharing the techniques of wilderness survival. Puritan clergymen tried to save their neighbors' souls, going so far as to translate the Bible into dialects, but they were not as successful at conversion as the French Jesuits and Spanish Franciscans. Attempts at coexistence did not smooth over the tension between the English and the Indians. They did not see eye to eye, for example, about the uses of the environment. Indian agriculture, in the eyes of English settlers, was neither intense nor efficient. Native Americans observed that white settlers consumed larger amounts of food per person and cultivated not only for themselves but also for other towns and villages that bought the surplus. Subsistence farming collided with the market economy.

Large-scale violence erupted in the 1670s. In the Virginia piedmont, frontiersmen led by Nathaniel Bacon attacked tribes living in the Appalachian foothills, while throughout New England the Wampanoags, Narragansetts, Mohegans, Podunks, and Nipmucks united to stop the encroachments into their woodlands and hunting grounds. King Philip's War lasted from June 1675 to September 1676 with isolated raids stretching on until 1678. Casualties rose into the hundreds and Anglo-Indian relations deteriorated.

In the next century Spain, France, and England disputed each other's North American claims and Native Americans joined sides, usually as the allies of France against England. These great wars of the eighteenth century ended in 1763 with England's victory, but disputes over territorial expansion continued. Colonial officials objected to the Proclamation of 1763 by which King George III's imperial government forbade his subjects from settling west of the Appalachian watershed. The area from those mountains to the Mississippi River, acquired from France at the negotiated Peace of Paris, was designated as an Indian reservation. From 1763 to 1783, as Anglo-colonial relations moved from disagreement to combat to independence, the London government consistently sided with the Native Americans.

Alden Vaughan explores the relations between Native Americans and European colonists by focusing upon color consciousness as an important explanation for European racism. Eighteenth-century racial theories, Vaughan contends, combined with frustration over Indian rejections of Christianity, inflated the Anglo-American emphasis upon Indian hostility. Significantly, European connotations of the color "red" prevented colonists from accepting Native Americans on a basis of equality.

Richard Johnson, on the other hand, emphasizes the positive relations between Native Americans and Europeans. In New England, he demonstrates, some Indians adopted the white man's religion, and many provided essential military service that bred lasting friendships and bonds of loyalty. These elements of mutual dependence, Johnson concludes, remained intact despite sporadic clashes.

YES

Alden T. Vaughan

FROM WHITE MAN TO REDSKIN: CHANGING ANGLO-AMERICAN PERCEPTIONS OF THE AMERICAN INDIAN

Documenting the shifts in the Anglo-American perceptions of Indian color is easier than explaining them. Contemporary authors were oblivious to the changes; they were too close to the phenomena and too involved in them. To a large extent, of course, the reasons for changing attitudes can only be surmised, for they reflect a vast and complicated alteration in millions of disparate individuals whose perceptions of the Indian cannot be precisely recontructed. Nonetheless, Anglo-American writings of the eighteenth century offer important clues to the psychological imperatives that encouraged "white" Americans to believe that Indians were significantly and irrevocably darker than themselves. At least three major interrelated and mutually reinforcing influences are apparent: the Anglo-Americans' anger at Indian hostility, their frustration over Indian rejection of Christianity and "civility," and their adoption of eighteenth-century racial theories.

First, chronologically, was the transformation of the Indian in English eyes from potential friend to inveterate enemy. That change took place gradually and unevenly, occurring at different times in different places, as military conflict increasingly characterized Indian-English contact. From the standpoint of Anglo-American attitudes, the causes of conflict were irrelevant: Englishmen at home or in America almost invariably blamed the Indians for hostilities and, hence, came to think of them as incorrigibly aggressive and ruthless. It was only a short step from regarding the Indians as bloodthirsty foes to perceiving them as naturally inferior in morality and humanity, and eventually in color.

The initial Anglo-American view of the Indians was largely amiable and optimistic. Most of the "savages," imperial spokesmen contended, would be friendly. They would also be eager for commerce and the gospel, partly because it would be in their own self-interest but mainly because the English

From the *American Historical Review* 87 (October 1982). Reprinted by permission.

professed to come peacefully, offering voluntary acceptance of English culture and religion. (By contrast, English imperialists viewed Spanish settlement as a model of how to alienate and exterminate the natives.) The Indians would therefore welcome English outposts, willingly sell surplus land, engage in mutually profitable trade, and enthusiastically embrace Protestantism. Yet, from the earliest days of English colonialism, its champions predicted—judging from a century of European experience in America—that some natives would oppose settlement no matter how fairly they were treated. And Indians who persisted in hostility or obstinately rejected free trade and proselytizing, the imperialists argued, deserved no quarter; the English never seriously questioned their own right to occupy part of America, by force if necessary. England's deeply ingrained ethnocentrism (a characteristic other European nations possessed, but apparently to a lesser degree), and England's determination to make profits and converts, which it hoped would emulate Spanish success but not Spanish methods, would brook no native opposition. Even the usually benign younger Hakluyt minced no words on this point: "To handle them gently, while gentle courses may be found to serve . . . be without comparison the best: but if gentle polishing will not serve, then we shall not want hammerours and rough masons enow, I meane our old soldiours trained up in the Netherlands, to square and prepare them to our Preachers hands." With the few recalcitrants chastised, colonization would proceed peacefully, to the benefit of settlers and Indians alike.

Such expectations died early. At Roanoke Island in the 1580s, most of the Indians turned against the colonists, for justifiable reasons, and the neighboring Powhatans probably exterminated the "Lost Colony" of 1587. In Virginia, settlers and natives clashed almost incessantly from 1607 to 1613, often in open warfare, sometimes in sporadic skirmishes, occasionally in bloodless but hostile negotiations. Nearly a decade of relative calm followed the captivity and conversion of Pocahontas in 1613; the brief and imperfect respite from hostilities ended suddenly with the massacre of 1622, which almost exterminated the colony. Even though responsibility for the massacre ultimately belonged with the English, as their own accounts unwittingly reveal, the Anglo-American attitude toward the Indians quickly shifted from contempt to hatred—a sentiment intensified by the ensuing decade of blatant carnage and by a similar massacre in 1644.

New England's experience offers some parallels and some marked contrasts to Virginia's. Unlike Virginia, the New England colonies had generally peaceful relations with the local tribes until 1675. To a considerable extent that reflected New England's unusual population ratio: epidemics in 1616-17 and 1633-34 greatly reduced the natives while barely touching the colonists, which lessened Indian resistance and further encouraged Puritan immigrants to believe that God intended them to create a New English Zion. So did the Pequot War of 1637, which briefly threatened New England's view of the Indians as potential friends and converts. The decisive victory over the Pequots further reduced Indian numbers, and, when most of the tribes remained neutral or actively supported the colonists, the Puritans' confidence in their own invincibility and in the Indians' vulnerability was reinforced rather than undermined. By contrast, early Virginians faced an Indian population that vastly outnumbered them and that had enough political cohesion to use its numerical strength effectively.

But numbers do not tell the whole story. Important too was the strong missionary impulse among New England's founders, an impulse that eventually enjoyed a quarter-century of modest achievement. New England's missionary activity began belatedly in the 1640s, but its success from then until King Philip's War seemed to justify earlier expectations. The uprisings of 1675—once again an Indian response to colonial encroachment and abuses—dashed Puritan assumptions about the eventual transformation of the Indians into proper Englishmen. Henceforth, the British colonists in New England joined those in the Chesapeake and elsewhere in a growing conviction that Indians in general were their enemies. That conviction hardened in the late seventeenth century and throughout the eighteenth as the British colonial frontier became a vast English-Indian battleground, often exacerbated by troops or agents from other colonial powers. Even Pennsylvania, after the effective withdrawal of the Quakers from political control and after the influx of a predominantly non-Quaker population, had its share of racial conflict.

Frequent and ferocious hostilities, regardless of who was at fault, inevitably corroded the earlier Anglo-American view of the Indians and reshaped its vocabulary. References to the Indians, never especially flattering, now became almost universally disparaging. In the aftermath of 1622, Anglo-American spokesmen portrayed the Virginia native as "having little of Humanitie but shape," "more brutish than the beasts they hunt," and "naturally born slaves." New Englanders reacted similarly to King Philip's War. The Indians were "Monsters shapt and fac'd like men," wrote one New England poet, and most of his compatriots undoubtedly agreed. Even book titles reflect the shift in attitude. In 1655 John Eliot could write hopefully of the Indians' progress toward conversion in *A Late and Further Manifestation of the Progress of the Gospell amongst the Indians in New England: Declaring Their Constant Love and Zeal to the Truth, with a Readiness to Give Account of Their Faith and Hope, as of Their Desire to Be Partakers of the Ordinances of Christ.* Twenty years later, in the midst of New England's struggle for survival, an anonymous pamphleteer suggested a far different view of the Indians in a *Brief and True Narration of the Late Wars Risen in New-England, Occasioned by the Quarrelsome Disposition, and Perfidious Carriage of the Barbarous, Savage, and Heathenish Natives there.* As warfare increasingly became the dominant mode of English-Indian contact, the image of the Indian as vicious savage made deep inroads on the Anglo-American psyche. Cotton Mather, whose rhetorical flights often exaggerated but seldom misrepresented colonial sentiments, gave revealing advice to New England's soldiers in King William's War: "Once you have but got the Track of those Ravenous howling Wolves, then pursue them vigourously; *Turn not back till* they *are consumed. . . .* Beat them small as the *Dust before the Wind . . . Sacrifice them to the Ghosts of Christians whom they have Murdered. . . . Vengance, Dear Country-men! Vengance upon our Murderers.*" The culmination of a century and a half of military escalation came in 1776 in the Declaration of Independence's only reference to the Indians:

The king "has endeavored to bring on the inhabitants of our frontiers, the merciless Indian savages, whose known rule of warfare is an undistinguished destruction of all ages, sexes and conditions." Nearly a decade of border warfare exacerbated the revoluntionaries' fear and hatred of the Indians. "The white Americans," observed a British traveler in 1784, "have the most rancorous antipathy to the whole race of Indians; and nothing is more common than to hear them talk of extirpating them totally from the face of the earth, men, women, and children."

War-bred animosities did not require a difference in color perception, but the unconscious temptation to tar the Indian with the brush of physical inferiority—to differentiate and denigrate the enemy—appears to have been irresistible. Wartime epithets have often invoked outward appearance, however irrelevant (witness the "yellow Japs" of World War II), and British Americans frequently resorted to pejorative color labels. In the late seventeenth and early eighteenth centuries, as war raged along the northern New England frontier, Cotton Mather castigated "those Tawny Pagans, than which there are not worse Divels Incarnate upon Earth," and "a *swarthy* Generation of *Philistines* here; the *Indian Natives*, I mean, whom alone we are like to have any *Warrs withal.*" Nearly a century later, when the bulk of the Indians sided with Great Britain during the American Revolution, Henry Dwight complained of "copper Colour'd Vermine" and hoped that an American army would "Massacre those Internal Savages to such a degree that [there] may'nt be a pair of them left, to continue the Breed upon the Earth." Logically enough, "redskins" eventually emerged as the epithet for enemies who usually used red paint on the warpath. Not coincidentally, perhaps, the first reported use of that term appears in a passage about Indian assaults on frontier settlements. In a sentence that suggests the impact of war on changing English attitudes, Samuel Smith of Hadley, Massachusetts, recalled in 1699 that several decades earlier his father had endured Indian raids in the Connecticut Valley. "My Father ever declardt," Smith remembered, "there would not be so much to feare iff ye Red Skins was treated with suche mixture of Justice & Authority as they cld understand, but iff he was living now he must see that wee can do nought but *fight* em & that right heavily."

The Indians' refusal to adopt English concepts of civility and religion poisoned Anglo-American attitudes as thoroughly as did warfare. Sixteenth- and seventeenth-century expectations of rapid and wholesale anglicization met constant rebuff; by the end of the seventeenth century it must have been clear to all but the more optimistic missionaries that most Indians would never be Christian in faith or English in allegiance and customs. Converts in the southern and middle colonies numbered only a handful; most of John Eliot's "praying towns" had been scuttled by King Philip's War and its aftermath; and even the Quakers in Pennsylvania, despite a commendable effort to treat the Indians fairly, had won few to English ways or beliefs. Occasional successes notwithstanding, the missionary movement had failed. Even less successful was the broader mission of eliminating customs that Englishmen subsumed under the heading of "savagery," such as nakedness, scarification, tribal law and government, hunting instead of herding, and, perhaps most important of all, an exclusively oral

27064

language. Some technological assimilation had occurred, as had some imaginative blending of religious ideas, but the overwhelming majority of Indians steadfastly held to their traditional ways and rejected most of the alien culture's offerings.

Who was to blame? The most obvious scapegoat was the Indian himself. He stubbornly resisted spiritual and material improvement, his critics charged, and they eventually concluded that his resistance stemmed either from a deeply ingrained antipathy to "civilization" or from a natural incapacity for improvement. Benjamin Franklin explained to a correspondent in 1753 that "Little Success . . . has hitherto attended every attempt to Civilize our American Indians in their present way of living. . . . When an Indian Child has been brought up among us, taught our language and habituated to Our Customs, yet if he goes to see his relations and make one Indian Ramble with them, there is no perswading him ever to return." Franklin did not consider the Indians inherently incapable of adopting English ways; they simply and obstinately preferred their own. Many of Franklin's contemporaries were less charitable. The editor of the 1764 edition of William Wood's *New England's Prospect*, for example, thought the Indians incurably barbarian and pagan. "The christianizing the Indians," he noted,

> scarcely affords a probability of success; for their immense sloth, their incapacity to consider abstract truth . . . and their perpetual wanderings, which prevent a steady worship, greatly impede the progress of Christianity, a mode of religion adapted to the most refined temper of the human mind. . . . The feroce manners of a native Indian can

> never be effaced, nor can the most finished politeness totally eradicate the wild lines of his education.

Almost predictably, the editor believed that Indians were not born white: with few exceptions, contempt for Indians correlated highly with a belief in their innate darkness.

A third major influence toward perceiving the Indians as inherently tawny or red came from eighteenth-century naturalists. Few of them had first-hand information about the American Indians—most were European scholars who never visited the New World—but in their frantic attempt to classify systematically all plant and animal life, including the principal divisions of mankind, they contributed directly to the notion of Indians as inherently red and indirectly at least to the belief in their inferiority.

Initially, the naturalists' categories had no hierarchical intent. Their taxonomies were horizontal, not vertical, and each branch of humanity enjoyed equality with all others. Before long, however, the subdivisions of *homo sapiens* acquired descriptive judgments that suggest a relative superiority in Europeans and corresponding inferiority in other races. Such a view meshed perfectly with the eighteenth century's emphatic belief in natural order, mataphorically expressed as a "Great Chain of Being," in which all creatures from microorganisms to angels had permanent places on a hierarchical continuum. The idea of an orderly chain of life had existed for centuries; it flourished in the fifteenth century, for example, when Sir John Fortescue recorded a classic description: "In this order angel is set over angel, rank upon rank in the Kingdom of Heaven; man is set over man, beast over beast, bird over bird, and fish over fish . . . so that there is no worm that crawls upon the ground, no bird that flies on high, no fish that swims in the depths, which the chain of this order binds not in most harmonious concord." Not until the eighteenth century, however, did ranks *within* humankind receive much attention. Then, because natural scientists almost invariably chose skin color as the principal criterion of racial identity, darkness of hue became "scientifically" linked to other undesirable qualities. As Winthrop Jordan has pointed out, for Africans the "Great Chain of Being" soon became a "Great Chain of Color" on which whites regarded blacks as divinely relegated to a lesser rank of humanity. In the eighteenth century, American Indians also became victims, though not quite so pejoratively, of the color chain's invidious implications. . . .

American racial thought in the post-Revolutionary era underwent subtle but significant changes. Ever since the sixteenth century, Europeans had viewed Africans and Indians as fundamentally different from each other in postdiluvian biological development and in their prospects for absorption into British-American society. In the eighteenth century, the gap gradually closed as the Indian became, in the eyes of most white observers, inherently tawny. As earlier, most Anglo-Americans considered Africans immutably black; in the late eighteenth and early nineteenth centuries some writers further debased the Afro-American by contriving polygenic theories to explain what they believed to be the black race's irredeemable physical and behavioral inferiority. Indians, by contrast, were sometimes lauded for superior appearance, virtue, or ability, yet increasingly they too suffered the stigma that white America attached to peoples of darker skin.

That the Indian was, in fact, inherently darker than the European, and that his pigmentation was the sign of a separate branch of mankind, had become axiomatic by the outbreak of the American Revolution. What remained for the Jeffersonian generation and its early nineteenth-century successors was to determine the Indians' proper color label and to reach a rough consensus on the implications of a racial status that was clearly inferior to the white man's but also superior to the black's. . . .

Once red became a viable designation, it seems to have satisfied everyone. To the Indians' bitterest critics, red could signify ferocity, blood, and anger; to their most avid supporters and to the Indians themselves, red could suggest bravery, health, and passion; to those who fell between the judgmental extremes, red could mean almost anything or nothing. In short, red was sufficiently flexible and ambiguous to meet the metaphysical imperatives of a society that did not wholly agree about the Indian's basic character or social and political fate. . . .

Even among their supposed supporters, however, the Indians fared badly, as a host of examples from Jefferson through Thomas McKenney and Lewis Cass amply illustrate. Such "friends" of the Indians contended that in the long run the Indian must be incorporated into the American mainstream, but increasingly in the nineteenth century the number of such advocates declined and the duration of the Indians' expected tutelage expanded. The Indians, assimilationists argued, must become farmers, landowners, and citizens; they must adopt "white" America's language, laws, and customs. They must cease to be Indians—even if it took centuries to reach that end. Along the way, Indian desires were rarely considered. Although the overwhelming majority wanted to retain their land and their culture, the Eastern tribes had little choice. In the first half of the nineteenth century, the basic options were assimilation or extermination, with removal to the West as a temporary stage in either case.

Some assimilationists advocated miscegenation as the surest path to de-Indianization. Ironically, the biological solution emerged almost simultaneously with laws in many states against Indian-white intermarriage. Such laws hint at hypocrisy and racial intransigence among the majority of Americans and reveal the implausibility of intermarriage as a solution to race relations in nineteenth-century America. But whatever the solution—miscegenation, allotment of farmlands in the East, removal to the West, or education in white-controlled boarding schools—the Indian was marked for gradual extinction by the uneasy coalition of his friends and foes. For both groups, as well as for the bulk of Americans who were neither friend nor foe but merely indifferent, the conviction that the Indians were innately and ineradicably "redmen" underlay their concern, or lack of it, for the Indians' fate. And to most white observers—certainly to the Indians' foes and almost certainly to the millions who scarcely cared—the stereotypical color carried a host of unfavorable associations that prevented the Indians' full assimilation into the Anglo-American community and simultaneously precluded their acceptance as a separate and equal people. Although a few dissenters resisted the prevailing color taxonomy and its correlative racial policies, the surviving literature, both factual and fictional, shows that the Indian was no longer considered a member of the same race; he remained forever distinct in color and character. Even relatively sympathetic spokesmen now believed the Indians to be permanently different. "No Christianizing," declares Natty Bumppo in Cooper's *Pathfinder* (1840), "will ever make even a Delaware [Indian] a white man, nor any whopping and yelling convert a paleface into a redskin." Bumppo earlier—in *The Prairie* (1827)—puts the same idea more succinctly: "Red natur' is red natur'."

NO

Richard R. Johnson

THE SEARCH FOR A USABLE INDIAN: AN ASPECT OF THE DEFENSE OF COLONIAL NEW ENGLAND

Two questions remain. [Why] did the Indians, for their part, cooperate with the whites? [What] does this episode contribute to an understanding of relations between the races in this period? Answers to both these questions are, unfortunately, limited by the same deficiencies of evidence that have largely restricted the study of the Indian's relations with the white to that of white attitudes toward the Indian. There are very few materials on which to base an interpretation of the Indian's side of the relationship and fewer still that have not passed through the refracting glass of white transcription. Nevertheless, by attempting to understand the wider context of white and Indian cooperation, it is possible to suggest motives and effects to an extent that casts some additional light upon the character of racial relations in early America.

The Iroquois' motives for encouraging New England's courtship are the least difficult to reconstruct. They risked little and gained much by its prolongation. Indeed, only if their warriors had tried and failed to subdue the eastern Indians might the bubble of illusion have been pricked. Clearly, the very lack of evidence concerning Indian motives may mislead scholars into reading diplomatic skills into what may have been no more than a profiting from fortunate circumstances. In the case of the Iroquois, however, both the relative abundance of the records of their diplomacy and its conspicuous success in preserving the confederacy as a major independent power in North America until the Revolution attest to their consistent and clear-sighted realism. Their negotiations with New England were characteristic. In return for a purely rhetorical commitment, they reaped a harvest of political prestige, several hundred pounds' worth of presents, and even, as in 1689, military assistance.

The motives of the New England Indians who served with the colonial forces are necessarily more conjectural. The frequent wranglings over money

From the *Journal of American History* 64 (December 1977). Reprinted by permission.

and the care taken by such leaders as Church to ensure that the Indians and their families received their due compensation indicate that pay and bounties were as powerful an inducement for Indian volunteers as for white. At a time when the New England Indians were being stripped of their lands, military service was an important source of income. In addition, and in contrast to such alternatives as apprenticeship, whaling, and domestic service, it allowed young men to earn their manhood in the traditional ways frowned upon by a surrounding white society. The ease with which Church often persuaded former Indian adversaries to enlist under his command demonstrates that Europeans were not the only race whose members sometimes found the attractions of waging war as a way of life greater than other, more social, loyalties.

A study of those groups that furnished New England with the bulk of its Indian auxiliaries—the Mohegans of Connecticut and the Praying Indians of Massachusetts and Plymouth—suggests, however, that these economic and cultural motives were but a part of a more complex Indian dependence on white society. This dependence, in turn, resulted from the fundamental shift in the balance of Indian-white relations that occurred over the course of the seventeenth century. The first military alliances between white and Indian in New England had been those of independent peoples seeking mutual advantage, as when Pilgrim and Wampanoag formed a common front against the Narragansetts, or when the latter in turn joined forces with the Connecticut settlers in 1637 to exterminate their troublesome Pequot neighbors. The colonists' arrival initially added only a new ingredient to conflict still centered around domestic Indian factionalism and inter-tribal rivalries. But the growing predominance of the whites tilted the balance of these relationships, compelling their Indian allies in turn to reassess their commitments. Some, like the Narragansetts and the Wampanoags, ultimately forsook old enmities in a last attempt to stem the English tide, only to meet with defeat and dispersal in King Philip's War. And those others, such as the Mohegans and the Praying Indians, who chose to remain committed to the whites, emerged from the struggle more dependent clients than allies as the very aid they furnished to the colonists enabled the latter to achieve a decisive local supremacy. None succeeded in preserving or profiting from a balance of forces of the kind which enabled the Iroquois to remain at once indispensable and autonomous.

Those Indians remaining within "white" New England by the last years of the seventeenth century, therefore, were necessarily those who had best accommodated themselves to the colonists' ways and needs. In addition, the Mohegans and the Praying Indians were peculiarly bound into a close relationship with the whites by the circumstances under which they had first established their separate identities. For the Praying Indians, this identity was defined by their acceptance of the colonists' religious beliefs and by the processes of socialization and acculturation that accompanied conversion. As recent studies have shown, the missionary program promoted by the Massachusetts and Plymouth governments was not limited to the provision of churches and schools for the Indians; it also resettled them in "praying towns" safely removed from tribal influences, set them under the supervision of English guardians, and commenced the reshaping of their behavior to "civilized" white Christian standards with codes of conduct suppressing many of the remaining manifestations of Indian cultural life. The thoroughness of this training in conformity to white practices and beliefs and its considerable measure of success in comparison to the efforts of colonial governments elsewhere does much to explain the willingness of a majority of Praying Indians to side with the English in time of war. Similarly, the early expression of this conformity in the practice of Indians from the praying towns hiring themselves out as laborers to neighboring farmers doubtless prepared the way, on both sides, for their subsequent employment as soldiers.

The Mohegans were also a product of the period of white colonization, but under circumstances that were primarily political rather than religious or social. They were born of intra-tribal factionalism, in a struggle over leadership within the Pequots that resulted in the secession in 1636 of a dissident group of "Mohegans" headed by the unsuccessful claimant, Uncas. They elected from the first to consolidate their separate identity through alliance with the whites, as when they promptly joined in the coalition already forming against their own Pequot kinsmen and shared the spoils of victory. This balanced and mutually profitable interdependence remained the theme of subsequent Mohegan-white relations, as Uncas deftly maneuvered the colonists into eliminating all rivals to his local hegemony, and they in turn profited from the Mohegans' military skills and willingness to admit new settlers to their lands. Moreover, by rebuffing the half-hearted proselytizings of the Connecticut authorities, Uncas and his successors succeeded in staving off the cultural and political pressures that had overwhelmed the Praying Indians. A measure of their success in preserving their traditional authority and their people's cohesion can be seen in the manner of their military service: the Mohegans continued to fight in separate companies alongside the whites at a time when the Massachusetts Indians were generally conscripted on an individual basis.

Ultimately, of course, the enveloping pressures of white settlement overwhelmed Mohegans and Praying Indians alike. By the mid-eighteenth century, the allies of King Philip's War had dissolved into scattered bands confined to shrinking reservations and fast disappearing amidst the surrounding English. This deepening dependence was clearly instrumental in inducing the New England Indians to remain in the service of the whites. Enlistment was even then, as it had continued to be, the refuge of those newly rootless or in transition between two worlds. Those Indian peoples whose way of life or political status had been most deeply affected by association with white society served in greatest numbers with the colonial forces. Yet the evident complexity of this association does not show that this service was a form of tribute paid by subservient peoples, and this does not support the modern moral that New England Indians were never more than either the white man's victims or his dupes. The example of the Mohegans demonstrates how even Indian peoples directly in the path of white expansion could turn the newcomers' presence to their own advantage, to the extent that some were able to found their own brief power and prosperity upon the trading of one form of assistance for another. Others were less fortunately situated or less skillful in their diplomacy. But even those who, like the Praying Indians, acquiesced in the pressures exerted upon them by white society, chose a path of accommodation over the alternatives of resistance or withdrawal. From this perspective, the Indians of New England were not merely being used by the whites; their military service was also a personal strategy for survival, a revealing and neglected phase in their response to the dislocations inflicted by European colonization.

This examination of the motives behind the military cooperation of Indian and white has already led far into the field of relations between the two races in the early colonial period. The search for the usable Indian can properly be seen as a significant phase in the evolution of these relations; to what extent did it also influence their subsequent development, shaping the ways in which Indian and white regarded and treated one another in New England? Did it heighten or alleviate the tensions between the races?

Prejudice is commonly tempered by the hope of advantage, and the policies and attitudes of the New England governments often reflected their recognition of the value of Indian aid. They learned to cater to the Indians' own shrewd assessment of their bargaining power. "If now our Indians are kindly used," wrote James Fitch to Massachusetts in 1696, "you may hereafter have more, if other wise non will stir." Grumblings at such presumption gave way to acquiescence; by 1712, Dudley was pressing a New Hampshire subordinate to treat the enlisted Indians with justice, for "I shall never get an Indian to

serve for your province again if they want a shilling of their due." Public recognition was less apparent, but it evidently extended to the point of tolerating an integrated indulgence in the white man's vices. John Neesnummin, an Indian minister visiting Boston, was denied lodging in the town, but Indian recruits were freely entertained at local taverns, hospitality to which sympathetic observers attributed their notorious weakness for liquor.

Appropriately, the greatest solicitude was lavished on those most conscious of their strength and from whom most was expected: the Five Nations of the Iroquois. The Massachusetts magistrates suppressed the province's first newspaper partly on account of a disparaging reference to the Mohawks, and in 1709, a year after Neesnummin had been refused accommodation, two successive delegations of Iroquois chiefs were royally entertained in Boston at the province's expense. The extent to which a desire for cordial relations with the confederacy could govern official policy was graphically demonstrated after the killing of several settlers at Deerfield and Hadley in 1693 and 1696. In both cases the evidence pointed to the Iroquois or their allies as the culprits—at Deerfield a wounded settler identified several Mohawks as his assailants. But urgent representations from Boston, Hartford, and New York pointed out the dangers of any verdict which might alienate the confederacy. After much correspondence two of the four suspects at Hadley were executed. But at Deerfield political considerations—"the English Interest"—outweighed "the Inquisition after Blood" as the Boston government took advantage of some flimsy circumstantial evidence throwing the blame on French Indians to order the prisoners' release.

Yet expediency rather than trust and affection inspired this solicitude and, in the long term, it would seem that the colonists' perception of the Indian's military potential did more to deepen than to heal divisions between the races. It prompted the employment of the Mohegans and missions to the Iroquois, but it also reinforced the image of the Indian as a dangerous and incorrigible warrior. The early settlers had anticipated that the Indian could be civilized out of his savagery. Conversion would distinguish Christian from pagan, not white from red. But by the late seventeenth century this optimism had subsided into the grimmer realization that Indians—all Indians—were somehow irredeemably different from the whites. Hopes of assimilation gave way to policies of segregation and discriminatory legislation. The use of Indian aid did not cause this change: both were consequences of the conflict that set the seal upon the breakdown of racial and cultural coexistence. Within the context of such prejudice, however, the colonists' perception of the Indians' military skills heightened their suspicions of those who remained in New England, Indians who had now, in the words of one Rhode Islander, "seen ye Englishes Slowness & therein weaknes & thyr owne nimblenes & strength." Hence the frequent questioning of the surviving Indians' loyalty, the proposals that those accounted but "pretended Freinds" should be driven from New England, and the widespread rumors that new uprisings backed by "Popish Treachery" were in preparation amongst the tribes. Fairness to the Indians, therefore, remained a pragmatic rather than a moral obligation, designed, in the revealing phrase of one frontier leader, "Least we or till we declare all indians to be Enemyes."

The search for Indian aid was not wholly devoid of warmer feelings. Among whites who served with the Indians, wartime comradeship often spun lasting bonds of loyalty and friendship. Aspinwall rescued from jail two Indians he believed to have been unjustly convicted of complicity in the murder of a settler; Fitch, Mason, and Avery spoke out boldly in defense of the Mohegans and Pequots they befriended; and Church successfully lobbied for a grant of land at Tiverton for the families of his Indian veterans. But such ties were uncommon, and, like the efforts of Gookin and his fellow "Indian-lovers" to protect the Praying Indians during King Philip's War, their character demonstrates more the reality of prejudice than its absence. Moreover, the very nature of the search for a usable Indian fostered a darker view of the Indian. It not only led the colonists to discover the Indian's military potential but also to desire that potential's most effective expression. In seeking Indian aid, the whites were requiring the Indian to be precisely what they most detested in him—savage, bloodthirsty, relentless, skulking, terrorizing and tearing the scalp from his opponents. Ironically, these qualities were in many ways more akin to white methods of total warfare than to the traditional Indian preference for a more symbolic and less destructive form of combat. But the whites ascribed to others what they feared to perceive in themselves, thereby moving a further step toward the belief that all Indians, because they embodied qualities deemed to be characteristically Indian, were too dangerous and different to be allowed to remain in contact with white society.

The Indian played the martial role allotted to him too well to allay these feelings. They burst out most strongly upon the frontier where, as one observer noted in 1696, the settlers were "exceedingly possessed with a vehement spirit against all Indians not indureing the sight of them as to the present." Certainly the frontier regions bore the brunt of suffering and attack. The perennial political division between angry frontiersmen demanding protection and coastal settlers and governments more concerned with matters of trade and taxes was already taking shape. Yet, a part of that anger and that "vehement spirit against all Indians" also grew out of the frontiersmen's impotent frustration at the Indian's superiority in border warfare—a superiority made all the more galling by the attempts of their own governments to enlist the Indian to protect them. If so, then the roots of racial prejudice lay in envy as well as ignorance and fear. One outlet for this frustration was the mistreatment of those Indians remaining within reach, as during King Philip's War. As one perceptive contemporary noted, "the vollgar cry is kill all indians when they cannot kill one."

New England's search for Indian aid serves in microcosm to illuminate the development and interrelation of larger themes of the roots of prejudice, the pattern of Indian-white relations, the changing face of war in America, and the colonists' adjustment to a world of international conflict. As policy, it proved to be a temporary expedient rather than a lasting solution. Yet, Indian auxiliaries shouldered much of the burden of defending New England for almost half a century; and the colonists' determined pursuit of aid from the Iroquois left a lasting imprint on their diplomatic and strategic perspectives. Moreover, its very transitoriness sets it more firmly in the stream of early American history. It mirrors New England's passage through a period when its colonists found themselves forced to look beyond their own resources, to the Indians and ultimately to England, for assistance. And it exemplifies an often neglected stage in early Indian-white relations, one where illusions and optimism had subsided but where the elements of a mutual dependence remained. From this longer perspective, New England's search for a usable Indian forms a strand in the fragile thread of collaboration between Indian and white that runs beyond the colonial period to reappear in such unexpected forms as the Indian auxiliaries of Andrew Jackson and George Custer and the Navaho radio operators of World War II. Sadly, such collaboration between the two races had bred no enduring coexistence; as in the case of New England, its character has served rather to define the terms of their segregation.

POSTSCRIPT

Was Conflict Unavoidable Between Native Americans and Colonists?

The complexities associated with the relations between Native Americans and colonists from Europe are evident from the foregoing essays by Vaughan and Johnson. Together they suggest the difficulty associated with efforts to generalize about the clash of cultures that occurred on New World shores. A case in point is the history of Indian-white relations in early Virginia. The colonists participating in the Jamestown expedition, for example, were attacked by a group of Indians almost as soon as they set foot on American soil. A few months later, however, Powhatan, the dominant chief in the region, provided essential food supplies to the Jamestown residents who were suffering from disease and hunger. By the latter part of 1608, however, the colonists, under the leadership of John Smith, had begun to take an antagonistic stance toward Powhatan and his people. Smith attempted to extort food supplies from the Indians by threatening to burn their villages and canoes. These hostilities continued long after Smith's departure from Virginia and did not end until the 1640s, when colonial leaders signed a formal treaty with the Powhatan Confederacy.

There is an extensive literature which addresses the relationship between Native Americans and Europeans in the seventeenth and eighteenth centuries. Gary Nash, *Red, White, and Black: The Peoples of Early America*, 2d ed. (Prentice-Hall, 1982) is an excellent survey for the colonial period. Two works by James Axtell—*The European and the Indian: Essays in the Ethnohistory of British America, 1607–1789* (Oxford University Press, 1981) and *The Invasion Within: The Contest of Cultures in Colonial North America* (Oxford University Press, 1985)—are indispensable. Karen Ordahl Kupperman, *Settling with the Indians: The Meeting of English and Indian Cultures in America, 1580–1640* (Rowman and Littlefield, 1980) and Bernard Sheehan, *Savagism and Civility: Indians and Englishmen in Colonial Virginia* (Cambridge University Press, 1980) offer conflicting explanations for the nature of Indian-white relations in the colonies. The themes of coexistence and coercion in relation to contacts between Native Americans and Englishmen in New England are assessed in Neal E. Salisbury, *Manitou and Providence: Indians, Europeans, and the Beginnings of New England* (Oxford University Press, 1982); and Francis Jennings, *The Invasion of America: Indians, Colonialism, and the Cant of Conquest* (University of North Carolina Press, 1975). Douglas E. Leach, *Flintlock and Tomahawk: New England in King Philip's War*, rev. ed. (Norton, 1966) is a well-written study of that clash. Every student interested in the history of Native American societies should read Anthony F. C. Wallace's classic anthropological and historical work, *The Death and Rebirth of the Seneca* (Alfred A. Knopf, 1970).

ISSUE 3

Was the Colonial Period a "Golden Age" for Women in America?

YES: Lois Green Carr and Lorena S. Walsh, from "The Planter's Wife: The Experience of White Women in Seventeenth-Century Maryland," *William and Mary Quarterly* (October 1977)

NO: Lyle Koehler, from *A Search for Power: The "Weaker Sex" in Seventeenth-Century New England* (University of Illinois Press, 1980)

ISSUE SUMMARY

YES: Carr and Walsh identify several factors that coalesced to afford women in seventeenth-century Maryland a higher status with fewer restraints on their social conduct than those experienced by women in England.
NO: Koehler contends that the division of labor that separated work into male and female spheres and Puritan attitudes towards rights of inheritance severely limited opportunities for upward mobility among New England women.

Students in American history classes have for generations read of the founding of the colonies in British North America, their political and economic development, and the colonists' struggles for independence without ever being confronted by a female performer in this magnificent historical drama. The terms "sons of liberty" and "founding fathers" reflect the end result of a long tradition of gender-specific myopia. In fact, only in the last two decades have discussions of the role of women in the development of American society made their appearance in standard textbooks. Consequently, it is useful to explore the status of women in colonial America.

The topic, of course, is quite complex. The status of colonial women was determined by the cultural attitudes that were exported to the New World from Europe, by the specific conditions confronting successive waves of settlers—male and female—in terms of labor requirements, and by changes produced by colonial maturation over time. It would be impossible to pinpoint a single, static condition in which *all* colonial women existed.

What was the status of women in the British North American colonies? To what degree did the legal status of women differ from their *de facto* status? A half century of scholarship has produced the notion that colonial women enjoyed a more privileged status than either their European contemporaries or their nineteenth-century descendants. This view, developed in the writings of Richard B. Morris, Elizabeth Dexter, and Mary Beard, was reinforced in the 1970s by John Demos and Roger Thompson. For example, Demos contends that despite the fact that Plymouth Colony was based on a patriarchal model in which women were expected to subordinate themselves to men, women still shared certain responsibilities with their husbands in some business activities and in matters relating to their children. At the same time, however, women were closed off from any formal public power in the Colony even when they performed essential economic functions within the community. They not only performed all the household duties but also assisted the menfolk with agricultural duties outside the home when the necessity arose. Still, society as a whole viewed women as "weaker vessels."

Women were crucial to the economic success of the colonial experiments and performed numerous functions in various occupations and professions. Women in colonial America and during the American Revolution practiced law, pounded iron as blacksmiths, trapped for furs and tanned leather, made guns, built ships, and edited and printed newspapers. At the same time, colonial society viewed women as subordinate beings. They held no political power within the individual colonies and still were suspect as the transmitters of evil, simply because they were the daughters of Eve. Nor was it a coincidence that most suspected witches were female. As Carol F. Karlsen has argued recently, 78 percent of 344 alleged witches in New England were female. Many of those accused were older women who had inherited land that traditionally would have gone to males. Such patterns of inheritance, she contends, disrupted the normative male-dominated social order. Witchcraft hysteria in colonial America, then, was a by-product of economic pressures *and* gender exploitation.

The following essays explore the status of women in seventeenth-century America. Lois Green Carr and Lorena S. Walsh assess this issue against the backdrop of four factors in colonial Maryland: the predominance of an immigrant population; the early death of male inhabitants; the late marriages of women due to their indentured servitude; and the sexual imbalance in which men greatly outnumbered women. As a result of these conditions, Maryland women experienced fewer restraints on their social conduct and enjoyed more power than did their English counterparts. Most who survived became planter's wives, enjoyed considerable freedom in choosing their husbands, and benefited from a substantial right to inherit property.

Lyle Koehler's study of seventeenth-century New England women provides a sharp contrast to the portrait presented by Carr and Walsh. Puritan views, Koehler argues, limited the economic independence of New England women by preventing fathers and husbands from providing their daughters and wives with an inheritance. Despite labor shortages in the colonies, women did not benefit by taking on traditionally male jobs. Hence, upward mobility for the New England woman could be achieved only through a fortuitous marriage.

YES

Lois Green Carr and
Lorena S. Walsh

THE PLANTER'S WIFE: THE EXPERIENCE OF WHITE WOMEN IN SEVENTEENTH-CENTURY MARYLAND

Four facts were basic to all human experience in seventeenth-century Maryland. First, for most of the period the great majority of inhabitants had been born in what we now call Britain. Population increase in Maryland did not result primarily from births in the colony before the late 1680s and did not produce a predominantly native population of adults before the first decade of the eighteenth century. Second, immigrant men could not expect to live beyond age forty-three, and 70 percent would die before age fifty. Women may have had even shorter lives. Third, perhaps 85 percent of the immigrants, and practically all the unmarried immigrant women, arrived as indentured servants and consequently married late. Family groups were never predominant in the immigration to Maryland and were a significant part for only a brief time at mid-century. Fourth, many more men than women immigrated during the whole period. These facts—immigrant predominance, early death, late marriage, and sexual imbalance—created circumstances of social and demographic disruption that deeply affected family and community life.

We need to assess the effects of this disruption on the experience of women in seventeenth-century Maryland. Were women degraded by the hazards of servitude in a society in which everyone had left community and kin behind and in which women were in short supply? Were traditional restraints on social conduct weakened? If so, were women more exploited or more independent and powerful than women who remained in England? Did any differences from English experience which we can observe in the experience of Maryland women survive the transformation from an immigrant to a predominantly native-born society with its own kinship networks and community traditions? The tentative argument put forward here is that the answer to all these questions is Yes. There were degrading aspects of

From the *William and Mary Quarterly*, 3d ser., 34 (October 1977). Reprinted by permission.

servitude, although these probably did not characterize the lot of most women; there were fewer restraints on social conduct, especially in courtship, than in England; women were less protected but also more powerful than those who remained at home; and at least some of these changes survived the appearance in Maryland of New World creole communities. . . .

Whatever their status, one fact about immigrant women is certain: many fewer came than men. Immigrant lists, headright lists, and itemizations of servants in inventories show severe imbalance. On a London immigrant list of 1634-1635 men outnumbered women six to one. From the 1650s at least until the 1680s most sources show a ratio of three to one. From then on, all sources show some, but not great, improvement. Among immigrants from Liverpool over the years 1697-1707 the ratio was just under two and one half to one.

Why did not more women come? Presumably, fewer wished to leave family and community and venture into a wilderness. But perhaps more important, women were not as desirable as men to merchants and planters who were making fortunes raising and marketing tobacco, a crop that requires large amounts of labor. The gradual improvement in the sex ratio among servants toward the end of the century may have been the result of a change in recruiting the needed labor. In the late 1660s the supply of young men willing to emigrate stopped increasing sufficiently to meet the labor demands of a growing Chesapeake population. Merchants who recruited servants for planters turned to other sources, and among these sources were women. They did not crowd the ships arriving in the Chesapeake, but their numbers did increase.

To ask the question another way, why did women come? Doubtless, most came to get a husband, an objective virtually certain of success in a land where women were so far outnumbered. The promotional literature, furthermore, painted bright pictures of the life that awaited men and women once out of their time; and various studies suggest that for a while, at least, the promoters were not being entirely fanciful. Until the 1660s, and to a less degree the 1680s, the expanding economy of Maryland and Virginia offered opportunities well beyond those available in England to men without capital and to the women who became their wives.

Nevertheless, the hazards were also great, and the greatest was untimely death. Newcomers promptly became ill, probably with malaria, and many died. What proportion survived is unclear; so far no one has devised a way of measuring it. Recurrent malaria made the woman who survived seasoning less able to withstand other diseases, especially dysentery and influenza. She was especially vulnerable when pregnant. Expectation of life for everyone was low in the Chesapeake, but especially so for women. A woman who had immigrated to Maryland took an extra risk, though perhaps a risk not greater than she might have suffered by moving from her village to London instead.

The majority of women who survived seasoning paid their transportation costs by working for a four- or five-year term of service. The kind of work depended on the status of the family they served. A female servant of a small planter—who through about the 1670s might have had a servant—probably worked at the hoe.

Such a man could not afford to buy labor that would not help with the cash crop. In wealthy families women probably were household servants, although some are occasionally listed in inventories of well-to-do planters as living on the quarters—that is, on plantations other than the dwelling plantation. Such women saved men the jobs of preparing food and washing linen but doubtless also worked in the fields. In middling households experience must have varied. Where the number of people to feed and wash for was large, female servants would have had little time to tend the crops.

Tracts that promoted immigration to the Chesapeake region asserted that female servants did not labor in the fields, except "nasty" wenches not fit for other tasks. This implies that most immigrant women expected, or at least hoped, to avoid heavy field work, which English women—at least those above the cottager's status—did not do. What proportion of female servants in Maryland found themselves demeaned by this unaccustomed labor is impossible to say, but this must have been the fate of some. . . .

The woman who immigrated to Maryland, survived seasoning and service, and gained her freedom became a planter's wife. She had considerable liberty in making her choice. There were men aplenty, and no fathers or brothers were hovering to monitor her behavior or disapprove her preference. This is the modern way of looking at her situation, of course. Perhaps she missed the protection of a father, a guardian, or kinfolk, and the participation in her decision of a community to which she felt ties. There is some evidence that the absence of kin and the pressures of the sex ratio created conditions of sexual freedom in courtship that were not customary in England. A register of marriages and births for seventeenth-century Somerset County shows that about one-third of the immigrant women whose marriages are recorded were pregnant at the time of the ceremony—nearly twice the rate in English parishes. There is no indication of community objection to this freedom so long as marriage took place. No presentments for bridal pregnancy were made in any of the Maryland courts.

The planter's wife was likely to be in her mid-twenties at marriage. An estimate of minimum age at marriage for servant women can be made from lists of indentured servants who left London over the years 1683-1684 and from age judgments in Maryland county court records. If we assume that the 112 female indentured servants going to Maryland and Virginia whose ages are given in the London lists served full four-year terms, then only 1.8 percent married before age twenty, but 68 percent after age twenty-four. Similarly, if the 141 women whose ages were judged in Charles County between 1666 and 1705 served out their terms according to the custom of the country, none married before age twenty-two, and half were twenty-five or over. When adjustments are made for the ages at which wives may have been purchased, the figures drop, but even so the majority of women waited until at least age twenty-four to marry. Actual age at marriage in Maryland can be found for few seventeenth-century female immigrants, but observations for Charles and Somerset counties place the mean age at about twenty-five.

Because of the age at which an immigrant woman married, the number of children she would bear her husband was small. She had lost up to ten years of her childbearing life—the possibility of perhaps four or five children, given the usual rhythm of childbearing. At the same time, high mortality would reduce both the number of children she would bear over the rest of her life and the number who would live. One partner to a marriage was likely to die within seven yeas, and the chances were only one in three that a marriage would last ten years. In these circumstances, most women would not bear more than three or four children—not counting those stillborn—to any one husband, plus a posthumous child were she the survivor. The best estimates suggest that nearly a quarter, perhaps more, of the children born alive died during their first year and that 40 to 55 percent would not live to see age twenty. Consequently, one of her children would probably die in infancy, and another one or two would fail to reach adulthood. Wills left in St. Mary's County during the seventeenth century show the results. In 105 families over the years 1660 to 1680 only twelve parents left more than three children behind them, including those conceived but not yet born. The average number was 2.3, nearly always minors, some of whom might die before reaching adulthood.

For the immigrant woman, then, one of the major facts of life was that although she might bear a child about every two years, nearly half would not reach maturity. The social implications of this fact are far-reaching. Because she married late in her childbearing years and because so many of her children would die young, the number who would reach marriageable age might not replace, or might only barely replace, her and her husband or husbands as child-producing members of the society. Con-

sequently, so long as immigrants were heavily predominant in the adult female population, Maryland could not grow much by natural increase. It remained a land of newcomers. . . .

A hazard of marriage for seventeenth-century women everywhere was death in childbirth, but this hazard may have been greater than usual in the Chesapeake. Whereas in most societies women tend to outlive men, in this malaria-ridden area it is probable that men outlived women. Hazards of childbirth provide the likely reason that Chesapeake women died so young. Once a woman in the Chesapeake reached forty-five, she tended to outlive men who reached the same age. . . .

However long they lived, immigrant women in Maryland tended to outlive their husbands—in Charles County, for example, by a ratio of two to one. This was possible, despite the fact that women were younger than men at death, because women were also younger than men at marriage. Some women were widowed with no living children, but most were left responsible for two or three. These were often tiny, and nearly always not yet sixteen.

This fact had drastic consequences, given the physical circumstances of life. People lived at a distance from one another, not even in villages, must less towns. The widow had left her kin 3,000 miles across an ocean, and her husband's family was also there. She would have to feed her children and make her own tobacco crop. Though neighbors might help, heavy labor would be required of her if she had no servants, until—what admittedly was usually not difficult—she acquired a new husband.

In this situation dying husbands were understandably anxious about the welfare of their families. Their wills reflected their feelings and tell something of how they regarded their wives. In St. Mary's and Charles counties during the seventeenth century, little more than one-quarter of the men left their widows with no more than the dower the law required— one-third of his land for her life, plus outright ownership of one-third of his personal property. If there were no children, a man almost always left his widow his whole estate. Otherwise there were a variety of arrangements.

During the 1660s, when testators begin to appear in quantity, nearly a fifth of the men who had children left all to their wives, trusting them to see that the children received fair portions. Thus in 1663 John Shircliffe willed his whole estate to his wife "towards the maintenance of herself and my children into whose tender care I do Commend them Desireing to see them brought up in the fear of God and the Catholick Religion and Chargeing them to be Dutiful and obedient to her." As the century progressed, husbands tended instead to give the wife all or a major part of the estate for her life, and to designate how it should be distributed after her death. Either way, the husband put great trust in his widow, considering that he knew she was bound to remarry. Only a handful of men left estates to their wives only for their term of widowhood or until the children came of age. When a man did not leave his wife a life estate, he often gave her land outright or more than her dower third of his movable property. Such bequests were at the expense of his children and showed his concern that his widow should have a maintenance which young children could not supply.

A husband usually made his wife his executor and thus responsible for paying his debts and preserving the estate. Only 11 percent deprived their wives of such powers. In many instances, however, men also appointed overseers to assist their wives and to see that their children were not abused or their property embezzled. Danger lay in the fact that a second husband acquired control of all his wife's property, including her life estate in the property of his predecessor. Over half of the husbands who died in the 1650s and 1660s appointed overseers to ensure that their wills were followed. Some trusted to the overseers' "Care and good Conscience for the good of my widow and fatherless children." Others more explicit made overseers responsible for seeing that "my said child . . . and the other [expected child] (when pleases God to send it) may have their right Proportion of my Said Estate and that the said Children may be bred up Chiefly in the fear of God." A few men— but remarkably few—authorized overseers to remove children from households of stepfathers who abused them or wasted their property. On the whole, the absence of such provisions for the protection of the children points to the husband's overriding concern for the welfare of his widow and to his confidence in her management, regardless of the certainty of her remarriage. Evidently, in the politics of family life women enjoyed great respect.

We have implied that this respect was a product of the experience of immigrants in the Chesapeake. Might it have been instead a reflection of the English culture? Little work is yet in print that allows comparison of the provisions for Maryland widows with those made for the widows of English farmers. Possibly, Maryland husbands were making traditional wills which could have been written in the communities they left behind. However, Margaret Spufford's recent study of three Cambridgeshire villages in the late sixteenth century and early seventeenth century suggests a different pattern. In one of these villages, Chippenham, women usually did receive a life interest in the property, but in the other two they did not. If the children were all minors, the widow controlled the property until the oldest son came of age, and then only if she did not remarry. In the majority of cases adult sons were given control of the property with instructions for the support of their mothers. Spufford suggests that the pattern found in Chippenham must have been very exceptional. On the basis of village censuses in six other counties, dating from 1624 to 1724, which show only 3 percent of widowed people heading households that included a married child, she argues that if widows commonly controlled the farm, a higher proportion should have headed such households. However, she also argues that widows with an interest in land would not long remain unmarried. If so, the low percentage may be deceptive. . . .

Remarriage was the usual and often the immediate solution for a woman who had lost her husband. The shortage of women made any woman eligible to marry again, and the difficulties of raising a family while running a plantation must have made remarriage necessary for widows who had no son old enough to make tobacco. One indication of the high incidence of remarriage is the fact that there were only sixty women, almost all of them widows, among the 1,735 people who left probate inventories in four southern Maryland counties over

the second half of the century. Most other women must have died while married and therefore legally without property to put through probate.

One result of remarriage was the development of complex family structures. Men found themselves responsible for stepchildren as well as their own offspring, and children acquired half-sisters and half-brothers. Sometimes a woman married a second husband who himself had been previously married, and both brought children of former spouses to the new marriage. They then produced children of their own. The possibilities for conflict over the upbringing of children are evident, and crowded living conditions, found even in the households of the wealthy, must have added to family tensions. Luckily, the children of the family very often had the same mother. In Charles County, at least, widows took new husbands three times more often than widowers took new wives. The role of the mother in managing the relationships of half-brothers and half-sisters or stepfathers and stepchildren must have been critical to family harmony.

Early death in this immigrant population thus had broad effects on Maryland society in the seventeenth century. It produced what we might call a pattern of serial polyandry, which enabled more men to marry and to father families than the sex ratios otherwise would have permitted. It produced thousands of orphaned children who had no kin to maintain them or preserve their property, and thus gave rise to an institution almost unknown in England, the orphans' court, which was charged with their protection. And early death, by creating families in which the mother was the unifying element, may have increased her authority within the household.

When the immigrant woman married her first husband, there was usually no property settlement involved, since she was unlikely to have any dowry. But her remarriage was another matter. At the very least, she owned or had a life interest in a third of her former husband's estate. She needed also to think of her children's interests. If she remarried, she would lose control of the property. Consequently, property settlements occasionally appear in the seventeenth-century court records between widows and their future husbands. Sometimes she and her intended signed an agreement whereby he relinquished his rights to the use of her children's portions. Sometimes he deeded to her property which she could dispose of at her pleasure. Whether any of these agreements or gifts would have survived a test in court is unknown. We have not yet found any challenged. Generally speaking, the formal marriage settlements of English law, which bypassed the legal difficulties of the married woman's inability to make a contract with her husband, were not adopted by immigrants, most of whom probably came from levels of English society that did not use these legal formalities.

The wife's dower rights in her husband's estate were a recognition of her role in contributing to his prosperity, whether by the property she had brought to the marriage or by the labor she performed in his household. A woman newly freed from servitude would not bring property, but the benefits of her labor would be great. A man not yet prosperous enough to own a servant might need his wife's help in the fields as well as in the house, especially if he were paying rent or still paying for land. Moreover, food preparation was so time-consuming that even if she worked only at household duties, she saved him time he needed for making tobacco and corn. The corn, for example, had to be pounded in the mortar or ground in a handmill before it could be used to make bread, for there were very few water mills in seventeenth-century Maryland. The wife probably raised vegetables in a kitchen garden; she also milked the cows and made butter and cheese, which might produce a salable surplus. She washed the clothes and made them if she had the skill. When there were servants to do field work, the wife undoubtedly spent her time entirely in such household tasks. A contract of 1681 expressed such a division of labor. Nicholas Maniere agreed to live on a plantation with his wife and child and a servant. Nicholas and the servant were to work the land; his wife was to "Dresse the Vitualls milk the Cowes wash for the servants and Doe allthings necessary for a woman to doe upon the s[ai]d plantation." . . .

Historians have only recently begun to explore the consequences of the shift from an immigrant to a predominantly native population. We would like to suggest some changes in the position of women that may have resulted from this transition. It is already known that as sexual imbalance disappeared, age at first marriage rose, but it remained lower than it had been for immigrants over the second half of the seventeenth century. At the same time, life expectancy improved, at least for men. The results were longer marriages and more children who reached maturity. In St. Mary's County after 1700, dying men far more often than earlier left children of age to maintain their widows, and widows may have felt less inclination and had less opportunity to remarry.

We may speculate on the social consequences of such changes. More fathers were still alive when their daughters married, and hence would have been able to exercise control over the selection of their sons-in-law. What in the seventeenth century may have been a period of comparative independence for women, both immigrant and native, may have given way to a return to more traditional European social controls over the creation of new families. . . .

We may also find the wife losing ground in the household polity, although her economic importance probably remained unimpaired. Indeed, she must have been far more likely than a seventeenth-century immigrant woman to bring property to her marriage. But several changes may have caused women to play a smaller role than before in household decision-making. Women became proportionately more numerous and may have lost bargaining power. Furthermore, as marriages lasted longer, the proportion of households full of stepchildren and half-brothers and half-sisters united primarily by the mother must have diminished. Finally, when husbands died, more widows would have had children old enough to maintain them and any minor brothers and sisters. There would be less need for women to play a controlling role, as well as less incentive for their husbands to grant it. The provincial marriage of the eighteenth century may have more closely resembled that of England than did the immigrant marriage of the seventeenth century.

If this change occurred, we should find symptoms to measure. There should be fewer gifts from husbands to wives of property put at the wife's disposal. Husbands should less frequently make bequests to wives that provided them with property beyond their dower. A wife might even be restricted to less than her dower, although the law allowed her to choose her dower instead of a bequest. At the same time, children should be commanded to maintain their mothers.

St. Mary's County wills show some of these symptoms. Wives occasionally were willed less than their dower, an arrangement that was rare in the wills examined for the period before 1710. More important, there was some decrease in bequests to wives of property beyond their dower, and a tendency to confine the wife's interest to the term of her widowhood or the minority of the oldest son. On the other hand, children were not exhorted to help their mothers or give them living space. Widows evidently received at least enough property to maintain themselves, and husbands saw no need to ensure the help of children in managing it. Still, St. Mary's County women lost some ground, within the family polity. Evidently, as demographic conditions became more normal, St. Mary's County widows began to lose ground to their children, a phenomenon that deserves further study.

NO

Lyle Koehler

WOMEN IN WORK AND POVERTY: THE DIFFICULTIES OF EARNING A LIVING

For some time now, many scholars of early American history have asserted that the absence of sufficient manpower resulted in extensive economic freedom for the "weaker sex." As Page Smith puts it, "There were, in the early years, very few negative definitions—that this or that activity was unsuitable or inappropriate for a woman to engage in. In consequence colonial women moved freely into most occupations in response to particular needs and opportunities rather than abstract theories of what was proper." Eleanor Flexner has more emphatically concluded, "In a struggling society in which there was a continuous labor shortage, no social taboos could keep a hungry woman idle." Barbara Mayer Wertheimer enthusiastically catalogues many of the jobs held by colonial women, and asserts that the earliest female settlers possessed "power and responsibility such as they had never known in seventeenth-century England or on the European continent . . . [They labored at] many kinds of work outside the home from which they were later barred.

Despite such assertions, there has been no systematic effort to determine the exact occupations available to women, and the extent to which these utilized skills *not* focused strictly around the domesticity and nurturance of the conventional female role. Moreover, we do not know how many women worked at some occupation other than that of housewife and mother, or how much they earned. Because the characterization of woman as the weaker sex affected Puritan views of sexual behavior, intelligence, and social privilege, we might suspect that it also deterred women from supporting themselves. In fact, as we shall see, economic factors discouraged productive, independent activity on the part of women.

LIMITATIONS ON SEARCHING OUT A CALLING

Puritans certainly believed in the efficacy of work. Detesting those who lived "idle like swine," they felt that labor brought "strength to the body, and vigour to the mynde," thereby providing an outlet for energies which could otherwise

From *A Search for Power: The "Weaker Sex" in Seventeenth-Century New England* by Lyle Koehler (Urbana, Chicago and London: University of Illinois Press, 1980). Reprinted by permission.

lead one to sin. The authorities encouraged each person to search out a suitable calling through apprenticeship, self-training, or hiring out. Boys had considerably more options than girls; apprenticeship contracts specified that the latter be taught only housewifely duties like cooking and sewing, while boys could learn the "secrets" of any number of trades, including blacksmithing, husbandry, shop management, milling, carpentry, and seamanship. It is unlikely that those daughters who never served as apprentices learned any of the male occupational "secrets," because limited opportunities for occupational training, as well as denial of access to public schools, put at a disadvantage any "strong-minded" woman who wished to advance in the world of work. Even if she could overcome the limits of her socialization for domesticity, or use that training to hire herself out in a female vocation, a young woman still could not readily accrue the funds necessary to set herself up in a business or trade; besides, she was unable to earn very much at women's jobs.

Moreover, fathers neglected to give their daughters a portion of the family estate as a nest egg, while they did sometimes convey realty to sons. . . . The daughter who inherited very much from her father's estate was quite a rarity in seventeenth-century Connecticut; only the daughter of a very wealthy man could actually have taken steps to become economically self-sufficient after her father's demise. Furthermore, daughters tended to receive their share in personalty, not realty which could be converted into a permanent productive income, whereas for sons the reverse was true. In fact, daughters inherited proportionally smaller legacies than had been customary in late medieval England.

The mean and median (£22) values of daughters' inheritances yielded some immediate purchasing power, but did little to increase their occupational possibilities. The average inheritance did not allow a daughter money enough to purchase a home lot near the town's center, which sold for £80 or £100. Nor could she rent a shop and stock it with goods. While the young man could work at a trade and save a tidy sum by his late twenties, the young women possessed no similar option. Hartford County records indicate that seventeenth-century inheritance patterns made it virtually impossible for a maiden, whose access to employment was already limited by her training and lack of education, to become part of the property-holding group which ran New England affairs.

THE SINGLE WOMAN AS SERVANT

While her parents were still alive, or after she inherited too little to buy her own financial independence, a single woman could strive to earn money at only one occupation before 1685. Domestic servitude did little more than insure that the young woman would continue to exist as a member of the submissive, inferior, financially dependent class. Female servants assisted with household duties, child care, and garden maintenance—but always under the supervision of a "mistress" or "master," whose orders had to be obeyed unless they violated criminal law. Servants received meals, clothing, and a place to sleep, but generally earned no financial remuneration in return for their valuable work. The few women who hired themselves out (unlike those invariably single ones who served as apprentices, redemptioners, indentured domestics, and even slaves) enjoyed a small measure of economic reward. Their typical annual salary was just £3 or £4, only 50 to 60 percent of the male hired servant's wage. Even with the addition of a sum for the room and board furnished by the master, the female domestic drew one of the lowest annual incomes of any working person.

Since before 1650 domestic servitude was considered an honorable occupation for a woman, some newly arrived single women sought employment in that capacity. These females, whose mean age was 20.7 years, often lived briefly in Puritan households under conditions of relative equality, and then married into the best families. Still, their actual numbers were few; in addition, male domestics migrating to New England outnumbered females three to one. . . .

In the first three decades of settlement, then, a handful of women used servitude as a vehicle for marital advancement, although not as a means to accumulate money for future investment. Since such women labored as indentured servants or redemptioners (usually for seven years, in return for the cost of their passage), before 1650 there is no instance of a female hiring out her own time. After that date, however, the image of the servant deteriorated so remarkably that only a severely impoverished single woman would want to become a domestic. Scottish, Irish, Indian, black, and poor English servants soon replaced the earlier "most honourable" English. . . .

The deterioration of servant status after 1650 made domestic work no longer a realistic option for the "middling" and "better sorts." Because women of those classes no longer became servants, opportunities for them to leave home and hire out their labor decreased. Nor did the poor English, Scottish, Irish, black, and

Indian women who became servants and slaves gain even a small measure of control over their own lives. For sustenance, every women had to rely on a father, master, or husband; marriage became literally basic to survival for many New England women.

As a result, housewifery served as the chief "occupation" for almost all New England women, and it no more facilitated financial independence than had other forms of domestic servitude. Women certainly contributed to the productivity of the family farm. Although they did not often work outdoors planting and harvesting crops, as English farm wives did, many spent a good deal of time cleaning house, spinning flax, dipping candles, canning preserves, roasting meat, caring for children, and performing untold other tasks. Some spun and made stockings, shirts, or breeches, which they sold to neighbors for an occasional shilling. Goodwives also sold poultry, butter, cheese, and garden produce, or bartered such items for desired commodities in the informal village trade networks. However, woman's work in the home was assumed to be less dangerous and time-consuming than men's—a conclusion which may have rankled Puritan women as much as it has irritated housewives in more modern times. Above all else, the wife was not to use her presumed "free time" to exceed her ordained station by taking an interest in commercial activities or any other "outward matters." She could contract for rents and wages, sell goods, and collect debts only when her husband had so authorized. The records from seventeenth-century civil cases reveal that New England husbands granted their wives such privileges in only 6 or 7 percent of all families. The wife's access to experience in "outward matters" which could have provided her with some income in either marriage or widowhood was, therefore, much circumscribed.

THE NURTURANT CALLINGS OF WET NURSE, TEACHER, DOCTOR, AND MIDWIFE

Of course, Puritans did allow married women to labor at activities other than housewifery; but those activities also centered around the female's assumed nurturance, and were unremunerative and part-time. Serving as a wet nurse was one such activity, even though its short-term and low-demand characteristics made it a very insubstantial "occupation." Wet nurses enjoyed some popularity because, despite the strong cultural ideal affirming maternal breast-feeding, Puritan mothers sometimes found it impossible to perform that "duty." Puerperal fever or other serious illnesses incapacitated mothers and, it was believed, could be transmitted through the milk. Sore or inverted nipples, breast inflammations, and scanty milk also necessitated the occasional use of a wet nurse. Fear of the presumed toxic effects of colostrum caused mothers to observe a taboo on suckling infants for three or four days after delivery, which increased possibilities for wet nursing. Still, wet nurses rarely received more than temporary employment, and the payment for that service was probably never very great. In fact, such short-term help may have been freely given, much the way neighboring wives helped out during measles or other epidemics. There is no record of New Englanders "farming out" babies to wet nurses for anywhere from ten to nineteen months, as was common in England. Indeed, Puritan women who

wet nursed infants probably did not even think of themselves as being employed at an occupation.

Like wet nurses, teachers maternally provided for the needs of the young. At dame schools, where a wife or "poor patient widow sits/And awes some twenty infants as she knits," the female teacher instructed her neighbor's younger offspring for 10s. to £2 per year, 1/10th to 1/120th of the salary for male teachers in the public schools. As early as 1639 Mistress Jupe taught pupils at the Ipswich dame school; before the century's end, twenty-three or twenty-four other women assisted young scholars in reading, writing, and religion at fourteen different New England locales. These schoolmarms were expected to rely upon their husbands' or ex-husbands' estates for sustenance, not upon any salary for their own work. Moreover, they were barred from working with the upper grades (over age nine or ten), lest the difficulty of the material studied at those levels overtax a woman's "weak" intellectual ability. They constituted only 12.6 percent (25 of 199) of all schoolteachers this researcher could locate in the seventeenth-century Puritan records.

The practice of medicine was another nurturant occupational activity open to married women. Many English housewives and their American counterparts learned "chirurgery"—the use of herbs, potions, and poultices to cure any number of maladies. Knowledge of the medicinal properties of wild herbs passed through the female line in some families for generations. Alice Apsley, Lady Fenwick, one of the first women to settle at Ft. Saybrook, Connecticut, distributed homegrown herbs to sick callers at her residence from 1639 until her departure from the colony in 1645. Mistress Field of

Salem prepared a green "sympathetic oynment" which purportedly healed sprains, aches, cramps, scaldings, cuts, mange in cattle, stench blood, tumors, the bites of "Venomous Beasts," and "old Rotten Sores." Doctor Margaret Jones of Charlestown, Massachusetts, secured some reputation as a witch because the aniseed, liquors, and small doses of herbs she administered produced "extraordinary violent effects." Hannah Bradford of Windsor, Connecticut, was such a capable physician that she reputedly "taught the first male doctor much of his medical lore." At least three women proved to be able surgeons. Henry Winthrop's widow reportedly "hath very good successe" in her "Surgerye"; Mistress Allyn patched up wounded soldiers as any army surgeon during King Philip's War; and, on Martha's Vineyard, Mistress Blande dispensed "Phisicke and Surgery" to many sick Indians.

Altogether, women comprised 24 percent (42 of 175) of New England's medical practitioners. These female doctors, nurses, and midwives earned the respect of their neighbors, but evidence suggests that they received little income for their services. Medicine in the seventeenth century lacked the financial advantages of ministry, governorship, or commerce; not until the 1690s did physicians begin to achieve some recognition as highly paid, self-conscious professionals. Before that, almost all doctors practiced medicine as a second profession, spending the bulk of their working hours in the ministry, the magistracy, husbandry, or housewifery. . . .

In the 1690s, the professionalization of medicine had severe consequences for female physicians. Men trained through apprenticeship to male doctors began displacing local female chirurgeons. One

can search the colonial records in vain for some mention of female physicians during that decade. For the first time, particularly in urban areas, Puritans began distinguishing between male "doctors" and female "nurses," even though such "nurses" assisted Boston wives in recovering from childbirth, cared for infants' ailments, and treated cases of smallpox. Sam Sewall mentions seven different male physicians in his diary for the years 1674 to 1699, but all women who treat illnesses are referred to either as midwives or as nurses.

Throughout the seventeenth century both sexes dispensed medical advice, but one realm of experience, midwifery, remained the exclusive province of women. (In fact, the York County authorities fined one man fifty shillings "for presuming to Act the Part of a Midwife.") Women learned midwifery from personal experience, from other midwives, or from standard obstetrical texts like Nicholas Culpeper's *Directory for Midwives* (1651). There were no medical examinations to pass in New England, nor did a prospective midwife take out a license to practice, as was required in England and in nearby New Amsterdam.

Midwives occupied a position of some influence. They were given the important function of examining women accused of premarital pregnancy, infanticide, or witchcraft; often the guilt or innocence of the accused rested on the findings of these female juries. In return for this necessary service, the town selectmen sometimes issued grants of land to widowed midwives. However, that happened only in a few instances, and it is significant that this researcher has found no account book or other record which mentions a midwife receiving any reward for her services. . . .

WOMEN IN BUSINESS

Limitations on daughters' inheritances and the lack of remunerative work for single women meant that few could join the property-holding group which controlled capital investment in land. So, too, did the paltry wages of midwives, physicians, teachers, and wet nurses, along with husbandly control over their incomes, prevent working wives from acquiring the economic security which would have enabled them to become property owners. As urbanization increased, especially late in the century, working women were generally unable to accumulate the capital necessary to participate in the Commercial Revolution enveloping New England.

Of course, some women who possessed both money and prestige also maintained small-scale businesses. As early as 1640 Philippa Hammond operated a shop at Boston. So did Widow Howdin (1645), Alice Thomas (before 1672), Ann Carter (1663), Jane Bernard (1672-76), Abigail Johnson (1672-73), Mistress Gutteridge (1690), Elizabeth Connigrave (1672-74), Rebecca Windsor (1672-74), and Mary Castle (1690). Almost all of these women ran coffee or cook shops, thereby utilizing their domestic training. Mary Avery and Susanna Jacob kept shop between 1685 and 1691, but whether they were owners or merely employees is unknown. Esther Palmer, a merchant, located in the metropolis in 1683, and Florence Mackarta, in partnership with two men, constructed a slaughterhouse on Peck's Wharf in 1693. A 1687 Boston tax list gives the names of forty-eight different women who derived some income from a trade or their estates—11.4 percent of all such persons rated. But business-women were rarer than the initial impression suggests. For example, it is not actually specified how many of the women on the 1687 list owned businesses and how many merely drew income from the estates of their deceased husbands. What *is* clear is that fully 85.4 percent of these women were widows.

Businesswomen, whether married or widowed, were few throughout New England. The paucity of early businesswomen can be readily demonstrated by searching through transcriptions of courtroom proceedings, town records, and other sources. . . . In all of New England outside Boston there are records of only nine women who worked at a trade or who ran a business other than innkeeping. By late century Margaret Barton of Salem, a chair frame maker, had accrued a fortune in "ventures at sea." In Hartford County, Elizabeth Gardner, Mary Phelps, and Mary Stanly owned interests in (respectively) an iron mill, a grist mill, and a shop. Jane Stolion appeared in court in 1645-46, accused of charging excessive prices at her New Haven dress and cloth shop. Mistress Jenny came before the Plymouth General Court in 1644 for not keeping the mortars at her mill clean, nor the bags of corn there from spoiling. Elizabeth Cadwell operated her husbands' ferry across the Connecticut River at Hartford after his death in 1695. One Maine widow, Elizabeth Rowdan, maintained a blacksmith shop and mill. Other women may have worked in their husband's bakery, cook, or apparel shops, or may have tailored clothing for sale; but the records observe a rigorous silence on that score, mentioning only one female baker at Salem (1639). Altogether, only 2.3 percent (23 of 988) of all tradespeople-merchants (again excluding innkeepers) were members of the "weaker sex."

An examination of those licensed to keep inns or sell alcoholic beverages indicates that few women supported themselves in this occupation, at least before the 1690s. Since all innkeepers had to secure licenses from the authorities, the records are quite complete. The first female innkeeper does not appear until 1643. Between 1643 and 1689 at least fifty-seven other women operated inns; however, they constituted but 18.9 percent of Boston's innkeepers and only 5 percent of those in the remainder of New England. On Ebenezer Peirce's *Civil, Military, and Professional Lists of Plymouth and Rhode Island Colonies* just three of seventy Plymouth innkeepers are female. In the 1690s, with large numbers of men away fighting in the Maine Indian wars, the New England total increased sharply, to eighty-four women—eight in Maine, twenty-four in New Hampshire, and fifty-two in the Bay Colony. Women then comprised over half of the tavernkeepers in Boston and approximately 20 percent of those in other locales. . . .

Although innkeeping or some other business may have given the individual woman some measure of personal satisfaction and self-sufficiency, the Boston tax list of 1687 suggests that businesswomen fared less well than businessmen. An occasional woman like the Widow Kellond might derive an annual income as high as £80 from her trade and estates, but she was much the exception. Only nineteen members of the "weaker sex"—39.6 percent of all tradeswomen—earned £10 or more from their trades and estates, while 74 percent of all tradesmen earned that much. The forty-eight female traders made £580 over the previous year, an average of £12, whereas the 373 male traders made £7,383, or £20 each.

There were several reasons why tradeswomen, when they managed to open shops, earned only 60 percent as much as tradesmen. Since the women possessed little training, their businesses tended to accent service in a way that was compatible with female sex-role stereotyping. Distributing beer, maintaining a cook shop, keeping an inn, and operating a millinery shop utilized talents common to housewives, but ones which returned little profit. Women in such businesses could not easily attract customers on the open market, for they lacked the mobility of carpenters, bricklayers, blacksmiths, and coopers. They could not advertise in newspapers, for none existed. They could not reap the benefits of an international trade, since they lacked ties to the great English trading houses and familiarity with foreign markets. Even credit was a problem. As milliner Hannah Crowell complained in 1696, "being a Woman [I] was not able to ride up and down to get in debts."

Women also lacked the capital necessary to establish large scale businesses. Only after her husband died did the typical woman strike out on her own, with the help of her widow's portion. Of all women who were licensed to sell spirituous liquors, some 71.1 percent were widows. Innkeeping was a ready source of sustenance for any widow whose husband left her house and little else. Working at a trade became an acceptable means of support for widows of artisans, but even they could only rarely increase the net value of their estates over the amounts they inherited. Age, decreased mobility, and a lack of appropriate training or education each took a toll. Moreover, husbands were often reluctant to provide for their wives by leaving them a full or part interest in their trade tools or their shops. Only two of fifty-seven Hartford County artisans, merchants, and shopkeepers bequeathed their widows interest in their businesses. Another man left a shop at Hartford to his sister.

Even those few widows who enjoyed some occupational independence were expected to restrict their activities to nurturant, housewifely, and comparatively low-status occupations. High-status positions such as public grammar-school teaching, the ministry, and major public offices were limited to men. Elizabeth Jones, appointed the Boston poundkeeper in 1670, 1676, and 1689, was the only woman to serve as a public official on even a minor level.

The woman who wished to work "by her own hand," whether widowed, married, or single, faced still other disadvantages. Before 1647 the Maine General Court forbade any woman from inhabiting the Isles of Shoales, thereby making it impossible for females to help out with the fishing or to operate stores at which the fishermen might buy provisions. Perhaps deterred by the sentiment expressed in Maine law, no woman of record ever fished at sea for a profit. Nor could women become sailors—when one dressed as a man and left Massachusetts on a vessel, her fellow seamen, upon discovering her sex, tarred and feathered her in a nearly fatal maltreatment. The presence of working women on the Atlantic was so inconceivable to Puritans that when a mysterious "Shallop at Sea man'd with women" was reported, men attributed the phenomenon to witchcraft.

WEALTH AND POVERTY

The limited, poorly paid, comparatively low status employment opportunities available to early New England women meant that they could not really participate in the expanding possibilities opened by the Commercial Revolution. Despite such disabilities, some observers might argue that dependent wives were rewarded in the end, by inheriting sizable properties (although not businesses) from their deceased husbands. Such widows could enjoy some independence in their later years. The tax lists seem to provide some evidence for this view; women appear as heads of families approximately 6 percent of the time, and fare well when their estates are compared to those of male family heads. . . .

It would be incorrect to assume, however, that as a group widows in Puritan New England were comparatively well-to-do, for most never appeared on a tax list. . . . Many husbands, well aware that their wives might have difficulty maintaining an estate, specified that their widows live with one or more sons in the family dwelling unit. Such men usually reserved one room, a garden, a cow, and some household goods for their widow's use. In one-tenth of all wills (30 of 282) fathers directed children to maintain their mother with annual supplies or a monetary allotment. The annual maintenance payment rarely amounted to much, however, averaging £9 13s.; most widows received less that £7. . . .

Although one-sixth or one-fifth of all widows (those of the middling and better sorts) enjoyed limited affluence, many more suffered poverty. . . .

The appointment of "keepers" for the indigent, or lodging them in the almshouse under a male attendant's supervision, blatantly reinforced female dependence. Such control angered some poor women, and at least two of them entirely rejected the dependence entailed in any form of relief. Mary Webster, a "wretched woman" of Hadley, Massachusetts, protested the efforts of church deacon Philip Smith to mitigate her indigence, expressing herself so sharply "that he declared himself apprehensive of receiving mischief at her hands" (ca. 1684). Jane Bourne of Cambridge refused to accept an allotment from the town for her food and lodging, instead moving out of town to secure employment elsewhere as a servant (1663). A third woman, Abigail Day, was "full of Discontent" and "Impatience under her Afflictions" while at the Boston almshouse. She would "thank neither God nor man" for the objectionable diet there, and she complained that her keeper "had several times made attempts upon her chastity" (1697).

The dissatisfaction of poor women like Abigail Day, Jane Bourne, and Mary Webster is readily understandable, for the paternalism of the Puritan system of poor relief too easily reflected women's difficulties in searching for gainful employment or starting businesses. Wherever they turned, women encountered the fruits of Puritan sexism—in low pay, lack of education and job training, decreased opportunities to secure the funds needed to open a business, and limitations on the kinds of employment available. . . . The great majority of women in early New England worked under a condition of dependence, whether as servants under the control of masters, poor women under the control of almshouse attendants or other keepers, widows under the relative control of their children, or (in the most common occupation of all) housewives under the control of their husbands.

The circumstances of life in seventeenth-century Puritan New England hardly had an emancipating effect. New England wives sometimes maintained family businesses in their husband's absence, or occasionally ran shops of their own; but so did English women. In fact, Alice Clark's research indicates that English women, as members of a more urbanized society, labored at many more occupations than did their New England counterparts. . . . While all of the information is not yet in, it is striking that 40 percent of New England's adult population comprised just 25 percent of all servants, 24 percent of all medical practitioners (if nurses and midwives are subtracted, the percentage drops to 9.6), 12.6 pecent of all schoolteachers, 18 percent of all innkeepers, and 2.3 percent of all tradespeople-merchants. Moreover, these women received much less remuneration than their male counterparts. Although labor shortages were frequent in the first few decades of settlement, such times did not lead to more women on the job market, or to women doing men's work. Inheritance patterns in agrarian locales made it virtually impossible for daughters and wives to exercise much control over capital investment in land. All but a few urban women were similarly unable to acquire real estate or capital which would have enabled them to expand their incomes. The only way for women to experience any upward mobility was to marry well. Seventeenth-century New England was a "Garden of Eden" only for the woman who pursued economic opportunity dependently, as the rib of a (hopefully) prospering and generous Adam.

POSTSCRIPT

Was the Colonial Period a "Golden Age" for Women in America?

The Koehler and Carr and Walsh studies focus upon two different regions in the seventeenth century. Their respective essays indicate that what might have been true for women in colonial New England might not hold true for women who migrated from Europe to the Chesapeake region. Moreover, there is no guarantee that the status of women remained constant throughout the colonial period.

Changes in the status of colonial women have been explored in Mary Beth Norton, "The Evolution of White Women's Experience in Early America," *American Historical Review* (June 1984). Norton surveys the basic elements of the "golden-age theory" and perceptively pronounces that theory to be "simplistic and unsophisticated" because it concentrates primarily upon the economic function of women in colonial society. The experiences of early American women, she asserts, are best explored within three chronological divisions: (1) 1620 to 1660; (2) 1660 to 1750; and (3) 1750 to 1815.

Surveys of American women's history which address the colonial period include June Sochen, *Herstory: A Woman's View of American History* (Alfred Publishing Company, 1974); Mary P. Ryan, *Womanhood in America: From Colonial Times to the Present* (New Viewpoints, 1975); and Nancy Woloch, *Women and the American Experience* (Knopf, 1984). Support for the "golden-age theory" can be found in Richard B. Morris, *Studies in the History of American Law*, 2d ed. (Octagon Books, 1964); Elizabeth Anthony Dexter, *Colonial Women of Affairs*, 2d ed. (Houghton Mifflin, 1931); Mary Ritter Beard, *Woman as Force in History* (Macmillan, 1946); Eleanor Flexner, *Century of Struggle* (Belknap Press, 1959); Roger Thompson, *Women in Stuart England and America: A Comparative Study* (Routledge and Kegan, 1974); and Page Smith, *Daughters of the Promised Land: Women in American History* (Little, Brown, 1977). For the relationship between women and witchcraft, see John Putnam Demos, *Entertaining Satan: Witchcraft and the Culture of Early New England* (Oxford University Press, 1982); and Carol F. Karlsen, *The Devil in the Shape of a Woman: Witchcraft in Colonial New England* (Norton, 1987). Women in the age of the American Revolution are treated in Mary Beth Norton, *Liberty's Daughters: The Revolutionary Experience of American Women, 1750–1800* (Little, Brown, 1980); and Linda K. Kerber, *Women of the Republic: Intellect and Ideology in Revolutionary America* (University of North Carolina Press, 1980). N. E. H. Hull, *Female Felons: Women and Serious Crime in Colonial Massachusetts* (University of Illinois Press, 1987) is a recent work which concludes that men and women received equal justice in the colonial period.

ISSUE 4

Did American Slaves Develop a Distinct Afro-American Culture in the Eighteenth Century?

YES: Alan Kulikoff, from *Tobacco and Slaves: The Development of Southern Cultures in the Chesapeake, 1680–1800* (University of North Carolina Press, 1986)

NO: Jean Butenhoff Lee, from "The Problem of Slave Community in the Eighteenth-Century Chesapeake," *William and Mary Quarterly* (October 1986)

ISSUE SUMMARY

YES: Kulikoff claims that Chesapeake slaves developed their own social institutions and a distinct indigenous culture in the half century between 1740 and 1790.

NO: Lee emphasizes the difficult and often unsuccessful efforts of slaves to create a stable family and community life in eighteenth-century Maryland.

The arrival at Jamestown, Virginia, in 1619 of a Dutch frigate carrying twenty Africans marked a momentous event for the future development of England's North American colonies. The introduction of a new racial component generated political, economic, and social repercussions that still are felt in modern America. And with the development of black slavery, American colonists set the stage for a long-term moral dilemma that ultimately produced the bloodshed and destruction of civil war.

In the last thirty years, historians have given considerable attention to colonial American slavery. Their research, however, has left unresolved a question regarding those first Africans in Jamestown: Were the first blacks in England's North American colonies immediately bound out as slaves? While the evidence is inconclusive, there is strong reason to believe that the first Africans brought to Jamestown became indentured servants and were freed after fulfilling their contracts to their masters. These individuals, therefore, formed the basis for the nation's free black population, which by 1860 would number approximately five hundred thousand.

If slavery did not originate with those first Africans, when did the institution appear? The process was remarkably gradual in the Chesapeake where the first slave codes were not enacted by the Virginia and Maryland legislatures until the 1660s. Some extant records, however, suggest that the status of "slave" was being given to black servants at least twenty years prior to the appearance of a *de jure* system. In 1640, John Punch, a black servant, was arrested with two white fellow servants for running away. All were found guilty, and the two white men were whipped and given additional time to serve on their indentures. Punch, however, was only whipped. The court record revealed that since he already was serving his master for life, no time could be added on. In other words, John Punch was a slave.

By 1750, the institution of slavery had emerged in all the British colonies in North America. The preponderance of male bondsmen, however, prevented American slave populations from expanding through natural increase. Masters, therefore, depended upon shipments from Africa for new slaves until the sex ratio achieved greater parity. In addition, heavy concentrations of slaves did not appear until the rise of large plantations. In New England, such plantations were limited to Rhode Island's Narragansett Valley; in the Middle Colonies, New Yorkers and Pennsylvanians acquired some extensive lands worked by slaves; and in the South, large plantations cultivating tobacco and rice appeared in the eighteenth century.

This, however, tells us little about the slaves themselves. How did they live? What was the scope of their lives? Was there a slave community in the colonial period? These questions are explored in the following two essays.

Allan Kulikoff contends that only with a more equal sex ratio, large plantations, and concentrated numbers of bondsmen could slaves develop a community life apart from that of their masters. These characteristics emerged in the Chesapeake area between 1740 and 1790 and permitted slaves to establish a recognizable, autonomous Afro-American culture.

Jean Lee agrees that the development of Afro-American slave community life was a gradual process, but she challenges Kulikoff's conclusions regarding the emergence of an autonomous slave community. By focusing on a single county, Charles County, Maryland, Lee determined that Afro-American family and communal life was quite fragile and subject to constant disruption. The contacts among slaves on a single plantation or on adjacent plantations, she asserts, were so limited as to preclude the kind of community life Kulikoff describes.

YES

Allan Kulikoff

ORIGINS OF BLACK SOCIETY

Although the eighteenth-century Chesapeake planter looked upon newly enslaved Africans as strange and barbaric folk, he knew that American-born slaves could be taught English customs. Hugh Jones, a Virginia cleric, commented in 1724 that "the languages of the new Negroes are various harsh jargons" but added that slaves born in Virginia "talk good English, and affect our language, habits, and customs." How readily did slaves in Maryland and Virginia accept English ways? Did the preponderance of whites in the region's population and their power force slaves to accept Anglo-American beliefs, values, and skills? Or did slaves succeed in creating their own institutions despite white repression? . . .

How readily slaves could form their own culture depended upon both the pattern of forced African immigration to the Americas and the economic and demographic environment that awaited new slaves. Black forced immigrants came from hundreds of different communities and did not have a common culture. Their religious beliefs, kinship systems, and forms of social organization differed substantially. Nevertheless, West Africans did share some values and experiences. For example, each West African group developed different kinship practices, but throughout the region each person located his place in society by his position in his kin group and lineage. When Africans arrived in the New World, their cultural differences were initially of greater significance than the values they shared. They shared only their experience as slaves and labored to make a new society out of their common beliefs and values. The features of the society they formed depended upon the demands of the white masters, the characteristics of the economy, the demography of slave and white populations, and the extent of ethnic division among blacks. As they interacted daily, slaves learned to cope with ordinary problems of working, eating, marrying, and child rearing under the adverse conditions of slavery. The social institutions they developed were neither imposed by Europeans nor directly taken from African communities, but were a unique combination of elements borrowed from the European enslavers and from the common values of various African societies. As soon as slaves formed social institutions, internal conflict diminished, and blacks could place a new Afro-American culture into a settled social context.

The size of working units that masters organized, the number of Africans they bought from slavetraders, and the crops they grew, as well as the rules they required their slaves to follow, influenced the kind of communities their slaves could form. Economic decisions by thousands of masters determined both the density of the black population and the proportion of whites in the population, and these demographic patterns in turn set limits on the intensity of slave community life. The choice of crops was crucial. Some crops required large plantations; others could be grown on small farms. Since large plantations needed more slaves than small farms, large planters purchased greater numbers of African slaves, and consequently, regions dominated by large plantations had greater concentrations of slaves and a larger proportion of Africans in their slave population than regions dominated by farms. Slaves who lived on a large plantation in a region where a substantial majority of the people were enslaved and the density of the slave population was high probably had more opportunities to worship their gods, begin stable families, and develop their own communities than did slaves who lived on small quarters in a preponderantly white country. A slave who lived with many Africans in a place where continual heavy importation of blacks kept the proportion of Africans high was more likely to adopt African customs than the slave

who lived where importation was sporadic, the proportion of immigrants among black adults low, and the number of whites great.

This model explains the development of black society in the Chesapeake colonies quite well. African and Afro-American slaves developed a settled life there very slowly. Three stages of community development can be discerned. From roughly 1650 to 1690, blacks assimilated the norms of white society, but the growth of the number of blacks also triggered white repression. The period from 1690 to 1740 was an era of heavy slave imports, small plantation sizes, and social conflicts among blacks. The infusion of Africans often disrupted newly formed slave communities. Finally, from 1740 to 1790, imports declined and then stopped, plantation sizes increased, the proportion of blacks in the population grew, and divisions among slaves disappeared. Consequently, native blacks formed relatively settled communities. . . .

TOWARD AFRO-AMERICAN SLAVE COMMUNITIES

The demographic conditions that prevented blacks from developing a cohesive social life before 1740 changed during the quarter of a century before the Revolution, as immigration of Africans to the Chesapeake declined sharply. Only 17 percent of Virginia's adult blacks in 1750 and 15 percent in 1755 had arrived within the previous ten years, and these newcomers went in relatively greater numbers to newer piedmont counties than had their predecessors. . . .

As the number of enslaved Africans in tidewater declined, the internal division among blacks diminished. These recent arrivals were under greater pressure than their predecessors to acquire the language, values, and beliefs of the dominant native majority. Like new Negroes before them, they sometimes ran away, but with less success. On arrival, they found themselves isolated and alone. Olaudah Equiano, for example, was brought to Virginia in 1757 at age twelve. "I was now exceedingly miserable," he later wrote, "and thought myself worse off than any . . . of my companions; for they could talk to each other, but I had no person to speak to that I could understand. In this state I was constantly grieving and pining, and wishing for death." But once slaves like Equiano learned English, they became part of the Afro-American community. Bob, twenty-nine, and Turkey Tom, thirty-eight, were new Negroes who lived on the home plantation of Charles Carroll of Carrollton in 1773. Since Bob and Tom were apparently the only two recent immigrant slaves on any of Carroll's many plantations, they both could participate fully in plantation life. Bob was a smith, a position usually reserved for natives; he married the daughter of a carpenter and lived with her and their two children. Tom, a laborer, also found a place in the plantation's kinship networks: his wife was at least a third-generation Marylander. Very few Africans probably ever became artisans, but so few Africans were imported that most Africans in tidewater could find wives among the native majority. . . .

The size of quarters increased after 1740 throughout tidewater, providing greater opportunities for slaves to develop a social life of their own. The proportion who lived on units of more than twenty slaves doubled in St. Mary's County, increased by half in York and

Anne Arundel counties, and grew, though more slowly, in Prince George's. In the 1780s, one-third to two-thirds of the slaves in eleven tidewater counties lived on farms of more than twenty slaves, and only a sixth to a tenth lived on units of fewer than six. If these counties were typical, 44 percent of tidewater's blacks lived on farms of more than twenty slaves, and another 26 percent lived on medium-sized units of eleven to twenty. The number of very large quarters also grew. Before 1740 few quarters housed more than thirty slaves, but by the 1770s and 1780s the wealthiest gentlemen ran home plantations with more than one hundred slaves and quarters with thirty to fifty. . . .

Because plantation sizes increased, more lived on quarters away from the master's house and his direct supervision. On small plantations the quarter could be located in an outbuilding or in a single dwelling. On large plantations, the quarters resembled small villages. Slave houses and the yards that surrounded them were centers of domestic activity. The houses were furnished with straw bedding, barrels for seats, pots, pans, and usually a grindstone or handmill for beating corn into meal. Agricultural tools and livestock were scattered outside the houses, and the quarter was surrounded by plots of corn and tobacco cultivated by the slaves.

Afro-Americans made the quarters into little communities, usually organized around families. Because the African slave trade largely ceased, the adult sex ratio decreased. Almost all men and women could marry, and by the 1770s many slaves had native grandparents and great-grandparents. The quarter was the center of family activity every evening and on Sundays and holidays, for except during the harvest, slaves had these times to themselves. Nonresident fathers visited their wives and children; runaways stayed with friends or kinfolk. In the evenings native men sometimes traveled to other quarters, where they passed the night talking, singing, smoking, and drinking. On occasional Sundays they held celebrations at which they danced to the banjo and sang bitter songs about their treatment by the master. . . .

After 1740, the density of the black population and the proportion of slaves in the population of tidewater both increased, and, as a result, the area's slave society gradually spread out to embrace many neighboring plantations in a single network. Ironically, masters provided slaves with several tools they could use to extend these cross-quarter networks. Slave sales tore black families asunder, but as masters sold and transferred their slaves, more and more kinfolk lived on neighboring quarters, and naturally they retained ties of affection after they were separated. Whites built numerous roads and paths to connect their farms and villages, and their slaves used these byways to visit friends or run away and evade recapture. By the 1770s and 1780s, Afro-Americans numerically dominated many neighborhoods and created many cross-plantation networks. . . .

Quarters were connected by extensive networks of roads and paths, which grew remarkably complex during the eighteenth century. For example, Prince George's County had about 50 miles of public roads in 1700, but 478 in 1762, or one mile of public road for every square mile of taxed land in the county. This elaboration of roads made it easier for slaves to visit nearby plantations. Whites could not patrol all these roads, let alone private paths not maintained by the county, without a general mobilization of the white population. . . .

The Afro-Americans made good use of these opportunities to create their own society. In the years before the Revolution, they developed a sense of community with other slaves both on their own plantations and in the neighborhood. This social solidarity can be shown in several ways. In the first place, Afro-Americans often concealed slaves from within the neighborhood on their quarters. Since masters searched the neighborhood for runaways and placed notices on public buildings before advertising in a newspaper, many runaways, especially truants who were recaptured or returned voluntarily after a few days' absence, were not so advertised. The increasing appearance of such advertisements in the *Maryland Gazette* during the thirty years before the Revolution suggests that slaves were becoming more successful in evading easy recapture. The numbers of runaways in southern Maryland rose in each five-year period between 1745 and 1779, except the years 1765-1769, and the increase was especially great during the Revolution, when some escaped slaves were able to reach British troops. . . .

The slave community, of course, had its share of conflicts, and on occasion a slave assaulted or stole from another slave. Nonetheless, accounts of several of these incidents suggest that the rest of the slave community united against the transgressors. Slaves sometimes refused to testify against their fellows, especially when blacks stole goods from whites, but when a member of the black community was hurt, slaves testified against the guilty person to protect themselves or their property. In May 1763 Jack poisoned Clear with a mixture of rum and henbane; she became ill and died the following February. Six slaves who belonged to Clear's master informed him of the act and testified against Jack in Prince George's court. They were joined by three slaves who lived on nearby plantations. The jury found Jack guilty, and he was sentenced to hang. Similarly, when Tom (owned by Richard Snowden, a prominent ironmaker) broke into Weems's quarter (near the Snowden ironworks) in Anne Arundel County and took goods belonging to Weems's slaves, six men and women owned by James and David Weems testified against him. He was found guilty and hanged.

There were limits to slave solidarity. Though native-born slaves often remained loyal to immediate kinfolk and friends on their own quarters, to more distant kinfolk, and to slaves on nearby or distant plantations, these loyalties sometimes clashed with each other or with the demands of the master. Then slaves had to choose sides in intricate master-slave conflicts. The development of these alliances can be seen in the response of Landon Carter and of his slaves when Simon, Carter's ox-carter, ran away in March 1766. Carter had Simon outlawed, and joined the militia to hunt for him. Simon was aided directly by at least six residents of his quarter, including an uncle, a brother, and a sister-in-law. Nonetheless, several other kinfolk, who lived on other quarters, were forced by Carter to inform against him. Finally, after two weeks, Talbot (another of Carter's slaves who lived some distance from Simon) shot Simon in the leg and, with the aid of several other slaves, recaptured him.

THE ORIGINS OF AFRO-AMERICAN CULTURE

Slaves in the Chesapeake, unlike those in the West Indies, took several generations to form a semiautonomous Afro-American culture. West Africans needed settled communities to develop the bundle of common values and beliefs they brought over with them into a syncretic culture, but the demographic environment of the early eighteenth-century Chesapeake was extremely hostile to the formation of settled communities. Heavily white populations, high black sex ratios, continually declining proportions of Africans among slaves, conflicts between African and creole slaves, and small unit sizes all made the development of both slave communities and slave culture difficult. African forced migrants did not forget these values, however, but used behavioral symbols of them whenever they could. These Africans practiced their beliefs in disconnected and often private episodes, not in daily social interaction with many other slaves. African slaves in the Chesapeake made tribal drums, strummed on their banjos, poisoned their enemies as did African witches and cunning men, passed on a few African words to their descendants, and sometimes engaged in private devotions to Allah or their tribal gods.

Afro-American slaves had developed strong community institutions on their quarters by the 1760s and 1770s, but the values and beliefs they held are difficult to ascertain. Since blacks in the Chesapeake region did not achieve a settled social life until after a heavy African slave trade stopped and since whites continued to live in even the most densely black areas, one would expect slave culture in the region to reflect white values and beliefs. Even native-born slaves had little choice either about their work or about the people who lived with them in their quarters. Nevertheless, they had a small measure of self-determination in their family life, in their religion, and in the ways they celebrated and mourned. When they could choose, Afro-American slaves simultaneously borrowed from whites and drew on the values and beliefs their ancestors brought from West Africa to form a culture not only significantly different from that of Anglo-Americans but also different from the culture of any West African group or any other group of North American slaves.

The ways Afro-American slaves organized their family life indicates most clearly how they used both African and Euro-American forms to create a new institution compatible with their life under slavery. By the time of the Revolution, most slaves lived in families, and slave households were similar to those of their white masters. About as many creole slaves as whites lived in two-parent and extended households. Whites lived in monogamous families, and only scattered examples of the African custom of polygyny can be found among creole blacks. Slavery forced the kinfolk of extended families to live very close to one another on large plantations, where they played and worked together. By contrast, whites only occasionally visited their extended kinfolk and worked in the fields only with their children, not with adult brothers and sisters. This closeness fostered a sense of kin solidarity among Afro-Americans. They named their children after both sides of the family (but interestingly enough, daughters were not often named after their mothers). And they sometimes refused to marry

within the plantation even when sex ratios were equal: many of the available potential partners were first cousins, and black slaves apparently refused to marry first cousins. This may have represented a transformation of African marriage taboos that differed from tribe to tribe but tended to be stricter than those of Chesapeake whites, who frequently married first cousins.

West African religions varied remarkably among themselves, yet enslaved Africans shared a similar way of viewing the world, which they passed on to their native black children. All activities, Africans believed, were infused with sacredness, each in its own particular way. Religion was not universal but was practiced only within a communal context. God, spirits, animals, and plants were all seen in relation to people in the community, and certain men—rainmakers, medicine men, priests, sorcerers—had special powers over spirits or material life not available to most people.

In contrast, the Anglican faith practiced by most slaveholders in the Chesapeake before the Revolution radically separated the sacred from the secular: Anglicans attended church services in isolated buildings on Sundays but often ignored religious ceremonies the rest of the week. Although native slaves occasionally accepted the outward signs of Christian belief, few became convinced Protestants. Their children were baptized, and sometimes they received religious instruction. All three Anglican clergymen of Prince George's County reported in 1724 that they baptized slave children and adults (especially native-born adults) and preached to those who would listen. In 1731 one Prince George's minister baptized blacks "where perfect in their Catechism" and "visit[ed] them in their sickness and married them when called upon." Similar work continued in Virginia and Maryland in the generation before the Revolution. Nonetheless, Thomas Bacon, a Maryland cleric and publisher of a compendium of the colony's laws, believed that these baptized slaves were often "living in as profound Ignorance of what Christianity really is, (except as to a few outward Ordinances) as if they had remained in the midst of those barbarous Heathen Countries from whence their parents had been first imported."

Native-born slaves continued to observe African forms of mourning and celebrating, but they did not place these forms within the structure of Anglican religion, nor did masters give them time enough to expand these occasional ceremonies into an indigenous Afro-American religion. Whites sometimes observed these strange practices. Thomas Bacon, for instance, preached to blacks on Maryland's Eastern Shore in the 1740s at services they directed "at their *funerals* (several of which I have attended)—and to such small congregations as their *marriages* have brought together." Two early nineteenth-century observers connected similar services they saw to the slaves' remote African past. Henry Knight, who traveled to Virginia in 1816, explained that masters permitted slaves a holiday to mourn the death of a fellow slave. The day of the funeral, "perhaps a month after the corpse is interred, is a jovial day with them; they sing and dance and drink the dead to his new home, which some believe to be in old Guinea," the home of their grandparents and great-grandparents. A Charlotte County, Virginia, cleric saw more solemn but equally emotional services. He contended that there were "many remains . . . of the savage customs of Africa. They cry and bawl and howl around the grave and roll in the dirt, and make many expressions of the most frantic grief . . . sometimes the noise they make may be heard as far as one or two miles."

The slaves' music and dance, though often unconnected to their religion, displayed a distinctly African character. Afro-American slaves continued to make and to play two instruments (the banjo and balafo) of African origin. In 1774 Nicholas Cresswell, a British visitor, described slave celebrations in Charles County, Maryland. On Sundays, he wrote, the blacks "generally meet together and amuse themselves with Dancing to the Banjo. This musical instrument . . . is made of a Gourd something in the imitation of a Guitar, with only four strings." "Their poetry," Cresswell reported, "is like the music—Rude and uncultivated. Their Dancing is most violent exercise, but so irregular and grotesque. I am not able to describe it." Cresswell's reaction to the dancing suggests that it contained African rhythms unknown in European dance. If the form was African, it was placed in an American context: the slave songs Cresswell heard "generally relate the usage they have received from their Masters or Mistresses in a very satirical stile and manner."

Native slaves retained folk beliefs that may have been integral parts of West African religions. Slaves sometimes turned to magic, sorcery, and witchcraft to resolve conflicts within their own community or to strike back at harsh or unreasonable masters. Some African medicine men, magicians, sorcerers, and witches migrated and passed on their skills to other slaves. These men were spiritual leaders (or powerful, if evil men) in many African communities, including those of the Ibos, and they continued to practice among creole slaves who believed in their powers. Several examples suggest the prevalence of these beliefs. William Grimes was born in King George County, Virginia, in 1784; his narrative of his life as a runaway suggests that he was terrified by a woman he thought was a witch, that he feared sleeping in the bed of a dead man, and that he consulted fortune-tellers. Dissatisfied slaves might consult conjurers to discover how to poison their masters. In 1773, for instance, Sharper was accused by his master, Peter Hansbrough of Stafford County, Virginia, of "Endeavouring to Procuring Poison from a Negroe Doctor or Conjurer as they are Call'd" for an unknown but dangerous purpose after Hansbrough had "discovered Some behaviour in . . . Sharper which occasioned [him] to be more Strict in inquiring into . . . where he Spent his time in his absent hours." Similarily, two slave blacksmiths in Spotsylvania County were convicted of attempting to poison their master in 1797, but seventy-six local residents petitioned the state for clemency because the slaves had been influenced by "a Negro Wench, or conjurer of Mr. James Crawford."

Afro-American slaves did not transform these disparate fragments of African cultures into a new slave religion until the development of white evangelical religion during the decades before and after the Revolution. Revivalist preachers permitted and even encouraged slaves to adapt African forms to the Christian faith. The most intensive black religious activity was in southside and central piedmont Virginia, areas with the Chesapeake's highest concentrations of new Negroes. The first evangelical mission to slaves began in 1755, when two

white Baptists organized a black congregation on William Byrd's plantation in Mecklenburg County; that group of Christians lasted until the Revolution. Samuel Davies, a Presbyterian clergyman who practiced in Hanover County, and several of his colleagues converted as many as a thousand slaves to evangelical Protestantism in the 1750s. Davies thought that these blacks were true Christians, not only acquainted with "the important doctrines of the Christian Religion, but also a deep sense of things upon their spirits, and a life of the strictest Morality and Piety." They placed African music into Protestant liturgy: "The *Negroes*," Davies commented, "above all of the human species that ever I knew, have an ear for Music, and a kind of delight in Psalmody." Some of his converts even "lodged all night in my kitchen; and sometimes, when I have awakened about two or three a-clock in the morning, a torrent of sacred harmony poured into my chamber, and carried my mind to heaven.

The numbers of Afro-Americans attracted to evangelical Protestantism rose slowly in the 1770s and then increased rapidly during the awakenings of the 1780s and 1790s. By 1790, about 7 percent of Virginia's black adults were members of Baptist or Methodist churches, and far more were affected by the revivals in both piedmont and tidewater counties. Slave work patterns and the authority of masters might be affected by this new and all-encompassing religiosity. For instance, some members of the Episcopal church in King George County complained in the mid-1780s that "Preachers or Exhorters" daily gathered "together Multitudes of People in the Woods most of them Slaves, alienating their minds from their Daily Labour and their Masters Interest."

Blacks accepted the exhortations of Baptist and Methodist preachers in the 1780s and 1790s far more enthusiastically than did whites. They answered the preacher's call with crying, shouting, shaking, and trembling. Their reaction was perhaps in part dictated by their African past: the ceremonies of revivals were similar to those of some African religions, and African forms meshed well with the emerging theology of evangelical Protestantism. Revivals, unlike the liturgy of rational religion, allowed slaves to reduce the distinctions between sacred and secular and return to a holistic, African kind of religiosity.

Afro-American slaves developed their own social institutions and indigenous culture during the second half of the eighteenth century. A period of great disruptions among blacks early in the century was followed by a time of settled communities. Newly enslaved Africans came to the Chesapeake colonies in large enough numbers to cause conflicts between native slaves and new Negroes, but the migration was too small to allow Africans to develop syncretic communities and cultures. It was only when native adults began to predominate that earlier conflicts among blacks were contained and families and quarter communities began to emerge. The culture these creole slaves forged put African forms of behavior into Euro-American familial and religious structures. Creole slaves by that time were two or three generations removed from Africa and (except in southside Virginia) infrequently saw Africans. They may not have been aware of the complicated origins of their behavior.

For the slaves, the origins of their culture were less important than its auton-

omy. White observers agreed that the music, dance, and religiosity of black slaves differed remarkably from those of whites. The emergence of black culture, and especially the beginnings of Afro-Christianity, played an important role in the development of slave solidarity. Slaves possessed little power over their lives: they suffered the expropriation of the fruits of their labor by their masters; they could be forced to move away from family and friends at a moment's notice; they were subject to the whip for any perceived transgressions. The practice of a distinctive culture within their own quarters gave them some small power over their own lives and destinies they otherwise would not have possessed.

The development of an indigenous black community life and culture had a great impact upon the social structure of the entire region. Afro-Americans became both an enslaved working class and a racial caste, separate from their white masters. They had their own system of social relations among themselves, within the context of slavery. Even though whites continued to possess remarkable power over blacks, they had to relate to slaves as a group with a structure and culture they could not entirely control. Afro-American communal life and culture, then, set minimal bounds on white behavior and encouraged black solidarity.

NO

Jean Butenhoff Lee

THE PROBLEM OF SLAVE COMMUNITY IN THE EIGHTEENTH-CENTURY CHESAPEAKE

In the spring of 1774, a young Englishman named Nicholas Cresswell crossed the Atlantic, entered Chesapeake Bay, and came to safe anchorage on the Rappahannock River. From there, three black oarsmen rowed him north on the bay as far as the broad mouth of the Potomac River, then upriver along the shores of St. Mary's and Charles counties, Maryland. On the afternoon of May 21, Cresswell reached his destination, the tiny village of Nanjemoy in southwestern Charles County.

A week later, as he was becoming acquainted with the sights and sounds of the Tobacco Coast, Cresswell attended what he called a "Negro Ball" near Nanjemoy. "Sundays being the only days these poor creatures have to themselves," he wrote, "they generally meet together and amuse themselves with Dancing to the Banjo," a four-stringed gourd "something in the imitation of a Guitar." Some of the slaves also sang "very droll music indeed," songs in which "they generally relate the usage they have received from their Masters or Mistresses in a very satirical stile and manner." The newcomer pronounced the music and verse "Rude and uncultivated," the dancing "most violent excercise . . . irregular and grotesque." With a hint of disbelief he concluded that the slaves "all appear to be exeedingly happy at these merry-makings and seem as if they had forgot or were not sensible of their miserable condition."

Cresswell's account is the kind of infrequent literary evidence that historians of the black experience in early America cherish for its clues to social intercourse among the enslaved, to their distinctive and expressive folk art, their use of leisure hours, and their resistance to the slave labor system, if only in lyrical satire. That Sunday in 1774 the Englishman observed a manifestation of what several scholars have argued was a recent development in the Chesapeake tidewater: stable Afro-American communities, a distinctive amalgam forged in the demographic experience of blacks during

From the *William and Mary Quarterly*, 3d Ser., 43 (July 1986). Reprinted by permission.

the preceding century. By the era of the American Revolution, it is argued, slave population growth had proceeded far enough that many blacks could exercise substantial control over their labor and leisure. They maintained reasonably stable family lives, extensive kin networks, and social intercourse that transcended plantation boundaries. The present article describes this interpretation more fully, offers a general critique of it, and employs quantifiable and narrative sources to examine slave life in the heavily black tidewater county that Cresswell observed. The evidence from Charles County does not deny that slaves sought to create communal life but emphasizes what a difficult—and often unsuccessful—effort it must have been.

RELYING ON PROBATE INVENTORIES COMpiled between 1658 and 1730 in Charles and three adjacent counties on Maryland's lower Western Shore, Russell R. Menard has suggested that the few slaves who lived there in the seventeenth century must have endured an isolated and dehumanizing existence. Most were adult males. Housed mainly on small plantations, they lived out their brief lives in a dreary round of clearing land, tending livestock, and growing tobacco and corn. They were cut off from their African culture, no longer part of kin groups through which African societies were organized, and often unable to find wives and form families. Importation of large numbers of Africans during the late seventeenth and early eighteenth centuries exacerbated the sexual imbalance among blacks, for adult males predominated in slave cargoes.

Allan Kulikoff hypothesizes that skewed sex ratios, small plantations, and the presence of many Africans persisted until about 1740. These conditions, he holds, impeded the development of a distinctive Afro-American culture because the experiences of Chesapeake and African slaves were different. Blacks who were born in the Chesapeake or who lived there for some time presumably were more or less assimilated to life in the white-dominated society of the Tobacco Coast. Periodically their lives were disrupted by the arrival of newcomers fresh from Africa, people of many ethnic groups who spoke a babel of languages, worshiped an array of deities, were bereft of family ties, and had to learn new ways of life and labor. Successive infusions of Africans, Kulikoff argues, therefore delayed formation of a society that was distinctively Afro-American.

Menard and Kulikoff agree that important demographic changes in the eighteenth century heralded the emergence of more settled social conditions and greater cultural homogeneity among slaves. First, the black population began to grow by natural increase, and importations from Africa declined. As a result, the proportion of children increased, and the ratio of men to women improved. In other words, as the slave population changed from largely immigrant to native-born, it gradually acquired more normal demographic characteristics. Second, slave population density increased, as did the number of large plantations. These factors allegedly led to widened opportunities within bondage. Some slaves escaped wearisome toil in the fields to become artisans or domestics. Others gained a measure of autonomy over their lives by being assigned to quarters where whites were not regularly present. For many more, a growing, sexually balanced, and largely native-born population clustered on large plantations was conducive, in Menard's words, to "social contact, intimate personal relationships, and a stable family life." By 1790, Kulikoff contends, "native blacks formed relatively settled communities," both within and among plantations. The linchpin of this argument is demographic change: as a native-born, sexually balanced black population experienced natural growth, and as population density and plantation size also increased, these conditions provided the basis for family and community life, occupational diversity, and autonomy.

Kulikoff has located this important transition in the years 1740 to 1790. He has also attempted to establish the distribution of the Chesapeake slave population and to explore some of the social and cultural consequences. He cautions that research on the region is incomplete, that his conclusions are based at least partly on unprovable assumptions, and that relationships between demographic and economic conditions, on the one hand, and slave society and culture, on the other, are "difficult to determine." He nevertheless believes that between 1740 and the American Revolution, in the area from "just north of the Patuxent" River in Anne Arundel and Prince George's counties, Maryland, "to just south of the James" River in Virginia, "plantations were large, black population density was high, few whites were present," and "well developed" road networks linked plantations. Slaves in this broad region "could create a rudimentary cross-plantation society," a process whites facilitated by selling slaves within their neighborhoods. Whereas blacks rarely lived in groups of more than thirty before 1740, "by the 1770s and 1780s the wealthiest gentlemen ran home plantations with more than one hundred

slaves and quarters with thirty to fifty." By the 1780s, Kulikoff argues, perhaps 44 percent of the enslaved resided on large quarters (those with more than twenty blacks); another 4 percent were men on smaller units located near "many large quarters." Yet another 26 percent lived on middling plantations, in groups of eleven to twenty, "and could participate in the family and community activities of their quarters." Composing the last one-fourth of the slaves, he contends, were "women and children who lived on small plantations . . . [and] usually did not travel from quarter to quarter but had to wait for husbands and fathers to visit them."

Kulikoff holds that, before the Revolution, slaves "developed strong community institutions on their quarters" and formed complex, cross-plantation kin networks. Balanced sex ratios enabled most men and women to marry, and by the 1770s the majority of Afro-Americans lived in families and had households "similar to those of their white masters. About as many creole slaves as whites lived in two-parent and extended households." Grandparents and even great-grandparents were common. A family or two usually inhabited the small plantations, while "extended families in which most residents were kinfolk" occupied the large units. Because slave dwellings on large plantations usually were located, Kulikoff claims, at some distance from the master's house, their occupants spent many hours of their lives free of direct white supervision. By the 1780s, one-half to three-fourths of the slaves living in the Chesapeake tidewater "enjoyed some sort of social life not controlled by their masters." Slaves socialized with one another, tended gardens located in the yards surrounding their quarters, sang and danced at gatherings like the one Nicholas Cresswell witnessed in 1774, traveled from one plantation to another to visit friends and relatives, gave food and other help to runaways, and protected themselves from harm at the hands of fellow bondsmen and bondswomen.

THIS CONCEPTION OF BLACK LIFE NOW DOMinates discussion of slavery in the eighteenth-century Chesapeake. Yet it remains unproven. The obscurity in which most slaves lived obstructs historians' efforts to reconstruct their lives, nor have scholars made full use of the sources that are available. Information on the number of Africans carried to Maryland and Virginia—blacks who allegedly intruded upon existing slave communities—is incomplete. Data on their dispersal are fragmentary. Historians have little notion who purchased the Africans, whether they were bought singly or in groups, and whether they joined preexisting black households. The rate at which Africans reproduced, when natural increase began, and when a largely native-born black population emerged in the Chesapeake have not been determined with any precision.

Attempts to identify Afro-American family connections, moreover, often prove futile. Marriage and birth registers are rare for slaves. Masters' wills and inventories of estates only occasionally reveal kinship ties among a decedent's human chattels; when they do, these sources often link only a mother and her youngest child. The disruptions to which slaves were subjected—assignment to outlying quarters, hiring out, sale, and dispersal through gift or bequest—preclude any confident expectation that blacks who lived near one another were necessarily related. Nor does procreation

by itself signify marriage or other enduring family commitments. The best evidence for slave families comes from the papers of a few great planters, but it is questionable whether kin connections that can be identified on some of the largest units were duplicated elsewhere, especially on smaller plantations.

The ruling interpretation leaves many questions to be answered with greater specificity. One would expect that growing population densities enhanced blacks' abilities to interact, find spouses, raise families, and create an Afro-American culture. But how dense was the slave population in the eighteenth-century Chesapeake? How many tidewater planters managed home plantations with more than one hundred blacks and quarters with thirty to fifty? How distant, typically, were slave dwellings from the master's house? If one-half to three-fourths of the blacks had "some sort of social life not controlled by their masters," is it believable that masters entirely controlled the lives of the rest of the enslaved?

Another problem concerns slaves' ability to interact across plantation boundaries. Road networks, high black population densities, and the practice of selling or otherwise disposing of slaves—especially relatives and friends—within neighborhoods obviously increased opportunities for contact. How often contacts were actually made is, of course, another matter. As yet we know little about how slaves were dispersed geographically, about the extent of road and path networks across the Chesapeake, or about how easily slaves could travel—either furtively or with their masters' permission—from one plantation to another. We shall never know how many mothers walked through the night in order to lie with their children for a few hours, as Frederick Douglass remembered his mother doing in the nineteenth century. Nor shall we ever know how often a slave hurried to a neighboring plantation to warn a relative of imminent danger, as Charles Ball's grandfather did in the late eighteenth century when he learned that his son was about to be sold to a slave dealer. But we can be reasonably certain that most of the black laborers of the Chesapeake spent no more than a small part of their time en route to or visiting friends and relatives who were not housed on their own quarters. For most of their lives, slaves' chances for social interaction were limited to the fields and meadows, the quarters and woods, of their home plantations.

It is to the groups in which slaves passed most of their daily lives, then, that we need to look for whatever *regular* occasions existed for family life and social interaction. The first Federal census of 1790, which is extant for Maryland but not Virginia, offers an opportunity to glimpse the spatial distribution of blacks. The returns show that, for the end of the eighteenth century, generalizations about large plantations, high slave density, and the presence of few whites are overdrawn. Whites were not few; they outnumbered slaves by 43,091 to 42,681 in the five lower Western Shore counties of the Maryland sector of the Patuxent-to-James region. The average number of whites in slaveholding families was 5.2 to 5.5 by county; these families possessed an average of 7.8 to 11.4 blacks. Nor were large plantations the norm: the proportion of slaveholding families with 20 or more slaves was less than one in ten in three of the four counties for which such data are extant. In the other, Prince George's, 15.5 percent of the plantations

can be classified as large. When families that did not have slaves are included, the percentages fall below 10 percent in all four counties. These figures hardly convey the impression that few whites and large plantations characterized the Maryland portion of the region. Before drawing conclusions, then, about opportunities for family formation and the development of Afro-American society and culture in the eighteenth-century Chesapeake, the spatial distribution of slaves deserves closer attention. Here is a subject for which many data exist, in the form of tax lists, censuses, and estate inventories. In fact, for the majority of blacks who toiled in the Chesapeake before 1800, the most common, often the only, documentary record we have of their existence, is their aggregate numbers. We need to get these numbers straight.

Charles County, in the heart of the region, is an advantageous place to examine the distribution of slaves. Its planters were heavily committed to tobacco production and slave labor. Furthermore, during the eighteenth century the number of large plantations, the proportion of slaves whose masters owned more than twenty blacks, and the ratio of blacks to whites in the whole population and in slaveholding households all increased. By 1790, black slaves were approaching a majority, and the county ranked third in Maryland in the number of black inhabitants, second in percentage of blacks, and first in the proportion of slaveowning families. . . .

For Charles County, the extant list enumerated two-thirds of both the white and slave populations. The distribution of slaves in 1782 exhibited some marked similarities to that of the 1750s. So far as can be documented, the proportion of households with adult slave laborers was about the same at the end of the War for Independence as it had been thirty years earlier. The highest concentration of blacks was still found in the lower hundred of William and Mary Parish, the lowest in Durham Parish in the western part of the country. In Pomonkey Hundred, slaveholding still hovered around 50 percent. Yet if the proportion of slaveholders and the concentration of blacks in the civil subdivisions of the county look much alike in the 1750s and early 1780s, the distribution of blacks among households does not. The taxable labor force became more heavily black during the intervening years. Moreover, the proportion of slaves whose masters owned more than ten taxable blacks increased, while the proportion whose masters held five or fewer declined. We also find that 81.4 percent of plantations had five taxable slaves or fewer in 1758, but that figure fell to 57.4 percent a generation later. And while less than 1 percent . . . of the plantations accounted for in the earlier set of tax records had adult slave labor forces in excess of twenty men and women, in 1782 the percentage stood at 5.8. . . .

During the era of the Revolution, then, Charles County slaves were experiencing the kind of demographic change that Menard predicted and Kulikoff has affirmed for the Chesapeake—a movement toward larger plantations where the possibilities for communal ties, family formation, and the sharing of tribulation and joy, of dreams and despair, presumably were significantly greater than in the period before 1730 when plantations were small and the average slave population density was much lower. How does the 1782 distribution of slaves in the ten hundreds of the county compare with

what Kulikoff believes likely for the Chesapeake tidewater generally by the 1780s? First, notwithstanding the growth of the slave population, whites remained numerically dominant, 6,457 to 5,411. Second, Kulikoff's conjectures on plantation size, if applied to Charles County, consistently exaggerate the extent to which basic · spatial distribution enhanced opportunities for slave family and communal life. His figures appreciably underestimate the proportion of slaves living in small groups of ten or fewer (44.9 percent in the county, 26 percent according to Kulikoff), are closer to the mark for the percentage living in groups of eleven to twenty (30.2 versus 26 percent), and significantly overestimate the proportion living on large plantations (25 percent versus 44 percent). Finally, no slaveowner held one hundred or more persons in bondage. Rather, the largest holding was sixty.

The 1782 assessment itself probably *overstates* the size of some slave groups because of the way it was taken. If a master had slaves in more than a single hundred of the county, they were counted for the hundred where they lived. But the tax lists do not reveal whether or how masters divided their slaves *within* hundreds. Owners of large tracts of land or separate tracts may well have stationed blacks on several quarters. In addition, slaves who were hired out were nevertheless credited to the master. Thus slaves were probably more scattered and less able to maintain regular contact with one another than the records disclose.

The wealth of data in the 1782 assessment enables one to move beyond generalizations about the number of slaves per master and to scrutinize at closer range 776 groups containing a total of 5,411 persons. Every slave, whether living in daily isolation from other blacks or in the largest group, can be placed in one of five age categories, and those in the most productive years of life can be distinguished by gender. From this evidence of the distribution of the youngest children and those who survived early childhood, of the comparative numbers of women and men of reproductive age, and of the proportion of slaves whose age and condition reduced their economic value, the most elementary boundaries of slave life emerge. . . .

Only on plantations with slaves in all five age/gender categories could the full range of daily contacts occur, between young and old, male and female, parent and child and perhaps grandparents. More than one-half of the slaves . . . tallied in the tax lists did *not* have that opportunity. Among the rest . . ., the opportunity was realized only if none of the groups was fragmented among quarters or through hiring out—a highly improbable circumstance. When one examines the age and gender groups plantation by plantation, moreover, it becomes obvious that many blacks endured a truncated existence of one kind or another, even if masters kept them all together. Examination of the holdings of masters who owned slaves in up to three of the age/gender categories reveals some distinctly constricted living arrangements in Charles County. On some quarters, children were without regular parental supervision and guidance. On others, men and women returning from the fields did not hear the voices of black children. Older slaves had no audience of young listeners to whom they could pass along memories of Africa, religious instruction, or advice about making the most of bondage. Women and children or, less commonly, men and children were the only occupants of some quarters; there young Afro-Americans lacked continuous contact not only with one parent but with any black adult of the absent gender who could serve as a model. . . .

The tax records demonstrate constraints that plantation agriculture placed upon blacks' ability to live in groups that, although not of their own choosing, at least included friends and relatives, males and females, young and old. The drawback of these records is that they yield a static picture. They reveal nothing about the experiences of slaves at other times in their lives, and they cannot even hint at the dislocations slaves endured at the whim of masters who hired or loaned them out, used them to satisfy debts, gave them away, or sold them for financial reasons or because they were recalcitrant. As probate records disclose, dislocation also occurred when masters died—a point deserving attention. In Charles County during the eighteenth century, slaves and land were the most valuable forms of wealth. Of these, the former were movable and easily more divisible. When a master died intestate, Maryland law prescribed that the slaves in the estate be divided among the widow, the surviving children, and the lineal descendants of children who had predeceased the parent. When masters wrote wills, they, too, customarily adopted partible inheritance of slave property. Significantly, among all parent-testators whose wills were filed for probate in the county between 1740 and 1784, daughters received a higher proportion of slave bequests than did sons. And it was daughters who, at marriage, usually moved to their husbands' land and took their slaves with them. Thus, for numerous reasons, no slave family or community escaped the threat of being torn apart. . . .

Many owners probably broke up slave groups with no more disquietude than merchant Thomas Howe Ridgate expressed when he wrote, "so adieu to [the] Negro's." When the tobacco crop was in the shed, when funds had to be raised to satisfy a debt or pay for a child's education, when children came of age, daughters married, or a widow died, when a slave mother weaned her infant, or when "any of the negroes shou'd misbehave, or . . . my Executors shou'd think it more to the advantage of my children that some of the negroes should be sold," then blacks who had endured bondage together were torn apart. In 1768 Roger Smith bequeathed to his wife a lifetime estate in two slave families, a couple with seven children and a woman with two. When Mrs. Smith remarried, her blacks came under the mastery of her new husband, though he could not sell or mortgage them. At her death these families descended intact to her brother-in-law, Basil Smith; but when he died in 1774, just six years after the initial bequest, the two slave families were parceled out in four lots. Another testator, Ann Dent, in 1764 gave mulatto Tom to one married daughter, Tom's wife Cate to a second married daughter, and the couple's son to a granddaughter. Whether or how often this slave family thereafter was allowed to reunite, even briefly, thus depended upon the location and decision of three different masters. Such parceling out, repeated again and again through several generations, certainly established dispersed kin networks, but how successful Afro-Americans were in using those networks, or how often they simply lost contact with parents, siblings, and spouses, is unknown.

The 1782 tax assessment lists and testamentary evidence show that it was not uncommon for children to be separated from their mothers, even at an early age. Sometimes masters planned to dispose of children still in the womb; at other times they deliberated what to do with a woman's "future increase." Ann Cornish decided that "as she had not a negroe apiece for each of her Grand Children she wou[ld] give them as they came into the World." Cebberamous, a bondswoman of Elizabeth Askin, was destined to lose "the first Child that . . . [she] shall bring to good." Theodocia Speake's slave Sue was similarly to be stripped of "the first Child that . . . [she] Brings that liveth a year & if in Case it Dieth in a year then the next Child the aforesaid negro Sue bringeth." Mothers—and fathers, too, if they were present—whose children remained with them only a year abruptly lost them just as they were beginning to explore the world on foot. Richard Maston's pregnant slave Venus kept her infant until it could babble and toddle but then had to relinquish it to a white couple who were to "take the Child . . . under their own immediate Care so soon as it . . . shall arrive at the Age of two years." Almost as if he were dealing out cards, Maximillion Matthews of Durham Parish in 1770 gave the first child of his slave woman Henny to his daughter, the second to his wife, and the third to his son, "and so Alternatively and respectively for all the increase that the said negro Henny may have."

Members of slave communities who were allocated among masters' wives, sons, daughters, and grandchildren could hope to see one another at least occasionally. And blacks who were temporarily hired out could look forward to returning to their home plantations at the termination of their contracts. Slave sales, especially public auctions, were a different matter. Masters who had a surplus of blacks or needed to raise funds, and executors who needed to clear an estate of debt, could not afford to be much concerned about ties among blacks. Nor would they have gone to the trouble and expense of advertising in the *Maryland Gazette* and Virginia newspapers had they expected to dispose of slaves entirely in the immediate neighborhood.

Dispersal of Benjamin Fendall's blacks illustrates what could happen among even the largest slaveholders. Fendall owned a well-developed plantation on the Potomac River, rented some of his lands to tenants, and operated several mills and a bakery that sold ship bread to passing vessels. In addition to field hands, his slaves included a blacksmith, an "ingenious fellow" who "is a Carpenter, Cooper, Shoemaker, and Tanner," a waiter, and "a fine Cook Wench, who is a good Seamstress, and can do any Kind of House-work." During his lifetime Fendall gave some of his slaves to his adult children. At his death in 1764, twenty-nine remained. These he willed to be sold, with the rest of his estate, to pay his debts and provide legacies for two children who were minors. Sale of the slaves was not swift: it was accomplished in two public auctions held six months apart. At the first, in the midst of the growing season in July 1764, seven males aged fourteen and above, one woman, and three children were sold. Then in January 1765 the executors disposed of all but one of the remaining slaves: eight males aged fourteen and above, six women, and four children. The twenty-nine slaves went to seventeen different masters. . . .

UNTIL RECENTLY, HISTORIANS HAVE PORtrayed North American slavery with too little sensitivity to time or place, so that it appeared a static rather than dynamic institution. They have also studied slavery mainly at what Ira Berlin has called its point of maturity: the antebellum years, which composed less than one-quarter of the time the institution existed in North America. Recent scholarship has helped to redress that imbalance by focusing on the preceding, formative centuries, and in that regard a paradigm based on Chesapeake demographic conditions is valuable. For most blacks in the Chesapeake before 1800, the only documentary evidence of their existence is their aggregate numbers set down in census and tax records and—for those listed in estate inventories—their names, gender, and age. The eighteenth-century data from Charles County suggest that it is time to refine and clarify the paradigm—to examine Chesapeake slave distribution more fully at the plantation level, to be sensitive to regional variations, and to establish more precisely the timing of demographic change.

In Charles County, the development of stable slave communities proceeded much more slowly than Menard or Kulikoff hypothesized in their pioneering work. Demographic encouragement of stability, moreover, never seems to have been as favorable as the current paradigm would suggest. True, the number of large plantations, the proportion of slaves living on those plantations, and the proportion of slaves in the county's population increased during the eighteenth century. Nonetheless, it would distort reality to apply to the county the prevailing interpretation of slave distribution in the Chesapeake tidewater. As late as 1782, large plantations, few whites, and high black population densities did not characterize Charles County. Rather, 45 percent of the enslaved were held by masters who owned ten or fewer slaves, and another 30 percent by masters who had eleven to twenty. Whites continued to outnumber blacks, as they had throughout the eighteenth century. These demographic factors need to be considered in relation to masters' treatment of slaves as property, to be acquired and disposed of at pleasure. The result was an Afro-American family and communal life that was markedly fragile and subject to disruption.

POSTSCRIPT

Did American Slaves Develop a Distinct Afro-American Culture in the Eighteenth Century?

The essays by Kulikoff and Lee both suggest that the emergence of a cohesive Afro-American community life was a gradual process that occurred over the course of two centuries. They differ not on the question of whether slaves attempted to create a communal life for themselves in the Chesapeake, but rather on the degree of success achieved by bondservants in gaining control over their community institutions. Kulikoff's conclusions are supported by Russell Menard, whose demographic studies provide a wealth of information on the colonial Chesapeake region. See "The Maryland Slave Population, 1658 to 1730: A Demographic Profile of Blacks in Four Counties," *William and Mary Quarterly* (January 1975); and "From Servants to Slaves: The Transformation of the Chesapeake Labor System," *Southern Studies* (Winter 1977). Although attention has focused largely on colonial Virginia and Maryland, you can examine further support for the Kulikoff thesis in William D. Piersen, *Black Yankees: The Development of an Afro-American Subculture in Eighteenth-Century New England* (University of Massachusetts, 1988).

How much of Afro-American culture was inspired by African survivals? How much cultural baggage did Africans bring with them to the New World? Anthropologist Melville Herskovits argued in *The Myth of the Negro Past* (1941) that numerous elements of West African culture survived the "middle passage" and were adapted by salves to their New World environment.

Despite the fact that historians of slavery have generally focused upon the antebellum period, there is a significant body of literature pertaining to the colonial period. The details of the Atlantic slave trade are treated best in Basil Davidson, *Black Mother: The African Slave Trade: Precolonial History, 1450–1850* (Little, Brown, 1961); Daniel P. Mannix, *Black Cargoes: A History of the Atlantic Slave Trade, 1518–1865* (Viking Press, 1962); and Philip D. Curtin, *The Atlantic Slave Trade: A Census* (University of Wisconsin, 1969). The origins of slavery in the British mainland colonies are debated in Oscar and Mary Handlin, "The Origins of the Southern Labor System," *William and Mary Quarterly* (April 1950); Carl N. Degler, "Slavery and the Genesis of American Race Prejudice," *Comparative Studies in History and Society* (October 1959); and Winthrop Jordan, "Modern Tensions and the Origins of American Slavery," *Journal of Southern History* (February 1962). The development of black slavery in various British mainland colonies is treated in Mechal Sobel, *The World They Made Together: Black and White Values in Eighteenth-Century Virginia* (Princeton University Press, 1987), and Peter H. Wood, *Black Majority: Negroes in Colonial South Carolina from 1670 Through the Stono Rebellion* (Knopf, 1974).

ISSUE 5

Was the Great Awakening a Key to the American Revolution?

YES: William G. McLoughlin, from " 'Enthusiasm for Liberty': The Great Awakening as the Key to the Revolution," in Jack P. Greene and William G. McLoughlin, *Preachers & Politicians: Two Essays on the Origins of the American Revolution* (American Antiquarian Society, 1977)

NO: Jon Butler, from "Enthusiasm Described and Decried: The Great Awakening as Interpretative Fiction," *Journal of American History* (September 1982)

ISSUE SUMMARY

YES: McLoughlin claims that the Great Awakening, by promoting religious revitalization, intercolonial unity, and democracy, paved the way for the American Revolution.

NO: Butler challenges the validity of the term "the Great Awakening" and argues that a link between the eighteenth-century colonial religious revivals and the American Revolution was virtually nonexistent.

Although generations of American school children have been taught that the British colonies in North America were founded by persons fleeing religious persecution in England, the truth is that many of those early settlers were motivated by other factors, some of which had little to do with theological preferences. To be sure, the Pilgrims and Puritans of New England sought to escape the proscriptions established by the Church of England. Many New Englanders, however, did not adhere to the precepts of Calvinism and, therefore, were viewed as outsiders. The Quakers who populated Pennsylvania were mostly fugitives from New England, where they had been victims of religious persecution. But to apply religious motivations to the earliest settlers of Virginia, South Carolina, or Georgia is to engage in a serious misreading of the historical record. Even in New England the religious mission of (the first governor of the Massachusetts Bay Colony) John Winthrop's "city upon a hill" began to erode as the colonial settlements matured and stabilized.

Although religion was a central element in the lives of the seventeenth- and eighteenth-century Europeans who migrated to the New World, proliferation of religious sects and denominations, emphasis upon material gain in all parts of the colonies, and the predominance of reason over emotion that is associated with the Deists of the Enlightenment period all contributed to a gradual but obvious movement of the colonists away from the church and clerical authority. William Bradford (the second governor of Plymouth Colony), for example, expressed grave concern that many Plymouth residents were following a path of perfidy, and William Penn (founder of Pennsylvania) was certain that the "holy experiment" of the Quakers had failed. Colonial clergy, fearful that a fall from grace was in progress, issued calls for a revival of religious fervor. The spirit of revivalism that spread through the colonies in the 1730s and 1740s, therefore, was an answer to these clerical prayers.

The episode known as the First Great Awakening coincided with the Pietistic movement in Europe and England and was carried forward by dynamic preachers such as Gilbert Tennent, Theodore Frelinghuysen, and George Whitefield. They promoted a religion of the heart, not of the head, in order to produce a spiritual rebirth. Although the degree to which the Great Awakening influenced the colonies is disputed, several consequences can be firmly established. The revivals, for example, reinvigorated American Protestantism. Many new congregations were organized as a result of irremediable schisms between "Old Lights" and "New Lights." Skepticism about the desirability of an educated clergy sparked a strong strain of anti-intellectualism. Also, the emphasis on conversion was a message to which virtually anyone could respond, regardless of age, sex, or social status.

For some historians, the implications of the Great Awakening extend beyond the religious sphere into the realm of politics and the American Revolution. To what extent is the argument suggesting a relationship between religion and revolution valid?

William G. McLoughlin contends that the roots of the War for Independence were clearly imbedded in the Great Awakening. The Revolution, McLoughlin argues, reflected the postmillennial philosophy initiated by the Great Awakening. As Americans came to view themselves as residents of a "New Israel," they supported the goal of breaking ties with the oppressive government embodied in King George III and the Parliament. Additionally, the democratic ideals associated with the American Revolution were spawned, says McLoughlin, by the itinerant preachers of the Great Awakening who encouraged greater democracy in the religious lives of their listeners. The Revolution, then, was nothing less than a political revitalization of a people whose religious regeneration began with the Great Awakening.

Jon Butler, by claiming that the link between the revivals and the American Revolution was virtually nonexistent, dismisses the relationship suggested by McLoughlin. This period of revivalism, he argues, generated democracy only minimally and provided little focus for intercolonial unity. He concludes with a suggestion that historians abandon the concept of the "Great Awakening" because, in reality, the mid-eighteenth-century revivals did not produce the kinds of dramatic changes, religious or political, frequently ascribed to them.

YES

William G. McLoughlin

THE GREAT AWAKENING AS THE KEY
TO THE REVOLUTION

No one doubts that the Americans were basically a very religious people. The First Great Awakening in the 1730s (which we associate with the preaching of Jonathan Edwards, George Whitefield, Theodore Frelinghuysen, Samuel Davies, and Gilbert Tennet) and the Second Great Awakening in the early nineteenth century (which we associate with the frontier camp meetings) prove that. It can also be shown that American patriots (with the possible exception of Thomas Jefferson) intended to create, and did so, not a secular nation but a Christian nation (with paid chaplains for Congress and the military, tax exemption for all church property, and 'In God We Trust' on our coinage). But the intransigent problem continues to plague us when we seek precisely for any implicit or overt religious aspects of the Revolution.

One way to solve this puzzle is to define religion in such a broad way as to describe the Revolution itself as a quasi-religious movement. . . . But there is another strategy which I am convinced is equally important and which I shall utilize here. That is to demonstrate that the roots of the Revolution as a political movement were so deeply imbedded in the soil of the First Great Awakening forty years earlier that it can be truly said that the Revolution was the natural outgrowth of that profound widespread religious movement.

The anthropologist Kenelm Burridge has said, "All religions are basically concerned with power. . . . Religions are concerned with the systematic ordering of different kinds of power": the power of God over life and death, disease and health; the power of the parent over the child or the husband over the wife; the power of the law over the criminal or the state over the citizen. "No religious movement," Burridge argues, "lacks a political ideology." That is to say, no religious movement can avoid having some assumptions about the right and wrong ways in which power and authority can be used. What we call "politics" is really our agreement as groups or nations as to how we wish to enforce a particular code of behavior (which is assumed to be godly) upon those who dissent from it.

From *Preachers and Politicians: Two essays on the Origins of the American Revolution* by William G. McLoughlin (Worcester, MA: American Antiquarian Society, 1977). Reprinted by permission.

If we accept this broad anthropological definition of religion, we can begin to understand why the Great Awakening of 1735 to 1765 was so important, and why it had such a profound impact upon the Revolution. During this generation the British colonists revised in very drastic ways their conception of how God's power should and would operate in North America—and, by extension, how it ought to operate everywhere in the world. In the end the Founding Fathers were fighting, as they said, not just for the rights of Englishmen but for the rights of mankind. . . .

The central feature of the great revivals of the 1730s and 1740s was the experience of individual conversion. New Light ministers (Whitefield, Edwards, Davies, Tennent, Frelinghuysen) told their congregations that men and women did not gain favor or forgiveness from God simply by learning or by conforming to the man-made creeds of a church or to the prevailing moral standards of their community. God demanded a higher standard of spiritual commitment than that. He demanded total submission to his will, complete repentance for sins and utter obedience to his commands. And for a variety of reasons multitudes of Americans felt the need for such forgiveness and submission.

Historians have now shown pretty convincingly that Americans in the early years of the eighteenth century were very uncertain of their relationship to God as well as of their relations with one another. The original zeal of the earlier generations of pious settlers, struggling to win a beachhead on the stern frontier along the coast, had worn thin. In all the colonies the people were badly divided over questions of mercantile and land development. Times were prosperous.

There were many opportunities to grow rich. Neighbor began to vie with neighbor, merchant with merchant, in aggressive, competitive ways, scrambling to make the most of the New World's fabulous resources Normally decent people began to cut moral corners, to abuse their offices, to slight their social responsibilities in order to engage in sharp dealing for private profit. This in turn produced an increasing number of lawsuits over alleged frauds or violations of contract. Town meetings became bitter, quarrelsome affairs and frequently one part of a town or county petitioned the legislature to settle problems which the local judicial or political system could not. Parish ministers were unable to appeal effectively to conscience, moral law, or communal harmony to reconcile angry factions within their congregations and were themselves often at odds with their parishioners over salaries or religious taxes. The poor began to accuse the rich of oppression and to attack the learned clergy for siding with the upper class against the common interest. Though few acknowledged it, increasing social and economic tensions produced increasing guilt feelings and pangs of conscience. People seemed to have lost that close relationship with God and each other which had marked the earlier generations of settlers.

Looking back, the historian can see these anxieties as part of the growing pains of the colonies as they adjusted to the New World environment and began to abandon the old ways they had known in Europe. As towns matured and land became scarce and expensive, the old patriarchal relationships and community spirit gave way to change and migration. The rapid expansion of seaports and market towns and the growing size of the population and its rapid movement westward in search of cheaper land and greater opportunities could not help but affect loyalty, the ties of friendship, the covenant of the church, and the respect for the parish minister. As these institutional constraints failed to preserve order, the more devout churchgoers began to lose faith in the authority of the church and the state. Somehow the old system seemed to be breaking down. The old ways of acting and believing, sharing and trusting no longer carried authority. The institutions of the old corporate social order were suffering what the sociologists call a crisis of cultural legitimacy. But no one knew what to do about it.

In this uneasy state of affairs the emergence of revival ministers preaching a doctrine of immediate repentance from sin and immediate conversion to God aroused an inordinate amount of attention after 1735. Pious people were anxious to know why God was angry with them and seemed to have departed from their midst. They wanted to regain their standing in God's good graces. When the Reverend George Whitefield arrived from England in 1739, he had already established a reputation as a successful revivalist in the old country. Americans found his style of preaching strikingly different from what they had been hearing in their local parish churches. Many were caught up in the enthusiasm aroused by this twenty-three-year-old evangelist as he traveled from town to town along the whole Atlantic coast of North America. Even Benjamin Franklin, who went to hear him with considerable skepticism in Philadelphia, was so excited by his words that he emptied his pockets into the collection plate. Jonathan Edwards's wife in Massachusetts said that it is "wonderful to see what a

spell he casts over an audience. . . . I have seen upwards of a thousand people hang on his words with breathless silence, broken only by an occasional half-suppressed sob." One ordinary farmer in Connecticut who saddled his horse, hoisted his wife up behind him, and rode madly into town to hear Whitefield said that when the preacher mounted the platform erected for him on the village green, "He lookt almost angellical, a young, slim, slender youth before some thousands of people & with a bold, undaunted countenance, & my hearing how god was with him everywhere as he came along, it solumnized my mind & put me in a trembling fear before he began to preach, for he looked as if he was Cloathed with Authority from the great god." Americans believed in God, in heaven and hell, in damnation, and in miracles. Their suppressed guilt and anxiety were overwhelmed when they were persuaded that Whitefield was a prophet of God, a man sent as God's messenger to arouse a sinful people from their wicked ways. And not only did God raise up Whitefield, but he raised up a host of other eloquent young revivalists to call the people back to the ways of God.

In describing the kinds of feelings which swept over them in these revival meetings or in retrospect afterwards, most converts agreed that what struck them most forcefully was not God's anger but his concern, his interest in helping them to mend their ways. The revivalists preached hellfire for the wicked but they also promised rewards to the repentant. . . .

What this kind of conversion experience seemed to be telling Americans as it swept over the colonies was that God does not work through kings and bishops, through a learned clergy or an upper class of the rich and wellborn, but through the people themselves. Out of the death of the old covenanted ideal of the corporate community was born the new republican ideal of government by consent. . . . It was fortunate perhaps that after 1765 the king and Parliament began to tighten imperial control over the colonies, for in doing so it allowed the new force unleashed by the Awakening to turn against this outside, alien foe rather than against the internal authorities in the colonies. The guilt which had been internalized prior to 1735 and which had caused such turmoil during the Awakening was projected outward after 1765 upon a common enemy. New Light religion absorbed social anxiety and private guilt into a political reformation which, the colonists told themselves, was as much for the purification of old England as for the reformation of New America. . . . Religious and political regeneration merged in a triumphant effort to realize the rising glory of God in America.

In addition to changing American social and ecclesiastical institutions the Awakening brought about a very critical turning point in American theology. As a result of the Awakening American pietists came to believe that they had a special role to play in God's providential plan for the redemption of mankind. By 1765 the whole significance of millennialism had been transformed in America. Prior to the Awakening theologians in America had universally preached that the millennium would occur only when Christ returned to earth to set right the wicked ways of this world. The second coming had to precede the millennium because men themselves were too wicked ever to create a perfect social and moral order. Increase Mather had been so fearful of the barbarous influence of the frontier environment that he predicted "that in the glorious times promised to the Church on Earth, America will be Hell." But by 1745 the glorious showers of blessing spread by God throughout the colonies had caused a far different and more optimistic interpretation to arise. American theologians began to argue that perhaps God meant to convert all the people of America and then to enlist them to help prepare the way for Christ's return by creating a perfect social order in the New World. No less a theologian than Jonathan Edwards expounded this new postmillennial optimism in a series of sermons in 1742. Christ will not return to earth before the millennium, he said, but after it. What was more, the New Jerusalem would not be accomplished all at once "by some miracle" but will be "gradually brought to pass" through the work of man. "It is not unlikely that this work of God's Spirit [the Awakening], so extraordinary and wonderful, is the dawning, or at least a prelude of that glorious work of God so often foretold in Scripture which, in the progress and issue of it, shall renew the world of mankind. . . . We cannot reasonably think otherwise than that the beginning of this great work of God must be near. And there are many things that make it probable that this work will begin in America." In this postmillennial view of American destiny it was manifest that Americans were the successors of the Jewish nation, the chosen people of God, God's New Israel. As such they had a mission to serve as the avant-garde of God's millennial kingdom on earth.

As this opinion spread after 1742 throughout the colonies, many came to believe that Americans could not effectively fulfill this mission so long as they were tied to a corrupt, oppressive, and tyrannical monarch and Parliament in England. In the years 1765 to 1775 those imbued with this new light God had shed during the Awakening became convinced that God was trying to show them how much more important it was to adhere to his higher laws than to the man-made laws of Parliament. Regardless of a man's denomination, this post-millennial optimism influenced many colonists to believe in 1775 that God had ordained, planned, and guided the British colonies to that moment when they must take their destiny into their own hands. Only in a purified and perfect republican social order, which guaranteed political and religious liberty to all men, could their mission to the world be accomplished. Thereafter the rights of Englishmen became the inalienable rights of mankind and the Americans felt obliged to bring the blessings of liberty to the rest of the world. . . .

[W]hen the crisis of institutional authority began in the colonies in the 1730s and when the old hierarchical, corporate order seemed unable to provide harmony and leadership, the common folk began to have serious doubts about its validity. The efforts of the "authorities" to oppose the religious enthusiasm of the Great Awakening only contributed . . . to the downfall of the old order. The upper orders in church and state insisted that the revivalists were fanatical demagogues causing disorder in the parishes and invading the rights and privileges of the settled parish ministers; by causing schisms in the churches and disputes over religious taxes they were undermining the laws. So itinerant preachers were fined, jailed, and banished, and when

their converts accused the parish ministers of being enemies to God and opponents of his divine outpouring of grace, many of them were put in jail for refusing any longer to pay taxes to support such sadducees and pharisees. In Anglican Virginia the Baptists were regularly jailed and mobbed right up until 1775 on the grounds that their revivals disturbed the civil peace and their churches were not properly licensed by the state.

The Awakening also produced bitter quarrels and schisms in the Middle Colonies where there was no established church system but where conservative ministers in the Dutch Reformed and Presbyterian churches opposed the fervent religious enthusiasm of the revival. It is significant that even George Whitefield and Gilbert Tennent (though not Jonathan Edwards) encouraged pious converts to leave their parish churches and go to hear New Light preaching if their parish ministers were not converted and therefore could not support God's work. Over 125 parishes in New England were split between New Lights and Old Lights by the 1750s and many more such schisms took place in the middle and southern colonies.

These decisions, made by thousands upon thousands of individuals, thinking and acting entirely upon their own responsibility and risking their livelihood, their status, and the welfare of their families, constitute the religious foreshadowing of the political decisions taken in 1775 for or against separation from the empire. The New Light nonconformists would not contribute in person or in purse to the continued support of corrupt religious institutions which opposed God's law, denied the freedom of conscience of individuals, and utilized the power of the state to oppress those who did God's will. These dissenters from the established order in parishes and counties across the colonies were taken to jail, fined, or had their household goods sold at auction by the local sheriff for engaging in civil disobedience to the powers that be. But they chose to obey God rather than man. Having done so once, they were fortified to do so again after 1765 in protest against the injustices of the Stamp Act, the Coercive Acts, the Admiralty laws, and the tea tax. Something crucial happened in the Awakening: in that great religious upheaval the colonists learned to judge for themselves and to act out of their own consciences. By 1776 it had become axiomatic that "disobedience to tyrants is obedience to God."

Fortunately for the Christian churches in the colonies the great majority of their ministers eventually came to agree with the New Lights. They concluded that the Great Awakening was truly a work of God. Hence America was spared that anticlericalism which wreaked such havoc in the French and Russian revolutions where the clergy allied themselves with the old order. By 1765 the New Lights had come to predominate in most of the Protestant denominations and even had strongly influenced the young Catholic churches in the colonies. Only, as might be expected, in a hierarchy where church appointments derived directly from the secular authority of the king, that is, in the Anglican Church, did the parish priests side with the ancien régime.

The Awakening also helped the colonies to develop a new kind of intercolonial unity. Some historians have seen this unity deriving essentially from the interdenominational concert among non-Anglican ministers after 1760 to oppose the appointment of an Anglican bishop for the colonies. Actually intercolonial unity preceded rather than followed this plan for "Christian Union" (as Ezra Stiles called it). The true basis for intercolonial unity lay in the system of itinerant preaching which played so important a part in spreading the New Light revival spirit after 1735. Itinerant preachers of all denominations, lay and clerical, followed Whitefield's example and toured from one colony to another gathering converts for their particular denominations or for all denominations. As the dissenting churches grew in number, the itinerants helped to unite them throughout the colonies. From these informal ties came the formal nationalization of the major Protestant denominations. Out of seeming disunity emerged a new order of union. The Revolutionary motto, "e pluribus unum," had its practical beginning in the religious unity of the New Light preachers. Although each particular Christian persuasion devoutly believed that its way of faith and practice was the one true way prescribed by God, all of them agreed that God's truth would prevail through religious freedom and did not need coercive uniformity. . . .

Less attention has been paid to the equally important fact that the itinerant revivalism of the generation of the Awakening fostered a new system of mass communication in America. Much has been made of the importance of colonial newspapers in spreading the word of republic ideology. Professor Harry Stout has recently noted that we must give equal attention to the role of itinerant preachers in spreading the word of God's New Light ideology which was its spiritual counterpart. When Stout argues that itinerancy must be studied in terms of Marshall McLuhan's axiom that 'the medium is the message,' he does not mean to denigrate the religious or doctrinal content of the New Light preachers. He does mean that itinerants conveyed a message of free and voluntary individual choice in religious affairs simply by offering their message in village squares or private homes as an alternative to the official word from the parish, tax-supported, church. But equally as important was the way in which the itinerants preached that message of free choice. Not being cloaked with the authority of the state or with the familiarity of the local community. the itinerant spoke simply as one individual to another; he spoke outside of any temporal or territorial location. And in doing so he freed Americans forever from the Old World view that religious stability relied on having roots in a fixed place or parish. Itinerant preaching freed the individual to travel where he would by assuring him that wherever he went the word of God through divinely ordained messengers would reach him. And since itinerant preachers played down doctrinal and ecclesiastical differences in order to lay stress upon individual repentance and conversion, mobile Americans could rest assured that whatever denominational exhorter followed them to the frontier or from rural farm to coastal city the essential spiritual message he would hear would be the same: repent, throw yourself on God's mercy, and he will save and protect you personally by sending his spirit to dwell in your heart wherever you may roam or whatever community you may temporarily reside in.

At the same time, the itinerant, who frequently lacked any formal education and almost never had a college education, spoke to other men as equals. Not only did he eschew the parish church but he stood on the same ground as the people to whom he spoke; he lived at their level and spoke in their language. Itinerancy democratized America's religion before the Revolution democratized its government. In preaching, the itinerant did not, because he knew he could not, order or command his hearers to conform. He was clothed only with spiritual authority and his power was based solely on his ability to persuade the individual listener to act upon his own free will. People who were rebellious against parental authority, or that of town fathers or legislators or royal governors or Parliament or their royal father in Buckingham Palace, could nevertheless accept attacks upon their sins and salvation for their guilt from an equal who had experienced the same psychological and spiritual problems. . . . Out of the Awakening came an individualized, non-theological, voluntary, and migratory ecclesiastical order perfectly suited to the needs of a people who had to shake off the institutional restrictions of an Old World order if they were ever to spread across the New World continent. . . .

Much has been made by social historians of the fact that the Enlightenment ushered in an era of concern for the benevolent care of the poor, the sick, the orphan, and the criminal. Philanthropic effort seemed to go hand-in-hand with the belief that science was teaching men better ways to heal and to rehabilitate those who had previously been considered inveterate sinners or children of the devil. Yet we can also credit the Great Awakening with a very similar impulse toward humanitarian reform. Jonathan Edwards defined true Christian virtue in 1756 as "interested benevolence to Being in general." Edwards's pupil Samuel Hopkins interpreted disinterested benevolence to mean devout Christian concern for the care and freedom of our fellow human beings. In 1773 Hopkins joined with Ezra Stiles (a minister who had not been overly friendly toward the New Light movement) in attacking the slave trade. And that same year some New Light Baptists in Boston, joined by others in the remote town of Ashfield, issued public broadsides against slavery itself. Here again we can see how the rationalists and pietists, starting from different parts of the republican-Christian world view, had arrived by 1775 at very similar positions. Jefferson, for his part, wrote into the Declaration of Independence a clause justifying rebellion on the grounds that George III had forced slavery upon his colonies.

Finally we can note that John Adams, though a Unitarian, and the Reverend John Witherspoon, a New Light Presbyterian, shared the same concern for the importance of public virtue in the new republic. Adams spoke of the United States of America as a "Christian Sparta"—a nation whose citizens should be as willing to sacrifice themselves for the good of their country as the Spartans at Thermopylae and at the same time as dedicated to God as the Christians who were thrown to the lions by the Emperor Nero. Witherspoon, who served in the Continental Congress while at the same time remaining president of the New Light college in Princeton, New Jersey, said, "In free States where the body of the people have the supreme power properly in their own hands and must be ultimately resorted to on all great matters if there be a general corruption of manners there can be nothing but confusion. So true is this that civil liberty cannot long be preserved without virtue. A monarchy may subsist for ages, and be

better or worse under a good or bad prince; but a republic once equally poised must either preserve its virtue or lose its liberty." Adams and Witherspoon, the rationalist and the pietist, represent the two sides of the Revolutionary coin, the connection between the Awakening and the Revolution. The Enlightened rationalist provided Americans with a theory of political science which stated that it was a natural law that government must be by the consent of the governed, that it must preserve inalienable natural rights, that it must have checks and balances, but that it must depend ultimately upon the willingness of the individual citizen to sacrifice his own comfort and welfare for the good of the commonwealth. The pietist provided Americans with a religious ideology which said that God's power inhered essentially in the free and voluntary consent of the individual, that Americans were God's chosen people, that true virtue required disinterested benevolence toward all mankind, and that without total commitment to God's higher law as expressed in his holy word no nation could save itself from corruption and tyranny.

. . . [T]he Revolution can be described as the political revitalization of a people whose religious regeneration began in the Great Awakening. Regeneration or cultural rebirth was the key which unlocked the door to the new household of the republic.

NO

Jon Butler

THE GREAT AWAKENING

How do historians describe "the Great Awakening"? Three points seem especially common. First, all but a few describe it as a Calvinist religious revival in which converts acknowledged their sinfulness without expecting salvation. These colonial converts thereby distinguished themselves from Englishmen caught up in contemporary Methodist revivals and from Americans involved in the so-called Second Great Awakening of the early national period, both of which imbibed Arminian principles that allowed humans to believe they might effect their own salvation in ways that John Calvin discounted. Second, historians emphasize the breadth and suddenness of the Awakening and frequently employ hurricane metaphors to reinforce the point. Thus, many of them describe how in the 1740s the Awakening "swept" across the mainland colonies, leaving only England's Caribbean colonies untouched. Third, most historians argue that this spiritual hurricane affected all facets of prerevolutionary society. Here they adopt [Jonathan] Edwards's description of the 1736 Northampton revival as one that touched "all sorts, sober and vicious, high and low, rich and poor, wise and unwise," but apply it to all the colonies. Indeed, some historians go farther and view the Great Awakening as a veritable social and political revolution itself. Writing in the late 1960s, [Richard] Bushman could only wonder at its power: "We inevitably will underestimate the effect of the Awakening on eighteenth-century society if we compare it to revivals today. The Awakening was more like the civil rights demonstrations, the campus disturbances, and the urban riots of the 1960s combined. All together these may approach, though certainly not surpass, the Awakening in their impact on national life."

No one would seriously question the existence of "the Great Awakening" if historians only described it as a short-lived Calvinist revival in New England during the early 1740s. Whether stimulated by Edwards, James Davenport, or the British itinerant George Whitefield, the New England revivals between 1740 and 1745 obviously were Calvinist ones. Their sponsors vigorously criticized the soft-core Arminianism that had reputedly

From the *Journal of American History* 69 (September 1982). Copyright © Organization of American Historians, 1969. Reprinted by permission.

overtaken New England Congregational-ism, and they stimulated the ritual re-newal of a century-old society by reintroducing colonists to the theology of distinguished seventeenth-century Puri-tan clergymen, especially Thomas Shep-ard and Solomon Stoddard.

Yet, Calvinism never dominated the eighteenth-century religious revivals ho-mogenized under the label "the Great Awakening." The revivals in the middle colonies flowed from especially disparate and international sources. . . . The re-vivals among English colonists in Vir-ginia also reveal eclectic roots. Presbyterians brought Calvinism into the colony for the first time since the 1650s, but Arminianism underwrote the power-ful Methodist awakening in the colony and soon crept into the ranks of the colony's Baptists as well.

"The Great Awakening" also is diffi-cult to date. Seldom has an "event" of such magnitude had such amorphous beginnings and endings. In New Eng-land, historians agree, the revivals flour-ished principally between 1740 and 1743 and largely ended by 1745, although a few scattered outbreaks of revivalism oc-curred there in the next decades. Estab-lishing the beginning of the revivals has proved more difficult, however. Most historians settle for the year 1740 because it marks Whitefield's first appearance in New England. But everyone acknowl-edges that earlier revivals underwrote Whitefield's enthusiastic reception there and involved remarkable numbers of col-onists. Edwards counted thirty-two towns caught up in revivals in 1734–1735 and noted that his own grandfather, Stoddard, had conducted no less than five "harvests" in Northampton before that, the earliest in the 1690s. Yet revivals in Virginia, the site of the most sustained

such events in the southern colonies, did not emerge in significant numbers until the 1750s and did not peak until the 1760s. At the same time, they also contin-ued into the revolutionary and early na-tional periods in ways that make them difficult to separate from their prede-cessors.

Yet even if one were to argue that "the Great Awakening" persisted through most of the eighteenth century, it is ob-vious that revivals "swept" only some of the mainland colonies. They occurred in Massachusetts, Connecticut, Rhode Is-land, Pennsylvania, New Jersey, and Vir-ginia with some frequency at least at some points between 1740 and 1770. But New Hampshire, Maryland, and Geor-gia witnessed few revivals in the same years, and revivals were only occa-sionally important in New York, Dela-ware, North Carolina, and South Carolina. The revivals also touched only certain segments of the population in the colonies where they occurred. The best example of the phenomenon is Pennsyl-vania. The revivals there had a sustained effect among English settlers only in Presbyterian churches where many of the laity and clergy also opposed them. The Baptists, who were so important to the New England revivals, paid little at-tention to them until the 1760s, and the colony's taciturn Quakers watched them in perplexed silence. Not even Germans imbibed them universally. At the same time that Benjamin Franklin was empty-ing his pockets in response to the preaching of Whitefield in Philadelphia—or at least claiming to do so—the resi-dents of Germantown were steadily leav-ing their churches, and Stephanie Grauman Wolf reports that they re-mained steadfast in their indifference to Christianity at least until the 1780s. . . .

Historians also exaggerate the cohesion of leadership in the revivals. They have accomplished this, in part, by overstressing the importance of Whitefield and Edwards. Whitefield's early charismatic influence later faded so that his appearances in the 1750s and 1760s had less impact even among evangelicals than they had in the 1740s. In addition, Whitefield's "leadership" was ethereal, at best, even before 1750. His principal early importance was to serve as a personal model of evangelical enterprise for ministers wishing to promote their own revivals of religion. Because he did little to organize and coordinate integrated colonial revivals, he also failed to exercise significant authority over the ministers he inspired.

The case against Edwards's leadership of the revivals is even clearer. Edwards defended the New England revivals from attack. But, like Whitefield, he never organized and coordinated revivals throughout the colonies or even throughout New England. Since most of his major works were not printed in his lifetime, even his intellectual leadership in American theology occurred in the century after his death. Whitefield's lack of knowledge about Edwards on his first tour of American in 1739–1740 is especially telling on this point. Edwards's name does not appear in Whitefield's journal prior to the latter's visit to Northampton in 1740, and Whitefield did not make the visit until Edwards had invited him to do so. Whitefield certainly knew of Edwards and the 1734–1735 Northampton revival but associated the town mainly with the pastorate of Edwards's grandfather Stoddard. As Whitefield described the visit in his journal: "After a little refreshment, we crossed the ferry to Northampton, where no less than three

hundred souls were saved about five years ago. Their pastor's name is Edwards, successor and grandson to the great Stoddard, whose memory will be always precious to my soul, and whose books entitled 'A Guide to Christ,' and 'Safety of Appearing in Christ's Righteousness,' I would recommend to all."

What were the effects of the prerevolutionary revivals of religion? The claims for their religious and secular impact need pruning too. One area of concern involves the relationship between the revivals and the rise of the Dissenting denominations in the colonies. Denomination building was intimately linked to the revivals in New England. There, as C. C. Goen has demonstrated, the revivals of the 1740s stimulated formation of over two hundred new congregations and several new denominations. This was accomplished mainly through a negative process called "Separatism," which split existing Congregationalist and Baptist churches along prorevival and antirevival lines. But Separatism was of no special consequence in increasing the number of Dissenters farther south. Presbyterians, Baptists, and, later, Methodists gained strength from former Anglicans who left their state-supported churches, but they won far more recruits among colonists who claimed no previous congressional membership.

Still, two points are important in assessing the importance of revivals to the expansion of the Dissenting denominations in the colonies. First, revivalism never was the key to the expansion of the colonial churches. Presbyterianism expanded as rapidly in the middle colonies between 1710 and 1740 as between 1740 and 1770. Revivalism scarcely produced the remarkable growth that the Church of England experienced in the eighteenth century unless, of course, it won the favor of colonists who opposed revivals as fiercely as did its leaders. [Edwin] Gaustad estimates that between 1700 and 1780 Anglican congregations expanded from about one hundred to four hundred, and Bruce E. Steiner has outlined extraordinary Anglican growth in the Dissenting colony of Connecticut although most historians describe the colony as being thoroughly absorbed by the revivals and "Separatism."

Second, the expansion of the leading evangelical denominations, Presbyterians and Baptists, can be traced to many causes, not just revivalism or "the Great Awakening." The growth of the colonial population from fewer than three hundred thousand in 1700 to over two million in 1770 made the expansion of even the most modestly active denominations highly likely. This was especially true because so many new colonists did not settle in established communities but in new communities that lacked religious institutions. As Timothy L. Smith has written of seventeenth-century settlements, the new eighteenth-century settlements welcomed congregations as much for the social functions they performed as for their religious functions. Some of the denominations reaped the legacy of Old World religious ties among new colonists, and others benefited from local anti-Anglican sentiment, especially in the Virginia and Carolina backcountry. As a result, evangelical organizers formed many congregations in the middle and southern colonies without resorting to revivals at all. The first Presbyterian congregation in Hanover County, Virginia, organized by Samuel Blair and William Tennent, Jr., in 1746, rested on an indigenous lay critique of Anglican theology that had turned resi-

dents to the works of Martin Luther, and after the campaign by Blair and Tennent, the congregation allied itself with the Presbyterian denomination rather than with simple revivalism.

The revivals democratized relations between ministers and the laity only in minimal ways. A significant number of New England ministers changed their preaching styles as a result of the 1740 revivals. [Alan] Heimert quotes Isaac Backus on the willingness of evangelicals to use sermons to "insinuate themselves into the affections' of the people" and notes how opponents of the revivals like [Charles] Chauncy nonetheless struggled to incorporate emotion nd "sentiment" into their sermons after 1740. Yet revivalists and evangelicals continued to draw sharp distinctions between the rights of ministers and the duties of the laity. Edwards did so in a careful, sophisticated way in *Some Thoughts concerning the Present Revival of Religion in New England*. Although he noted that "disputing, jangling, and contention" surrounded "lay exhorting," he agreed that "some exhorting is a Christian duty." But he quickly moved to a strong defense of ministerial prerogatives, which he introduced with the proposition that "the Common people in exhorting one another ought not to clothe themselves with the like authority, with that which is proper for ministers." Gilbert Tennent was less cautious. In his 1740 sermon *The Danger of an Unconverted Ministry*, he bitterly attacked "Pharisee-shepherds" and "Pharisee-teachers" whose preaching was frequently as "unedifying" as their personal lives. But Gilbert Tennent never attacked the ministry itself. Rather, he argued for the necessity of a *converted* ministry precisely because he believed that only preaching brought men and women to Christ and that only ordained ministers could preach. Thus, in both 1742 and 1757, he thundered against lay preachers. They were "of dreadful consequence to the Church's peace and soundness in principle. . . . [F]or Ignorant Young Converts to take upon them authoritatively to Instruct and Exhort publickly tends to introduce the greatest Errors and the greatest anarchy and confusion." . . .

Did itinerants challenge this ministerial hegemony? [William G.] McLoughlin has framed such an argument in exceptionally strong terms. He has argued that the itinerant significantly changed the early American social and religious landscape because he usually lacked formal education, "spoke to other men as equals" in a traditionally deferential society, "eschew[ed] the parish church," refused to "order or command his hearers to conform," and was "clothed only with spiritual authority [so that] his power was based solely on his ability to persuade the individual listener to act upon his own free will."

Actually, itinerancy produced few changes in colonial American society and religion and is frequently misunderstood. Although some itinerants lacked institutionally based formal educations, none are known to have been illiterate. The most famous itinerant of the century, Whitefield, took an Oxford degree in 1736, and the most infamous, Davenport, stood at the top of his class at Yale in 1732. Itinerants usually bypassed the local church only when its minister opposed them; when the minister was hospitable the itinerants preached in the church building. One reason itinerants eschewed the coercive instruments of the state was that they never possessed them before the Revolution. But after the

Revolution the denominations they represented sought and received special favors from the new state governments, especially concerning incorporation, and won the passage of coercive legislation regarding morality and outlawing blasphemy. Finally, itinerants seldom ventured into the colonial countryside" clothed only with spiritual authority." Instead, itinerants acknowledged the continuing importance of deference and hierarchy in colonial society by stressing denominational approbation for their work. Virtually all of them wore the protective shield of ordination—the major exceptions are a few laymen who itinerated in New England in the early 1740s and about whom virtually nothing is known—and nearly all of them could point to denominational sponsorship. Even Virginia's aggressive Samuel Davies defended himself to the Bishop of London, Gov. William Gooch, and the sometimes suspicious backcountry settlers to whom he preached by pointing to his ordination and sponsorship by the Presbytery of New Castle. Only Davenport ventured into the countryside with little more than the spirit (and his Yale degree) to protect him. But only Davenport was judged by a court to have been mentally unstable.

In this context, it is not surprising that the eighteenth-century revivals of religion failed to bring significant new power—democracy—to the laity in the congregations. Although Gilbert Tennent argued that the laity had an obligation to abandon unconverted, unedifying ministers in favor of converted ones, it is not possible to demonstrate that the revivals increased the traditional powers that laymen previously possessed or brought them new ones. Congregations throughout the colonies had long exercised considerable power over their ministers through their effective control of church spending and fund raising as well as through the laity's ability simply to stop attending church services at all. As examples, witness alone the well-known seventeenth-century disputes between ministers and their listeners in Sudbury and Salem Village in Massachusetts and the complaints against ministers brought by the laity to the Presbytery of Philadelphia between 1706 and 1740. Yet, although the revivals should have increased this lay willingness to complain about ministerial failings, no historian ever has demonstrated systematically that this ever happened. . . .

What, then, of the relationship between the revivals and the American Revolution? Obviously, the revivals provided little focus for intercolonial unity in the way some historians have described. They appeared too erratically in too few colonies under too many different auspices to make such generalizations appropriate. The eighteenth-century colonial wars are more appropriate candidates for the honor. They raised significant legislative opposition to the crown in many colonies and cost many colonists their lives, especially in the last and most "successful" contest, the French and Indian War. Nor is it possible to demonstrate that specific congregations and denominations associated with the revivals originated anti-British protest that became uniquely important to the Revolution. Nathan O. Hatch has noted that Andrew Crosswell's revivalist congregation in Boston had all but collapsed by 1770, and no historian ever has demonstrated that similar congregations elsewhere served as isolated cells of anti-British protest. The connection is equally difficult to make with denomina-

tions. Connecticut New Lights and Pennsylvania Presbyterians played important roles in the colonial protests, but their activity does not, in itself, link revivals to the Revolution in any important way. First, the revivals in both places occurred a quarter of a century before the Revolution began. Second, neither group expanded in the 1740s or sustained its membership later exclusively because of the revivals. Third, the British probably angered laymen of both groups because the latter were important politicians rather than because they were New Lights and Presbyterians. Or, put another way, they were political leaders who happened to be New Lights and Presbyterians rather than Presbyterians and New Lights who happened to be politicians.

This is not to say that colonial revivalism did not reinforce anti-British protest in some way. Heimert has argued that the Calvinism of the revivals "provided pre-Revolutionary America with a radical, even democratic, social and political ideology" and contained millennialist themes that bore equally dangerous implications for British rule. But the secret to the success of anti-British and revolutionary protests lay in the expanse of their ideological foundations. Millennialism was indeed important to the American revolutionaries because, as Hatch as argued, it crossed Old Light-New Light boundaries, while Bernard Bailyn has demonstrated in his capsule biographies of the New England clergymen Andrew Eliot, Jonathan Mayhew, and Stephen Johnson that both Calvinism and theological liberalism produced positive responses on questions of democracy and the Revolution. And, of course, some historians still argue for the importance of the secular Enlightenment in shaping revolutionary ideology, whether it be in the thought of John Locke, John Trenchard, and Thomas Gordon, or in newfound Scottish philosophers.

Some historians have argued that the eighteenth-century revivals had a more subtle, yet still profound, effect on the colonies in fostering a new system of mass communications among settlers. Stout has written that itinerancy and extemporaneous preaching—but specifically not the intellectual content of the sermons reached—stimulated social and political egalitarianism in the colonies. They created a "spirit of liberty" that tore at traditional social and political deference and fitted Americans superbly for the contests of the 1760s and 1770s. Here again problems of timing and effect intrude. The political ramifications of extemporaneous sermons delivered by itinerant or resident preachers were unclear at best and were delayed for as long as twenty-five years. Moreover, the Revolution they presumably underwrote made only the most modest contributions to social egalitarianism and democracy, of which they probably were not the sole cause.

Yet the real Achilles heel of Stout's interpretation may center on the extent of extemporaneous preaching itself. Stout—and McLoughlin, who has echoed him—did not study the frequency of extemporaneous preaching in the revivals. They built their argument on the assumption that it was the key to the revivals and the dominant mode of revival preaching, just as revival critics claimed. This may not be the case, however. As used in the eighteenth century, the term "extempore preaching" did not mean preaching without preparation. Rather, it meant preaching without a written text or notes in a way that, ac-

cording to Stout, allowed the minister greater flexibility in shaping his subject and communicating with his audience. Although extemporaneous preaching was notorious at the height of the 1740 revivals, not all revival ministers engaged in the practice. Edwards probably never gave extemporaneous sermons despite the fact that he relaxed his sermon style after 1740. Gilbert Tennent, who appears to have preached extemporaneously through about 1743, apparently reduced this practice in the next decade. In 1762, Gilbert Tennent opposed the appointment of a man who preached extemporaneously as an assistant minister in Tennent's Philadelphia congregation, and he attacked extemporaneous preaching in a important but unpublished treatise he wrote in the same year. In the surviving draft of this document, Gilbert Tennent argued that ministers who favored extemporaneous preaching frequently overstressed emotion and that, ideally, ministers ought to mix their preaching styles by preaching with notes "in the morning to inform the mind" and by preaching extemporaneously "in the afternoon to affect the Heart." But in an observation obviously meant to deflate proponents of extemporaneous preaching, he also commented that in his own experience "the Difference between the two modes of preaching with or without notes is So Small, that if you Shutt your eyes or Sit where you don't See the Speaker, you will be often at a Loss to Distinguish which mode is used."

The caution of Edwards and Gilbert Tennent in eschewing or abandoning extemporaneous preaching and the fact that nearly all reports about its frequency come from revival critics raise important questions about its real influence in the colonies. Did Whitefield, for example, memorize texts, speak from brief notes, or simply begin preaching without previously having given the sermon extended thought? Did other ministers speak extemporaneously on some occasions but revert, on others, to reading their sermons or delivering them from extensive notes? And between 1730 and 1770 did ministers adopt or abandon extemporaneous preaching in different denominations at different times? Since we do not yet have the answers to these questions, generalizations about the political implications of extemporaneous preaching in the revivals are premature.

What, then, ought we to say about the revivals of religion in prerevolutionary America? The most important suggestion is the most drastic. Historians should abandon the term "the Great Awakening" because it distorts the character of eighteenth-century American religious life and misinterprets its relationship to prerevolutionary American society and politics. In religion it is a deus ex machina that falsely homogenizes the heterogeneous; in politics it falsely unites the colonies in slick preparation for the Revolution. Instead, a four-part model of the eighteenth-century colonial revivals will highlight their common features, underscore important differences, and help us assess their real significance.

First, with one exception, the prerevolutionary revivals should be understood primarily as regional events that occurred in only half the colonies. Revivals occurred intermittently in New England between 1690 and 1745 but became especially common between 1735 and 1745. They were uniformly Calvinist and produced more significant local political ramifications—even if they did not democratize New England—than other colonial revivals except those in Virginia. Revivals in the middle colonies occurred primarily between 1740 and 1760. They had remarkably eclectic theological origins, bypassed large numbers of settlers, were especially weak in New York, and produced few demonstrable political and social changes. Revivals in the southern colonies did not occur in significant numbers until the 1750s, when they were limited largely to Virginia, missed Maryland almost entirely, and did not occur with any regularity in the Carolinas until well after 1760. Virginia's Baptist revivalists stimulated major political and social changes in the colony, but the secular importance of the other revivals has been exaggerated. A fourth set of revivals, and the exception to the regional pattern outlined here, accompanied the preaching tours of the Anglican itinerant Whitefield. These tours frequently intersected with the regional revivals in progress at different times in New England, the middle colonies, and some parts of the southern colonies, but even then the fit was imperfect. Whitefield's tours produced some changes in ministerial speaking styles but few permanent alterations in institutional patterns of religion, although his personal charisma supported no less than seven tours of the colonies between 1740 and his death in Newburyport, Massachusetts, in 1770.

Second, the prerevolutionary revivals occurred in the colonial backwaters of Western society where they were part of a long-term pattern of erratic movements for spiritual renewal and revival that had long characterized Western Christianity and Protestantism since its birth two centuries earlier. Thus, their theological origins were international and diverse rather than narrowly Calvinist and uniquely American. Calvinism was important in some revivals, but Arminianism and Pietism supported others. This theological heterogeneity also makes it impossible to isolate a single overwhelmingly important cause of the revivals. Instead, they appear to have arisen when three circumstances were present—internal demands for renewal in different international Christian communities, charismatic preachers, and special, often unique, local circumstances that made communities receptive to elevated religious rhetoric.

Third, the revivals had modest effects on colonial religion. This is not to say that they were "conservative" because they did not always uphold the traditional religious order. But they were never radical, whatever their critics claimed. For example, the revivals reinforced ministerial rather than lay authority even as they altered some clergymen's perceptions of their tasks and methods. They also stimulated the demand for organization, order, and authority in the evangelical denominations. Presbyterian "New Lights" repudiated the conservative Synod of Philadelphia because its discipline was too weak, not too strong, and demanded tougher standards for ordination and subsequent service. After 1760, when Presbyterians and Baptists utilized revivalism as part of their campaigns for denominational expansion, they only increased their stress on central denominational organization and authority.

Indeed, the best test of the benign character of the revivals is to take up the challenge of contemporaries who linked them to outbreaks of enthusiasm" in Europe. In making these charges, the two leading antirevivalists in the colonies, Garden of Charleston and Chauncy

of Boston, specifically compared the colonial revivals with those of the infamous "French Prophets" of London, exiled Huguenots who were active in the city between 1706 and about 1730. The French Prophets predicted the downfall of English politicians, raised followers from the dead, and used women extensively as leaders to prophesy and preach. By comparison, the American revivalists were indeed "conservative." They prophesied only about the millennium, not about local politicians, and described only the necessity, not the certainty, of salvation. What is most important is that they eschewed radical change in the position of women in the churches. True, women experienced dramatic conversions, some of the earliest being described vividly by Edwards. But, they preached only irregularly, rarely prophesied, and certainly never led congregations, denominations, or sects in a way that could remotely approach their status among the French Prophets.

Fourth, the link between the revivals and the American Revolution is virtually nonexistent. The relationship between prerevolutionary political change and the revivals is weak everywhere except in Virginia, where the Baptist revivals indeed shattered the exclusive, century-old Anglican hold on organized religious activity and politics in the colony. But, their importance to the Revolution is weakened by the fact that so many members of Virginia's Anglican aristocracy also led the Revolution. In other colonies the revivals furnished little revolutionary rhetoric, including even millennialist thought, that was not available from other sources and provided no unique organizational mechanisms for anti-British protest activity. They may have been of some importance in helping colonists make moral judgments about eighteenth-century English politics, though colonists unconnected to the revivals made these judgments as well.

In the main, then, the revivals of religion in eighteenth-century America emerge as nearly perfect mirrors of a regionalized, provincial society. They arose erratically in different times and places across a century from the 1690s down to the time of the Revolution. Calvinism underlay some of them, Pietism and Arminianism others. Their leadership was local and, at best, regional, and they helped reinforce—but were not the key to—the proliferation and expansion of still-regional Protestant denominations in the colonies. As such, they created no intercolonial religious institutions and fostered no significant experiential unity in the colonies. Their social and political effects were minimal and usually local, although they could traumatize communities in which they upset, if only temporarily, familiar patterns of worship and social behavior. But the congregations they occasionally produced usually blended into the traditional social system, and the revivals abated without shattering its structure. Thus, the revivals of religion in pre-revolutionary America seldom became proto-revolutionary, and they failed to change the timing, causes, or effects of the Revolution in any significant way.

Of course, it is awkward to write about the eighteenth-century revivals of religion in America as erratic, heterogeneous, and politically benign. All of us have walked too long in the company of Tracy's "Great Awakening" to make our journey into the colonial past without it anything but frightening. But as Chauncy wrote of the Whitefield revivals, perhaps now it is time for historians "to see that Things have been carried too far, and that the Hazard is great . . . lest we should be over-run with *Enthusiasm*."

POSTSCRIPT

Was the Great Awakening a Key to the American Revolution?

Even if McLoughlin's thesis (that the revivals of the mid-eighteenth century were a "key" that helped open the door to the war for independence) is not valid, there is room to argue that the Revolution was not without its religious elements. In his book *Religion in America: Past and Present* (Prentice-Hall, 1961), Clifton E. Olmstead argues for a broader application of religious causes to the origins of the American Revolution. First, and consistent with McLoughlin, Olmstead contends that the Great Awakening did foster a sense of community among American colonists, thus providing the unity required for an organized assault on England. Moreover, the Awakening further weakened existing ties between colonies and Mother Country by drawing adherents of the Church of England into the evangelical denominations that expanded as a result of revivalistic Protestantism. Second, tensions were generated by the demand that an Anglican bishop be established in the colonies. Many evangelicals found in this plan evidence that the British government wanted further control over the colonies. Third, the Quebec Act, enacted by Parliament in 1774, not only angered American colonists by nullifying their claims to western lands but also heightened religious prejudice in the colonies by granting tolerance to Roman Catholics. Fourth, ministers played a significant role in encouraging their parishioners to support the independence movement. Olmstead claims that this revolutionary movement in the colonies was defended overwhelmingly by Congregationalist, Presbyterian, Dutch Reformed, and Baptist ministers. Finally, many of the revolutionaries, imbued with the American sense of mission, believed that God was ordaining their revolutionary activities.

Further support for the views expressed by William McLoughlin can be found in Alan Heimert, *Religion and the American Mind from the Great Awakening to the Revolution* (Cambridge University Press, 1966); William Warren Sweet, *The Story of Religion in America* (New York, 1950); Cedric B. Cowing, *The Great Awakening and the American Revolution: Colonial Thought in the Eighteenth Century* (University of Chicago, 1971); Richard Hofstadter, *America at 1750: A Social Portrait* (Knopf, 1973); Rhys Isaac, *The Transformation of Virginia, 1740–1790* (University of North Carolina Press, 1982); Ruth H. Bloch, *Visionary Republic* (Cambridge University Press, 1985); Harry S. Stout, *The New England Soul: Preaching and Religious Culture in Colonial New England* (Oxford University Press, 1986); and Patricia U. Bonomi, *Under the Cope of Heaven: Religion, Society, and Politics in Colonial America* (Oxford University Press, 1986). Alan Heimert's views have been challenged by Sidney Mead and Bernard Bailyn. Students interested in the Great Awakening should consult Edwin Scott Gaustad, *The Great Awakening in New England* (Harper & Bros., 1957); David S. Lovejoy, *Religious Enthusiasm and the Great Awakening* (Prentice-Hall, 1969); and Marilyn J. Westerkamp, *Triumph of the Laity: Scots-Irish Piety and the Great Awakening, 1625–1760* (Oxford University Press, 1987). George Athan Billias, ed., *The American Revolution: How Revolutionary Was It?* (Holt, Rinehart and Winston, 1965) offers different perspectives on the war for independence, as does Bernard Bailyn in *Ideological Origins of the American Revolution* (Harvard University Press, 1967).

PART 2

The New Nation

As America grew and became more established, its people and leaders struggled with implementing the ideals that had sparked the Revolution. What had been abstractions before the formation of the new government had to be applied and refined in day-to-day practice. The nature of post-revolutionary America, the stability of government, the transition of power, the reality of citizens' civil rights, as well as the role of women, had to be worked out.

Can the Revolution Serve as a Developmental Model for Third World Nations Today?

The Constitution: Was It an Economic Document?

Did President Jefferson Outfederalize the Federalists?

Did Women Achieve Greater Autonomy in the New Nation?

ISSUE 6

Can the Revolution Serve as a Developmental Model for Third World Nations Today?

YES: Richard B. Morris, from "The American Revolution: Model for Emerging Nations," *The Emerging Nations and the American Revolution* (Harper & Row, 1970)

NO: Carl N. Degler, from "The American Past: An Unsuspected Obstacle in Foreign Affairs," *American Scholar* (Spring 1963)

ISSUE SUMMARY

YES: Historian Richard F. Morris argues that the American Revolution was both a war of decolonization and a movement of wide-ranging political, social, and economic changes.
NO: Pulitzer Prize-winning author Carl N. Degler believes that, because of its unique conservative attempt to maintain the "status quo," the American Revolution is meaningless as a model for Third World nations to imitate.

After America's Vietnam war, many Third World nations complained that the United States had become a counterrevolutionary power. The complaints may not be invalid. In fact, there is good reason to suspect that the American Revolution may not have been a genuine revolution after all. Compared with the radical changes wrought by the Russian and Chinese Revolutions in this century, the American Revolution seems tame. Was the American Revolution a true revolution? The answer depends on your definition of the term. Two writers have recently outlined twelve different definitions of revolution. For the purpose of simplification, it is useful to discuss two approaches to defining revolution: *strict constructionists* perceive revolution as productive of significant and deep societal change; *loose constructionists* define the term as "any resort to violence within a political order to change its constitution, rulers, or policies." Everyone agrees that American revolutionaries fulfilled the second definition since they successfully fought a war that resulted in the overthrow of their English rulers and established a government run by themselves. If one defines revolution as the strict constructionists do, however, historians disagree over the amount of social and economic changes that took place in America. Some even argue that America was a middle-class democracy before the American Revolution and, therefore, there was no need for a social revolution.

Earlier historians, like George Bancroft, advanced the Whig or pro-American interpretation of the war. America won, he said, because God was on our side. Much of Bancroft's ten-volume *History of the United States (1834–1874)* was written during the period of Jacksonian democracy when belief in the destiny of the United States to spread the ideas of freedom, progress, and democracy was at its highest point.

The Whig view of the American Revolution has been kept alive by television series, grammar school textbooks, and the mid-1970s bicentennial celebrations. Professional historians revived the neo-Whig interpretation after World War II partly in response to the need for a consensus of values with which Americans could draw upon to fight the Russians in the Cold War and partly to win over neutral Third World nations.

Two groups of historians disagreed with the neo-Whig interpretation of the American Revolution. The Imperial historians viewed the Revolution from the perspective of the British empire. Arguing for a more objective approach, their writings tended to be sympathetic to the economic and political difficulties that Great Britain faced in running an empire in the late eighteenth century. In 1909, Carl Becker paved the way for a different interpretation of the Revolution when he concluded that the American Revolution created a struggle not only for home rule but also for who should rule at home. The Progressive historians searched for the social and economic conflicts among groups struggling for political power. Often a quasi-Marxist approach to the Revolution was taken. In state after state, the struggle for who should rule at home was viewed as a contest between the lower classes and the local aristocracy of merchants and large landowners. This progressive interpretation dominated most of the writings on the American Revolution from 1910 through 1945. It has been revived again in a more sophisticated manner by a new generation of scholars who were influenced by the events of the 1960s when protests against the "status quo" questioned the consensus of values that had glued America together in the preceding decades.

The following two selections discuss the influence of the American Revolution on the rest of the world. Both historians write within the framework of comparative history; yet both view the American Revolution from the Progressive and neo-Whig perspectives. In the first essay, the distinguished colonial historian Richard F. Morris argues that as the first great revolution of modern times, the American Revolution was both a war of decolonization and a movement of wide-ranging political, social, and economic changes. In the second essay, Stanford University historian Carl Degler thinks that because of its unique conservative attempt to maintain the "status quo," the American Revolution is meaningless as a model for Third World nations to imitate.

YES

Richard B. Morris

THE AMERICAN REVOLUTION: MODEL FOR EMERGING NATIONS?

In a ritual or in substance, all the emerging nations of our time have paid obeisance to the American Revolution. As the first successful decolonization movement of the modern world, it serves as an object lesson even for emerging nations who have obtained their independence not through overt rebellion, as did the Americans, but through that piecemeal liquidation of empires by which the Great Powers have in most cases abdicated colonial rule since the Second World War.

If the American Revolution had done nothing more than to pioneer that historic movement of peoples from colonialism to national independence, it would still have enormous relevance for the emerging nations. The fact is, however, that the Revolution provided more than a set of guidelines for revolutionary tactics and strategy; it led to a total transformation of American society, and thus it has special pertinence in an age of revolutionary social change.

At first glance it might seem incredible that there should be any affinity in spirit between a superpower like the United States and the young nations rising phoenix-like from the ashes of colonialism, handicapped by poverty, illiteracy, overpopulation, and landlordism. Many striking analogies may be demonstrated, however. At Independence the United States was both young and relatively weak. The Chinese called the youthful United States "The New People," while Europe's tradition-bound statesmen considered America not only young, but crude, undeveloped, and even primitive. Few if any of Europe's statesmen had faith in the lasting powers of a republic which extended its sway over so vast a territory as did the Thirteen States. Instead, they confidently expected that the centrifugal forces of sectionalism would soon rip it asunder. Even if America managed to survive as a political entity, Englishmen assumed that economic imperatives would once again attach the erstwhile insurgents to the mother country, and that the Thirteen States would resume a subordinate and dependent commercial role in the temporarily aborted relationship of Metropolis and Colony.

From *The Emerging Nations and the American Revolution* by Richard B. Morris (New York: Harper & Row, 1970). Reprinted by permission of the author.

How like the posture assumed today by the Great Powers toward the young nations that have just emerged or are in the process of emerging from colonialism. Because so many Americans are not heedful of their revolutionary past it may come as a shock to many of them to have so powerful and affluent a nation as their own compared with Nigeria or Kenya, with Burma or Indonesia. Striking dissimilarities there are, to be sure, and they seem too obvious to need spelling out, but it is the appropriateness of the analogy in certain areas which should command our attention.

All of the devices to which the emerging nations have resorted in achieving independence for themselves can be discovered in that first anticolonial revolution waged by Thirteen Colonies against a powerful world empire. In that revolutionary process the Americans, like latter-day revolutionaries, utilized the weapons of non-cooperation, civil disorder, provisional congresses, and finally war itself, even before issuing their declaration of independence. The Patriot or Revolutionary forces drew unity and inspiration from a charismatic leadership and fought a long and bitter war to a successful conclusion against seemingly hopeless odds.

First of all, though, the American Revolution determined the ritual observed by most later revolutions. Virtually all of the nations recently emerging from colonial status have felt obliged to justify their revolutions by declarations couched in language very similar to that utilized by the Americans in 1776. Even the Democratic Republic of Vietnam in its proclamation of September 2, 1945, made an open and intended levy on Jefferson's Great Declaration.

Secondly, in the use of sustained guerilla operations over a period of years the American Revolution bears comparison with recent so-called "wars of national liberation." Except for climactic battles like Saratoga and Yorktown, the Patriot operation depended on maintaining a fighting force in being through mobility, withdrawal, and surprise counterattack. Operating with lightening speed from inaccessible bases which they changed frequently, Marion, Pickens, and Sumter, leaders of irregular forces, struck blows in rapid succession at isolated British and Tory camps, garrisons, and convoys in the lower South. Theirs indeed was a tactic of terror, which William Cullen Bryant has captured in his "Song of Marion's Men." The same kind of tactic has been exploited by such modern revolutionaries as Mao Tse-tung and the late Che Guevara. . . .

A recent scholar has referred to the "crisis of legitimacy" that confronts all post-revolutionary societies, the need to create new bonds of loyalty to replace the old. The Americans resolved that crisis with great facility. They insisted upon the legality of their revolution, and fought for the rights of Englishmen as they believed them to be guaranteed by the British Constitution, and for the rights of man as they understood them to be guaranteed by Nature and Nature's God. Step by step they trimmed down Parliament's authority over the colonies until the King was the sole remaining tie. This, too, they deftly sundered. The Declaration cites "a long train of abuses" suffered by the colonies, and, taking a leaf from Tom Paine's *Common Sense*, presents the "history of the present King of Great Britain" as a "history of repeated injuries and usurpation." Denouncing as "unfit to be the ruler of a free people," "a prince whose character is thus marked by every act which may define a tyrant," The Great Declaration goes on to declare "these United Colonies" to be "free and independent states" and then to absolve them from "all political connection" with Great Britain. Thus the "crisis of legitimacy" was ingeniously resolved. . . .

If nationalism is the yeast which produces the revolutionary ferment of emerging nations, the analogy from the world of the present to young America is by no means strained. The American nation was born of revolution, and from its infancy it possessed characteristics which set it apart from the nations of the Old World. Goethe caught that essential difference in his *Poems of Wisdom* when he wrote:

America, you fare much better
Than this old continent of ours
No basalt rocks your land enfetters
No ruined towers . . .

In its emergence America was destined to fix the character of much of modern nationalism. Leaders like Washington and John Jay were concerned about establishing a national character. To start, the common tongue, the English language, had to be Americanized— Noah Webster saw to that. Even before Webster the process was going forward. "You speak American Well," the French traveler Chastellux reported to be a common remark as early as 1782. Education had to be made more available and pragmatic, the divisive force of religious intolerance mitigated, and the penal code modernized to fit a more humane society. The statesman John Jay did more than coin a phrase when he observed in 1797, "I wish to see our people more Americanized, if I may use that expression; until we feel and act as an indepen-

dent nation, we shall always suffer from foreign intrigue."

Accordingly, when the Irish Free State compels its children to study Gaelic, when Israel adopts Hebrew as its official language, when the Vietnamese require all foreign signs removed and replaced by those in the Vietnamese language, and when fanatical Indian patriots riot to make Hindi, not English, the language of instruction, we must bear in mind that they are taking the same basic steps in building national character that Americans themselves assumed without a venerated national tradition, with but few national myths, and with heroes chosen from an immediate past. . . .

It has been the fashion of commentators to consider the American Revolution as legalistic and as exhibiting a tender concern for property unlike such twentieth-century revolutions as those of Mexico and Cuba, for example. Like all oversimplifications, this one fails to take into account the complex currents which swept the American Revolutionary movement and the wide range of socioeconomic ideas which the leaders espoused. Time after time minority groups sought to move their states in leveling directions not acceptable to the majority. By way of example, the preliminary draft of Pennsylvania's Declaration of Rights contained an article stating "that an enormous Proportion of Property vested in a few Individuals is dangerous to the Rights, and destructive of the Common Happiness of Mankind," and should accordingly be discouraged by the laws of the state. Many of the states fixed price and wage ceilings during the Revolution, along with regulations against profiteering and monopolizing, and various legislatures in post-Revolutionary years enacted paper money and stay laws.

They provide documentation attesting to the widespread conviction that property values should not be elevated above human values, and that the property owner and creditor should not on all occasions be awarded their pound of flesh. . . .

In disputes with underdeveloped nations over such issues as the confiscation of American and other foreign-owned property and the honoring of debts, the United States has invariably, if not inflexibly, applied long-accepted Hamiltonian standards generally observed in the more stable democracies of the Free World. As a Revolutionary nation the United States honored these standards in the breach. The American states during and after the Revolution confiscated the estates of the Loyalists. The initial purpose of such confiscatory measures was not to universalize freeholding, since a very broad class of freeholders already existed, but to punish notorious dissidents and raise funds desperately needed to carry on the war. However, the confiscated estates either at the beginning, as in cases where manor tenants were allowed to exercise pre-emption rights and thus transformed into freeholders, were broken up, or in the long run they were sold by insiders and speculators to small holders. Either way, the long-range effect was egalitarian. In some cases the objective was clearly the breaking up of land monopoly. Thus the estates of the Penn family in Pennsylvania were taken over, as one correspondent reminded Lady Juliana Penn in the summer of 1782, "not in a way of confiscation, but upon principles of policy and expedience." They thought the estate "two [sic] large for a subject to possess, supposing it dangerous to the public that so much property should rest in the hands of one family."

If the Soviet Union refuses to honor the Czarist debts, its actions are hardly unique among revolutionary states. For a generation Southern planters in the American states, buttressed by legal devices adopted by their state governments, refused to pay their prewar debts owing to English and Scottish merchants. The evidence of such indebtedness is massive and the devices employed to avoid payment provide some of the strongest arguments for considering the War for Independence a social revolution. Despite the provision of the Treaty of Peace that creditors on either side should meet with no lawful impediment to the recovery in full value of their debts, many Virginians remained adamant on the subject. George Mason remarked to Patrick Henry that the question most frequently raised in conversation was: "If we are now to pay the debts due to the British merchants, what have we been fighting for all this while?" . . .

We are accustomed to associating recent revolutions, whether the Bolshevik Revolution of 1917 or the Cuban Revolution of 1959, with violent social upheaval. In contrast, the American Revolution, with its sober and affluent leadership and its emphasis on legitimacy and moderation, seemingly accomplished its social transformation in a less explosive fashion. To the Loyalists who were forced to emigrate and whose property was seized, the social revolution seemed violent enough, to be sure. The estimate of the emigré Loyalists who went to Canada or England during the American Revolution ranges as high as 100,000, with perhaps an equal number of black people joining the exodus. As one perceptive scholar of revolutions has pointed out, this represents a far higher percentage of displaced persons for the

American than for the French Revolution.

To fill the places of the Loyalists many new men came into business and government, and many new fortunes were created by the special opportunities afforded by the Revolution in such areas as privateering, war manufacturing and supplies, and by the establishment of new trade patterns and the speculative opportunities afforded by inflation. In addition, in most cases representation in the state legislatures was enlarged to the advantage of newly settled areas and men of less established families. In the Sixty-second *Federalist* James Madison stresses "the mutability in the public councils" which he attributed to "a rapid succession of new members," and asserts that "every new election in the States is found to change one half of the representatives." Madison's contention that within the American Revolutionary states the new governments were operated by new men, many of whom could hardly have expected to attain prominence had the colonies remained British, is sustained by a comparative study of the membership of colonial legislatures on the eve of independence and shortly after independence had been obtained. In three states the proportion of those in the lowest socioeconomic category, denominated as being in "moderate" circumstances, rose from 17 percent of the legislatures in 1770 to 62 percent in 1784, with a corresponding decline recorded in the ranks of the "wealthy" and the "well-to-do." Even in the South the "wealthy" lost their predominance in the legislatures. The proportion of merchants and lawyers in the state legislatures suffered a startling decline while the representation of the farmers doubled during these years. If, then, socio-economic upthrust is an essential criteria of a true revolution, one headed in a democratic direction, the American Revolution, with its partial, if not total, displacement of the colonial "upper" or "aristocratic" class, must be considered a social revolution. . . .

Remarkable as was the transformation of the American white society, nevertheless the American Revolution tragically failed to confront the issue of black inequality fairly and squarely. . . .

Serious moves to end slavery were in fact put in motion. Into the 1776 Virginia Constitution Jefferson tried unsuccessfully to write a provision that "no person hereafter coming into the state would be held in slavery." When he included the slave trade as one of the evils ascribed to George III in the Declaration, his fellow delegates had the reference stricken out. Even before the Great Declaration the North took steps to end slavery, a process which the war accelerated. In 1774 Rhode Island provided that all slaves brought into the colony should be free henceforth. After 1776, states like Massachusetts and Vermont abolished slavery outright, while others, like Pennsylvania in 1780 and Connecticut and Rhode Island in 1784, began to make provisions for gradual emancipation. Indeed, the 1780's saw the burgeoning of manumission societies, as well as widespread manumissions of slaves in some of the Southern states.

The harsh fact is that the Patriot side numbered most of the big slaveowners of the South, who were intensely provoked by various offers of freedom held out by royal officials to the Negro slave in exchange for loyalty to the Crown. To men with strong antislavery convictions like the New York statesman John Jay, the failure of the American Revolution to end slavery and discrimination against the Negro made the Declaration of Independence a continuing commitment. Having failed to come to grips with the subject of black inequality in the Revolution and managing to evade the issue during the federal Convention, the Founding Fathers postponed to some remote time the implementation of the principles and promises embodied in the Declaration of Independence. The long history of the antislavery and civil rights movement in the United States provides continuous and abundant proof that men of conscience in America consider Negro inequality the great unfulfilled commitment of the American Revolution. That was what Abraham Lincoln meant when, in speaking of Jefferson's generation, he remarked in 1857: "They meant to set up a standard maxim for free society, which should be . . . constantly looked to, constantly labored for, and even though never perfectly attained, constantly approximated, and thereby constantly spreading and deepening its influence and augmenting the happiness and value of life to all people of all colors everywhere."

Although America stands as the classic example of a nation which enjoyed a phenomenal degree of economic growth since its establishment, it is seldom realized how great a spur to development the casting off of the shackles of colonialism proved. On balance, the entire mercantilist program of external control of trade embraced under the rubric of Parliament's Navigation Laws was disadvantageous to the economy of the mainland. Yet some historians play down the trade laws as an issue between colonies and mother country and would minimize the hardships imposed upon the colonial economy by the trade laws. If the colonists complained comparatively little about the Navigation Laws before 1763, it may well have been because they were so loosely administered. Powerful and articulate segments of the colonial population considered the strict enforcement of the acts after 1763, along with the revenue measures, as a serious grievance.

The anticolonial stance of the Americans represented a protest against the permanent debtor status assigned the colonies in the imperial economic scheme. In that respect it is not unlike the anticolonialism of emerging nations seeking to free themselves from economic dependency upon one or another of the Great Powers. What Jefferson felicitously called "the pursuit of happiness" was a concept embracing a variety of freedoms, including social mobility, freedom of occupational choice, freedom of monopolistic restraints, security, and a more abundant life, including a fair sharing of the nation's resources.

That America has achieved these goals for most of its citizens cannot be denied, nor can one controvert the fact that in some measure these achievements stem from the liberative effect of the American Revolution on the economy. The federal principle in the new Constitution gave America an instant common market, still unmatched in the world to date. Emulated by the Common Market nations of Europe, it serves as an example to Latin America and to the new states of East Africa now engaged in setting up their own common market. The sound fiscal policies inaugurated by Alexander Hamilton made abundant credit available to business, while the government's land programs encouraged the farmer just as the innovative and inventive climate of America spurred the manufacturer.

Whether one would date the take-off into a self-sustained economic growth with the adoption of the Constitution, or with the 1840's, or perhaps with even a later period, America did manage to win economic as well as political independence. Without the former the latter would have proven a hollow gain indeed. That sustained rate of growth and that degree of affluence which America did achieve still makes the United States the envy of the older nations whose economies it has surpassed. And if it may be said that the revolutions which have swept the underdeveloped world are a response to rising expectations, then the United States through the image of affluence it has projected is as much responsible for these insurgent movements as are dread subversives reared on the gospels of Marx, Lenin, and Mao.

To sum up the durable contribution of the American Revolution and its relevance to today's revolutionary world, it should be acknowledged at the start that the American War for Independence was a revolution of enormous consequences for the world. . . .

As the first great revolution of modern times, the American Revolution was both a war of decolonization and a movement of broad social change and reform. Waged to establish an independent nation, sovereign and equal with all the nations of the earth, it constituted at the same time a movement to support the rights of man, of all men, and women too. And, in that wider sense, the American Revolution, with its egalitarian overtones, has enormous relevance to the revolutions of the emerging nations of later times and, not least of all, to our own time.

NO

Carl N. Degler

THE AMERICAN PAST

AN UNSUSPECTED OBSTACLE IN FOREIGN AFFAIRS

Increasingly, it is fashionable to discern a connection between our own successful revolt against colonial rule and the revolt against Europe that is the essence of the nationalist ferment in Asia and Africa. In the July, 1961, issue of *Foreign Affairs*, for example, Henry Wriston wrote: "Familiarity with our record will end much of the difficulty in understanding current revolutions. For 1961 is still a part of the Age of Revolution that was launched in 1776." Later in the same article he added, "Read aright, our Declaration of Independence makes us kin to all the new nations which escaped from the status of wards and attained the stature of independence." A year later, in the *Saturday Evening Post*, also coinciding with the anniversary of the nation's birth, Secretary of State Dean Rusk took up the same theme, observing that it was his "conviction that the ideas which inspired the American Revolution and have guided our national development are the most powerful forces at work in the world today." Since then, Alan Westin in the *New York Times Magazine* has made a similar connection between our history and that of the newly independent states of the world.

To be sure, there is some reason to see such an analogy. After all, our own revolution was the first colonial rebellion to succeed in modern times. But a closer inspection of the American past suggests that our experience is too special to be a guide to the life of other people; to suppose that what we did can be done by others simply because we did it, is to misread our history and, more important, to confuse our people and to misunderstand what is going on in the underdeveloped world.

Take the example of our colonial revolution from Great Britain. On the surface it is a simple war for independence against the greatest power of the day. Viewed as such it appears strikingly similar to the Indian movement for independence or the Indonesian revolt against the Dutch. But once we probe beneath the surface the analogy quickly evaporates.

Reprinted from THE AMERICAN SCHOLAR, Volume 32, Number 2, Spring 1963. Copyright © 1963 by the publisher. By permission of the publisher.

A salient feature of our revolution was that [its] purpose was deeply conservative. The colonials revolted against British rule in order to keep things as they were, not to initiate a new era. The well-known argument of the colonists that they would not accept taxation without representation was not a demand for new liberties, but an appeal for the retention of rights long enjoyed and only recently taken away by a reinvigorated British government's efforts to impose a tax on stamps and later on tea. Indeed, the whole revolutionary decade from 1765 to 1776 can be viewed as a conservative response to the colonials to the British government's various schemes for dealing in a new and more rational way with the governance of its empire now that the French had been successfully ejected from North America. Anyone who runs through the colonial protests of those years cannot help being impressed by their underlying similarity: Let us return to the ways of government known before 1760 when there were none of the objectionable taxes, laws and interferences by Britain in the affairs of the colonies. What the colonials hoped for was a restoration of those years of "salutary neglect," as Edmund Burke named them.

The demand for independence came only reluctantly and after years of trial and agitation and when the imperial purpose of the British seemed incapable of being turned aside in any other fashion. As late as July 6, 1775—two months after the fray at Concord and Lexington—the Continental Congress officially denied "any designs of separation from Great Britain and establishing independent states." We have taken up arms, the Congress carefully explained, "in defense of the freedom that is our birthright, and which we ever enjoyed til the late violation of it. . . ." That same reluctance to move to revolution was remembered by John Adams over a half-century later. "That there existed a general desire of independence of the crown, in any part of America before the Revolution," he wrote in 1821, "is as far from the truth as the zenith is from the nadir. For my own part, there was not a moment during the Revolution, when I would not have given everything I ever possessed for a restoration to the state of things before the contest began, provided we could have had any sufficient security for its continuance." as Adams implied, prior to the 1760's British rule was unobjectionable. The Declaration of Independence itself testifies to this, for the "crimes" of George III listed therein are those of the preceding ten years. Nothing was said about the rest of the century and a half of British rule.

What analogy can there be between this history and that of the newly independent people? There was in America no long-drawnout, underground independence movement as in India under Ghandi or in Ghana under Nkrumah. Independence became a goal for Americans only as a "dernier resort," as Washington was fond of saying. The men who pushed the American Revolution were not nationalists compelled to spend years in the jails of the colonial power, but political leaders seeking only to continue their free governments as they knew them all their lives. Fully three-quarters of the men who signed the Declaration of Independence held office under the Crown before the Revolution and under the state governments immediately after the Revolution. What other colonial country today can show a similar degree of continuity of leadership across the chasm of its revolution for independence?

More is at stake here than simple historical accuracy. Our whole conception of what a revolution is and how independence is achieved has been shaped by our historical experience. It is true, of course, as has been pointed out by a number of commentators, that as a result of their own successful revolt Americans in the eighteenth, nineteenth and twentieth centuries were prone to welcome revolutions elsewhere. But the significant fact is that when these revolutions did not emulate the American pattern of quickly leading to orderly, democratic societies, American public opinion found these foreign revolutions disappointing, if not hostile. That was what happened with the French Revolution after 1793, with the Latin American revolts of the nineteenth century and with the Russian Revolution of 1917, to name only the most obvious. And it is happening today with the revolutions in Asia and Africa. Our revolutionary experience bears almost no resemblance to the turmoil and authoritarianism of the modern nationalist revolutions around the globe. Certainly there was violence against Tories and conflict among the chief economic groups during and after our Revolution, but the overriding social fact was that the transition from colonial status to independence was carried out smoothly and without any serious breakdown in political authority. In the course of a century and a half, during which they built their version of English representative government, Americans had learned how to operate a system of self-government and to put their trust in peaceful solutions to political problems rather than in violence or one-man rule. At the time of the Revolution, most white males were already a part of the political process, for if the latest scholarly studies of the colonial suffrage are to be believed—and I think they are—then at the very least a majority of white men voted and could participate in government years before Paul Revere made his famous ride. Probably most Americans, at least the males, could read and write at the time of independence, and probably most of them owned their own land. Thus, as a self-governing people before the Revolution, the Americans struck for independence in order to *retain* their freedom and to resist what they interpreted as British *intentions* of tyranny.

The colonial or newly independent peoples today, on the other hand, struggle for or cherish self-government as a new, albeit desirable, thing. For them the forms and practices of self-government are unfamiliar because of either lack of time to develop them or lack of opportunity to practice them. Happily they repudiate that past, looking expectantly toward freedom in the future. The American Revolution, to be sure, like many other great events, went beyond the intentions of those who started it, but between a revolution that is intended to overthrow the past and one that is intended to perpetuate it lies the vast gulf between a radical and a conservative habit of mind. . . .

Furthermore, contrary to the impression given by public figures today, our revolutionary fathers were not so sure that the American Revolution was exportable or reproducible. John Adams and Thomas Jefferson, for example, in their famous correspondence during their declining years, agreed that even new countries like the newly independent republics of South America were not fit for either free government or independence. "I enter in all your doubts as to the events of the revolution of South America," Jefferson wrote to Adams in 1818. "They will succeed against Spain," he correctly prophesied. "But the dangerous enemy is within their breasts. Ignorance and superstition will chain their minds and bodies under religious and military despotism. I do believe it would be better for them to obtain freedom by degrees only. . . ." Both men continued to harbor such doubts up to the close of their lives in 1826.

Another analogy often made between the history of the United States and the newly emergent nations is that America began as an underdeveloped country, successfully making the transition to industrialization without government controls or interference with individual initiative. Therefore, it is argued, if Americans could do it in the past, then these new nations can today. Why, then, many Americans today ask in rising anger, do these nations need foreign aid, why do they lean so sympathetically toward socialistic measures and state intervention in economic affairs?

Again the answer must be that the analogy is wrong. It is true that in the early years of the Republic the United States was largely agrarian in economy, deceptively similar in character to those traditional societies now emerging into statehood. But the United States was an agricultural society in which the ratio between man and land was low. "Here every one may have land to labor for himself," Jefferson pointed out in 1813. Sometimes the land speculator made the acquisition of land more difficult or more expensive than might otherwise have been the case, but as early as 1820, an eighty-acre piece of land could be purchased from the government for one hundred dollars. In a nation where most men were landowners, few Americans had to contend with landlords or moneylenders, as has been the case with Indians crowded upon their tiny plots in Bengal and the Oudh. And when they did, as in New York State in the 1830' and 1840's, the force of the rest of society supported the overthrow of feudal encumbrances. . . .

An American in the early nineteenth century, as a result of his own hard labor, could accumulate a surplus, even buy more land (and, if he lived in the South, more slaves) and greatly improve his material position in his own lifetime. The thirty-eight million immigrants who entered the United States between 1820 and 1930 were living testimony to the belief in and the actuality of the opportunity. The immigrants came also because wages were high in the United States, for in the new country there was a chronic, if variable, shortage of labor. High wages in turn encouraged a rising rate of productivity through the use of machines and labor-saving devices on farms and in factories. (Even slave labor was too expensive at times and so Yankee ingenuity and Southern profit-seeking combined to produce a cotton gin.) In the new nations of the world, the two great problems that inhibit economic growth are low agricultural productivity and a high ratio of men to the land. America in its rise to economic abundance has not had to contend with such difficult obstacles.

There is a further reason why the economic growth of the United States offers few analogies for the new nation. One of the consequences of the abundance of natural resources was that the nation could afford to leave economic activity up to individual initiative, with all that that meant in offering a powerful incentive to production. A less well-endowed society could not have afforded to give free rein to the individual, for, as is evident in American history, individual enterprise is often rather free and easy in its use of national resources. Waste, contrary to Vance Packard, is not an invention of modern Americans. From the very beginning of our history foreign travelers have commented upon the slovenly agriculture of Americans. In the South of the eighteenth century, one historian has written, "Planters bought land as they might buy a wagon—with the expectation of wearing it out." Even in New England where good land was hard to come by, staunch defenders of the region like Timothy Dwight in 1821 had to admit that "the husbandry of New England is far inferior to that of Great Britain." In a country so richly endowed, the federal government itself could afford, literally, to give away the national domain, as it did through the Homestead Act and the grants to the railroads, in an effort to spur individual economic enterprise. . . .

If our history is a poor guide for understanding the world today, it is also an obstacle to the world's understanding of us. Self-righteous Northerners too often assume that the subordination of the Negro in American culture is an unfortunate, but largely Southern phenomenon, not typical of our society as a whole. To any objective observer, though, it is evident that throughout history, down to the present, the black man has been a problem for white Americans, north as well as south of Mason's and Dixon's line. For a long time in our history, because the Negro was a slave, the question of his proper place in society was ignored. But even as Northerners argued against slavery in the South in the years before the

Civil War, it was evident that opposition to slavery did not mean that the black man was accepted as an equal with the white. Lincoln himself, although a staunch foe of slavery, admitted in his debates with Douglas in 1858 that "I have no purpose to introduce political and social equality between the white and black races. There is a physical difference between the two, which in my judgment, will probably forever forbid their living together upon the footing of perfect equality; and inasmuch as it becomes a necessity that there must be a difference, I, as well as Judge Douglas, am in favor of the race to which I belong having the superior position. . . . I agree with Judge Douglas," he added, that the negro "is not my equal in many respects—certainly not in color, perhaps not in moral or intellectual endowment."

As President and just before he made public his preliminary Emancipation Proclamation, Lincoln met with a group of free Negroes to encourage them to emigrate to Central America. In the course of his remarks, he made clear his belief that white and black Americans could not live together as equals. Typically, Lincoln began his talk by getting to the central question of why Negroes should leave the country of their birth. "You and we," he said, "are different races. We have between us a broader difference than exists between almost any other two races. Whether it is right or wrong I need not discuss, but this physical difference is a great disadvantage to us both, as I think your race suffer very greatly, many of them living among us, while ours suffer from your presence. In a word, we suffer on each side." He went on to say that slavery and the Negro were the cause for "our white men cutting one another's throats" in civil war, "But for your race among us there could not be war, although many men engaged on *either* side do not care for you one way or the other."

After slavery was abolished, the question of the Negro's place in a white man's country troubled Americans for decades and it still does, both in the North and in the South, although today the constitutional basis for the equality of the Negro is more widely accepted than at any time in our history. The point being made here should not be misunderstood. There is no question that ever since the Fourteenth Amendment, at least, the ideals of America has enshrined in our documents stand for equality for all men, without distinction of race or color. But that principle is not yet a matter of practice today, any more than it has been throughout our history.

Because our society is working to close the gap between principle and practice, we feel the world should understand our history and therefore excuse our shortcomings in the matter of race relations. Here the shoe is on the other foot, for we find that our history has limited us, as the history of other peoples prevents them from emulating our political stability and our economic growth. Moreover, to most Americans our history appears to be a valid if unfavorable explanation for the subordination of the black man. Was not Tocqueville correct when he ascribed to the long history of slavery the discriminatory behavior white Americans adopt toward Negroes? "Among the moderns," Tocqueville wrote in *Democracy in America*, "the abstract and transient fact of slavery is fatally united with the physical and permanent fact of color. The tradition of slavery dishonors the race, and the peculiarity of the race perpetuates the tradition of slavery. . . .

Thus the Negro transmits the eternal mark of his ignominy to all his descendents; and although the law may abolish slavery, God alone can obliterate the traces of its existence." Certainly the long history of slavery helps to explain the peculiarly American attitude toward the Negro. Furthermore, Americans are surely right in thinking that European superiority about our racial problem is unjustified simply because no European people has tested its alleged lack of racial bias under circumstances similar to those in the American past—that is, with large numbers of Negroes reared in slavery. Indeed, now that substantial numbers of West Indian Negroes, congregating in London, are arousing hostility from whites, Englishmen can no longer be sure that their vaunted lack of racism is any more than lack of opportunity.

But in entertaining such thoughts, Americans usually overlook the examples of peoples who do have a history of receiving without discrimination a large number of Negroes into their culture. Negro slaves, after all, made up a large part of the population of several of the countries of Latin America. Brazil, for example, has a history of slavery longer than ours, but for a variety of reasons this has not resulted in the kind of discrimination against the Negro that has been taken as a matter of course in the United States. On the contrary, the races in Brazil have mingled intimately, publicly and privately. Even during the nineteenth century under slavery, the free Negro in Brazil and elsewhere in South America attained governmental and ecclesiastical posts that were often of an eminence not yet achieved by Negroes in the United States today. Cuba, as Castro has not hesitated to remind us, is a conspicuous example of a society where the

Negro has been accepted as an equal. In fact, General Batista, whose government Castro overthrew, is a Negro. Other Negroes as well have played important roles in the life of Cuba in the past.

Thus when the newly emergent peoples of the world, nearly all of whom are colored, criticize the American attitude toward the Negro, they are doing more than merely objecting to the treatment they might receive here. They are objecting to our history; they are finding in us a deficiency that is not in the nature of man but in the nature of our history. It might after all, have been different. Therefore, despite all our good intentions and regardless of the correctness of the Supreme Court's decisions, our slowness in eradicating racial discrimination is as difficult for the colored peoples of the world to understand as their political and economic backwardness is for us.

There is yet another burden that the past places upon Americans in confronting the world of the mid-twentieth century. Leaders in the contest of global dimensions are expected to have a philosophy, an ideology, for by having one they can make their aims clear and they can attract followers. America, though, as Daniel Boorstin has pointed out, lacks an ideology. The new life and new ways of thought that Americans like to think they brought into being on this continent are the result not of plan or ideology, but of circumstances. As the example of the Revolution reminds us, Americans look to a political utopia in the past, not in the future. We talk of progress in material things, but rarely do we talk of political progress, although we frequently lament the sorry decline in the level of our political behavior. In Walter Lippmann's *The Public Philosophy*, for example, he lamented our departure from what he considered the golden age of political discourse in the eighteenth century.

The whole structure of our political life is pragmatic and without plan. Our political parties have always been collections of diverse interests and only by the greatest of effort have historians and political scientists been able to find differences between them. Indeed, as Louis Hartz has shown, both parties historically have drawn their principles from the same pool of liberal ideas. As a government, we have dealt with problems as they came up and without any regard to logic or preconceived ideology. Thus when canals were needed to open the Ohio valley and the Middle West, we did not hesitate to let the state governments build or help to build them, although at the same time we talked of individual enterprise as the motive force in the economy—and it was, too. More recently, resolutely rejecting socialism as a political faith, we nevertheless set up, and retained under both parties, public power projects because the progress of the country seemed to require them.

Significantly, our great statements of political purpose have come into existence as a result of dealing with specific problems, peculiar to our history. Compare, for example, our Declaration of Independence—incidentally, the most cosmopolitan of all our great documents, for it was intended as a justification to the world—with the Declaration of the Rights of Man and the Citizen that emanated from the French Revolution. Our declaration is an indictment of a specific government—actually a single man, George III—at a definite time in history. So tied to circumstances and time is it that no one, except students of the Revolution, ever reads the main part, which is a list of George's crimes. That main part says nothing to men in different times and different places. The French declaration, on the other hand, was a statement of intention, of goals for Frenchmen and, by easy extension, of goals for all men who lived under an absolutist state. It is not accidental that it became the model for the liberal state in the revolutions of the nineteenth century.

For another example take the greatest of American political treatises, *The Federalist* of Hamilton, Madison and Jay. Its historical interest and importance for Americans are immense, for in it the Constitution at the formative stage is expounded by men of exceptional political acumen. But it says little to men elsewhere who may be dealing with problems of government and constitutions. *The Federalist* is too specific, too wrapped up in the special nature of the American situation. Even Madison's perceptive essay Number Ten, which Charles Beard once tried to make into a precursor of Marx's economic interpretation of history, is, in fact, an explanation of why the United States did not fit the scheme of a general theorist like Montesquieu. (It has been Montesquieu's thesis that a republic was impossible in a large country and Madison tried to show that the breadth of the thirteen colonies actually nullified Montesquieu's objections.) Similar limitations are to be found in the well-known Lincoln-Douglas debates; they are important for Americans, but no one reads them for their general principles; in fact, there are no general principles to be derived from the debates, as, for example, one finds in Burke's *Reflections on the French Revolution*. What Tocqueville recognized as true over a century ago still holds. "The spirit of Americans is averse to general ideas; it does not seek theoretical discoveries.

Neither politics nor manufactures direct them to such speculations; and although new laws are perpetually enacted in the United States, no great writers there have hitherto inquired into the general principles of legislation. The Americans have lawyers and commentators but no jurists; and they furnish examples rather than lessons to the world." There still is no book or treatise by an American comparable in intention, much less in reputation, to Montesquieu's *Spirit of the Laws*, Rousseau's *Social Contract*, or Locke's great treatises on government. Indeed, the two most incisive statements of our central tendency as a polity and society have been written by foreigners, Tocqueville in the 1830's and Bryce in the 1880's.

The American political tradition, rich as it is, is overwhelmingly pragmatic and conservative. It keeps what works as long as it works, regardless of how illogical an institution or a device it may be. The Electoral College is a case in point. Designed as a means for keeping the selection of the President out of the hands of the masses, the Electoral College today is defended by liberals as a support to the underrepresented urban regions in national elections!

Perhaps the most obvious example of a distinctively American idea is the principle of separation of church and state. As an idea in the late eighteenth century, it was revolutionary. No Western state in almost two thousands years had dared to rule without the support of the church and no state had dared to leave the church unsupported by the political power. And although we rigidly adhere to it as if it were an ideology—how else is one to explain our refusal to send a representative to the Vatican or to take a religious census—it, too, is more pragmatic than it appears. On its face, the doctrine prohibits any support of religion by the state, yet our Presidents proclaim religious holidays like Thanksgiving; our states support churches and religious schools by tax exemption at the same time that they are forbidden to permit prayers to be said in the classroom. Children may be released from school ahead of time for religious instruction, but only if that instruction takes place outside public property. The states may and do provide textbooks and buses to children attending religious schools, and the armed forces and the Congress maintain chaplains. In short, our principle of separation of church and state exhibits little of that internal consistency that any respectable ideology should. And the reason is that Americans do not think ideologically but pragmatically. Because they believe that religion is a good thing, they like to see it supported by their democratic government; yet they also believe that the mixing of religion and the state is divisive and ultimately destructive of religious freedom. Hence they have evolved this inconsistent but eminently workable compromise, leaving it to the Supreme Court to patch it up from time to time to keep it functioning.

A couple of years ago, in the depths of despair over the gains being made by the ideology of Communism, *Life* magazine and *The New York Times* commissioned a number of prominent Americans to articulate the national purpose. The results were disappointing. A similar effort by the President's Commission on National Goals also failed to strike fire at home or abroad. Such efforts at spelling out what America stands for, whoever is commissioned to undertake the task, are doomed to failure on at least two counts. For one thing, such efforts are too ideo-

logical for most Americans to accept; they smack of the European penchant for theory and manifestos that we distrust so much. Besides, as we have seen, the amorphous, inconsistent American way just does not fit into so neat a package. Nor, obviously, can such efforts say much to non-Americans.

The fact is that we have no ideology, for by definition an ideology is capable of being made universal. Our peculiar history cannot be spelled out, attractively packaged and sold to people with a quite different historical experience. In this respect we are at a grave disadvantage in the world struggle of ideas with Communism. Communism, after all, was designed as an ideology and only later was forcibly adapted to the circumstances and uses of a single country, or, more recently, several countries. Here, too, our history has been of no help.

It has often been observed that, from the time of the first Puritans down to the days of the New Frontier, Americans have been a people with a sense of mission. But the mission has been neither a proselytizing nor an aggressive one. Each of our forays into imperialism has been attended by strong reservations on the part of large minorities of the population. This was true at the time of the Mexican War, it was true after the Spanish-American War. Indeed, the burden of the anti-imperialist argument in 1898 was that the newly conquered peoples like the Puerto Ricans and the Filipinos could not adapt to our peculiar institutions. (Usually the argument was put less charitably and delicately than that; it was said that darkskinned Catholics were not equal to the high demands of Anglo-Saxon, Protestant American customs.) And in a short time—as empires are wont to do—we relinquished the Philippines. Even when we have engaged in imperialist ventures, as in Central America and the Caribbean, our aim has never been to carry our way of life to the heathen, so to speak, as it has been for the French and to a lesser extent for the British. We have been content merely to send in the Marines, establish order and redeem the defaulted bonds. With the culture we had little to do. In short, the Puritan ideal of a city upon a hill-setting an example for all, but making no effort at conversion of the Gentiles—has been our model.

Despite the rhetoric of Tom Paine and a few other enthusiastic propagandists for support of the Revolutionary War effort, the founding fathers were convinced of the essential differences between America and the rest of the world. Writing to Lafayette in 1788, George Washington expressed his renewed belief in the special destiny of America now that a new constitution had been written. "You see," he wrote, "I am not less enthusiastic than ever I have been, if a belief that peculiar scenes of felicity are reserved for this country, is to be denominated enthusiasm. Indeed, I do not believe, that Providence has done so much for nothing." About the same time, from Paris, Jefferson exulted to his friend James Monroe on the differences between America and Europe. "My God!" he exclaimed, "how little do my countrymen know what precious blessings they are in possession of; and which no other people on earth enjoy. I confess I had no idea of it myself." He urged all Americans to see Europe, to better appreciate the United States and to learn "how much it is their interest to preserve, uninfected by contagion those peculiarities in their governments and manners, to which they are indebted for those bless-

ings." America was so different from Europe, he told J.B. Say in 1804, that the principles in Say's treatise on economics because they were drawn from European experience might not be applicable in America.

Lincoln, echoing a remark of Jefferson's, called America the last, best hope of man. For most of the nineteenth century, the mission of America was what could be achieved here, not what could be exported to other peoples. If the downtrodden peasant of Central Europe or the unfranchised worker of a London slum wished to realize the dream for which America stood, he was not urged to reproduce America in his own country, but to come here. And does not this belief that America is unique, that the mission is to create the city on the hill help to explain that tendency of Americans to reproduce their home environment wherever they may be, whether it is Saigon, Berlin or Addis Ababa? If there is something arrogant and parochial about the behavior of Americans stationed in foreign countries, as we have been led to believe from books like *The Ugly American*, that is not accidental. Our sense of mission has also been arrogant and provincial.

There was a time, undoubtedly, when our awareness of the unique character of our history was tinged, if not suffused, with a sense of superiority. My purpose has not been to perpetuate the feeling; the object in emphasizing the unique features of the American past does not stem from any sense of arrogant pride. The aim has been quite different. In an age when America is a model for the whole world, it is important for us to remember that our history is irrelevant for most other peoples. If we do remember that then we will not expect other nations to follow our path and will save ourselves from disappointment arising out of misjudgment.

Frequently in our history the unique character of the American past was used as a support for isolation from the rest of the world. But that has not been my intention, either. No nation, least of all the United States, is an island unto itself in the present world. Nevertheless, the burdens that our peculiar history places upon us as an international leader should not be ignored, or, as some would try to do, speciously transmuted into assets. Our history has neither fitted us for nor warned us of the international role that we now play. In this restricted, if important sense, our history is a burden to us and irrelevant to the future of others.

POSTSCRIPT

Can the American Revolution Serve as a Developmental Model for Third World Nations Today?

These two historians approach the world-wide effects of the American Revolution from opposite perspectives. Carl Degler believes the American revolutionary experience is virtually meaningless to the emerging nations today. He makes some telling points about the uniqueness of the American experience. Unlike Third World nations, the American colonists had years of political experience running the lower houses of their legislature before rebelling. The orientation of the American political system is pragmatic, not ideological; conservative, not radical. The two-party democratic system with an elected presidency has not been the model for Third World nations. Nor do our large-scale agricultural systems and highly technical industrial systems seem very appealing to nations who lack large amounts of land, labor, and capital, and an entrepreneurial middle class.

Professor Morris provides us with a useful corrective to the more extreme arguments of Degler. He points out that, in the eighteenth century, it was revolutionary to set up a republican form of government. Also unique was the idea that a government could be based on a written constitution of fundamental laws grounded on the consent of the people instead of a king who received his authority from God. It appears that new political and economic opportunities were opened for lower class citizens when the Loyalists left the country during the war. A number of these citizens became not only landowners but also members of their respective state legislatures. If Morris is correct in arguing that many ex-Loyalists' lands were taken over by former tenants and other landless farmers, perhaps the American Revolution more closely resembles the strict constructionist models of the twentieth-century Russian and Chinese Revolutions than neo-Whig historians are willing to concede.

Scholarly works on the Revolution have proliferated over the past two decades. The two most influential books which stress the intellectual currents of the era are Bernard Bailyn's *The Ideological Origins of the American Revolution*

(Belknap Press, 1967) and *The Creation of the American Republic 1776–1787* (University of North Carolina Press, 1969), a massive but highly influential study by Bailyn's student Gordon S. Wood. The bicentennial celebration in 1976 enabled a number of historians and intellectuals to reconsider the period. Current political agendas often influenced a number of these reassessments. Conservative thinking is represented by *America's Continuing Revolution: An Act of Conservation* (American Enterprise Institute, 1975) and Robert H. Horwitz, ed., *The Moral Foundations of the American Republic*, 3d ed. (University Press of Virginia, 1986). The most important and recent collection of essays by historians, which also tends to the conservative, is Richard M. Fulton, ed., *The Revolution That Wasn't* (Kennikat, 1981). There have also been a number of neo-Progressive assessments of the Revolution. Edward Countryman, *The American Revolution* (Hill and Wang, 1985) is the best summary. It should be compared with Edmund S. Morgan's concise neo-Whig assessment, written over thirty years ago, of the *Birth of the Republic, 1763–1789* (University of Chicago Press, 1956). Neo-Progressive monographic studies by Countryman, Gary B. Nash, and Rhys Issac have been published. A summary of their views is conveniently collected in Alfred F. Young, ed., *The American Revolution: Exploration in the History of American Radicalism* (Northern Illinois University Press, 1976). Very few scholars have considered the impact of the American Revolution on other nations. The classic account is R. R. Palmer, *The Age of the Democratic Revolution: A Political History of Europe and America, 1760–1800, Volume I: The Challenge* (Princeton, 1959). Sung Bok Kim, "The American Revolution and the Modern World," in another bicentennial collection of *Legacies of the America Revolution* (Utah State University, 1978) leans more towards Degler than Morris in his discussion. But Morris's *The Emerging Nations and the American Revolution* (Harper & Row, 1970), from which the first essay in this issue was taken, remains the best discussion of this subject and deserves to be read in its entirety.

ISSUE 7

The Constitution: Was It an Economic Document?

YES: Michael Parenti, from *Democracy for the Few*, 5th ed. (St. Martin's Press, 1988)

NO: Henry Steele Commager, from "The Economic Interpretation of the Constitution Reconsidered," *The Search for a Usable Past* (Knopf, 1967)

ISSUE SUMMARY

YES: Political scientist Michael Parenti argues that the Constitution was framed by financially successful planters, merchants, and creditors in order to protect the rights of property ahead of the rights and liberties of persons.
NO: Well-known essayist and historian Henry Steele Commager maintains the Constitution was essentially a political document designed to solve the problem of the distribution of power between the national government *and* the state and local governments.

The United States possesses the oldest written Constitution of any major power. The 55 men who attended the Philadelphia Convention in 1787 could scarcely have dreamed that two hundred years later the nation would venerate them as the most "enlightened statesmen" of their time. James Madison, the principal architect of the document, may have argued that the Founding Fathers had created a system that might "decide forever the fate of Republican Government which we wish to last for ages." But Madison also told Jefferson in October 1787 that he did not think the document would be adopted, and if it was, it would not work.

While the enlightened statesman view of the Founding Fathers became the accepted interpretation among the general public, professional historians began to challenge this view. In 1913 Columbia University Professor Charles A. Beard wrote *An Economic Interpretation of the Constitution of the United States* (The Free Press, 1986). It caused instant controversy because it humanized the Founding Fathers and questioned their motivations. The Founding Fathers supported the creation of a stronger, central government, argued Beard, not for patriotic reasons, but because they wanted to protect their own economic interests. *An Economic Interpretation* argues its thesis in a dull pedestrian manner, but seventy-five years later it remains the most influential book ever written in American history.

Beard's research method was fairly simple. Drawing upon a batch of old, previously unexamined treasury records in the National Archives, Beard discovered that a number of delegates to the Philadelphia Convention and later state ratifying conventions held substantial amounts of continental securities, which would sharply increase in value if a strong national government were established. In addition to attributing economic motives to the Founding Fathers, Beard added a Marxist class conflict interpretation to his book. Those who supported the Constitution, he said, represented "personalty interests which had been adversely affected under the Articles of Confederation: money, public securities, manufactures, and trade and shipping." Those who opposed ratification of the Constitution were the small farmers and the debtors.

Beard's socioeconomic conflict interpretation of the supporters and opponents of the Constitution raised another issue. How was the Constitution ratified if a majority of Americans opposed it? Beard's answer was fairly direct. Most Americans couldn't vote because they didn't own property. Therefore, the entire process from the calling of the Philadelphia Convention to the state ratifying conventions was unrepresentative and undemocratic.

An Economic Interpretation was a product of its times. Economists, sociologists, and political scientists had been analyzing the conflicts which America had been experiencing as a result of the Industrial Revolution at the turn of the twentieth century. Beard joined a group of historians who were also interested in reforming the society in which they lived. These progressive historians also shared his discontent with the old-fashioned institutional approach. The role of the new historians was to rewrite history and discover the real reason why things happened. For the progressive historians, reality consisted of uncovering the social and economic causes of society.

During the 1920s, 1930s, and 1940s, there were two standard interpretations of the Founding Fathers. The enlightened statesman view was still held by the general public and could be found in the grammar school and high school textbooks. But college students were being given a second interpretation. Beard's thesis on the Constitution had become the new orthodoxy. Most college texts on American history and governing had incorporated Beard's conflict interpretation of the Constitution into their discussions of this period. A good example of Beard's influence lasting into the 1980s can be found in the first selection. Professor Michael Parenti argues that the Constitution is an elitist document framed by financially successful planters, merchants, and creditors, in order to protect the rights of property over the rights and liberties of persons.

In the second selection, Professor Henry Steele Commager emphasizes the political reasons why the Constitution was written. In a view somewhat reminiscent of the enlightened statesman argument, Commager takes Beard to task. He reminds us that the Constitution was essentially a political document designed to solve the problem of distributing power between the local and national governments.

YES

Michael Parenti

A CONSTITUTION FOR THE FEW

To help us understand the American political system, let us investigate its origins and its formal structure, the rules under which it operates, and the interests it represents, beginning with the Constitution and the men who wrote it. Why was a central government and a Constitution created? By whom? And for what purposes?

It is commonly taught that in the eighteenth and nineteenth centuries men of property preferred a laissez-faire government, one that kept its activities to a minimum. In actuality, while they wanted government to leave them free in all matters of trade and commerce, not for a moment did they desire a weak, inactive government. Rather, they strove to erect a civil authority that worked *for* rather than against the interests of wealth, and they frequently advocated an extension rather than a diminution of state power. They readily agreed with Adam Smith, who said that government was "instituted for the defense of the rich against the poor" and "grows up with the acquisition of valuable property."

CLASS POWER AND CONFLICT IN EARLY AMERICA

During the period between the Revolution and the Constitutional Convention, the "rich and the wellborn" played a dominant role in public affairs.

> Their power was born of place, position, and fortune. They were located at or near the seats of government and they were in direct contact with legislatures and government officers. They influenced and often dominated the local newspapers which voiced the ideas and interests of commerce and identified them with the good of the whole people, the state, and the nation. The published writings of the leaders of the period are almost without exception those of merchants, of their lawyers, or of politicians sympathetic with them.

The United States of 1787 has been described as an "egalitarian" society free from the extremes of want and wealth that characterized the Old World, but there were landed estates and colonial mansions that bespoke an impressive munificence. From the earliest English settlements, men of influence had received vast land grants from the crown. By 1700, three-fourths of the acreage in New York belonged to fewer than a dozen persons. In the interior of Virginia, seven persons owned a total of 1,732,000 acres. By 1760, fewer than 500 men in five colonial cities controlled most of the commerce, banking, mining, and manufacturing on the eastern seaboard and owned much of the land.

As of 1787, property qualifications left perhaps more than a third of the White male population disfranchised. Property qualifications for holding office were so steep as to prevent most voters from qualifying as candidates. Thus, a member of the New Jersey legislature had to be worth at least 1,000 pounds, while state senators in South Carolina were required to possess estates worth at least 7,000 pounds, clear of debt. In addition, the practice of oral voting, rather than use of a secret ballot, and an "absence of a real choice among candidates and programs" led to "widespread apathy." As a result, men of substance monopolized the important offices. Not long before the Constitutional Convention, the French *chargé d'affaires* wrote to his Foreign Minister:

> Although there are no nobles in America, there is a class of men denominated "gentlemen." . . . Almost all of them dread the efforts of the people to despoil them of their possessions, and, moreover, they are creditors, and therefore interested in strengthening the government, and watching over the execution of the law. . . . The majority of them being merchants, it is for their interest to establish the credit of the United States in Europe on a solid foundation by the exact payment of debts, and to grant to Congress powers extensive enough to compel the people to contribute for this purpose.

The Constitution was framed by financially successful planters, merchants, and creditors, many linked by kinship and marriage and by years of service in Congress, the military, or diplomatic service. They congregated in Philadelphia in 1787 for the professed purpose of revising the Articles of Confederation and strengthening the powers of the central government. They were aware of the weaknesses of the United States in its commercial and diplomatic dealings with other nations. There were also problems among the thirteen states involving trade, customs duties, and currency differences, but these have been exaggerated and in fact, some reforms were being instituted under the Articles.

Most toublesome to the framers of the Constitution was the increasingly insurgent spirit evidenced among the people. Fearing the popular takeover of state governments, the wealthy class looked to a national government as a means of protecting their interests. Even in states where they were inclined to avoid strong federation, the rich, once faced with the threat of popular rule "and realizing that a political alliance with conservatives from other states would be a safeguard if the radicals should capture the state government . . . gave up 'state rights' for 'nationalism' without hesitation."

The nationalist conviction that arose so swiftly among men of wealth during the 1780s was not the product of inspiration; it was not a "dream of nation-building" that suddenly possessed them. (If so, they kept it a secret in their public and private communications.) Rather, their newly acquired nationalism was a practical response to material conditions affecting them in a most immediate way. Their like-minded commitment to federalism was born of a common class interest that transcended state boundaries.

The populace of that day has been portrayed as irresponsible and parochial spendthrifts who never paid their debts and who believed in nothing more than timid state governments and inflated paper money. Most scholars say little about the actual plight of the common people, the great bulk of whom lived at a subsistence level. Most of the agrarian population consisted of poor freeholders, tenants, and indentured hands (the latter lived in conditions of servitude). Small farmers were burdened by heavy rents, ruinous taxes, and low incomes. To survive, they frequently had to borrow money at high interest rates. To meet their debts, they mortgaged their future crops and went still deeper into debt. Large numbers were caught in that cycle of rural indebtedness which is today still the common fate of agrarian peoples in many countries.

Throughout this period, newspapers complained of the "increasing numbers of young beggars in the streets." Economic prisoners crowded the jails. In 1786, one county jail in Massachusetts held eighty-eight persons of whom eighty-four were incarcerated for debts or nonpayment of taxes. Among the people there grew the feeling that the revolution against the English crown had been fought for naught. Angry armed crowds in several states began blocking foreclosures and forcibly freeing debtors from jail. Disorders of a violent but organized kind occurred in a number of states. In the winter of 1787, debtor farmers in western Massachusetts led by Daniel Shays took up arms. But their rebellion was forcibly put down by the state militia after several skirmishes that left eleven men dead and scores wounded.

CONTAINING THE SPREAD OF DEMOCRACY

The specter of Shays' Rebellion hovered over the delegates who gathered in Philadelphia three months later, confirming their worst fears. They were determined that persons of birth and fortune should control the affairs of the nation and check the "leveling impulses" of the propertyless multitude that composed "the majority faction." "To secure the public good and private rights against the danger of such a faction," wrote James Madison in *Federalist* No. 10, "and at the same time preserve the spirit and form of popular government is then the great object to which our inquiries are directed." Here Madison touched the heart of the matter: how to keep the *spirit* and *form* of popular government with only a minimum of the *substance*; how to construct a government that would win some popular support but would not tamper with the existing class structure, a government strong enough to service the growing needs of an entrepreneurial class while withstanding the democratic egalitarian demands of the popular class.

The framers of the Constitution could agree with Madison when he wrote in the same *Federalist* No. 10 that "the most common and durable source of faction has been the various and unequal distribution of property. Those who hold and those who are without property have ever formed distinct interests in society" and "the first object of government" is "the protection of different and unequal faculties of acquiring property." The framers were of the opinion that democracy was "the worst of all political evils," as Elbridge Gerry put it. Both he and Madison warned of "the danger of the leveling spirit." "The people," said Roger Sherman, "should have as little to do as may be about the Government." And according to Alexander Hamilton, "All communities divide themselves into the few and the many. The first are the rich and the well-born, the other the mass of the people. . . . The people are turbulent and changing; they seldom judge or determine right."

The delegates spent many weeks debating their interests, but these were the differences of merchants, slave owners, and manufacturers, a debate of haves versus haves in which each group sought safeguards within the new Constitution for its particular concerns. Added to this were disagreements about how best to achieve agreed-upon ends. Questions of structure and authority occupied a good deal of the delegates' time: How much representation should the large and small states have? How might the legislature be organized? How should the executive be selected? What length of tenure should exist for the different officeholders? Yet questions of enormous significance, relating to the new government's ability to protect the interests of property, were agreed upon with surprisingly little debate. On these issues, there were no dirt farmers or poor artisans attending the convention to proffer an opposing viewpoint. The debate between haves and have-nots never occurred. Thus Article I, Section 8 of the Constitution, which gives the federal government the power to support commerce and protect the interests of property, was adopted within a few days with little debate. It empowered Congress to:

1. Regulate commerce among the states and with foreign nations and Indian tribes
2. Lay and collect taxes and impose duties and tariffs on imports but not on commercial exports
3. Establish a national currency and regulate its value
4. "Borrow Money on the credit of the United States"—a measure of special interest to creditors
5. Fix the standard of weights and measures necessary for trade
6. Protect the value of securities and currency against counterfeiting
7. Establish "uniform Laws on the subject of Bankruptcies throughout the United States"
8. "Pay the Debts and provide for the common Defence and general Welfare of the United States"

Congress was limited to powers specifically delegated to it by the Constitution or implied as "necessary and proper" for the performance of the delegated powers. Over the years, under this "implied power" clause, federal intervention in the private economy grew to an extraordinary magnitude.

Some of the delegates were land speculators who expressed a concern about western holdings. Accordingly, Congress was given the "Power to dispose of and make all needful Rules and Regulations respecting the Territory or other Property belonging to the United States." Some delegates speculated in highly inflated and nearly worthless Confederation securities. Under Article VI, all debts incurred by the Confederation were valid against the new government, a provision that allowed speculators to make enormous profits when their securities, bought for a trifling, were honored at face value.

By assuming this debt, the federal government—under the policies of the first Secretary of the Treasury, Alexander Hamilton—"monetarized" the economy, using the public treasury to create a vast amount of credit for a propertied class that could then invest further in commerce and industry. The eventual payment of this assumed debt would come out of the pockets of the general public. In effect, the government helped greatly to finance the early process of capital accumulation. In assuming the debt, Hamilton was using the federal power to bolster not only the special interests of speculators and creditors but also the overall interest of an emerging capitalist class.

In the interest of merchants and creditors, the states were prohibited from issuing paper money or imposing duties on imports and exports or interfering with the payment of debts by passing any "Law impairing the Obligation of Contracts." The Constitution guaranteed "Full Faith and Credit" in each state "to the Acts, Records, and judicial Proceedings" of other states, thus allowing creditors to pursue their debtors across state lines.

Slavery—another form of property—was afforded special accommodation in the Constitution. Three-fifths of the slave population in each state were to be counted when calculating representation in the lower house. The importation of slaves was given constitutional protection for another twenty years. And slaves who escaped from one state to another had to be delivered up to the original owner upon claim, a provision that was unanimously adopted at the Convention.

The framers believed the states acted with insufficient force against popular uprisings, so Congress was given the task of "organizing, arming, and disciplining the Militia" and calling it forth, among other reasons, to "suppress Insurrections." The federal government was empowered to protect the states "against domestic Violence." Provision was made for "the Erection of Forts, Magazines, Arsenals, dock-Yards and other needful Buildings" and for the maintenance of an army and navy for both national defense and to establish an armed federal presence within the potentially insurrectionary states—a provision that was to prove a godsend to the industrial barons a century later when the army was used repeatedly to break strikes by miners and railroad and factory workers.

In keeping with their desire to contain the majority, the founders inserted "auxiliary precautions" *designed to fragment power without democratizing it*. By separating the executive, legislative, and judicial functions and then providing a system of checks and balances among the various branches, including staggered elections, executive veto, Senate confirmation of appointments and ratification of treaties, and a bicameral legislature, they hoped to dilute the impact of popular sentiments. They contrived an elaborate and difficult process for amending the Constitution, requiring proposal by two-thirds of both the Senate and the House, and ratification by three-fourths of the state legislatures. (Such strictures operate with anti-majoritarian effect to this day. Thus, although national polls show a substantial majority of Americans supports the Equal Rights Amendment, the proposal failed to make its way through the constitutional labyrinth.) To the extent that it existed at all, the majoritarian principle was tightly locked into a system of minority vetoes, making swift and sweeping popular action less likely.

The propertyless majority, as Madison pointed out in *Federalist* No. 10, must not be allowed to concert in common cause against the established social order. First, it was necessary to prevent a unity of public sentiment by enlarging the polity and then compartmentalizing it into geographically insulated political communities. The larger the nation, the greater the "variety of parties and interests" and the more difficult it would be for a majority to find itself and act in unison. As Madison argued, "A rage for paper money, for an abolition of debts, for an equal division of property, or for any other wicked project will be less apt to pervade the whole body of the Union than a particular member of it." An uprising of improvished farmers may threaten Massachusetts at one time and Rhode Island at another, but a national government will be large and varied enough to contain each of these and insulate the rest of the nation from the contamination of rebellion.

Second, not only must the majority be prevented from finding horizontal cohesion, but its vertical force—that is, its upward thrust upon government—should be blunted by interjecting indirect forms of representation. Thus, senators from each state were to be elected by their respective state legislatures. The chief executive was to be selected by an electoral college voted by the people but, as anticipated by the framers, composed of political leaders and men of substance who would gather in their various states and choose a president of their own liking. It was believed that they would usually be unable to muster a majority for any one candidate, and that the final selection would be left to the House,

with each state delegation therein having only one vote. The Supreme Court was to be elected by no one, its justices being appointed to life tenure by the president and confirmed by the Senate. In time, of course, the electoral college proved to be something of a rubber stamp, and the Seventeenth Amendment, adopted in 1913, provided for popular election of the Senate—demonstrating that the Constitution is modifiable in democratic directions, but only with great difficulty.

The only portion of government directly elected by the people was the House of Representatives. Many of the delegates would have preferred excluding the public entirely from direct representation: John Mercer observed that he found nothing in the proposed Constitution more objectionable than "the mode of election by the people. The people cannot know and judge of the characters of Candidates. The worst possible choice will be made." Others were concerned that demagogues would ride into office on a populist tide only to pillage the treasury and wreak havoc on all. "The time is not distant," warned Gouverneur Morris, "when this Country will abound with mechanics [artisans] and manufacturers [industrial workers] who will receive their bread from their employers. Will such men be the secure and faithful Guardians of liberty? . . . Children do not vote. Why? Because they want prudence, because they have no will of their own. The ignorant and dependent can be as little trusted with the public interest."

When the delegates finally agreed to having "the people" elect the lower house, they were referring to a select portion of the population. Property qualifications disfranchised the poorest White males in various states. Half the adult population was denied suffrage because they were women. American Indians had no access to the ballot. About one-fourth, both men and women, had no vote because they were held in bondage, and even of the Blacks who had gained their legal freedom, in both the North and the South, none was allowed to vote until the passage of the Fourteenth Amendment, after the Civil War.

PLOTTERS OR PATRIOTS?

The question of whether the framers of the Constitution were motivated by financial or national interest has been debated ever since Charles Beard published *An Economic Interpretation of the Constitution* in 1913. Beard believed that the "founding fathers" were guided by their class interests. Arguing against Beard are those who say that the framers were concerned with higher things than just lining their purses. True, they were moneyed men who profited directly from policies initiated under the new Constitution, but they were motivated by a concern for nation building that went beyond their particular class interests, the argument goes. To paraphrase Justice Holmes, these men invested their belief to make a nation; they did not make a nation because they had invested. "High-mindedness is not impossible to man," Holmes reminds us.

That is exactly the point: high-mindedness is a common attribute among people even when, or especially when, they are pursuing their personal and class interests. The fallacy is to presume that there is a dichotomy between the desire to build a strong nation and the desire to protect wealth and that the framers could not have been motivated by both. In fact, like most other people, they believed that what was good for themselves was ultimately good for the entire society. Their universal values and their class interests went hand in hand, and to discover the existence of the "higher" sentiment does not eliminate the self-interested one.

Most persons believe in their own virtue. The founders never doubted the nobility of their effort and its importance for the generations to come. Just as many of them could feel dedicated to the principle of "liberty for all" and at the same time own slaves, so could they serve both their nation and their estates. The point is not that they were devoid of the grander sentiments of nation building but that *there was nothing in their concept of nation that worked against their class interest and a great deal that worked for it.*

People tend to perceive issues in accordance with the position they occupy in the social structure; that position is largely—although not exclusively—determined by their class status. Even if we deny that the framers were motivated by the desire for personal gain that moves others, we cannot dismiss the existence of their class interest. They may not have been solely concerned with getting their own hands in the till, although enough of them did, but they were admittedly preoccupied with defending the wealthy few from the laboring many—for the ultimate benefit of all, as they understood it. "The Constitution," as Staughton Lynd noted, "was the settlement of a revolution. What was at stake for Hamilton, Livingston, and their opponents, was more than speculative windfalls in securities; it was the question, what kind of society would emerge from the revolution when the dust had settled, and on which class the political center of gravity would come to rest."

The small farmers and debtors, who opposed a central government that was even farther beyond their reach than the local and state governments, have been described as motivated by self-serving, parochial interests—unlike the supposedly higher-minded statesmen who journeyed to Philadelphia and others of their class who supported ratification. How and why the wealthy became visionary nation-builders is never explained. Not too long before, many of them had been proponents of laissez-faire and had opposed a strong central merchantile government. In truth, it was not their minds that were so much broader but their economic interests. Their motives were neither higher nor lower than those of any other social group struggling for place and power in the United States of 1787. They pursued their material interests as might any small freeholder. But possessing more time, money, information, and organization, they enjoyed superior results.

How could they have acted otherwise? For them to have ignored the conditions of governance necessary for the maintenance of the social order that meant everything to them would have amounted to committing class suicide—and they were not about to do that. They were a rising bourgeoisie rallying around a central power in order to develop the kind of national powers that would (a) better provide for the growing needs of a national commercial economy, (b) protect their overseas trading and diplomatic interests, and (c) defend their class interests from the competing claims of other classes within their own society. Some of us are quite willing to accept the existence of such a material-based nationalism in the history of other countries, but not in our own.

Finally, those who argue that the founders were motivated primarily by high-minded objectives consistently overlook the fact that the delegates repeatedly stated their intention to erect a government strong enough to protect the haves from the have-nots. They gave voice to the crassest class prejudices and never found it necessary to disguise the fact—as have latter-day apologists—that their concern was to diminish popular control and resist all tendencies toward class equalization (or "leveling," as it was called). Their opposition to democracy and their dedication to moneyed interests were unabashedly and openly avowed. Their preoccupation with their class interests was so pronounced that one delegate, James Wilson of Pennsylvania, did finally complain of hearing too much about how the sole or primary object of government was property. The cultivation and improvement of the human mind, he maintained, was the most noble object—a fine sentiment that evoked no opposition from his colleagues as they continued about their business.

If the founders sought to "check power with power," they seemed chiefly concerned with restraining mass power, while assuring the perpetuation of their own class power. They supposedly had a "realistic" opinion of the rapacious nature of human beings—readily evidenced when they talked about the common people—yet they held a remarkably sanguine view of the self-interested impulses of their own class, which they saw as inhabited largely by virtuous men of "principle and property." According to Madison, wealthy men (the "minority faction") would be unable to sacrifice "the rights of other citizens" or mask their "violence under the forms of the

Constitution." They would never jeopardize the institution of property and wealth and the untrammeled uses thereof, which in the eyes of the framers constituted the essence of "liberty."

AN ELITIST DOCUMENT

More important than to conjecture about the framers' motives is to look at the Constitution they fashioned, for it tells us a good deal about their objectives. The Constitution was consciously designed as a conservative document, elaborately equipped with a system of minority checks and vetoes, making it easier for entrenched interests to endure. It provided ample power to build the services and protections of state needed by a growing capitalist class but made difficult the transition of rule to a different class. The Constitution was a historically successful ruling-class undertaking whose effects are still very much with us. . . .

The Constitution championed the rights of property over the rights and liberties of persons. For the founders, liberty meant something different from and antithetical to democracy. It meant liberty to invest, speculate, trade, and accumulate wealth and to secure its possession without encroachment by sovereign or populace. The civil liberties designed to give all individuals the right to engage in public affairs won little support from the delegates. When Colonel Mason recommended that a committee be formed to draft "a Bill of Rights," a task he said could be accomplished "in a few hours," the other convention members offered little discussion on the motion and voted unanimously against it.

If the Constitution was so blatantly elitist, how did it manage to win ratifica-tion? Actually, it did not have a wide backing, initially being opposed in most of the states. But the same superiority of wealth, organization, and control of political office and the press that allowed the rich to monopolize the Philadelphia Convention enabled them to orchestrate a successful ratification campaign. The Federalists also used bribes, intimidation, and other discouragements against opponents of the Constitution. What's more, *the Constitution never was submitted to a popular vote*. Ratification was by state convention composed of delegates drawn mostly from the same affluent strata as the framers. Those who voted for these delegates were themselves usually subjected to property qualifications.

DEMOCRATIC CONCESSIONS

For all its undemocratic aspects, the Constitution was not without its historically progressive features. Consider the following:

1. The very existence of a written constitution with specifically limited powers represented an advance over more autocratic forms of government.

2. No property qualifications were required for any federal officeholder, unlike in England and most of the states. And salaries were provided for all officials, thus rejecting the common practice of treating public office as a voluntary service, which only the rich could afford.

3. The president and all other officeholders were elected for limited terms. No one could claim a life tenure on any office.

4. Article VI reads: "no religious Test shall ever be required as a Qualification to any Office or public Trust under the United States," a feature that represented a distinct advance over a number

of state constitutions that banned Catholics, Jews, and nonbelievers from holding office.

5. Bills of attainder, the practice of declaring by legislative fiat a specific person or group of people guilty of an offense, without benefit of a trial, were made unconstitutional. Also outlawed were ex post facto laws, the practice of declaring an act a crime and punishing those who had committed it *before* it had been unlawful.

6. As noted earlier, the framers showed no interest in a Bill of Rights, but supporters of the new Constitution soon recognized their tactical error and pledged the swift adoption of such a bill as a condition for ratification. So, in the first session of Congress, the first ten amendments were swiftly passed and then adopted by the states; these rights included freedom of speech and religion; freedom to assemble peaceably and to petition for redress of grievances; the right to keep arms; freedom from unreasonable searches and seizures, self-incrimination, double jeopardy, cruel and unusual punishment, and excessive bail and fines; the right to a fair and impartial trial; and other forms of due process.

7. The Constitution guarantees a republican form of government and explicitly repudiates monarchy and aristocracy; hence, Article I, Section 9 states: "No title of Nobility shall be granted by the United States. . . ." According to James McHenry, a delegate from Maryland, *at least twenty-one of the fifty-five delegates favored some form of monarchy.* Yet few dared venture in that direction out of fear of popular opposition. Furthermore, delegates like Madison believed that stability for their class order was best assured by a republican form of government. The time had come for the

bourgeoisie to rule directly without the baneful intrusions of kings and nobles.

Time and again during the Philadelphia Convention, this assemblage of men who feared and loathed democracy found it necessary to show some regard for popular sentiment (as with the direct election of the lower house). If the Constitution was going to be accepted by the states and if the new government was to have any stability, it had to gain some measure of popular acceptance; hence, the founders felt compelled to leave something for the people. While the delegates and their class dominated the events of 1787–1789, they were far from omnipotent. The class system they sought to preserve was itself the cause of marked restiveness among the people.

Land seizures by the poor, food riots, and other violent disturbances occurred throughout the eighteenth century in just about every state and erstwhile colony. This popular ferment spurred the framers in their effort to erect a strong central government *but it also set a limit on what they could do.* The delegates "gave" nothing to popular interests, rather—as with the Bill of Rights—they reluctantly made concessions under the threat of democratic rebellion. They kept what they could and grudgingly relinquished what they felt they had to, driven not by a love of democracy but by a fear of it, not by a love of the people but by a prudent desire to avoid popular uprisings. The Constitution, then, was a product not only of class privilege but of class struggle—a struggle that continued and intensified as the corporate economy and the government grew.

NO

Henry Steele Commager

THE ECONOMIC INTERPRETATION OF THE CONSTITUTION RECONSIDERED

By June 26, 1787, tempers in the Federal Convention were already growing short, for gentlemen had come to the explosive question of representation in the upper chamber. Two days later Franklin moved to invoke divine guidance, and his motion was shunted aside only because there was no money with which to pay a chaplain and the members were unprepared to appeal to Heaven without an intermediary. It was not surprising that when James Madison spoke of representation in the proposed legislature, he was conscious of the solemnity of the occasion. We are, he said, framing a system "which we wish to last for ages" and one that might "decide forever the fate of Republican Government."

It was an awful thought, and when, a few days later, Gouverneur Morris spoke to the same subject he felt the occasion a most solemn one; even the irrepressible Morris could be solemn. "He came here," he observed (so Madison noted),

> as a Representative of America; he flattered himself he came here in some degree as a Representative of the whole human race; for the whole human race will be affected by the proceedings of this Convention. He wished gentlemen to extend their views beyond the present moment of time; beyond the narrow limits . . . from which they derive their political origin. . . .
>
> Much has been said of the sentiments of the people. They were unknown. They could not be known. All that we can infer is that if the plan we recommend be reasonable & right; all who have reasonable minds and sound intentions will embrace it. . . .

These were by no means occasional sentiments only. They were sentiments that occurred again and again throughout the whole of that long hot summer, until they received their final, eloquent expression from the aged Franklin in that comment on the rising, not the setting, sun. Even during the most acrimonious debates members were aware that they were framing a constitution for ages to come, that they were creating a model for people everywhere on the globe; there was a lively sense of responsibility and even of destiny. Nor can we now, as we contemplate that Constitution which is the oldest written national constitution, and that federal system which is one of the oldest and the most successful in history, regard these appeals to posterity as merely rhetorical.

That men are not always conscious either of what they do or of the motives that animate them is a familiar rather than a cynical observation. Some 45 years ago Charles A. Beard propounded an economic interpretation of the Constitution—an interpretation which submitted that the Constitution was *essentially* (that is a crucial word) an economic document—and that it was carried through the Convention and the state ratifying conventions by interested economic groups for economic reasons. "The Constitution," Mr. Beard concluded, "was essentially an economic document based upon the concept that the fundamental private rights of property are anterior to government and morally beyond the reach of popular majorities."

At the time it was pronounced, that interpretation caused something of a sensation, and Mr. Beard was himself eventually to comment with justifiable indignation on the meanness and the vehemence of the attacks upon it—and him. Yet the remarkable thing about the economic interpretation is not the criticism it inspired but the support it commanded. For within a few years it had established itself as the new orthodoxy, and those who took exception to it were stamped either as professional patriots—perhaps secret Sons or Daughters of the Revolution—or naïve academicians who had never learned the facts of economic life.

The attraction that the economic interpretation had for the generation of the twenties and thirties—and that it still exerts—is one of the curiosities of our cultural history, but by no means an inexplicable one. To a generation of materialists Beard's thesis made clear that the stuff of history was material. To a generation disillusioned by the exploitations of big business it discovered that the past, too, had been ravaged by economic exploiters. To a generation that looked with skeptical eyes upon the claims of Wilsonian idealism and all but rejoiced in their frustration, it suggested that all earlier idealisms and patriotisms—even the idealism and patriotism of the framers—had been similarly flawed by selfishness and hypocrisy.

Yet may it not be said of *An Economic Interpretation of the Constitution* that it is not a conclusion but a point of departure? It explains a great deal about the forces that went into the making of the Constitution, and a great deal, too, about the men who assembled in Philadelphia in 1787, but it tells us extraordinarily little about the document itself. And it tells us even less about the historical meaning of that document.

What were the objects of the Federal Convention? The immediate objects were to restore order; to strengthen the public credit; to enable the United States to make satisfactory commercial treaties and agreements; to provide conditions in which trade and commerce could flourish; to facilitate management of the western lands and of Indian affairs. All familiar enough. But what, in the light of history, were the grand objects of the Convention? What was it that gave Madison and Morris and Wilson and King and Washington himself a sense of destiny?

There were two grand objects—objects inextricably interrelated. The first was to solve the problem of federalism, that is, the problem of the distribution of powers among governments. Upon the wisdom with which members of the Convention distinguished between powers of a general and powers of a local nature, and assigned these to their appropriate governments, would depend the success or failure of the new experiment.

But it was impossible for the children of the eighteenth century to talk or think of powers without thinking of power, and this was a healthy realism. No less troublesome—and more fundamental—than the problem of the distribution of powers, was the problem of sanctions. How were they to enforce the terms of the distribution and impose limits upon all the governments involved? It was one thing to work out the ideal distribution of general and local powers. It was another thing to see to it that the states abided by their obligations under the Articles of Union and that the national government respected the autonomy of states and liberty of individuals.

Those familiar with the Revolutionary era know that the second of these problems was more difficult than the first. Americans had learned how to limit government: the written constitutions, the bills of rights, the checks and balances. They had not yet learned (nor had anyone) how to "substitute the mild magistracy of the law for the cruel and violent magistracy of force." The phrase is Madison's.

Let us return to the *Economic Interpretation*. The correctness of Beard's analysis of the origins and backgrounds of the membership of the Convention, of the arguments in the Convention, and of the methods of assuring ratification, need not be debated. But these considerations are, in a sense, irrelevant and immaterial. For though they are designed to illuminate the document itself, in fact they illuminate only the processes of its manufacture.

The idea that property considerations were paramount in the minds of those assembled in Philadelphia is misleading and unsound and is borne out neither by the evidence of the debates in the Convention nor by the Constitution itself. The Constitution was not *essentially* an economic document. It was, and is, *essentially* a political document. It addresses itself to the great and fundamental question of the distribution of powers between governments. The Constitution was—and is—a document that attempts to provide sanctions behind that distribution; a document that sets up, through law, a standing rule to live by and provides legal machinery for the enforcement of that rule. These are political, not economic functions.

Not only were the principles that animated the framers political rather than economic; the solutions that they formulated to the great questions that confronted them were dictated by political, not by economic considerations.

Here are two fundamental challenges to the Beard interpretation: first, the Constitution is primarily a document in federalism; and second, the Constitution does not in fact confess or display the controlling influence of those who held that "the fundamental private rights of property are anterior to government and morally beyond the reach of popular majorities."

Let us look more closely at these two contentions. The first requires little elaboration or vindication, for it is clear to all students of the Revolutionary era that the one pervasive and over-branching problem of that generation was the problem of imperial organization. How to get the various parts of any empire to work together for common purposes? How to get central control—over war, for example, or commerce or money—without impairing local autonomy? How, on the other hand, preserve personal liberty and local self-government without impairing the effectiveness of the central government? This was one of the oldest problems in political science—as old as the history of the Greek city-states; as new as the recent debate over Federal aid to education or the Bricker amendment.

The British failed to solve the problem of imperial order; when pushed to the wall they had recourse to the hopelessly doctrinaire Declaratory Act, which was, in fact, a declaration of political bankruptcy; as Edmund Burke observed, no people is going to be argued into slavery. The Americans then took up the vexatious problem. The Articles of Confederation were satisfactory enough as far as the distribution of powers was concerned, but wholly wanting in sanctions. The absence of sanctions spelled the failure of the Articles—and this failure led to the Philadelphia Convention.

Now it will be readily conceded that many, if not most, of the questions connected with federalism were economic in character. Involved were such practical matters as taxation, the regulation of commerce, coinage, western lands, slavery, and so forth. The problem that presented itself to the framers was not whether government should exercise authority over such matters; it was *which* government should exercise such authority—and how should it be exercised?

There were, after all, no anarchists at the Federal Convention. Everyone agreed that *some* government had to have authority to tax, raise armies, regulate commerce, coin money, control contracts, enact bankruptcy legislation, regulate western territories, make treaties, and do all the things that government must do. But where should these authorities be lodged—with the state governments or with the national government they were about to erect, or with both?

This question was a political, not an economic, one. And the solution at which the framers arrived was based upon a sound understanding of politics, and need not be explained by reference to class attachments or security interests.

Certainly if the framers were concerned primarily or even largely with protecting property against popular majorities, they failed signally to carry out their purposes. It is at this point in our consideration of the *Economic Interpretation of the Constitution* that we need to employ what our literary friends call *explication du texte*. For the weakest link in the Beard interpretation is precisely the crucial one—the document itself. Mr. Beard makes amply clear that those who wrote the Constitution were members of the propertied classes,* and that many of

---

"A majority of the members were lawyers by profession.

"Most of the members came from towns, on or near the coast, that is, from the regions in which personalty was largely concentrated.

"Not one member represented in his immediate personal economic interests the small farming or mechanic classes.

"The overwhelming majority of members, at least five-sixths, were immediately, directly, and personally interested in the outcome of their labors at Philadelphia, and were to a greater or less extent economic beneficiaries from the adoption of the Constitution."

Beard, *An Economic Interpretation of the Constitution.*

them were personally involved in the outcome of what they were about to do; he makes out a persuasive case that the division over the Constitution was along economic lines. What he does not make clear is how or where the Constitution itself reflects all these economic influences.

Much is made of the contract clause and the paper money clause of the Constitution. No state may impair the obligations of a contract—whatever those words mean, and they apparently did not mean to the framers quite what Chief Justice Marshall later said they meant in *Fletcher v. Peck* or *Dartmouth College v. Woodward*. No state may emit bills of credit or make anything but gold and silver coin legal tender in payment of debts.

These are formidable prohibitions, and clearly reflect the impatience of men of property with the malpractices of the states during the Confederation. Yet quite aside from what the states may or may not have done, who can doubt that these limitations upon the states followed a sound principle—the principle that control of coinage and money belonged to the central, not the local governments, and the principle that local jurisdictions should not be able to modify or overthrow contracts recognized throughout the Union?

What is most interesting in this connection is what is so often overlooked: that the framers did not write any comparable prohibitions upon the United States government. The United States was not forbidden to impair the obligation of its contracts, not at least in the Constitution as it came from the hands of its property-conscious framers. Possibly the Fifth Amendment may have squinted towards such a prohibition; we

need not determine that now, for the Fifth Amendment was added by the *states* after the Constitution had been ratified. So, too, the emission of bills of credit and the making other than gold and silver legal tender were limitations on the states, but not on the national government. There was, in fact, a lively debate over the question of limiting the authority of the national government in the matter of bills of credit. When the question came up on August 16, Gouverneur Morris threatened that "The Monied interest will oppose the plan of Government, if paper emissions be not prohibited." In the end the Convention dropped out a specific authorization to emit bills of credit, but pointedly did not prohibit such action. Just where this left the situation troubled Chief Justice Chase's Court briefly three quarters of a century later; the Court recovered its balance, and the sovereign power of the government over money was not again *successfully* challenged.

Nor were there other specific limitations of an economic character upon the powers of the new government that was being erected on the ruins of the old. The framers properly gave the Congress power to regulate commerce with foreign nations and among the states. The term commerce—as Hamilton and Adair (and Crosskey, too!) have made clear—was broadly meant, and the grant of authority, too, was broad. The framers gave Congress the power to levy taxes and, again, wrote no limitations into the Constitution except as to the apportionment of direct taxes; it remained for the most conservative of Courts to reverse itself, and common sense, and discover that the framers had intended to forbid an income tax! Today, organizations that invoke the very term "constitutional" are agitating for an amendment placing a quantitative limit upon income taxes that may be levied; fortunately, Madison's generation understood better the true nature of governmental power.

The framers gave Congress—in ambiguous terms, to be sure—authority to make "all needful Rules and Regulations respecting the Territory or other Property" of the United States, and provided that "new states may be admitted." These evasive phrases gave little hint of the heated debates in the Convention over western lands. Those who delight to find narrow and undemocratic sentiments in the breasts of the framers never cease to quote a Gouverneur Morris or an Elbridge Gerry on the dangers of the West, and it is possible to compile a horrid catalogue of such statements. But what is significant is not what framers said, but what they did. They did not place any limits upon the disposition of western territory, or establish any barriers against the admission of western states.

The fact is that we look in vain *in the Constitution itself* for any really effective guarantee for property or any effective barriers against what Beard calls "the reach of popular majorities."

It will be argued, however, that what the framers feared was the *states*, and that the specific prohibitions against state action, together with the broad transfer of economic powers from state to nation, were deemed sufficient guarantee against state attacks upon property. As for the national government, care was taken to make that sufficiently aristocratic, sufficiently the representative of the propertied classes, and sufficiently checked and limited so that it would not threaten basic property interests.

It is at this juncture that the familiar principle of limitation on governmental authority commands our attention. Granted the wisest distribution of powers among governments, what guarantee was there that power would be properly exercised? What guarantees were there against the abuse of power? What assurance was there that the large states would not ride roughshod over the small, that majorities would not crush minorities or minorities abuse majorities? What protection was there against mobs, demagogues, dangerous combinations of interests or of states? What protection was there for the commercial interest, the planter interest, the slave interest, the securities interests, the land speculator interests?

It was Madison who most clearly saw the real character of this problem and who formulated its solution. It was not that the people as such were dangerous; "The truth was," he said on July 11, "that all men having power ought to be distrusted to a certain degree." Long before Lord Acton coined the aphorism, the Revolutionary leaders had discovered that power corrupts. They understood, too, the drive for power on the part of individuals and groups. All this is familiar to students of *The Federalist*, No. 10. It should be familiar to students of the debates in Philadelphia, for there, too, Madison sets forth his theory and supported it with a wealth of argument. Listen to him on one of the early days of the Convention, June 6, when he is discussing the way to avoid abuses of republican liberty—abuses which "prevailed in the largest as well as the smallest [states] . . ."

. . . And were we not thence admonished [he continued] to enlarge the sphere as far as the nature of the Government would admit. This was the only defence against the inconveniences of democracy *consistent with the democratic form of Government* [our italics]. All civilized Societies would be divided into different Sects, Factions & interests, as they happened to consist of rich & poor, debtors and creditors, the landed, the manufacturing, the commercial interests, the inhabitants of this district or that district, the followers of this political leader or that political leader, the disciples of this religious Sect or that religious Sect. In all cases where a majority are united by a common interest or passion, the rights of the minority are in danger. . . . In a Republican Govt. the Majority if united have always an opportunity [to oppress the minority. What is the remedy?] The only remedy is to enlarge the sphere, & thereby divide the community into so great a number of interests & parties, that in the first place a majority will not be likely at the same moment to have a common interest separate from that of the whole or of the minority; and in the second place, that in case they should have such an interest, they may not be apt to unite in the pursuit of it. It was incumbent on us then to try this remedy, and . . . to frame a republican system on such a scale & in such a form as will controul all the evils which have been experience.

This long quotation is wonderfully eloquent of the attitude of the most sagacious of the framers. Madison, Wilson, Mason, Franklin, as well as Gerry, Morris, Pinckney, and Hamilton feared power. They feared power whether exercised by a monarch, an aristocracy, an army, or a majority, and they were one in their determination to write into fundamental law limitations on the arbitrary exercise of that power. To assume, as Beard so commonly does, that

the fear of the misuse of power by majorities was either peculiar to the Federalists or more ardent with them than with their opponents, is mistaken. Indeed it was rather the anti-Federalists who were most deeply disturbed by the prospect of majority rule; they, rather than the Federalists, were the "men of little faith." Thus it was John Lansing, Jr., of New York (he who left the Convention rather than have any part in its dangerous work) who said that "all free constitutions are formed with two views—to deter the governed from crime, and the governors from tyranny." And the ardent Patrick Henry, who led the attack on the Constitution in the Virginia Convention—and almost defeated it—complained not of too little democracy in that document, but too much.

The framers, to be sure, feared the powers of the majority, as they feared all power unless controlled. But they were insistent that, in the last analysis, there must be government by majority; even conservatives like Morris and Hamilton made this clear. Listen to Hamilton, for example, at the very close of the Convention. Elbridge Gerry, an opponent of the Constitution, had asked for a reconsideration of the provision for calling a constitutional convention, alleging that this opened the gate to a majority that could "bind the union to innovations that may subvert the State-Constitutions altogether." To this Hamilton replied that

There was no greater evil in subjecting the people of the U.S. to the major voice than the people of a particular State. . . . It was equally desirable now that an easy mode should be established for supplying defects which will probably appear in the New System. . . . There could be no danger in giving this power, as the people would finally decide in the case.

. . . But we need not rely upon what men said; there is too much of making history by quotation anyway. Let us look rather at what men did. We can turn again to the Constitution itself. Granted the elaborate system of checks and balances: the separation of powers, the bicameral legislature, the executive veto, and so forth—checks found in the state constitutions as well, and in our own democratic era as in the earlier one— what provision did the framers make against majority tyranny? What provisions did they write into the Constitution against what Randolph called "democratic licentiousness"?

They granted equality of representation in the Senate. If this meant that conservative Delaware would have the same representation in the upper chamber as democratic Pennsylvania, it also meant that democratic Rhode Island would have the same representation as conservative South Carolina. But the decision for equality of representation was not dictated by considerations either economic or democratic, but rather by the recalcitrance of the small states. Indeed, though it is difficult to generalize here, on the whole it is true that it was the more ardent Federalists who favored proportional representation in both houses.

They elaborated a most complicated method of electing a Chief Executive, a method designed to prevent the easy expression of any majority will. Again the explanation is not simple. The fact was that the framers did not envision the possibility of direct votes for presidential candidates which would not conform to state lines and interests and thus lead to dissension and confusion. Some method, they thought, must be designated to overcome the force of state prejudices (or merely of parochialism) and get an election; the method they anticipated was a preliminary elimination contest by the electoral college and then eventual election by the House. This, said George Mason, was what would occur nineteen times out of twenty.* There is no evidence in the debates that the complicated method finally hit upon for electing a President was designed either to frustrate popular majorities or to protect special economic interests; its purpose was to overcome state pride and particularism.

Senators and Presidents, then, would not be the creatures of democracy. But what guarantee was there that senators would be representatives of property interests, or that the President himself would recognize the "priority of property"? Most states had property qualifications for office holding, but there are none in the Federal Constitution. As far as the Constitution is concerned, the President, congressmen, and Supreme Court justices can all be paupers.

Both General Charles Cotesworth Pinckney and his young cousin Charles, of South Carolina, were worried about this. The latter proposed a property qualification of $100,000 (a tidy sum in those days) for the Presidency, half that for the judges, and substantial sums for members of Congress. Franklin rebuked him. He was distressed, he said, to hear anything "that tended to debase the spirit of the common people." More surprising was the rebuke from that stout conserva-

*It has happened twice: Jefferson vs. Burr (1801) and J. Q Adams vs. Clay, Jackson, and Crawford (1825).

tive, John Dickinson. "He doubted," Madison reports, "the policy of interweaving into a Republican constitution a veneration for wealth. He had always understood that a veneration for poverty & virtue were the objects of republican encouragement." Pinckney's proposal was overwhelmingly rejected.

What of the members of the lower house? When Randolph opened "the main business" on May 29 he said the remedy for the crisis that men faced must be "the republican principle," and two days later members were discussing the fourth resolution, which provided for election to the lower house by the people. Roger Sherman of Connecticut thought that "the people should have as little to do as may be about the Government," and Gerry hastened to agree in words now well-worn from enthusiastic quotation that "The evils we experience flow from the excess of democracy." These voices were soon drowned out, however. Mason "argued strongly for an election . . . by the people. It was to be the grand depository of the democratic principle of the Govt." And the learned James Wilson, striking the note to which he was to recur again and again, made clear that he was for raising the federal pyramid to a considerable altitude, and for that reason wished to give it as broad a basis as possible." He thought both branches of the legislature—and the President as well, for that matter— should be elected by the people. "The Legislature," he later observed, "ought to be the most exact transcript of the whole Society."

A further observation is unhappily relevant today. It was a maxim with John Adams that "where annual elections end, there tyranny begins," and the whole Revolutionary generation was committed to a frequent return to the source of authority. But the framers put into the Constitution no limits on the number of terms which Presidents or congressmen could serve. It was not that the question was ignored; it received elaborate attention. It was rather that the generation that wrote the Constitution was better grounded in political principles than is our own; that it did not confuse, as we so often do, quantitative and qualitative limitations; and that—in a curious way—it had more confidence in the intelligence and the good will of the people than we seem to have today. It is, in any event, our own generation that has the dubious distinction of writing into the Constitution the first quantitative limitation on the right of the majority to choose their President. It is not the generation of the framers that was undemocratic; it is our generation that is undemocratic.

It is relevant to note, too, that the Constitution contains no property qualification for voting. Most states, to be sure, had such qualifications—in general a freehold or its equivalent—and the Constitution assimilated such qualifications as states might establish. Yet the framers, whether for reasons practical or philosophical we need not determine, made no serious efforts to write any property qualifications for voting into the Constitution itself.

The question of popular control came up clearly in one other connection as well: the matter of ratification. Should the Constitution be ratified by state legislatures, or by conventions? The practical arguments for the two methods were nicely balanced. The decisive argument was not, however, one of expediency but of principle. "To the people with whom all power remains that has not been given up in the Constitutions derived from them" we must resort, said Mason. Madison put the matter on principle, too. "He considered the difference between a system founded on the Legislatures only, and one founded on the people, to be the true difference between a *league* or *treaty* and a *Constitution.*" Ellsworth's motion to refer the Constitution to legislatures was defeated by a vote of eight to two, and the resolution to refer it to conventions passed with only Delaware in the negative.

Was the Constitution designed to place private property beyond the reach of majorities? If so, the framers did a very bad job. They failed to write into it the most elementary safeguards for property. They failed to write into it limitations on the tax power, or prohibitions against the abuse of the money power. They failed to provide for rule by those whom Adams was later to call the wise and the rich and the well-born. What they did succeed in doing was to create a system of checks and balances and adjustments and accommodations that would effectively prevent the suppression of most minorities by majorities. They took advantage of the complexity, the diversity, the pluralism, of American society and economy to encourage a balance of interests. They worked out sound and lasting political solutions to the problems of class, interest, section, race, religion, party.

Perhaps the most perspicacious comment on this whole question of the threat from turbulent popular majorities against property and order came, *mirabile dictu*, from the dashing young Charles Pinckney of South Carolina—he of the "lost" Pinckney Plan. On June 25 Pinckney made a major speech and thought it important enough to write out and give to Madison. The point of departure was the hackneyed one of the character of the second branch of the legislature, but the comments were an anticipation of De Tocqueville and Lord Bryce. We need not, Pinckney asserted, fear the rise of class conflicts in America, nor take precautions against them.

The genius of the people, their mediocrity of situation & the prospects which are afforded their industry in a Country which must be a new one for centuries are unfavorable to the rapid distinction of ranks. . . . If equality is . . . the leading feature of the U. States [he asked], where then are the riches & wealth whose representation & protection is the peculiar province of this permanent body [the Senate]. Are they in the hands of the few who may be called rich; in the possession of less than a hundred citizens? certainly not. They are in the great body of the people . . . [There was no likelihood that a privileged body would ever develop in the United States, he added, either from the landed interest, the moneyed interest, or the mercantile.] Besides, Sir, I apprehend that on this point the policy of the U. States has been much mistaken. We have unwisely considered ourselves as the inhabitants of an old instead of a new country. We have adopted the maxims of a State full of people . . . The people of this country are not only very different from the inhabitants of any State we are acquainted with in the modern world; but I assert that their situation is distinct from either the people of Greece or of Rome . . . Our true situation appears to me to be this—a new extensive Country containing within itself the materials for forming a Government capable of extending to its citizens all the blessings of civil & religious liberty—capable of making them happy at home. This is the great end of Republican Establishments. . . .

Not a government cunningly contrived to protect the interests of property, but one capable of extending to its citizens the blessings of liberty and happiness—was that not, after all, what the framers created?

POSTSCRIPT

The Constitution: Was It an Economic Document?

Michael Parenti is a radical political scientist. In *Democracy for the Few*, 5th ed., he extends the underlying assumptions of Beard's *An Economic Interpretation* throughout his own examination of the operations of our present-day American government. Like Beard, Parenti assumes that the Constitution was written to protect the economic interests of the upper classes. The checks and balances system, he argues, was designed to protect the property of the elite while pretending to give some political power to the masses.

Henry Steele Commager, on the other hand, concedes to Beard and Parenti that the members who wrote the Constitution came from the propertied classes and often were personally involved in the outcome. But Commager sees the major issues raised at Philadelphia as political. In his view the framers had to decide what power should be extended to the national government without usurping the rights of the states. Commager also demonstrates that many concessions in the Constitution were made to sentiments described by John Randolph as "democratic licentiousness." These included the elimination of property requirements for voting or holding office, equal representation for each state in the Senate regardless of size, and direct elections for members of the House of Representatives. If the Constitution was designed to place private property beyond the reach of the masses, says Commager, "the framers did a very bad job of it."

The most influential work on the Constitution in the last twenty years has been Gordon Wood's *The Creation of the American Republic 1776–1789* (North Carolina University Press, 1969). Attempts to move beyond Wood can be found in a symposium of a dozen historians on *The Creation of the American Republic, 1776–1789* in *The William and Mary Quarterly* (July 1987). A devastating critique of the methodological fallacies of Wood and other intellectual writers on this period can be found in Ralph Lerner's "The Constitution of the Thinking Revolutionary," in *Beyond Confederation: Origins of the Constitution and American National Identity*, Beeman et al., eds. (University of North Carolina Press, 1987).

The bicentennial celebration of the Constitution witnessed the publication of numerous works on this period. Edmund S. Morgan reviewed nineteen of them in *The New Republic* (June 29, 1987). Richard B. Morris, *The Forging of the Union, 1781–1789* (Harper & Row, 1987) summarizes a lifetime of scholarship by the most knowledgeable historian of this period. Michael Kammen, *A Machine That Would Go Of Itself: The Constitution in American Culture* (Knopf, 1986) elaborates on the place the Constitution has occupied "in the public consciousness and symbolic life of the American people."

ISSUE 8

Did President Jefferson Outfederalize the Federalists?

YES: Richard Hofstadter, from "Thomas Jefferson: The Aristocrat as Democrat," *The American Political Tradition and the Men Who Made It* (Random House, 1948)

NO: Forrest McDonald, from *The Presidency of Thomas Jefferson* (The University Press of Kansas, 1976)

ISSUE SUMMARY

YES: Pulitzer Prize-winning historian Richard Hofstadter argues that Thomas Jefferson was a moderate, practical politician who followed a course of action which eventually co-opted the major policies of the Federalists.
NO: Professor Forrest McDonald believes that President Jefferson attempted to replace Hamiltonian Federalist principles with a Republican ideology and wanted to restore America's agrarian heritage.

"Jefferson still lives," stated John Adams as he died on July 4, 1826, the fiftieth anniversary of Independence Day. Unknown to Adams, Jefferson had passed away a few hours earlier that same day. But Jefferson never really died. He was one of the few heroes of history to become a living legend.

There are two Jeffersons. The first was the true Renaissance man who knew a little about everything. "Not a sprig of grass shoots uninteresting to me," he once wrote to his daughter. As a philosopher who spoke to posterity, he waxed eloquent in his letters about civil liberties, the rights of man, states' rights, strict construction of the Constitution. and the virtues of the agrarian way of life. Our most intellectual president was also our most practical. He was an architect of the nation's capital, the University of Virginia, and his own home. Visitors to his Monticello plantation are amazed by the elaborate pulley and drainage systems that he devised. A respected member of the Virginia aristocracy who owned about 10,000 acres and from one hundred to two hundred slaves, Jefferson ran his farm in a self-sufficient manner and carefully studied the efficiency of employing slave labor. When he traveled, he recorded everything he observed in detailed journals. The newest inventions—steam engines, thermometers, elevators—fascinated him.

The second Jefferson was the man who has been ranked among the top half-dozen United States' presidents in every major poll taken by historians in the last thirty-five years. Does Jefferson deserve such an honor? It depends on how the functions of the presidency are perceived. One role that Jefferson disdained more than any other president in our history was the function of chief of state. So important to the modern presidency, the ceremonial role could have been played by the tall, dignified Virginia aristocrat as well as it was by George Washington, had he so desired. But Jefferson hated formalities. He walked to his inauguration and refused to wear a hat. Because he was a widower, he abandoned the practice of holding large, formal parties. He also felt they smacked too much of monarchy. He preferred small, intimate dinners with his intellectual friends and political cronies. A shy, soft-spoken individual with a slight speech impediment, the author of the Declaration of Independence did not campaign for office. He also refused to deliver an annual address to Congress, preferring to send them a written message. In short, if one uses modern terminology, Jefferson was not "mediagenic." In 1988, Jefferson might not have even been nominated by his party, much less elected to the office of the presidency.

In the first selection, Pulitzer Prize-winning historian Richard Hofstadter rejects the notion that Jefferson was an impractical visionary who thought that a rebellion every twenty years was an excellent idea. "Jefferson," said Hofstadter, "was a complex person who must be measured in whole, not in part, in action as well as thought." Using this criteria, Jefferson emerges as a cautious, practical politician with policies appealing to moderate Federalists and what today would be called Middle Americans. By 1820 Jefferson and his successors had totally eliminated the Federalist Party "but only at the cost of taking over its program."

Not all historians accept Hofstadter's non-ideological view of Jefferson. Forrest McDonald, for example, in the second essay sees Jefferson as a man staunchly opposed to Alexander Hamilton's Federalist programs and his philosophy of government. In his view, Jefferson wanted to take government away from the mercantile classes and return it to the farmers. According to McDonald, the Republican ideology consisted of the following program: "restore the separation of powers through the voluntary restraint of virtuous officials, cast out the monarchist and the money men, repeal the most oppressive of taxes, slash expenses, pay off the public debt, and thus restore America to the pristine simplicity of an Acadian past."

YES

Richard Hofstadter

THOMAS JEFFERSON:
THE ARISTOCRAT AS DEMOCRAT

Jefferson was a complex person who must be measured in whole, not in part, in action as well as thought. There were deep ambiguities in his thinking, which made any effort at consistency impossible. Although Federalist historians have cited these ambiguities as evidence of a moral taint, a constitutional shiftiness of mind, they may in fact be traced to a continuously ambivalent personal and political history. He valued much more highly the achievements of his father, whom he intensely admired, than the social status of his mother, whose influence he never acknowledged; but from the beginning he was aware of both the assurance of the aristocracy and the real merits and talents of men who came from unknown families. In his autobiography he remarked dryly of the Randolph genealogy: "They trace their pedigree far back in England and Scotland, to which let everyone ascribe the faith and merit he chooses." When he came to maturity, Jefferson was a slaveowner and yet a revolutionist, who could say that man's rights were "unalienable" at the very moment when he owned several dozen souls. All his life he circulated among men of wealth, learning, and distinction, and as befitted one who disliked acrimony he learned to accommodate himself to them—but he also absorbed the most liberal and questionable opinions of his age and associated on congenial terms with men like Thomas Paine and Joel Barlow. In American politics he became a leader of yeomen farmers—but also of great planters. He was the head of a popular faction that stood against the commercial interests—but it was also a propertied faction with acquisitive aspirations of his own. Well read in the best philosophical literature of his century, he accepted broad cosmopolitan ideas, but he was also an ardent American patriot. He was a pacifist in personal temperament and philosophy, a nationalist by training, and yet a Virginian with strong parochial loyalties. He wanted with all his heart to hold to the values of agrarian society, and yet he believed in progress. Add to all this the fact that he lived an unusually long life, saw many changes, and tried to adapt his views to changing circumstances.

Jefferson had warm impulses. His cosmopolitan mind refracted the most advanced and liberating ideas of his time. He believed in those ideas, and rephrased and reiterated them in language that has become classic; he was not in the habit of breaking lances trying to fulfill them. The generous and emancipating thoughts for which his name is so justly praised are to be found almost entirely in his *private* correspondence; after he wrote the Declaration of Independence and the Virginia Statute for Religious Freedom he avoided expressing his more unacceptable ideas in public. He understood that in the workday world of public activity his most lofty ideals were chiefly valuable to indicate the direction in which society should be guided. He never really expected them to be realized in his time and preferred to place his hopes in progress, in the promise that mankind would consummate his ideals in some magnificent future. ("Your taste is judicious," John Adams once taunted him, "in liking better the dreams of the future than the history of the past.")

Jefferson's practical activity was usually aimed at some kind of minimum program that could be achieved without keen conflict or great expenditure of energy. He hated vigorous controversy, shrank from asserting his principles when they would excite the anger of colleagues or neighbors. He tried to avoid a wide circulation of his *Notes on Virginia* because he did not want Virginians to read his bitter remarks on slavery and a few tart observations on the province's Constitution. Jefferson did not lack courage—his futile embargo policy, carried out under bitter protest from every part of the country, proves that—but rather that hardihood of spirit which

makes a political fight bearable. Although he had strong political prejudices and sometimes violent animosities, he did not enjoy power and could not bear publicity. He was acutely sensitive to criticism, admitting to Francis Hopkinson in 1789: "I find the pain of a little censure, even when it is unfounded, is more acute than the pleasure of much praise." Abnormally shy and troubled by a slight speech defect, he found it impossible to read his messages in person to Congress as Washington and Adams had done. He had not the temperament of an agitator, hardly even of a leader in the qualities that leadership requires under modern democracy. Not once did he deliver an exciting speech. His private life was one of enormous variety and interest, and there were many times when he would have been happy to desert public service to enjoy is farm, his family, and his books.

Jefferson's Federalist opponents feared, above all, power lodged in the majority. Jefferson feared power lodged anywhere else. In his First Inaugural Address he asked concerning the common observation "that man cannot be trusted with the government of himself": "Can he, then, be trusted with the government of others?" He would have agreed with Madison that power is "of an encroaching nature," and he was sure that power corrupts those who possess it. "If once the people become inattentive to the public affairs," he wrote Edward Carrington from Paris, "you and I and Congress and Assemblies, Judges and Governors, shall all become wolves. It seems to be the law of our general nature, in spite of individual exceptions."

Admitting that a majority will often decide public questions wrongly, Jefferson argued that "the duperies of the people are less injurious" than the self-interested policies of kings, priests, and aristocrats. He refused to be alarmed by popular uprisings like the Shays Rebellion. In the safety of his private correspondence he felt free to say that "honest republican governments" should be "so mild in their punishment of rebellions as not to discourage them too much." "A little rebellion now and then is a good thing, and as necessary in the political world as storms in the physical." The people are not always well informed, but it is better that they have misconceptions that make them restless than that they be lethargic—for lethargy in the people means death for republics.

Again and again Jefferson urged that the people be educated and informed through a broad common-school system and a free press. Although he had small faith in the power of republics to resist corruption and decay, he hoped that mass education would stem this degenerative process. Education not only would give stability and wisdom to the politics of a commonwealth, but would widen opportunities, bring out the natural talents that could be found in abundance among the common people. Throughout Jefferson's life there runs this humane concern for "the pursuit of happiness," for the development of the individual without regard to limitations of class.

By and large, however, when Jefferson spoke warmly of the merits and abilities of "the people" he meant "the farmers." He did not see a town until he was almost eighteen, and he believed deeply that rural living and rural people are the wellspring of civic virtue and individual vitality, that farmers are the best social base of a democratic republic. "Those who labor in the earth are the chosen people of God, if ever he had a chosen people," he proclaimed in his *Notes on Virginia*. "Corruption of morals in the mass of cultivators is a phenomenon of which no age nor nation has furnished an example."

> . . . generally speaking, the proportion which the aggregate of the other classes of citizens bears in any State to that of its husbandmen, is the proportion of its unsound to its healthy parts, and is a good enough barometer whereby to measure its degree of corruption. While we have lands to labor then, let us never wish to see our citizens occupied at a work bench or twirling a distaff. . . . Let our workshops remain in Europe

The American economy, then, should be preserved in its agricultural state. Manufacturers, cities, urban classes, should be held at a minimum. So Jefferson believed, at any rate, until the responsibilities of the White House and the conduct of foreign policy caused him to modify his views. He once went so far as to say that he hoped the United States would remain, with respect to Europe, on the same economic footing as China. Commerce he would encourage—it supplied the needs of agriculture—but this was the extent of his early concessions to the urban classes.

Thus far Jefferson, with his faith in the farmers, his distrust of the urban classes, and his belief in the long-range value of rebellions and social disturbances, seems at the opposite pole from the Constitution-makers—and so he might have been if his political theory had been elaborated into a coherent system. But he had more in common with the conservative thinkers of his age than is usually recognized. His differences with the political theory of the Constitution-makers were differences of emphasis, not of structure. He shared their primary fears. He did not think that political constitutions could safely rely on man's virtue. In a letter to Mann Page in 1795 he declared that he could not accept the idea of the Rochefoucaulds and Montaignes that "fourteen out of fifteen men are rogues." *"But I have always found that rogues would be uppermost*, and I do not know that the proportion is too strong for the higher orders and for those who, rising above the swinish multitude, always contrive to nestle themselves into the places of power and profit."* . . .

Jefferson, of course, accepted the principle of balanced government and the idea that the people must be checked. "It is not by the consolidation, or concentration of powers, but by their distribution that good government is effected," he wrote in his autobiography. He designed a constitution for Virginia in 1776 which employed the principle of checks and balances and required property qualifications of voters. Of the two houses of the legislature, only the lower was to be elected by the people; the senate was to be chosen by the house, as was the governor, so that two of the three parts of the lawmaking body were at once removed from the citizens. Five years later, criticizing the Constitution that had been adopted by Virginia instead of his own, he complained primarily of its lack of checks: the Senate and the House of Delegates were too much alike because both were chosen by the voters in the same way. *"The purpose of establishing different houses of legislation is to introduce the influence of different interests or different principles."* he continued:

All the powers of government, legislative, executive, and judiciary, result to the legislative body. The concentrating

these in the same hands is precisely the definition of despotic government. It will be no alleviation that these powers will be exercised by a plurality of hands and not by a single one. One hundred and seventy-three despots would surely be as oppressive as one. . . . As little will it avail us that they are chosen by ourselves. An *elective despotism* was not the government we fought for, but one which should not only be founded on free principles, but in which the powers of government should be so divided and balanced among several bodies of magistracy, as that no one could transcend their legal limits without being effectually checked and restrained by the others.

This would have been accounted sound doctrine at the Philadelphia Convention of 1787. A government that does not divide and balance powers in a system of checks is precisely what Jefferson means by despotic; the fact that the governing body is chosen by the people does not qualify his complaint; such a government, without checks, is merely "an elective despotism." Jefferson, then, refused to accept simple majority rule, adopting instead the idea that "different interests or different principles" should be represented in government.

All this sounds close to the theories of Madison and Adams. In fact, Jefferson did not differ with them strongly enough to challenge their conservative writings of the constitutional period. In 1788 he wrote to Madison praising the *Federalist* as "the best commentary on the principles of government which ever was written." Two years later, advising his nephew Thomas Mann Randolph on a course of reading, Jefferson praised Locke's work as being "perfect as far as it goes," and then added: "Descending from theory to practice, there is no better book than the Federalist." In 1787 he told John Adams that he had read his *Defence* "with infinite satisfaction and improvement. It will do great good in America. Its learning and its good sense will, I hope, make it an institute for our politicians, old as well as young."

When the text of the federal Constitution of 1787 reached him in France, Jefferson confessed to Adams that he was staggered at what had been attempted, but soon recovered his composure. He informed Madison that he saw many good features in it, but objected strongly to two things: the absence of a bill of rights (later included in the first ten amendments), and the eligibility of the president for more than one term. In the end he gave it a substantial endorsement: "It is a good canvas, on which some strokes only want retouching." His regard for it grew with the years.

As much as Madison or Morris, Jefferson disliked the idea of city mobs—"the panders of vice and the instruments by which the liberties of a country are generally overturned"—but he believed that they would not emerge in the calculable future because America's lands would be open to make substantial farmers of the ragged and discontented. In his First Inaugural he said that the land would last the American people "to the hundredth and thousandth generation"! The United States would be a nation of farmers, tilling their own soil, independent, informed, unexcitable, and incorruptible. Such a national destiny, he must have felt, would be secured by the Louisiana Purchase.

The future, then, would be founded on a propertied class in a propertied nation. Jefferson leaned strongly to the idea that a propertied interest in society is necessary to a stable political mentality. In 1800

he wrote a friend that he had always favored universal manhood suffrage; but this was one of those theoretical notions to which he was not firmly wedded. "Still I find some very honest men," he added, "who, thinking the possession of some property necessary to give due independence of mind, are for restraining the elective franchise to property." His 1776 draft of a constitution for Virginia had required that voters own either a freehold estate of twenty-five acres in the country or one fourth of an acre in town, or pay taxes within two years of the time of voting. Never did Jefferson try to introduce universal manhood suffrage anywhere.

The outstanding characteristic of Jefferson's democracy is its close organic relation to the agrarian order of his time. It seems hardly enough to say that he thought that a nation of farmers, educated, informed, and blessed with free institutions, was the best suited to a democratic republic, without adding that he did not think any *other* kind of society a good risk to maintain republican government. In a nation of large cities, well-developed manufactures and commerce, and a numerous working class, popular republicanism would be an impossibility—or at best an improbability.

Certainly the balance of Jefferson's good society is a tenuous thing: the working class is corrupt; merchants are corrupt; speculators are corrupt; cities are "pestilential"; only farmers are dependably good. Sunder human nature from its proper or "natural" nourishment in the cultivation of the soil and the ownership of real property, and he profoundly distrusts it. Sunder democracy from the farm and how much more firmly does he believe in it than John Adams? Yet this is just what the relentless advance of modern industrial cap-italism has done: it has sundered four fifths of society from the soil, has sepa-rated the masses from their property, and has built life increasingly on what Jefferson would have called an artificial basis—in short, has gradually emptied the practical content out of Jefferson's agrarian version of democracy. This pro-cess had its earliest beginnings during Jefferson's lifetime, and, as we shall see, he yielded a good part of his agrarian prejudices (like the pragmatic, un-doctrinaire soul that he was) without sacrificing his democratic preferences. But although he clung to his humane vision of democracy, he left it without the new economic rationale that it required.

In after years Jefferson declared that the struggle between his party and the Federalists was one between those who cherished the people and those who dis-trusted them. But he had been associated with a number of men like Elbridge Gerry, Pierce Butler, Charles Pinckney, and Edmund Randolph who did not cherish the people in the least, and the differences in abstract principle were hardly intense enough to account for the fierceness of the conflict or for the pecu-liar lines along which it was drawn. Al-though democratically minded Americans did stand with Jefferson, the line of divi-sion was essentially between two kinds of property, not two kinds of philosophy.

The Federalists during Hamilton's ser-vice as Secretary of the Treasury had given the government a foundation of unashamed devotion to the mercantile and investing classes. Through his method of funding the national debt, through his national bank, and through all the subsidiary policies of the govern-ment, Hamilton subsidized those who invested in manufactures, commerce, and public securities, throwing as much of the tax burden as possible on planters and farmers. The landed interests, how-ever, were in a majority, and it was only a matter of time before they could marshal themselves in a strong party of their own. Jefferson's party was formed to de-fend specific propertied interests rather than the abstract premises of democracy, and its policies were conceived and exe-cuted in the sober, moderate spirit that Jefferson's generation expected of prop-ertied citizens when they entered the political arena.

When Jefferson was elected in 1800, the more naïve Federalists, frightened to the marrow by their own propaganda, imagined that the end of the world had come. Fisher Ames anticipated that he would soon scent "the loathsome steam of human victims offered in sacrifice." Among those who knew the President-elect, however, there was no such hyste-ria—especially not among insiders who had private knowledge of the circum-stances under which he had been cho-sen.

The election of 1800 was unique in American history. Because no distinction had yet been made in the Constitution between ballots cast for presidential and vice-presidential candidates, Jefferson and his running mate, Aaron Burr, won the same number of votes in the electoral college. The tied contest was thrown into the House of Representatives, where it fell to Federalist Congressmen to choose between two Republicans. To some this seemed merely a choice of executioners; others, looking upon Jefferson as their supreme enemy, gravitated naturally to-ward Burr. Not so Alexander Hamilton, who had long been Burr's political rival in New York. In a remarkable letter to a Federalist Representative, Hamilton gave a shrewd estimate of Jefferson's character. He admitted that his old foe's views were "tinctured with fanaticism; that he is too much in earnest with his democracy." But it is not true, he continued, in an appraisal that is as penetrating in substance as it is unfair in phrasing,

> that Jefferson is zealot enough to do anything in pursuance of his principles which will contravene his popularity or his interest. He is as likely as any man I know to temporize—to calculate what will be likely to promote his own reputation and advantage; and the probable result of such a temper is the preservation of systems, though originally opposed, which, being once established, could not be overturned without danger to the person who did it. To my mind a true estimate of Mr. Jefferson's character warrants the expectation of a temporizing rather than a violent system. . . . Add to this that there is no fair reason to suppose him capable of being corrupted, which is a security that he will not go beyond certain limits

Not entirely satisfied with Hamilton's advice, Federalist leaders sought for assurance from Jefferson. The Virginian refused to commit himself in response to direct approach, but a friend who sounded him out informally was able to convey to the Federalists the comforting knowledge that Jefferson's intentions were moderate. That Jefferson abandoned any of his original plans, and in that sense bargained away any principles to win the office, is extremely unlikely; but when he entered the White House it was after satisfying the Federalists that he and they had come to some kind of understanding.

A little thought on the difficult position in which Jefferson now found himself should convince anyone that for a man of his moderate temperament there was small choice in fundamental policy. The Hamiltonian system, now in operation for twelve years, had become part of the American economy. The nation was faring well. To unscramble Hamilton's system of funding, banks, and revenues would precipitate a bitter struggle, widen the breach between the classes, and drive moderates out of the Republican ranks; it might bring depression, perhaps even rend the Union. And when the strife was over, there would always be the need of coming to terms with the classes that carried on commerce and banking and manufactures. Further, even if the landed interests were charged with the burden of Hamilton's debts, there was always the probability that they were better off when the system was working smoothing than they would be after a ruinously successful assault upon it. Jefferson, in short, found himself in a position much like that of modern social-democratic statesmen who, upon attaining power, find themselves the managers of a going concern that they fear to disrupt. Just as they have been incapable of liquidating capitalism, so Jefferson found himself unable to keep it from growing and extending its sway over the agrarian masses. Instead he wisely confined himself to trimming carefully at the edges of the Hamiltonian system.

Jefferson's First Inaugural Address was a conciliatory document contrived to bind up the wounds of the bitter period from 1798 to 1800 and to attract moderate Federalists to his support. "We are all republicans—we are all federalists," he declared. Soon the President was writing to Dupont de Nemours in words that show how well Hamilton had taken his measure:

When this government was first established, it was possible to have kept it going on true principles, but the contracted, English, half-lettered ideas of Hamilton destroyed that hope in the bud. We can pay off his debts in 15 years: but we can never get rid of his financial system. It mortifies me to be strengthening principles which I deem radically vicious, but this vice is entailed on us by the first error. In other parts of our government I hope we shall be able by degrees to introduce sound principles and make them habitual. What is practicable must often control what is pure theory

Jefferson kept his promises to friends and enemies alike. So successfully did he whittle away at the Federalist machinery by reducing expenditures that he was able to abolish the hated excise duties that stirred up the Whisky Rebellion and still make great inroads on the public debt. He tried hard to tame the federal judiciary—the last arm of the national government still under Federalist control—but to little effect. Through the Louisiana Purchase he widened the area for agrarian expansion. In 1811, two years after his terms were over, his party also allowed the First Bank of the United States to die upon the expiration of its charter.

But no attack was made upon other vital parts of the Hamiltonian system. No attempt was made to curb such abuses as speculation in public lands; nor did the well-organized Republican machines try hard to democratize the mechanics of government in the states or the nation. Limitations on the suffrage, for example, were left untouched. Professor Beard observes that the Republican states were "no more enamored of an equalitarian political democracy" than the Federalist states. Had Jefferson suggested a broad

revision of the suffrage, many of his state leaders who had no use for theoretical democracy would have looked at him askance; if he had been the crusading democrat of Jeffersonian legend he could not have been so successful a machine leader.

Since his policies did not deviate too widely from those of the Federalists, Jefferson hoped to win over the moderates from their ranks and planned to use the patronage in doing so. "If we can hit on the true line of conduct which may conciliate the honest part of those who were called federalists," he wrote to Horatio Gates soon after taking office, "and do justice to those who have so long been excluded from [the patronage], I shall hope to be able to obliterate, or rather to unite the names of federalists and republicans."

In politics, then, the strategy was conciliation; in economics it was compromise. Soon the Republican machines began flirting with the financial interests they had sworn to oppose. Republican state legislatures issued charters liberally to local banks, which, in turn, tended to cleave to the Republican Party in politics. Jefferson gave his benediction to this process of mutual accommodation. When the Bank of Baltimore applied to the administration for assistance, he wrote to Secretary of the Treasury Albert Gallatin:

> It is certainly for the public good to keep all the banks competitors for our favors by a judicious distribution of them and thus to engage the individuals who belong to them in support of the reformed order of things or at least in an acquiescence under it.

And:

> . . . I am decidedly in favor of making all the banks Republican by sharing deposits among them in proportion to

the disposition they show. . . . It is material to the safety of Republicanism to detach the mercantile interest from its enemies and incorporate them into the body of its friends. A merchant is naturally a Republican, and can be otherwise only from a vitiated state of things.

John Adams, in the quiet of his retirement at Quincy, might have been amused to see a new elite, closely linked to the fiscal interests, emerging in the heart of the Republican Party, but the militant agrarian John Taylor was deeply discouraged. In 1811 he wrote:

> . . . those who clearly discerned the injustice and impolicy of enriching and strengthening the federalists by bank or debt stock, at the publick expense, will seldom refuse to receive a similar sinecure. In short, a power in the individuals who compose legislatures, to fish up wealth from the people, by nets of their own weaving . . . will corrupt legislative, executive and judicial publick servants, by whatever systems constituted.

The inability of the Republicans to follow a pure policy of democratic agrarianism was matched by their inability to fashion a positive theory of agrarian economics. The predominant strain in their economic thinking was laissez-faire, their primary goal essentially negative—to destroy the link between the federal government and the investing classes. Acute and observant, their economic writing was at its best in criticism, but it offered no guide to a specific agrarian program. They had no plan; indeed, they made a principle of planlessness.

Jefferson has been described as a physiocrat by many writers—among them V. L. Parrington—but there is little more substance to this notion than there is to the preposterous idea that he was influ-

enced chiefly by French thought. He was naturally content to remain an eclectic in economics. "No one axiom," he wrote to J. B. Say in 1815, "can be laid down as wise and expedient for all times and circumstances." Their defense of free trade was responsible for whatever appeal the physiocrats had for Jefferson; but after he read *The Wealth of Nations* he became a convert to the doctrines of Adam Smith.

Like other theorists of the "natural law" era, Jefferson was quite ready to believe that the "natural" operations of the system of self-seeking private enterprise were intrinsically beneficent and should not normally be disturbed by government. In his First Inaugural he called for "a wise and frugal government, which shall restrain men from injuring one another, *which shall leave them otherwise free to regulate their own pursuits of industry and improvement,* and shall not take from the mouth of labor the bread it has earned." In a letter to Joseph Milligan, April 6, 1816, in which he discussed the proper limits of taxation, he concluded that the state ought not be aggressive in redistributing property:

> To take from one, because it is thought his own industry and that of his fathers has acquired too much, in order to spare to others, who, or whose fathers have not exercised equal industry and skill, is to violate arbitrarily the first principle of association, "the *guarantee* to everyone a free exercise of his industry and the fruits acquired by it."

John Taylor, perhaps the cleverest of the agrarian writers, likewise believed that "it is both wise and just to leave the distribution of property to industry and talents."

This conception of state policy was not anti-capitalist but anti-mercantilist. Jefferson and his followers had seen the unhappy effects of British governmental interference in American economic affairs, and they regarded Hamilton's system of state economic activity ("the contracted, English, half-lettered ideas of Hamilton") as merely a continuation at home of English economic ideas. Hamilton had set the government to helping the capitalists at the expense of the agrarians. The Jeffersonian response was not to call for a government that would help the agrarians at the expense of the capitalists, but simply for one that would let things alone. Where modern liberals have looked to government interference as a means of helping the poor, Jefferson, in common with other eighteenth-century liberals, thought of it chiefly as an unfair means of helping the rich through interest-bearing debts, taxation, tariffs, banks, privileges, and bounties. He concluded that the only necessary remedy under republican government would be to deprive the rich of these devices and restore freedom and equality through "natural" economic forces. Because he did not usually think of economic relationships as having an inherent taint of exploitation in them, he saw no necessity to call upon the state to counteract them. It was not the task of government to alter the economic order: the rich were not entitled to it and the poor would not find it necessary.

Jefferson rejected from his political philosophy the idea that one man has any intrinsic superiority over another; but he implicitly and perhaps unwittingly took it back again when he accepted competitive laissez-faire economics with its assumption that, so long as men were equal in law, and government played no favorites, wealth would be distributed in accordance with "industry and skill."

Such a philosophy seemed natural enough to American farmers and planters who were in their own rights entrepreneurs, businessmen, exporters, and often, in a small way, speculators with a weather eye on land values—men accustomed to stand on their own feet.

In due time, of course, Jeffersonian laissez-faire became the political economy of the most conservative thinkers in the country. Fifty years after Jefferson's death men like William Graham Sumner were writing sentences exactly like Jefferson's and John Taylor's to defend enterprising industrial capitalists and railroad barons from government regulation and reform. And one hundred years after the Jeffersonians first challenged John Adams at the polls, William Jennings Bryan, leading the last stand of agrarianism as an independent political power, was still striving to give his cause the color of respectability by showing that, after all, the farmer too was a businessman!

The practical conduct of foreign relations forced the Jeffersonians into a position no less frustrating than the maintenance of Hamilton's domestic system. In the East they found themselves almost as dependent on foreign commerce as were the sea traders of New England; their cheapest manufactured goods were bought abroad, and abroad their surplus was sold. In the West, where they looked about hungrily for new lands, fear of the Indians and of the closure of their trade outlet at New Orleans intensified their expansionist appetites. Expansion of their export market on the land and defense of it on the sea finally started them on a headlong retreat from Jeffersonian principles.

Jefferson himself was both a fierce patriot and a sincere pacifist. During the Napoleonic Wars, when England and

France began to prey upon American commerce, he tried to retaliate by a pacifistic policy of economic coercion. In December 1807 Congress passed his drastic Embargo Act, which simply confined American ships to port. His aim was to bring both sides to terms by withholding food and other supplies. This was the one doctrinaire and impractical measure of his career, and it proved a miserable failure. The Embargo not only failed to force Britain and France to respect American rights on the high seas, but also brought economic paralysis to the trading cities of the Northeast and the farms and plantations of the West and South. Jefferson finally admitted that the fifteen months of its operation cost more than a war. At the close of his second term the Embargo was replaced by a Nonintercourse Act, which opened trade with the rest of Europe but continued the costly ban on England and France.

Although Jefferson's successor, James Madison, continued to be harried by the maritime controversy, it was expansionism—what John Randolph called "agrarian cupidity"—rather than free trade that in the end brought the War of 1812. Southern planters wanted the Floridas and Northern farmers wanted Canada. Jefferson, always an ardent expansionist, approved of both aims and accepted the popular clichés with which expansion was justified. ("The possession of Canada," he wrote Adams in the summer of 1812, "secures our women and children forever from the tomahawk and scalping knife, by removing those who excite them.") As Julius W. Pratt has shown, enthusiasm for war with England raged along the broad arc of the frontier; resistance to war was hottest in the old Federalist and mercantile sections.

But if the United States was to withdraw from Europe economically, as under Jefferson, or to lose its best market through war, as under Madison, it had to find a way of employing its energies and supplying its people with manufactured goods. Accordingly, capital, cut off from its normal investment outlet in overseas commerce, began to turn to manufacturing. The period of the Embargo and the War of 1812 proved to be the seedtime of American industrialism; Henry Adams remarked on the ironic fact that "American manufactures owed more to Jefferson than to northern statesmen who merely encouraged them after they were established."

Jefferson, of course, realized the immediate implications of his desire to pursue an independent economic course and as early as 1805 became a convert to the development of manufactures. "The spirit of manufacture has taken deep root among us," he wrote Dupont in 1809, "and its foundations are laid in too great expense to be abandoned." "Our enemy," he wailed to William Short in 1814, "has indeed the consolation of Satan on removing our first parents from Paradise: from a peaceable and agricultural nation he makes us a military and manufacturing one." To another he wrote; "We must now place the manufacturer by the side of the agriculturist." If the United States was to be peaceful, it must be self-sufficient, must end its dependence on foreign goods and overseas trade. The Napoleonic Wars destroyed the Jeffersonian dream of an agrarian commonwealth. Since Jeffersonian democracy, as embodied in measures of public policy, was entirely dependent upon the agrarian order, these wars also erased the practical distinction between Republicans and Federalists.

Manufactures, if they were to be maintained, needed tariffs, especially when British capitalists, hoping to crush their new competitors at once, began dumping goods in the American market at the close of the war. In 1816 the Republicans passed a much higher tariff than Hamilton's. They, not the Federalists, began the American protective system.

And war must be financed. Hard hit by the economic drain of military operations and the financial sabotage of the Northeast, the Republicans were confronted with a bitter dilemma: either they must go begging to the fiscal interests for support, or they must charter a new national bank to fill the vacuum they had created by letting Hamilton's bank expire. They chose the second course—and soon Republican newspapers were reprinting Alexander Hamilton's arguments in favor of the constitutionality of the First Bank of the United States! In vain did Jefferson rage in his letters against the banking system. A second bank, similar in structure to Hamilton's, was chartered by the Republicans in 1816. By the end of that year Jefferson's party had taken over the whole complex of Federalist policies—manufactures, bank, tariffs, army, navy, and all—and this under the administration of Jefferson's friend, neighbor, and political heir, James Madison. As Josiah Quincy complained, the Republicans had "out-Federalized Federalism." By 1820 they had driven the rival party completely off the field, but only at the cost of taking over its program. Federalism, Jefferson wrote to Albert Gallatin in 1823, "has changed its name and hidden itself among us . . . as strong as it has ever been since 1800." Nathaniel Macon, one of the last of the intransigent agrarians, lamented: "The opinions of Jefferson and those who were with him are forgot."

NO

Forrest McDonald

THE FAITHFUL AND
THE CRISIS OF FAITH

By most objective criteria, the Americans of 1800 had abundant cause to be proud, confident, even smug. . . .

And yet a sense of decadence had plagued the land for five years and more. From the pulpit rang cries of despair and doom; dishonesty as well as panic had invaded the marketplace; liars and libelers made a travesty of freedom of the press; violence, hysteria, and paranoia infested the public councils. Those Americans who called themselves Federalists felt betrayed by an ungrateful people for whom they had labored long and well, and feared that the horrors of Jacobinism and anarchy were hourly imminent. Those who called themselves Republicans felt betrayed by the twin evils of money and monarchy, and feared that liberty was about to breathe its last. Many who embraced neither political sect, whether from apathy or disgust, nonetheless shared the general feeling that the nation was in an advanced state of moral rot.

What the Federalists thought was actually of little consequence, for they were soon to expire, in what Thomas Jefferson called the Revolution of 1800. Almost miraculously, with their demise—though not because of it—despair suddenly gave way to euphoria. The new optimism, like the pervasive gloom and the defeat of Federalism that preceded it, stemmed from an interplay of social, religious, ideological, and economic forces and institutions, and from certain ingrained American characteristics. If one would understand the Jeffersonian revolution—how it happened and how it affected the nation's destiny—one must seek first to understand those forces, institutions, and characteristics.

One of the tenets of Republicanism in America was that, contrary to the teachings of Montesquieu and other theorists, republican government was best adapted to large territories, since in an area as vast as the United States the very diversity of the people would prevent an accumulation of power inimical to liberty. If the principle, was sound, the Americans were truly blessed, for their culture was nothing if not plural. At first blush that

From *The Presidency of Thomas Jefferson* by Forrest McDonald (Lawrence/Manhattan/Wichita: The University Press of Kansas, 1976). Copyright © 1976. Reprinted by permission.

generalization might appear strong, or indeed entirely unfounded. Overwhelmingly, Americans were farmers or traders of British extraction and the Protestant faith; and even in politics, as Jefferson said in his inaugural address, "we are all republicans, we are all federalists." But the mother country itself was scarcely homogeneous, despite the amalgamation that financial and governmental power had brought to Great Britain in the eighteenth century; it comprised a host of different Celtic peoples—the Irish, the Welsh, the Cornish, and three distinct varieties of Scots—as well as Englishmen who differed from one another from north to south and east to west. Americans had proved slow to cast off the cultural baggage that they or their ancestors had brought with them; and a generation of independence, though building some sense of nationhood, had erased neither their original ethnic traits nor the intense localism that complemented and nourished those traits. As to differences in political principles, Jefferson was right in regarding them as largely superficial; yet they were substantive enough to lead many men to fight, and some to kill, one another. . . .

It should not be surprising that those who were saved through revivalism were also supporters of Jeffersonian Republicanism, for the theology of the one was psychologically akin to the ideology of the other. In part, to be sure, religious dissenters supported Jefferson because of his well-known championship of the cause of religious liberty. New England Baptists, for instance, having fought long and vainly for disestablishment, virtually idolized Jefferson. South and west of New England, however, establishment had long since ceased to be a live issue, and in much of that area Jefferson's religious views, to the extent that they were fully known, were if anything a political handicap. Rather, it was the compatibility of outlooks that made it possible for southern and western revivalists simultaneously to embrace evangelical Arminianism in religion and Republican ideology in politics.

Anglo-Americans, like the English themselves, were by and large nonideological people, but in 1800 the country was divided into two fiercely antagonistic ideological camps. In a loose, general sort of way, and with allowance for a number of exceptions, it can be said that the revival ideologies derived from contrasting views of the nature of man. The first view, that associated with the Hamiltonian Federalists, was premised upon the belief that man, while capable of noble and even altruistic behavior, could never entirely escape the influence of his inborn baser passions—especially ambition and avarice, the love of power and the love of money. The second, that espoused by the Jeffersonian Republicans, held that man was born with a tabula rasa, with virtually boundless capacity for becoming good or evil, depending upon the wholesomeness of the environment in which he grew. From the premise of the first it followed that government should recognize the evil drives of men as individuals, but check them and even harness them in such a way that they would work for the general good of society as a whole. From the premise of the second it followed that government should work to rid society of as many evils as possible—including, to a very large extent, the worst of evils, government itself. The one was positive, the other negative; the one sought to do good, the other to eradicate evil.

But the ideological division was more specifically focused than that. The High Federalists believed in and had fashioned a governmental system modeled upon the one that began to emerge in England after the Glorious Revolution of 1688 and was brought to maturity under the leadership of Sir Robert Walpole during the 1720s and 1730s. In part the system worked on the basis of what has often, simple-mindedly, been regarded as the essence of Hamiltonianism: tying the interests of the wealthy to those of the national government, or more accurately, inducing people of all ranks to act in the general interest by making it profitable for them to do so. But the genius of Hamilton's system ran much deeper. He erected a complex set of interrelated institutions, based upon the monetization of the public debt, which made it virtually impossible for anyone to pursue power and wealth successfully except through the framework of those institutions, and which simultaneously delimited and dictated the possible courses of government activity, so that government had no choice but to function in the public interest as Hamilton saw it. For instance, servicing the public debt, on which the whole superstructure rested, required a regular source of revenue that was necessarily derived largely from duties on imports from Great Britain. For that reason the United States could not go to war with Britain except at the risk of national bankruptcy, but could fight Revolutionary France or France's ally Spain, which were owners of territories that the United States avidly desired. Hamilton regarded this as the proper American foreign policy, at least for a time; and should circumstances change, he was perfectly capable of redefining the rules and rerigging the institutions so

as to dictate another policy. In domestic affairs, a wide range of implications of his system was equally inescapable.

The Jeffersonian Republicans regarded this scheme of things as utterly wicked, even as the English opposition had regarded Walpole's system. Indeed, though the Jeffersonians borrowed some of their ideas from James Harrington and other seventeenth-century writers and some from John Locke, their ideology was borrowed *in toto* from such Oppositionists as Charles Davenant, John Trenchard, Thomas Gordon, James Burgh, and most especially Henry St. John, First Viscount Bolingbroke. As a well-rounded system, it is all to be found in the pages of the *Craftsman*, an Oppositionist journal that Bolingbroke published from 1726 to 1737. The Republicans adjusted the ideology to fit the circumstances, to fit the United States Constitution and the "ministry" of Alexander Hamilton rather than the British constitution and the ministry of Robert Walpole; but that was all, and astonishingly little adjustment was necessary.

The Bolingbroke-Oppositionist *cum* Jeffersonian Republican ideology ran as follows. Corruption was everywhere, it was true; but given a proper environment, that need not be the way of things. Mankind could be rejuvenated through education and self-discipline, but that was possible only in the context of a life style that exalted living on, owning, and working the land. Only the land could give people the independence and unhurried existence that were prerequisite to self-improvement.

In some Edenic past, "the people"— which both Bolingbroke and Jefferson understood to mean the gentry and the solid yeomanry, and not to include aristocrats, money jobbers, priests, or the

NO Forrest McDonald / 165

scum in the cities—had enjoyed the proper atmosphere, and therefore had been happy. Relationships were based upon agriculture and its "handmaiden" commerce, upon ownership of land, honest labor in the earth, craftsmanship in the cities, and free trade between individuals. All men revered God, respected their fellows, deferred to their betters, and knew their place. Because they were secure in their sense of place, they were also secure in their identities and their sense of values; and manly virtue, honor, and public spirit governed their conduct.

scum in the cities—had enjoyed the proper atmosphere, and therefore had been happy. Relationships were based upon agriculture and its "handmaiden" commerce, upon ownership of land, honest labor in the earth, craftsmanship in the cities, and free trade between individuals. All men revered God, respected their fellows, deferred to their betters, and knew their place. Because they were secure in their sense of place, they were also secure in their identities and their sense of values; and manly virtue, honor, and public spirit governed their conduct.

Then a serpent invaded the garden. To Bolingbroke, the evil started with the Glorious Revolution, which begat two bastard offspring: the Financial Revolution and the system of government by ministry, rather than the system of separation of powers that had been embodied in the ancient English constitution. To Jefferson, things were slightly more complex. America had been spared the corruption that had poisoned England until the accession of George III, and when it began to infest America, the spirit of 1776 had saved the day. Yet the American Revolution, because of the Hamiltonians, was ultimately undermined in just the way the English revolution had been: both were waged to check executive power, and both ended in the worst form of executive tyranny, ministerial government. The instrument of corruption in both instances was money—not "real" money, gold and silver, but artificial money in the form of public debt, bank notes, stocks, and other kinds of paper— the acquisition of which had nothing to do with either land or labor. Government ministers assiduously encouraged people to traffic in such paper, and with that stimulus the pursuit of easy wealth proved irresistible. A frenzy for gam-

bling, stock-jobbing, and paper shuffling permeated the highest councils of state and spread among the people themselves. Manly virtue gave way to effeminacy and vice; public spirit succumbed to extravagance, venality, and corruption.

Jefferson never tired of telling a story which, to him, epitomized what had gone wrong. Early in Washington's first administration, Jefferson recalled, he had been engaged in a friendly discussion of political principles with Hamilton and Vice-President Adams. Jefferson had maintained that an agrarian republic was most conducive to human happiness. Adams disagreed and, to Jefferson's horror, said that monarchy was better, that if the British government were purged of corruption it would be the best system ever devised. Hamilton, to the astonishment of both his listeners, declared that if the British system were urged of corruption it would not work: it was, he said, the most perfect system of government as it stood, for corruption was the most suitable engine of effective government.

In the matter of foreign relations, Republicans opposed the corrupt new order on two interrelated sets of grounds, with the same logic and often the same language that the Oppositionists had used earlier. One was that it entangled the nation with foreign powers, making independent, self-determined action impossible. Not only had Hamilton's system prevented the United States from siding with Revolutionary France against Britain in the early 1790s—which the Republicans believed to be the moral course, as well as the one most advantageous to the country—but it continually subjected America to alien influences because foreigners owned a large percentage of the public debt and the stock of the Bank of the United States. This involvement, in turn, gave rise to the second set of grounds for objection: foreign entanglements necessitated standing armies and navies, the support of which added to an already oppressive tax burden. The gentry and yeomanry, the Republicans believed, had been carrying more than their share of the tax load, even when taxes had been mainly in the form of import duties; and when excise taxes were levied specifically to support the military during the quasi war with France in 1798, the new burden fell almost exclusively on the landed. Taxes to support standing armies and navies were doubly galling because a professional military corps, as a class distinct from the people, was a threat to liberty in its own right, and it could also be unleashed to collect taxes by force, thus making the people pay for their own oppression. (English Oppositionists had been afraid of standing armies, but not of navies, for they had regarded a strong naval establishment as necessary for the protection of British commerce. The American Republicans' fear of standing armies was largely abstract, since they believed that the traditional American reliance on militias would prevent the rise of dangerous armies; but their hostility to navies was immediate and strong, for navies seemed most likely to involve the United States in fighting, and besides, navies cost a lot of money for upkeep even when they were not actively employed.)

Given all that, a revolution in the form of a return to first principles was called for. The several branches of government must be put back into constitutional balance, the moneychangers must be ousted from the temples, the gentry and yeomanry must be restored to supremacy, commerce must be returned to its subordinate role as agriculture's handmaiden, and the values of the agrarian way of life must be cherished anew. In the undertaking, the Republicans had reason for hope—as, in reality, Bolingbroke and his circle had not—for it could all be done within the framework of the Constitution. The Constitution made it possible for the Republicans to gain control of the national government, and should they prove able to do so, only two major tasks needed to be done. The first was to purge government of extreme, irreconcilable monarchists. Jefferson believed that this could be done quickly and easily, for he thought that all but a handful of the people in government were men of sound and honorable principles. The second was to pay off the public debt as rapidly as possible, since that was the wellspring of the whole system of corruption. This would not be easy; but with good management, honest administration, and rigid economy, Jefferson believed that it could be accomplished within sixteen years.

That was the Republicans' ideology and the essence of their program: restore the separation of powers through the voluntary restraint of virtuous officials, cast out the monarchists and the money men, repeal the most oppressive of taxes, slash expenses, pay off the public debt, and thus restore America to the pristine simplicity of an Arcadian past.

It is to be observed that nothing has been said of strict construction of the Constitution and the extreme states'-rights doctrine of interposition, with which Jefferson was associated in his argument against the constitutionality of the Bank in 1791 and in his authorship of the Kentucky Resolutions against the

Alien and Sedition Acts in 1798 and 1799. The fact is that only a handful of people knew of those documents or knew that Jefferson had written them; they were not a part of his public identity. Moreover, they were arguments that had been coined in the first instance as matters of political expediency—as means of heading off what Jefferson regarded as dangerous activity by the Federalists—and he never thought of them as sacred principles of constitutional government.

It is also to be observed that nothing has been said of the federal judiciary or of territorial expansion, two matters that consumed much of the energy and attention of the Jeffersonians when they came to power. The judiciary was of merely tangential consequence in the Jeffersonians' thinking; it became important to them only when it loomed as an unexpected stumbling block. Territorial expansion was an integral part of their program, but only implicitly: it went without saying that the nation should expand as the opportunity arose, to make room for generations of farmers yet unborn.

The Republicans gained control of the national government, after twelve years of Federalist domination, in a bitterly contested election that began in April of 1800 and was not completed until February of 1801. Their triumph was not a popular mandate for the implementation of the Republican ideology, nor was it a popular mandate for anything else. The presidential electors were, for the most part, chosen by the state legislatures, who also chose all the members of the United States Senate. The decision was in the hands of no more than a thousand men, and for practical purposes it turned on the activities of two or three dozen factional leaders. The supporters of Thomas Jefferson proved to be more skillful as political manipulators and masters of intrigue than were the supporters of President John Adams—they had already proved, in capturing majorities in most legislatures, that they were better organized and more artful in arousing the voters—and that was the key to their success.

Nonetheless, their program had a broad basis of popular support, for it was peculiarly suited to the genius of the American people, and it appealed to their prejudices and interests as well. Moreover, there was no doubt that the Republicans had the talent, the energy, and the determination to carry the program into execution. But there was a question, a very large one. Republican theory was wondrous potent as an ideology of opposition. It remained to be seen whether it was a sound basis for administration.

Jeffersonian Republicanism was an ideology and an idea, a system of values and a way of looking at things; and as the aphorism goes, ideas and ideals have consequences. But it was also a program of action, carefully crafted and methodically executed; and as we are sometimes wont to forget, actions have consequences, too. To appraise Jefferson's presidency, it is therefore necessary to take both sets of criteria into account.

In the realm of ideas and ideology, Jeffersonian Republicanism was a body of thought that had been taken largely from the Oppositionist tradition of eighteenth-century England, principally as incorporated in the writings of Charles Davenant, John Trenchard, Thomas Gordon, James Burgh, and most particularly Henry St. John, Viscount Bolingbroke. This system of thought is explicated rather fully in the text, and it would be pointless to reiterate the effort here. It is useful, however, to remember that we are speaking of *oppositionist* thought: Bolingbroke and his predecessors and followers (whether calling themselves Tories or Commonwealthmen or Real Whigs) were condemning and seeking to undo the Financial Revolution and its attendant political corruption, as epitomized by the ministry of Sir Robert Walpole, In its stead, they proposed to restore a pristine and largely imaginary past in which life was rural, relationships were personal, the gentry ruled as a natural aristocracy, the main corpus of the citizenry was an honest yeomanry, commerce and craft-manufacturing existed only as handmaidens to agriculture, standing armies and privileged monopolies and fictitious paper wealth were all unknown, and government was limited—limited to an essentially passive function as impartial arbiter and defender of the existing social order, and limited by the unwritten but inviolable Constitution, dividing power among three separate, distinct, and coequal branches. In other words, the Jeffersonians' ideological forebears were reactionaries, swimming against the tide of history, for the world aborning was the depersonalized world of money, machines, cities, and big government.

The Jeffersonians, though castigated by their enemies as dangerous innovators and radicals, were likewise resisting the emergence of the modern world. They had seen the Hamiltonian Federalists attempting to transform and corrupt America, even as the Oppositionists had seen Walpole and the new monied classes transform and corrupt England, and they swallowed the Oppositionists' ideas and ideology whole. The Jeffersonians republicanized Bolingbroke, to be sure, developing the doctrine that absolute separation of powers, with a strictly limited presidency, was guaranteed by the written Constitution. In their hearts, however, they did not trust paper constitutions, and their view of Jefferson's mission as president did not differ substantively and significantly from Bolingbroke's idea of a Patriot King: a head of state who would rally the entire nation to his banner, and then, in an act of supreme wisdom and virtue, voluntarily restrain himself and thus give vitality and meaning to the constitutional system. The Republicans also added the doctrine of states' rights, but that was mainly a tactical position which most of them abandoned—except rhetorically—once they came into control of the national government. The only genuine changes they brought to the ideology were two. One was to relocate its social base, from that of an Anglican gentry to that of southern slaveholders, Celtic-American back-country men, and evangelical Protestants. The other was to put the ideology into practice.

If who they were and what they were seeking are thus understood, it is evident that they remained remarkably true to their principles throughout Jefferson's presidency—despite charges to the contrary by a host of critics, ranging from Alexander Hamilton to Henry Adams to Leonard Levy. Moreover, they were remarkably successful in accomplishing what they set out to do. They set out to destroy the complex financial mechanism that Hamilton had built around the public debt, and they went a long way toward that goal—so close that if war could have been avoided for another eight years, their success might have been total. They also set out to secure the frontiers of the United States by expanding the country's territorial domain into the vast wilderness, and they succeeded so well that it became possible to dream that the United States could remain a nation of uncorrupted farmers for a thousand years to come.

And yet on the broader scale they failed, and failed calamitously—not because of their own shortcomings, but because their system was incompatible with the immediate current of events, with the broad sweep of history, and with the nature of man and society. As an abstract idea, Bolingbrokism *cum* Jeffersonian Republicanism may have been flawless, and it was certainly appealing. In the real world, it contradicted and destroyed itself.

At the core of the Republicans' thinking lay the assumption, almost Marxian in its naïveté, that only two things must be done to remake America as an ideal society and a beacon unto mankind. First, the public debt must be extinguished, for with it would die stock-jobbing, paper-shuffling, "monopoly" banking, excisemen, placemen, and all the other instrumentalities of corruption that the Walpole/Hamilton system "artificially" created. Second, governmental power must be confined to its constitutional limits, which implied reduction of the functions of government but also, and more importantly, meant adherence to the rules of the separation of powers— that being the only legitimate method, in their view, whereby a free government could exercise its authority. If ancient ways were thus restored, the Jeffersonians believed, liberty and independence would inevitably follow. In turn, liberty and independence—by which they meant the absence of governmental restraint or favor and the absence of effective interference from foreign

powers—would make it possible for every man, equal in rights but not in talents, to pursue happiness in his own way and to find his own "natural" level in the natural order.

Things did not work out that way, especially in regard to relations with foreign powers: far from freeing the country from foreign interference, Republican policy sorely impaired the nation's ability to determine its own destiny. In their eagerness to retire the public debt, the Jeffersonians tried diligently to economize. Toward that end they slashed military and naval appropriations so much as to render the United States incapable of defending itself—at a time when the entire Western world was at war. Simultaneously, in their haste to destroy all vestiges of the Hamiltonian system, the Jeffersonians abolished virtually all internal taxes. This relieved the farmers and planters of an onerous tax burden and arrested the proliferation of hated excisemen, but it also made national revenues almost totally dependent upon duties on imports—which meant dependent upon the uninterrupted flow of international commerce, which in turn depended upon the will of Napoleon Bonaparte and the ministers of King George III.

For two or three years the Jeffersonians were extremely lucky. That is to say, during that period the kaleidoscope of events in Europe turned briefly and flukishly in their favor. They obtained Louisiana as a result of a concatenation of circumstances that was wildly improbable and was never to be repeated. They were able to pay off much of the public debt and to accumulate sizable treasury surpluses because Great Britain, out of consideration for its own interests, allowed the Americans to engage in a trade of debatable legality, thus swelling the volume of American imports and, concomitantly, the revenues flowing into the United States Treasury.

From 1803 onward, however, each turn of the international wheel was less favorable to the United States. By 1805 it was apparent that West Florida—for which the Jeffersonians hungered almost obsessively, since its strategic and economic value was considerably greater than that of all Louisiana excepting New Orleans— would not become American in the way that Louisiana had. In the same year it began to be clear that the British would not long continue to allow the United States to grow wealthy by trading with Britain's mortal enemies.

But for their ideology, the Jeffersonians could have reversed their earlier policy stance, embraced Britain, and become hostile toward France and Spain, thus enabling the nation to continue to prosper and expand. Given their ideological commitment, they could not do so. Moreover, given the consequences of their actions so far, they lacked the strength to make even a token show of force against Great Britain. Thus in 1807, when both Britain and France forbade the United States to engage in international commerce except as tributaries to themselves, the embargo—a policy of pusillanimity and bungling, billed as a noble experiment in peaceful coercion— was the only course open to them.

At home, as they became ever more deeply impaled upon the horns of their self-created international dilemma, the Jeffersonians became progressively less tolerant of opposition or criticism. From the beginning they had shown considerable disdain for the federal courts; as Jefferson's second term wore on, this disdain degenerated into contempt for due process of law and for law itself.

Thus the embargo became a program of domestic tyranny in inverse ratio to its ineffectiveness as an instrument of international policy: the more the policy was found wanting, the more rigorously was it enforced.

The embargo, then, both as a bankrupt foreign policy and as a reign of domestic oppression, was not a sudden aberration but the logical and virtually certain outcome of the Jeffersonian ideology put into practice: the ideology's yield was dependence rather than independence, oppression rather than liberty.

One other aspect of the Jeffersonian experience wants notice, and that concerns the Republicans' conception of the presidency as a limited branch of government, absolutely separate from the legislative branch. In practice, adherence to that ideal was impossible because of the very nature of the presidential office. For one thing, though some presidential powers are relatively independent, others are intermeshed with those of Congress. For another, the American executive branch is "republicanized," or kept from being monarchical, by being made elective for a fixed term of years. To be sure, the Republicans' political machinery was so effective that Jefferson could doubtless have been elected to a third and even a fourth term, had he chosen. But Washington's two-term precedent was strong, and, what was more telling, the psychic cost of the presidential office was and is frightful; by the seventh or eighth year Jefferson, like Washington before him and like most two-term presidents who followed him, was physically, emotionally, and spiritually exhausted. The second term was therefore a lame-duck term, and that fact subtly but significantly altered the relationship between the president and Congress. Pure though Jefferson's motives and the motives of many Republican congressmen were, it was important to them that his popularity would cease to be of use to them in seeking reelection, and it was important to him that he would not need their political support in 1808. In the circumstances, Jefferson did what lame-duck presidents normally do—that is, he gravitated toward the arena in which he had less to do with Congress, the area of foreign relations; and Congress, and especially the Senate, also followed the norm by rising at the end to regain powers that it believed had been more or less usurped from it.

Still another crucial aspect of the American presidency, one with which the Republicans were not at all prepared to cope, is that the Constitution vests in one office and one person two distinct and nearly incompatible roles which under the British system had come to be divided between the king and his ministers. One is the truly monarchical function, that of serving as the ritualistic symbol of the nation. The other is the purely executive function, that of fashioning policy and directing its implementation. Success in the one hinges upon the president's charisma, his leadership, and his abstract appeal to the whole people; success in the other hinges upon the president's skill in tangible dealings with small groups and individual human beings. The Republicans' conception of the presidency was, in these terms, entirely unrealistic: they disavowed the first role and wanted the president to fill the second by standing as aloof from Congress as a proper king stands from his subjects.

Jefferson was superbly gifted at playing both roles, and he was able to play them without offending Republican sen-

sibilities or prejudices. He ostentatiously disdained the pomp and pageantry that had marked the presidencies of Washington and Adams, but all the while he assiduously and effectively courted popularity. Foreign ministers and Federalist critics alike commented upon his inordinate love of popularity, and marked it as a weakness of character; perhaps it was, but it was also true wisdom, for reverence toward the Crown was a deep-rooted habit in the English-speaking world, and love of the president as king-surrogate was a crucial social adhesive for the diffuse and pluralistic infant United States. Indeed, in this respect Jefferson made a profound contribution toward the perdurance of the republic. Washington had been a veritable demigod and a symbol of the nation, and thus provided a sort of half-way house between monarchy and republicanism; Jefferson humanized the presidency and served as a symbol, not of the nation, but of the people, and thus made the transition complete.

In the role of policy-maker and administrator, Jefferson was even more skilled. After his inaugural he abandoned the monarchical practice of appearing in person before Congress; he never held court or levees, but invited congressmen in small groups for dinner, where he wore homespun and hosted them in the manner of a country squire; he never openly initiated legislation, and only deferentially suggested that Congress might look into one subject or another; he never vetoed a bill on policy grounds, and would not have dreamed of doing so. In sum, he allowed Congress to function with no overt presidential direction and with only the gentlest of presidential guidance. As to cabinet meetings, he conducted them as a democracy of equals. And yet, almost until the end, he ran Congress more successfully and more thoroughly than did any preceding president and precious few succeeding presidents, and the cabinet always reflected his will except when he had no firm opinions on a matter. Moreover, he did so without the use of bribery, patronage, corruption or coercion: it all flowed from the force of his intellect, his character, and his personality.

But, perversely, that too was a weakness of the Jeffersonian scheme of things: the system could be made to work only with a Thomas Jefferson at the helm. When Jefferson himself faltered, as he did on several occasions during his presidency, the government almost stopped functioning except in the routine operations of Galatin's Treasury machinery. When Jefferson left the office, all the shortcomings of his method of administration became manifest. The cabinet became a center of petty bickering and continuous cabalizing, and Congress split into irreconcilable factions and repeatedly asserted its will against the president.

For all these reasons, Jefferson's legacy to his successor was a can of serpents. Jefferson's second term was merely a calamity; Madison's first would be a disaster.

There is more to a presidency than the tangible events that happen during and in consequence of it: there are also the myths it inspires. For a time, of course, memories were too fresh, feelings were too strong, and events were too unpleasant to admit of the kind of romanticization that is a necessary prelude to myth-making. By 1826, however—when Jefferson along with John Adams died on the fiftieth anniversary of the Declaration of Independence—memories had mellowed, new rivalries had replaced the old, and artful and designing men were looking to the past for heroes whose lives could be used or misused to justify their own doings. Jefferson was admirably suited for such use and misuse, for he had written and acted in a greater variety of ways on a greater variety of subjects than any of the other Founding Fathers, and he was more quotable than any of them save possibly Adams alone.

But the Jefferson legend developed along curiously divided lines. In the realm of formal historical writing, he fared poorly until well into the twentieth century. . . .

Meanwhile, in the realm of folklore and political rhetoric, which ordinary Americans heard and heeded more frequently and more trustingly than they did the staid pronouncements of historians, Jefferson was exalted as the patron saint of all good things. The range of causes for which his name was invoked is staggering: democracy and partisanship, states' rights and nationalism, slavery and abolitionism, egalitarianism and racism, imperialism and isolationism, populism and laissez-faire capitalism, the planned and the decentralized society. In the nineteenth century, so long as rural values continued to prevail in America despite the relentless march of industrialization, Jefferson continued to be identified with the agrarian tradition; in the twentieth, when the center of American life and values became the city, his connection with that ideal was all but forgotten, and instead he came to be regarded as the champion of the "have-nots" against the "haves," of the "common man" (or the "forgotten man" or the "little fellow") against aristocrats and plutocrats.

In the 1920s and 1930s the two strands of the legend began to come together. The Democratic politician-historian Claude G. Bowers and the more scholarly Gilbert Chinard began the process of beatification through the written word, and though the Jefferson they described was one he would scarcely have recognized, the process has continued. Franklin Roosevelt's New Deal depicted itself as thoroughly Jeffersonian, though given to the use of "Hamiltonian means to accomplish Jeffersonian ends"—and while building a federal bureaucracy almost as large as the population of the entire country had been during Jefferson's time and while extending its regulatory power apace, it built Jefferson a monument which declared his true mission to have been as a libertarian. In time, and in our own time, "Jefferson" and "Jeffersonian" came to mean merely "good," or "that which the nation aspires to be."

The real Jefferson—the one who once lived in Virginia and once worked in the President's House—was lost in the shuffle. So, too, was the America he wanted his country to become; and in a nation of crime-ridden cities and poisoned air, of credit cards and gigantic corporations, of welfare rolls and massive bureaucracies, of staggering military budgets and astronomical public debts, of corruption and alienation, that loss is the more poignant. He and his followers set out to deflect the course of History, and History ended up devouring them and turning even their memory to its own purposes. History has away of doing that.

POSTSCRIPT

Did President Jefferson Outfederalize the Federalists?

It is interesting to note that neither Hofstadter or McDonald dwell upon the apparent reversals of Jefferson's states' rights and strict constructionist views of the Constitution when he became president. Hofstadter does not mention this because he considers Jefferson a pragmatist. McDonald argues that while Jefferson considered unconstitutional Hamilton's proposal for a national bank and Adams's Alien and Sedition Acts, he never thought of them as sacred principles of constitutional government.

Both writers also agree that the embargo and the subsequent War of 1812 with Great Britain undermined the attempts of Jefferson and his successors Madison and Monroe to maintain America as primarily an agrarian society. Both authors also note that the war forced the Republicans to accept manufacturing as an integral part of the American economy. But the two authors stress different consequences of the war. Hofstadter maintains that although the Federalist party disappeared soon after the war, the Republicans had totally adopted its political and economic philosophy of high tariffs, a national banking system, and the promotion of an industrial economy. McDonald, on the other hand, stresses that the failed embargo against England and France made Jefferson's administration intolerant of dissent and contemptuous of the law itself. "Thus," says McDonald, "the embargo became a program of domestic tyranny in inverse ratio to its ineffectiveness as an instrument of international policy: the more the policy was found wanting, the more rigorously was it enforced." McDonald could also have pointed out that Jefferson would not be the last president to have a reform program thwarted by the repressed atmosphere that war creates. Twentieth-century presidents Woodrow Wilson, Franklin Roosevelt, and Lyndon Johnson also saw their domestic reforms undone when the country put its energies into waging war.

It is not surprising that Jefferson's two major biographers, both professors at the University of Virginia for many years, have written sympathetic portraits. Dumas Malone's magisterial *Jefferson and His Times*, 6 volumes (Little, Brown, 1948–1981) and Merrill Peterson's 900-page opus *Thomas Jefferson and the New Nation: A Bibliography* (Oxford, 1970) contain detailed accounts of most facets of his life and are very useful as reference works. Peterson's *The Jeffersonian Images in the American Mind* (Oxford, 1960) is a wonderful account of the use and misuse of Jefferson's image in American politics since his death. Widely acclaimed by general reviewers though not by historians is Fawn M. Brodie's psycho-biography of *Thomas Jefferson: An Intimate History* (Norton, 1974), which accepts as true the liaison between Jefferson and Sally Hemings that led to five unacknowledged sons and daughters. A shorter version can be found in Brodie's "The Great Taboo," *American Heritage* (June, 1972). There are few modern critical portraits of Jefferson. One is Leonard Levy, *Jefferson and Civil Liberties: The Darker Side* (Quadrangle, 1973) which occasionally reads like a lawyer's brief but points out the contradictions between Jefferson's philosophical principles and his actions as president. More balanced, though critical, is Forrest McDonald's *Thomas Jefferson* (Kansas, 1976). No student should miss McDonald's concise critical summary of Washington's and Jefferson's precedent-setting impact on the American presidency in "A Mirror for Presidents," *Commentary* (December 1976).

The 1980s continue to produce books about the third president. A solid work of reasonable length which represents a lifetime of scholarship is Noble E. Cunningham, Jr., *In Pursuit of Reason: The Life of Thomas Jefferson* (Louisiana State University Press, 1987). Those who want to sample *Thomas Jefferson's Writings* should consult the 1600-page volume edited by Merrill Peterson for the Library of America in 1985. Peterson has also edited *Thomas Jefferson: A Reference Biography* (Scribner's, 1986), which contains twenty-five original essays that integrate the many interests of this "renaissance man." Finally, the Library of America has recently reissued Henry Adams's *History of the United States of America During the Administrations of Thomas Jefferson and James Madison*. Both volumes deserve the title "classic" and should be sampled by the serious student.

ISSUE 9

Did Women Achieve Greater Autonomy in the New Nation?

YES: Nancy Woloch, from *Women and the American Experience* (Alfred A. Knopf, 1984)

NO: Gerda Lerner, from "The Lady and the Mill Girl: Changes in the Status of Women in the Age of Jackson," *American Studies Journal* (Spring 1961)

ISSUE SUMMARY

YES: Woloch describes the exercise of autonomy and authority in the domestic life of middle-class wives.
NO: Lerner considers a spectrum of women's roles, emphasizing the subservient position of female industrial workers.

Social and economic changes after 1783 altered the economic status of women. Increased urbanization, the accumulation of wealth, and the imitation of European bourgeois values and habits combined to eliminate the androgynous workplace where previously women could display their skills alongside men. Perhaps a diminished concern over survival contributed to changes in behavior also. With the onset of industrialization, work which had been performed in homes was transferred to factories, and women usually worked only for a limited time, until they married. Residence and workplace were no longer one; the roles of wife, mother, and worker no longer could be juggled easily.

Most historians interpret the War for Independence as a negative influence on women's status. The opinions of foreign visitors, however, were mixed. Alexis de Tocqueville, acknowledged as the most acute of the early nineteenth-century observers of the United States, uncovered an interesting dichotomy. "In America, he wrote, "the independence of woman is irrevocably lost in the bonds of matrimony. If an unmarried woman is less constrained there than elsewhere, a wife is subjected to stricter obligations." Tocqueville was astonished because "Long before an American girl arrives at the marriageable age, her emancipation from maternal control begins; she has scarcely ceased to be a child when she already thinks for herself, speaks with freedom and acts on her own impulse."

Class distinctions separated American women into different groups. Moreover, different sources of family income—agriculture versus commerce or the professions—further complicate any generalizations. The sectional divisions of North, South, and West, which historians use to explain the alignment of general attitudes in the United States, must also be considered for a fuller understanding of women's behavior. The kind of household added still another dimension. For example, contrast the modest rural cottage, where the housewife prepared almost all foodstuffs and much of the clothing on the premises, with the plantation, where the concerns of the mistress were similar but whose duties were largely supervisory, and, then, with the urban home, where the woman possessed the opportunity to purchase most necessities if she wished, instead of making them. Recognizing that women did not represent a monolithic entity, it is not surprising that historians should offer clashing interpretations of women's status in the antebellum period. Some of these differences are evident in the following essays by Nancy Woloch and Gerda Lerner.

Professor Woloch focuses upon middle-class women for whom the home became a private retreat from the outside commercial world. As controller of this social space, these women, Woloch claims, acquired an independent role that added to their social prestige. This common sphere became the site for housekeeping, child rearing, and moral and religious instruction, activities that generally were carried out without the presence of a household patriarch. Hence, according to Woloch, women were able to exercise greater control over their everyday lives.

For Gerda Lerner, antebellum women confronted shrinking opportunities in the professions and trades. Native-born female workers, such as those employed as the original labor force at the Lowell, Massachusetts, textile mills, were being replaced by mid-century by immigrant workers. Work outside the home came to be viewed as employment unbefitting a "lady." In addition, she points out, women were excluded from the wave of political democracy that swept through the nation in the Jacksonian era. All classes of women remained politically disenfranchised. Given the improved status of white adult males in gaining suffrage rights, however, this actually amounted to a state of "relative deprivation" for women in antebellum America.

YES

Nancy Woloch

THE HOME AND THE WORLD

When the *Ladies Magazine* first appeared in 1828, a transformation in domestic life was well under way, at least in the commercial, urbanizing Northeast. During colonial days, when most families lived on farms, the household was a productive unit. All family members engaged in work to sustain it, work that was done in or near the home. As part of the family labor force, women and children were subordinate to paternal authority. But during the early nineteenth century, as a market economy developed, old patterns of life started to vanish. Men who once would have been farmers or craftsmen were now working outside the home to earn the income that supported it. The home was no longer a center of production, nor did family members work together for family sustenance. Within the emerging middle class, "home" became a private enclave, a retreat from the "world" and a refuge from commercial life. And within the home, women assumed a distinctive role.

The middle-class wife, like the *Ladies Magazine* reader of 1828, remained at home while her income-earning husband went to work outside it, in office or store, business or profession. While the man ventured forth into the world, the woman at home gained an independent realm of her own, one that was no longer constantly under male domination. Domestic life was now under female control. Nor was the wife tied down to wheel and loom, hearth and dairy. Once home manufacture was transferred to workplace, the woman at home was responsible primarily for housekeeping, child rearing, and moral and religious life. Within her own domestic space, however, she had gained both a new degree of autonomy and a new degree of authority over others.

The doctrine of sphere, as expounded in the *Ladies Magazine, Godey's Lady's Book,* and countless other publications, celebrated the new status of the middle-class woman, along with her distinctive vocation, values, and character. It also described an unspoken bargain between middle-class women and men. While men were still heads of families, their real domain was now in the world—a world of business, professions, politics, and money making.

Family status depended on their earned income and public roles. Women were expected to devote themselves entirely to private life, to the "chaste circle of the fireside," and to maintain an alternate world with separate values. But their roles at home also helped to define family status. Moreover, within the home, they had gained new clout and respect. The bargain was based on mutual gain. If men had the opportunity to rise in the world, women had the opportunity to rise in the home.

The middle-class woman's role was of course a dependent one. Her authority expanded only as the family's productive functions contracted, and those functions contracted, and those functions contracted only when family income went up. Rising income was at the center of woman's sphere. Only with substantial support could a married woman adopt the nonproductive role once reserved for the very wealthy or the anti-economic attitudes propounded by the *Ladies Magazine*. In reality, few women could sever themselves completely from either home production or physical work. Middle-class women and those who aspired to that status remained active contributors to the family economy. Most women, moreover, were only remote beneficiaries of the middle-class bargain. In rural areas, on farms in New England, in the South, and in the Midwest, traditional ways of life persisted. Household production continued, women and children were still part of the family labor force, and paternal authority as head of that labor force remained in effect, if not entirely intact. A woman's clout did not increase if a family was poor, or if she was not attached to a dependable, income-producing man. In many cases, the perquisites of woman's sphere—influence, autonomy, and authority—were little more than shared aspirations.

Nor were women of any class able to ignore worldly concerns. Within the growing middle class, woman's sphere was as precarious an ideal as its counterpart for men—the opportunity to rise in the world. The early-nineteenth-century family was likely to be in both financial and geographical motion. Income rose or fell according to personal fate and twists and turns of the economy such as the depression that diminished *Ladies Magazine* subscriptions in 1834. Buffeted by panics or elevated by good fortune, Americans faced the possibility of downward mobility at every turn. The "vicissitudes" were particularly precarious for women, who had little ability to determine family finances. When a husband died or a father failed in business, consequences could be dire. Shifts in family fortune, moreover, were usually linked to shifts in locale, to constant waves of internal migration—from rural areas to towns and cities, or from crowded areas to vacant land. Hardly insulated by sphere, early-nineteenth-century women were continually adapting to new homes, communities, associations, and economic situations.

But in important ways, woman's sphere was also a reality with which many women could identify, because their everyday patterns of life and work were becoming increasingly different from those of men. Even on the family farm, that most traditional of settings, men were now attuned to the market economy while women's responsibilities remained tied to the household economy. In towns and cities, differences between male and female work patterns were even more marked. During colonial times, as historian Nancy Cott points out, the work of both men and women was closely tied to the land. It was seasonal, discontinuous, and task oriented. But during the early nineteenth century, as the economy changed and as wage labor replaced family labor, male work patterns became oriented to time, not task. Whatever a man did for a living—laborer, businessman, tradesman, or clerk—he now had a clearly defined working day. His work, accordingly, became separated from the rest of life. Household work, however, remained in a time warp of task orientation. Women's work day expanded and contracted to fit the jobs at hand, whether the washing of clothes, baking of bread, or care of children—activities that all merged into life. In short, women's work and homebound world remained premodern, whereas men's was changing. A distinctive rhythm of labor and life style also defined woman's sphere.

Finally, women of all regions and all social levels could hope to benefit from the new importance now attributed to their shared vocation. In traditional society, household work and child-care had never drawn much acclaim. During the early nineteenth century, however, they were found to have social significance, to contribute to the well-being of society at large. Women's sphere was in fact a new social space, one that had not been recognized before. On the one hand, it was an enclosed, limited, private space. On the other, it was an improvement over having no space at all. Woman's sphere, according to popular literature, encompassed a now important social institution, the home. It linked all women together in a valuable vocation—domesticity and child rearing. It fostered a positive consciousness of gender, one that

had not existed in the colonial era. And it necessitated a redefinition of female character, one appropriate to the middle-class woman's elevated domestic status.

During the early nineteenth century, the home took on new significance, material and emotional. By mid-century, the middle class home had become a substantial place, with pantries and drawing rooms, mirrors and pianos, and at least some of the items featured in *Godey's Lady's Book*—upholstered sofas, elaborate furniture, carpets, and draperies. Its center was no longer the hearth, where colonial women did much of their work, but the parlor, where the family assembled. Since middle-class Americans had not only far more possessions but rising standards of neatness and cleanliness, "housework" quickly replaced "housewifery." Even with hired help, the middle-class women was hardly idle, since home maintenance and management was now a more elaborate procedure.

The middle-class home was also viewed as an emotional space, a refuge from the competitive world, and a source of stability and order in a society that weemed to be losing both. And it was now under feminine sway. Increasingly, the home was idealized as a bastion of feminine values, of piety and morality, affection and self-sacrifice—commodities that were in short supply outside it. Literature directed at women, especially, lost no opportunity to define the home as a feminine fief. "The family state . . . is the aptest earthly illustration of the heavenly kingdom and woman is its chief minister," educator Catherine Beecher declared in her *Treatise on Domestic Economy* in the 1840s. "The duties of the woman are as sacred and important as any ordained by man." By midcentury, the home was depicted as an insulated, privatized, feminized shrine. "Our homes—what is their corner-stone but the virtue of a woman, and on what does social well-being rest but in our homes?" asked *Godey's Lady's Book* in 1856.

Must we not trace all other blessings of civilized life to the doors of our private dwellings? Are not our hearth-stones guarded by holy forms, conjugal, filial and parental love, the corner-stone of church and state, more sacred than either, more necessary than both? Let our temples crumble and capitals of state be levelled with the dust, but spare our homes! Man did not invent, and he cannot improve or abrogate them. A private shelter to cover . . . two hearts dearer to each other than all in the world; high walls to exclude the profane eyes of every human being; seclusion enough for the children to feel that mother is a holy and peculiar name—this is home. . . . Here the church and state must come for their origin and support. Oh! spare our homes.

While the middle-class home expanded in size and significance, the family itself was getting smaller. Americans were having fewer children. In 1800, the national birth rate had been the highest in the world; but during the next few decades it rapidly fell, a process that would continue for the rest of the century. The mother of 7.04 in 1800 became the mother of 5.92 in 1850 and 3.56 by 1900. Although the decline was national, it was uneven. During the early nineteenth century, large families were still the rule in most agricultural regions, along the newly settled frontier and among immigrants and blacks. Rural fertility, in fact, was also falling, but urban fertility was consistently lower. The most precipitous drop was among the new middle class in towns and cities.

But as the family began to shrink, the value attached to motherhood rose. Though such mounting significance had already been suggested in post-Revolutionary rhetoric, during the early nineteenth century it increased dramatically. Once household production waned, child raising became the family's central focus and purpose. In the middle-class home, children were no longer family workers but rather *what* the family produced. More time was devoted to their upbringing, more resources to their education, more effort to instilling the values and traits that would keep them in the middle class. The increased importance of child rearing contributed to an authority shift in the family. Paternal power dropped a notch as maternal affection became the main psychological force at home. The mother was now the primary child rearer, the crucial dispenser of values and former of character. She could "generate those moral tendencies which cover the whole of existence," as a minister wrote in the *Ladies Magazine*. "Her character is felt throughout the intricate workings of society." By the 1830s, when the publishing industry began an era of rapid expansion, the mother's significance was celebrated on all sides.

Innumerable tracts and stories—like those in the *Ladies Magazine*—paid tribute to the mother of Washington. In prints and etchings, a new iconography of motherhood developed. Magazines featured scenes of mothers at home, surrounded by children, in affectionate poses. In literature directed at women, motherhood was celebrated as the ultimate opportunity for self-sacrifice and, simultaneously, the ultimate role of female power. "How entire and perfect is this dominion over the unformed character of your infant," *Ladies Magazine* author Lydia Sigourney exuded in her *Letters to Mothers* (1838). No opportunity was lost to celebrate the social utility of motherhood. It was mothers, as Lydia Maria Child declared in her popular *Mother's Book* (1831) "on whose intelligence and discretion the safety and prosperity of our nation so much depend."

Nor was the expansion of maternal influence just rhetorical. By midcentury, it began to be recognized in the law. Northern states started to alter the tradition of paternal custody in cases of separation and divorce. Courts began to consider the "needs" of young children and "parental fitness," as well as to award custody to the "innocent party." Women did not gain equal custody rights, to say nothing of preference, until the end of the century. But adulation of motherhood was not without some legal ramifications, at least in the North. In the antebellum South, where patriarchy remained intact, legal encroachments on paternal power were rejected.

While celebrations of woman's sphere stressed the significance of domestic roles and maternal influence, they also suggested a new and positive consciousness of gender. The polarity of spheres that segragated middle-class men and women was not without an emotional bonus. Since women shared a common vocation, values, and attitudes appropriate to the home, not the world, they did have more in common with one another than did men, as Sarah Hale contended in *Ladies Magazine*. And they profited from long-term, intense relationships with other women—relationships that continued for decades, despite marriage and geographical separation, often taking the form of lengthy visits and correspondence. Such correspondence, as historian Carroll Smith Rosenberg contends, reveals that "Women's sphere had an essential dignity and integrity that grew out of women's shared experiences and mutual affection." Within their self-contained female world—noncompetitive, empathetic, and supportive—women valued one another and thereby gained a sense of security and self-esteem. "Women, who had little status and power in the larger world of male concerns, possessed status and power in the lives of other women."

Historians disagree as to whether an intimate mother-daughter relationship lay at the heart of this female world, or whether the peer relationship was more important. In either case, early-nineteenth-century middle-class women assumed centrality in one another's lives, depended emotionally on one another, and appreciated their same-sex connections and friendships. The role of friendship as an outlet for shared "sentiments" was reflected in the New England letters and diaries analyzed by historian Nancy Cott. Men, in these documents, were usually remote, distant figures, often without names. Or they might be referred to, with muted sarcasm, as "the Lords of Creation," an expression favored by Sarah Hale in the *Ladies Magazine*. But affection among women was explicit. Friendship provided an opportunity to exchange "reciprocal views and feelings," wrote Eliza Chaplin to Laura Lovell in 1820. "To you I unfold my whole heart without apology." "I do not believe that men can ever feel so pure an enthusiasm for women as we can feel for one another," *Ladies Magazine* author Catherine Sedgwick revealed to her diary in 1834. "Ours is nearest to the love of angels."

The positive consciousness of gender suggested by personal documents reflected and supported a new assessment of female character. According to the doctrine of sphere, character traits, like social roles, were now divided between men and women. Men were expected to be competitive, assertive, individualistic, and materialistic so as to be able to make their way in the world. The woman at home needed a compensatory set of character traits. Dependent and affectionate, she was also pious, pure, gentle, nurturant, benevolent, and sacrificing. Such "softer" virtues had been filtering in throughout the eighteenth century, especially in advice tracts destined for the upwardly mobile. But during the early nineteenth century, the softer virtues became accepted as innate. Women, moreover, compared to men, were believed to have a firmer grip on religion and morals, a virtual monopoly on piety and purity, a positive sense of moral superiority. In traditional society, women were not assumed to be superior to men in any way. Now, piety and purity provided some leverage. They also involved a new set of bargains between women and men.

PIETY AND PURITY

During the early nineteenth century, ministers provided a vital bolster to the doctrine of woman's sphere. They opposed those forces antithetical to women's interests—materialism, immorality, intemperance, and licentiousness. They helped to formulate a new definition of female character. Christian virtues—such as humility, submission, piety, and charity—were now, they suggested, primarily female virtues. Most important, ministers confirmed female moral superiority. Women might be the weaker members of society, but they were now assured that they exceeded men in spiritual fervor and moral strength.

Religion was also one of the few activities beyond the home in which women might participate without abdicating their sphere. Their participation in the churches was in fact vital. Women formed the majority of congregants. Accordingly, female piety, and even activism, were heartily encouraged by their ministers. "We look to you, ladies, to raise the standard of character in our own sex," announced New England clergyman Joseph Buckminster in an 1810 sermon. "We look to you for the continuance of domestick purity, for the revival of domestick religion, for the increase of our charities, and the support of what remains of religion in our private habits and publick institutions." Under such circumstances, a mutually dependent relationship developed between Protestant clerics and their middle-class female parishioners. Both saw themselves as outsiders in a society devoted to the pursuit of wealth, as allies who strove for morality in a competitive world. It was no accident that women's publications such as the *Ladies Magazine* counted on ministers for articles exalting the character of women. Ministers in turn depended on women for their loyal support.

Despite clergymen's persistent fears that their authority was diminishing, religion was not on the wane. Protestantism flourished during the early nineteenth century. The Second Great Awakening of the first quarter of the century was surpassed by the great evangelical crusades of the second. Presbyterians and Congregationalists attracted members in New England, fiery waves of revivals swept over New York state, westerners flocked to camp meetings on the frontier, and Baptists and Methodists made gains nationwide. According to some estimates, formal church membership tripled. Throughout all this fervor, women remained prominent. Their affinity for piety became evident in a spate of revivals at the start of the century. The Second Great Awakening marked the beginning of the new alliance between women and ministers as well as of their unstated bargain: clerical endorsement of female moral superiority in exchange for women's support and activism.

Female converts outnumbered male converts three to two in the Second Great Awakening in New England, and women formed the bulk of congregations thereafter. They played an equally prominent role in revival-swept western New York. By 1814, for instance, women outnumbered men in the churches and religious societies of bustling Utica, and they could be relied on to urge the conversion of family members. A mother's conversion, ministers learned, could lead to those of her children and husband; a daughter's conversion might soon create a pious family. The most zealous activists of these early revivals, significantly, were women of the new middle class—the wives and daughters of men who worked outside the home. Church membership became a boost to upward mobility. But female religiosity also moved down the social scale, to wives of artisans and farmers, just as it spread to other regions. On the midwestern frontier, it was women who could be counted on to form congregations, join religious societies, and demand Sabbath observance. Piety had become female property. When Englishwoman Frances Trollope investigated American society in the 1830s, she claimed that she had never seen a country "where religion had so strong a hold upon the women, or a slighter hold upon the men."

If religion had a hold on women, however, they in turn had a hold on the clergy. Through weight of numbers, women gained a genuine influence in Protestant churches that they lacked elsewhere. They contributed, for instance, to a softening of doctrine: the old idea of infant damnation had little appeal to American mothers. Ministers, accordingly, granted that Christian nurture could outweigh original sin. Discarding predestination as an axiom, ministers now suggested that mothers, not God, were responsible for their children's souls. The "feminization" of religion and of child rearing went hand in hand. Ministers bolstered the authority not only of the pious mother but of any pious woman, even the once insignificant daughter. Evangelical magazines, for instance, celebrated female influence in tales of dying daughters who, to the end, sought the conversion of relatives and friends. Social weakness, even fatal illness, was no obstacle to spiritual strength.

While ministers accorded women a new degree of influence, religious commitment offered other advantages. It also provided a community of peers outside the home, among like-minded women in church-related associations. The passivity of the convert, once she was united with her sisters, could be transformed into activist zeal. Early-nineteenth-century women provided the constituency for a multitude of societies formed under clerical auspices. They joined Bible and tract societies, which distributed pious literature, and Sabbath school unions, such as those endorsed in the *Ladies Magazine*, and missionary societies, which raised funds for pious endeavors. They formed charitable associations to aid the indigent and maternal associations to foster Christian motherhood. Through voluntary religious groups, women gained one another's company, new routes to participation in the world, and clerical approval. "While the pious female . . . does not aspire after things too great for her," a minister told a women's charitable society in 1815, "she discovers that there is wide field opened for the exercise of all her active powers."

In many ways, the evangelical Protestant experience was loaded with potential for women. Conversion encouraged introspection and self-attention. Cooperative efforts in church groups inspired a conscious sense of sisterhood and mutual interest. And clerical assurance of moral superiority supported a new degree of authority over others. But religious activism also had built-in limitations; clerical support meant clerical control. In the heat of revivals, as female piety assumed new significance, ministers warned women to avoid leadership roles as, for example, revivalists. Their piety was to be limited to the private role of personal persuasion; "influence" was contingent on acceptance of limits. As long as a woman kept to her "proper place," a tract society pamphlet explained in 1823, she might exert "almost any degree of influence she pleases." This was part of the implicit bargain between clergymen and women parishioners. It was also a fundamental tenet espoused by Sarah Hale in the *Ladies Magazine*.

If piety became a vital component of female character, so did purity, a word with several meanings. One was pas-sionlessness, or lack of sexual feeling. According to the doctrine of sphere, the sexes were distinguished by features that were not merely different but opposite. Lust and carnality were male characteristics, or liabilities. Women, less physical, more spiritual, and morally superior, were indeed closer to "angels." This was of course a new development. In traditional society, women, like men, were assumed to be sexual beings. Since weaker of will, they were often assumed to be even more lustful, licentious, and insatiable than men. But early in the nineteenth century, around the time of the Second Great Awakening, purity became a female bargaining point. Like piety, it was now a prerequisite for influence. Sermons often warned that if purity gave away, all of the perquisities of sphere were lost. "let her lay aside delicacy," a minister held in 1837, "and her influence over our sex is gone."

Though ministers were the first authorities to endorse the female virtue of purity, they were not the only ones. By mid-century, the medical profession also confirmed that passionlessness was an innate and commendable female characteristic. "The majority of women (happily for them)," physician William Acton stated in a much-quoted medical treatise, "are not much troubled with sexual feeling of any kind." There were dissenting opinions within the profession. But in medical manuals aimed at the upwardly mobile middle class, midcentury physicians usually emphasized the debilitating effects of sexual indulgence, recommended infrequent intercourse, opposed contraception, and confirmed female asexuality. They also assured women that their physical health, and social roles, were determined by their reproductive organs. Doctors explained that the uterus was linked to the female nervous system, and that any malfunction affected the entire body, causing a gamut of ailments—headaches, backaches, indigestion, insomnia, and nervous disorders. Women's unusual physiology, indeed, determined her emotions, character, and vocation. "Mentally, socially, spiritually, [woman] is more interior than a man," a Philadelphia physician concluded in the 1860s. "The house, the chamber, the closet, are the centers of her social life and power."

Like other components of woman's sphere, purity encompassed both sanctions and benefits. The sanctions were stressed in the advice literature directed at middle-class women. Etiquette manuals, for instance, counseled prudent behavior that would serve to deter male advances. "Sit not with another in a space that is too narrow," warned the *Young Ladies Friend*. Magazine fiction offered tales about girls who lacked discretion, were consequently victimized by male predators, and ended up ruined, impoverished, ostracized, or dead. Such proscriptions were related to significant changes in courtship customs, since incidence of premarital pregnancy sharply declined—from a high of almost 30 percent of first births in the late eighteenth century to a new low of under 10 percent in the mid-nineteenth century. This precipitous drop, historians contend, suggests the acceptance by both young men and women of a new ideology of sexual restraint. Convictions about female purity imposed limitations not only on women but men as well.

Purity was also a code word for a new degree of female sexual control within marriage. During the early nineteenth century, when the fertility of white women began its precipitous decline, the shrinking family became a hallmark of the new middle class. It may also have been a result of the new clout of wives within middle-class homes. Now imbued with moral superiority, wives gained a right of refusal, an escape from "submission," and power to limit the frequency of sexual relations. They also gained more control over the number of children they had. Available methods of family limitation (beyond folk remedies and patent medicines) were abstinence, as recommended in medical literature, and withdrawal, which was condemned; abortion was also a possible last resort, at least until later in the century when it was outlawed. Although abstinence was not the sole effective means of curbing births, it probably was in widespread use. And female purity was probably an ideal on which middle-class men and women agreed, an asset for the family that wanted to rise in the world—a family in which children were no longer economic assets but, rather, liabilities. In the early nineteenth century, sexual restraint appeared to both serve family goals and enhance women's autonomy within the home.

Convictions about female purity also affected women's relation to the medical profession. Connections between women and doctors were hardly as clear-cut as the unstated bargain between women and ministers. Physicians were a far newer source of authority. Medicine became a recognized profession only after the turn of the century. By the 1820s, all states except three had laws requiring medical practitioners to be licensed, and most licensing laws required graduation from medical college. As a result, women were excluded from medical practice, and mid-wifery, once a female monopoly, began a slow decline. In rural areas and on the frontier, midwives continued to deliver babies, and also among the urban poor. The rural midwife, indeed, remained in business into the twentieth century. But the urbanizing East set the trend for the future. During the early nineteenth century, middle-class mothers in towns and cities turned to physicians. No longer a public female ritual, childbirth became a private event with two main participants, a woman and a male professional.

The physician's new role in childbirth brought both loss and gain. The entourage of women relatives and friends who had once played a supportive part gradually vanished. But middle-class women seemed to appreciate the use of the forceps (the physician's prerogative) as the means of a faster delivery with less suffering. Mothers, indeed, became the doctor's prime constituency, since a successful obstetric practice paved the way for a profitable family practice. Moreover, with the rise of the medical profession, female ill health assumed new visibility.

Middle-class women of the early nineteenth century were distinguished by their debilitating illnesses—nervousness, anemia, hysteria, headaches, backaches. The marked rise in female illness, much of it never diagnosed, may have been connected to physical causes—such as the spread of venereal disease—or psychological ones. Women's dependent status could have had debilitating effects on their health. Sickness might also have had a positive function, providing reprieve from domestic work. In any case, physical fragility became a female liability. When Catherine Beecher surveyed women's health across the nation in the 1850s, she concluded that sick women outnumbered the healthy three to one.

Reporting from one Illinois town, Beecher gave her version of the terrible state of women's health.

> Mrs. H. an invalid. Mrs. G. scrufula, Mrs. W. liver complaint, Mrs. S. pelvic disorders, Mrs. B. pelvic deseases very badly. Mrs. B. not healthy. Mrs. T. very feeble. Mrs. G. cancer. Mrs. N. liver complaint. Do not know one healthy woman in the place.

If all the facts and details of women's diseases were known, Catherine Beecher claimed, "It would send a groan of terror and horror over the land."

Even when chronically ill, however, women did not completely trust their doctors. The professionalization of medicine did not ensure its competence. At midcentury, as historian Regina Morantz explains, medicine was in a state of crisis. "Heroic" medicine—bleeding and enormous doses of dangerous substances—was being discarded, but it had not yet been replaced by anything better. Not only were well trained doctors unlikely to be very effective, but few were well trained. During the 1830s, any profit-minded doctor could open a medical college and, however lax its standards, produce hundreds of graduates to be licensed. Women had especial reason to be wary. Since female complaints of all sorts were believed to stem from uterine malfunction, the woman patient might well be subjected to "local treatment"—a proceducre involving uterine cauterization, injection of solutions, even the insertion of leeches. Not surprisingly, "local treatment" seemed a dire assault on female purity. And not surprisingly, middle-class women sought alternatives.

One set of alternatives were nonmedical remedies or fads—Grahamism (diet reform), water cures, animal magnetism, or phrenology. The *Ladies Magazine*, for instance, ran many features on phrenology, complete with huge charts of the human skull. Middle-class women also took refuge at spas, joined ladies' physiological societies, where health and medicine were discussed and accepted the views of health reformers. The latter usually favored preventive measures that would preclude the need to resort to physicians at all—such as exercise, fresh air, baths, and cereals. Similar measures were endorsed in the medical columns of *Godey's Lady's Book*, written by doctors. Women also turned to irregular practitioners—unlicensed dispensers of remedies and advice, who might well be women. Dr. Harriot Hunt, for instance, went into practice in Boston with her sister in the 1830s, after an apprenticeship with other irregulars. Opposed to the "heroic" methods of the licensed profession, which rejected her, she prescribed homeopathic, preventive measures and became interested in the psychological causes of women's ailments. An even less regular practitioner, Mary Gove Nichols, once a contributor to the *Ladies Magazine*, became a water cure therapist and health reformer, catering, like Hunt, to a female clientele. Although not committed to the female passionlessness, these leading irregulars were committed to the protection of women from male depravity.

Another response to the professionalization of medicine was explained in *Godey's Ladiy's Book*. Women, wrote Sarah Hale, should be allowed to enter the medical profession in order to minister to women and children. Her argument for women doctors was based on the sanctity of sphere. Propriety and morality dictated that women should be examined by women. The woman physician, moreover, would raise the moral tone of the profession and open to women new avenues for practicing their altruism, benevolence, and sympathy. Through the entry of women into medicine, woman's sphere would be not destroyed but preserved. Hale lent especial support to Elizabeth Blackwell, the first woman medical college graduate and licensed woman physician. Like Hunt and Nichols, Blackwell was hardly a subscriber to the doctrine of female asexuality. She was, however, a crusader against prostitution and obscenity, and a supporter of the moral purity movement.

The doctrine of woman's sphere, and its redefinition of female character, could therefore be used as a bargaining tool. Piety, purity, and moral superiority could be mobilized to increase women's authority at home and demand more influence outside it. The doctrine of sphere could also be used to bolster other demands, such as that for "advanced" education. Although only a small proportion of Americans had any education beyond the primary level, an increasing number of them were women. Sending a daughter to an academy or seminary was now a perquisite of the expanding middle class.

NO
Gerda Lerner

THE LADY AND THE MILL GIRL: CHANGES IN THE STATUS OF WOMEN IN THE AGE OF JACKSON

The period 1800–1840 is one in which decisive changes occurred in the status of American women. It has remained surprisingly unexplored. With the exception of a recent, unpublished dissertation by Keith Melder and the distinctive work of Elisabeth Dexter, there is a dearth of descriptive material and an almost total absence of interpretation. Yet the period offers essential clues to an understanding of later institutional developments, particularly the shape and nature of the woman's rights movement. This analysis will consider the economic, political, and social status of women and examine the changes in each area. It will also attempt an interpretation of the ideological shifts which occurred in American society concerning the "proper" role for women.

Periodization always offers difficulties. It seemed useful here, for purposes of comparison, to group women's status before 1800 roughly under the "colonial" heading and ignore the transitional and possible atypical shifts which occurred during the American Revolution and the early period of nationhood. Also, regional differences were largely ignored. The South was left out of consideration entirely because its industrial development occurred later.

The status of colonial women has been well studied and described and can briefly be summarized for comparison with the later period. Throughout the colonial period there was a marked shortage of women, which varied with the regions and always was greatest in the frontier areas. This (from the point of view of women) favorable sex ratio enhanced their status and position. The Puritan world view regarded idleness as sin; life in an underdeveloped country made it absolutely necessary that each member of the community perform an economic function. Thus work for women, married or single, was not only approved, it was regarded as a civic duty. Puritan town councils expected single girls, widows, and unattached women to be self-supporting

From *American Studies* (Spring 1961). Copyright © 1961 American Studies. Reprinted by permission of American Studies and the author.

and for a long time provided needy spinsters with parcels of land. There was no social sanction against married women working; on the contrary, wives were expected to help their husbands in their trade and won social approval for doing extra work in or out of the home. Needy children, girls as well as boys, were indentured or apprenticed and were expected to work for their keep.

The vast majority of women worked within their homes, where their labor produced most articles needed for the family. The entire colonial production of cloth and clothing and in part that of shoes was in the hands of women. In addition to these occupations, women were found in many different kinds of employment. They were butchers, silversmiths, gunsmiths, upholsterers. They ran mills, plantations, tan yards, shipyards, and every kind of shop, tavern and boarding house. They were gate keepers, jail keepers, sextons, journalists, printers, "doctoresses," apothecaries, midwives, nurses, and teachers. Women acquired their skills the same way as did the men, through apprenticeship training, frequently within their own families.

Absence of a dowry, ease of marriage and remarriage, and a more lenient attitude of the law with regard to women's property rights were manifestations of the improved position of wives in the colonies. Under British common law, marriage destroyed a woman's contractual capacity; she could not sign a contract even with the consent of her husband. But colonial authorities were more lenient toward the wife's property rights by protecting her dower rights in her husband's property, granting her personal clothing, and upholding prenuptial contracts between husband and wife. In the absence of the husband,

colonial courts granted women "femme sole" rights, which enabled them to conduct their husband's business, sign contracts, and sue. The relative social freedom of women and the esteem in which they were held was commented upon by most early foreign travelers in America.

But economic, legal, and social status tells only part of the story. Colonial society as a whole was hierarchical, and rank and standing in society depended on the position of the men. Women did not play a determining role in the ranking pattern; they took their position in society through the men of their own family or the men they married. In other words, they participated in the hierarchy only as daughters and wives, not as individuals. Similarly, their occupations were, by and large, merely auxiliary, designed to contribute to family income, enhance their husbands' business or continue it in case of widowhood. The self-supporting spinsters were certainly the exception. The underlying assumption of colonial society was that women ought to occupy an inferior and subordinate position. The settlers had brought this assumption with them from Europe; it was reflected in their legal concepts, their willingness to exclude women from political life, their discriminatory educational practices. What is remarkable is the extent to which this felt inferiority of women was constantly challenged and modified under the impact of environment, frontier conditions, and favorable sex ratio.

By 1840 all of American society had changed. The Revolution had substituted an egalitarian ideology for the hierarchical concepts of colonial life. Privilege based on ability rather than inherited status, upward mobility for all groups of society, and unlimited opportunities for individual self-fulfillment had become ideological goals, if not always realities. For men, that is; women were, by tacit consensus, excluded from the new democracy. Indeed, their actual situation had in many respects deteriorated. While, as wives, they had benefitted from increasing wealth, urbanization, and industrialization, their role as economic producers and as political members of society differed sharply from that of men. Women's work outside of the home no longer met with social approval; on the contrary, with two notable exceptions, it was condemned. Many business and professional occupations formerly open to women were now closed, many others restricted as to training and advancement. The entry of large numbers of women into low status, low pay, and low skill industrial work had fixed such work by definition as "woman's work." Women's political status, while legally unchanged, had deteriorated relative to the advances made by men. At the same time the genteel lady of fashion had become a model of American femininity, and the definition of "woman's proper sphere" seemed narrower and more confined than ever.

Within the scope of this essay only a few of these changes can be more fully explained. The professionalization of medicine and its impact on women may serve as a typical example of what occurred in all the professions.

In colonial America there were no medical schools, no medical journals, few hospitals, and few laws pertaining to the practice of the healing arts. Clergymen and governors, barbers, quacks, apprentices, and women practiced medicine. Most practitioners acquired their credentials by reading Paracelsus and Galen and serving an apprenticeship with an established practitioner. Among the semi-trained "physics," surgeons, and healers, the occasional "doctoress" was fully accepted and frequently well rewarded. County records of all the colonies contain references to the work of the female physicians. There was even a female Army surgeon, a Mrs. Allyn, who served during King Philip's war. Plantation records mention by name several slave women who were granted special privileges because of their useful service as midwives and "doctoresses."

The period of the professionalization of American medicine dates from 1765, when Dr. William Shippen began his lectures on midwifery in Philadelphia. The founding of medical faculties in several colleges, the standardization of training requirements, and the proliferation of medical societies intensified during the last quarter of the 18th century. The American Revolution dramatized the need for trained medical personnel, afforded first-hand battlefield experience to a number of surgeons and brought increasing numbers of semi-trained practitioners in contact with the handful of European-trained surgeons working in the military hospitals. This was an experience from which women were excluded. The resulting interest in improved medical training, the gradual appearance of graduates of medical colleges, and the efforts of medical societies led to licensing legislation. In 1801 Maryland required all medical practitioners to be licensed; in 1806 New York enacted a similar law, followed by all but three states. This trend was reversed in the 1830s and 40s when most states repealed their licensure requirements. This was due to pressure from eclectic, homeopathic practitioners, the public's dissatisfaction with the "heroic medicine" then practiced by licensed physicians, and to the distrust of state regulation, which was widespread during the Age of Jackson. Licensure as prime proof of qualification for the practice of medicine was reinstituted in the 1870s.

In the middle of the 19th century it was not so much a license of an M.D. which marked the professional physician as it was graduation from an approved medical college, admission to hospital practice and to a network of referrals through other physicians. In 1800 there were four medical schools, in 1850, forty-two. Almost all of them excluded women from admission. Not surprisingly, women turned to eclectic schools for training. Harriot Hunt, a Boston physician, was trained by apprenticeship with a husband and wife team of homeopathic physicians. After more than twenty years of practice she attempted to enter Harvard Medical school and was repeatedly rebuffed. Elizabeth Blackwell received her M.D. from Geneva (New York) Medical College, an eclectic school. Sarah Adamson found all regular medical schools closed against her and earned an M.D. in 1851 from Central College at Syracuse, an eclectic institution. Clemence Lozier graduated from the same school two years later and went on to found the New York Medical College and Hospital for women in 1862, a homeopathic institution which was later absorbed into the Flower-Fifth Avenue Hospital.

Another way in which professionalization worked to the detriment of women can be seen in the cases of Drs. Elizabeth and Emily Blackwell, Marie Zakrzewska, and Ann Preston, who despite their M.D.s and excellent training were denied access to hospitals, were refused recognition by county medical societies, and were denied customary referrals by male colleagues. Their experiences were similar to those of most of the pioneer women physicians. Such discrimination caused the formation of alternate institutions for the training of women physicians and for hospitals in which they might treat their patients. The point here is not so much that any one aspect of the process of professionalization excluded women but that the process, which took place over the span of almost a century, proceeded in such a way as to institutionalize an exclusion of women, which had earlier been accomplished irregularly, inconsistently, and mostly by means of social pressure. The end result was an *absolute* lowering of status for all women in the medical profession and a *relative* loss. As the professional status of all physicians advanced, the status differential between male and female practitioners was more obviously disadvantageous and underscored women's marginality. Their vital exclusion from the most prestigious and lucrative branches of the profession and their concentration in specializations relating to women and children made such disadvantaging more obvious by the end of the 19th century.

This process of pre-emption of knowledge, of institutionalization of the profession, and of legitimation of its claims by law and public acceptance is standard for the professionalization of the sciences, as George Daniels has pointed out. It inevitably results in the elimination of fringe elements from the profession. It is interesting to note that women had been pushed out of the medical profession in 16th-century Europe by a similar process. Once the public had come to accept licensing and college training as guarantees of up-to-date practice, the outsider, no mater how well qualified by years of experience, stood no chance in the competition. Women were the casualties of medical professionalization.

In the field of midwifery the results were similar, but the process was more complicated. Women had held a virtual monopoly in the profession in colonial America. In 1646 a man was prosecuted in Maine for practicing as a midwife. There are many records of well-trained midwives with diplomas from European institutions working in the colonies. In most of the colonies midwives were licensed, registered, and required to pass an examination before a board. When Dr. Shippen announced his pioneering lectures on midwifery, he did it to "combat the widespread popular prejudice against the man-midwife" and because he considered most midwives ignorant and improperly trained.

Yet he invited "those women who love virtue enough, to own their Ignorance, and apply for instruction" to attend his lectures, offering as an inducement the assurance that female pupils would be taught privately. It is not known if any midwives availed themselves of the opportunity.

Technological advances, as well as scientific, worked against the interests of female midwives. In 16th-century Europe the invention and use of obstetrical forceps had for three generations been the well-kept secret of the Chamberlen family and had greatly enhanced their medical practice. Hugh Chamberlen was forced by circumstances to sell the secret to the Medical College in Amsterdam, which in turn transmitted the precious knowledge to licensed physicians only. By the time the use of the instrument became widespread, it had become associated with male physicians and male midwives. Similarly in America, introduction of the obstetrical forceps was associated with the practice of male midwives and served to their advantage. By the end of the 18th century a number of male physicians advertised their practice of midwifery. Shortly thereafter female midwives also resorted to advertising, probably in an effort to meet the competition. By the early 19th century male physicians had virtually monopolized the practice of midwifery on the Eastern seaboard. True to the generally delayed economic development in the Western frontier regions, female midwives continued to work on the frontier until a much later period. It is interesting to note that the concepts of "propriety" shifted with the prevalent practice. In 17th-century Maine the attempt of a man to act as a midwife was considered outrageous and illegal; in mid-19th-century America the suggestion that women should train as midwives and physicians was considered equally outrageous and improper.

Professionalization, similar to that in medicine with the elimination of women from the upgraded profession, occurred in the field of law. Before 1750, when law suits were commonly brought to the courts by the plaintiffs themselves or by deputies without specialized legal training, women as well as men could and did act as "attorneys-in-fact." When the law became a paid profession and trained lawyers took over litigation, women disappeared from the court scene for over a century.

A similar process of shrinking opportunities for women developed in business and in the retail trades. There were fewer female storekeepers and business women in the 1830s than there had been in colonial days. There was also a noticeable shift in the kind of merchandise handled by them. Where previously women could be found running almost every kind of retail shop, after 1830 they were mostly found in businesses which served women only.

The only fields in which professionalization did not result in the elimination of women from the upgraded profession were nursing and teaching. Both were characterized by a severe shortage of labor. Nursing lies outside the field of this inquiry, since it did not become an organized profession until after the Civil War. Before then, it was regarded peculiarly as a woman's occupation, although some of the hospitals and the Army during wars employed male nurses. These bore the stigma of low skill, low status, and low pay. Generally, nursing was regarded as simply an extension of the unpaid services performed by the housewife—a characteristic attitude that haunts the profession to this day.

Education seems, at first glance, to offer an entirely opposite pattern from that of the other professions. In colonial days women had taught "Dame schools" and grade schools during summer sessions. Gradually, as educational opportunities for girls expanded, they advanced just a step ahead of their students. Professionalization of teaching occurred between 1820 and 1860, a period marked by a sharp increase in the number of women teachers. The spread of female seminaries, academies, and normal schools provided new opportunities for the training and employment of female teachers.

This trend, which runs counter to that found in the other professions, can be accounted for by the fact that women filled a desperate need created by the challenge of the common schools, the ever-increasing size of the student body, and the westward growth of the nation. America was committed to educating its children in public schools, but it was insistent on doing so as cheaply as possible. Women were available in great numbers, and they were willing to work cheaply. The result was another ideological adaptation: in the very period when the gospel of the home as woman's proper sphere was preached most loudly, it was discovered that women were the natural teachers of youth, could do the job better than men, and were to be preferred for such employment. This was always provided, of course, that they would work at the proper wage differential—30 to 50 percent of the wages paid male teachers was considered appropriate. The result was that in 1888 in the country as a whole 63 percent of all teachers were women, while the figure for the cities only was 90.04 percent.

It appeared in the teaching field, as it would in industry, that role expectations were adaptable provided the inferior status group filled a social need. The inconsistent and peculiar patterns of employment of black labor in the present-day market bear out the validity of this generalization.

There was another field in which the labor of women was appreciated and which they were urged to enter—industry. From Alexander Hamilton to Matthew Carey and Tench Coxe, advocates of industrialization sang the praises of the working girl and advanced arguments in favor of her employment. The social benefits of female labor particularly stressed were those bestowed upon her family, who now no longer had to support her. Working girls were "thus happily preserved from idleness and its attendant vices and crimes," and the whole community benefitted from their increased purchasing power.

American industrialization, which occurred in an underdeveloped economy with a shortage of labor, depended on the labor of women and children. Men were occupied with agricultural work and were not available or were unwilling to enter the factories. This accounts for the special features of the early development of the New England textile industry: the relatively high wages, the respectability of the job and relatively high status of the mill girls, the patriarchal character of the model factory towns, and the temporary mobility of women workers from farm to factory and back again to farm. All this was characteristic only of a limited area and of a period of about two decades. By the late 1830s the romance had won off: immigration had supplied a strongly competitive, permanent work force willing to work for subsistence wages; early efforts at trade union organization had been shattered, and mechanization had turned semiskilled factory labor into unskilled labor. The process led to the replacement of the New England-born farm girls by immigrants in the mills and was accompanied by a loss of status and respectability for female workers.

The lack of organized social services during periods of depression drove ever greater numbers of women into the labor market. At first, inside the factories distinctions between men's and women's jobs were blurred. Men and women were assigned to machinery on the basis of local need. But as more women entered industry the limited number of occupations open to them tended to increase competition among them, thus lowering pay standards. Generally, women regarded their work as temporary and hesitated to invest in apprenticeship training, because they expected to marry and raise families. Thus they remained untrained, casual labor and were soon, by custom, relegated to the lowest paid, least skilled jobs. Long hours, overwork, and poor working conditions would characterize women's work in industry for almost a century.

POSTSCRIPT

Did Women Achieve Greater Autonomy in the New Nation?

Disenchanted with lost economic opportunities and a relative deterioration in their political status, many women in the "age of Jackson" began to channel their frustration into a variety of reform efforts. Causes such as the abolition of slavery and the prohibition of alcohol attracted numerous female participants and offered women opportunities to exercise their leadership abilities. Several outstanding women later turned their attention from temperance and racial injustice to the benefit of their own sex. Lucretia Mott, Sarah and Angelina Grimke, Susan B. Anthony, and Elizabeth Cady Stanton organized their sisters to pursue the rights of women. In light of the favorable conditions attributed to middle-class women by Professor Woloch, it is significant that, according to Lerner, the women's rights movement was dominated by middle-class concerns. These concerns were clarified in 1848 by the Women's Rights Convention in Seneca Falls, New York. Here Elizabeth Cady Stanton presented the Declaration and Sentiments and Resolutions, which proclaimed that "all men and women are created equal" and which included a proposal for women's suffrage. That the struggle for voting rights would be a long, uphill battle was indicated by an article published in *Harper's Monthly Magazine* in 1853. Women's suffrage, the author wrote, "is avowedly opposed to the most time-honored propensities of social life; it is opposed to nature; it is opposed to revelation. . . . This unblushing female Socialism defies alike apostles and prophets. In this respect no kindred movement is so decidedly infidel, so rancorously and avowedly anti-biblical. . . . It is equally opposed to nature and the established order of society founded upon it."

There is a large and growing historiography of American women. In addition to the surveys by Sochen, Ryan, and Woloch cited in the postscript to Issue 3, students should consult Carl N. Degler, *At Odds: Women and the Family in America from the Revolution to the Present* (Oxford University Press, 1980). Barbara Welter, "The Cult of True Womanhood, 1820–1860," *American Quarterly* (Summer 1966) analyzes a concept addressed in both the Woloch and Lerner essays. Thomas Dublin, *Women at Work: The Transformation of Work and Community in Lowell, Massachusetts, 1826–1860* (Columbia University Press, 1979) and Alice Kessler-Harris, *Out to Work: A History of Wage-Earning Women in the United States* (Oxford University Press, 1982) focus upon the significant role played by working-class women. Hasia R. Diner, *Erin's Daughters in America: Irish Immigrant Women in the Nineteenth Century* (Johns Hopkins Press, 1983) is an important reminder that women outnumbered men in the Irish migration and, thus, deserve as much attention as their male counterparts have received from historians in the past. The lives of women in the South are assessed in two marvelous studies: Catherine Clinton, *The Plantation Mistress* (Pantheon, 1982), which attempts to overturn popular myths about this group; and Suzanne Lebsock, *The Free Women of Petersburg: Status and Culture in a Southern Town, 1784–1860* (Norton, 1984), which suggests a steady increase in the economic autonomy of Southern women, white *and* black. For another work treating the status of black women in the antebellum period, see Dorothy Sterling, ed., *We Are Your Sisters: Black Women in the Nineteenth Century* (Norton, 1984). For important studies related to the rise of the woman's movement and the reform activities of antebellum women, see Barbara J. Berg, *The Remembered Gate: Origins of American Feminism—The Woman and the City, 1800–1860* (Oxford University Press, 1978); Gerda Lerner, *The Grimke Sisters from Southern Carolina: Pioneers for Woman's Rights and Abolition* (Houghton Mifflin, 1967); Ellen C. Du Bois, *Feminism and Suffrage: The Emergence of an Independent Woman's Movement in America, 1848–1869* (Cornell University Press, 1978); and Barbara Leslie Epstein, *The Politics of Domesticity: Women, Evangelism, and Temperance in Nineteenth-Century America* (Wesleyan University Press, 1981).

PART 3

Antebellum America

Pressures and trends that began building in the early years of the American nation continued to gather momentum until conflict was almost inevitable. America had to respond to challenges from members of society who felt alienated from or forgotten by the new nation. The ideals of human rights and democratic participation that guided the founding of the nation had been applied only to selected segments of the population. Changes in the nature of the voting population and the ways in which Americans viewed their place in the world had dramatic implications for the future. The level and quality of participation in the "American experiment" by disenfranchised or disaffected members of the society became an important issue for America.

Did the Election of 1828 Represent a Democratic Revolt of the People?

Was Antebellum Reform Motivated Primarily by Humanitarian Goals?

Was U.S. Foreign Policy in the Early Nineteenth Century Imperialistic?

Did Slavery Destroy the Black Family?

San Jacinto Museum of History Association

199

ISSUE 10

Did the Election of 1828 Represent a Democratic Revolt of the People?

YES: Robert V. Remini, from "Election of 1828," Arthur M. Schlesigner, Jr., ed., *The Coming to Power: Critical Presidential Elections in American History* (McGraw-Hill, 1972)

NO: Richard P. McCormick, from "New Perspectives on Jacksonian Politics," *American Historical Review* (January 1960)

ISSUE SUMMARY

YES: Professor Robert V. Remini argues that the 1828 presidential election symbolized the people's arrival at political responsibility and began a genuine, nationally organized, two-party system that came of age in the 1830s.
NO: Historian Richard P. McCormick maintains that voting statistics demonstrate that a genuine political revolution did not take place until the presidential elections of 1840, when fairly well-balanced political parties had been organized in virtually every state.

According to conventional wisdom, Andrew Jackson's election to the presidency in 1828 began the era of the common man, in which the mass of voters, no longer restrained from voting by property requirements, rose up and threw the elite leaders out of our nation's capital. While recent historians are not quite sure what constituted Jacksonian democracy or who supported it, and they question whether there ever existed such an era of egalitarianism, American history textbooks still include the obligatory chapter on the age of Jackson.

There are several reasons the old-fashioned view of this period still prevails. In spite of the new scholarly interest in social history, it is still easier to generalize about political events. Consequently, most texts continue to devote the major portion of their pages to detailed examinations of the successes and failures of various presidential administrations. Whether Jackson was more significant than other presidents is difficult to assess because "Old Hickory's" forceful personality, compounded with his use of strong executive authority, engendered constant controversy in his eight years in office.

Another reason the traditional concept of Jacksonian democracy has not been abandoned is because critics of the progressive interpretation have not been able to come up with an acceptable alternative view. Culminating with Arthur Schlesigner, Jr.'s, Pulitzer Prize-winning and beautifully written *The Age of Jackson* (Little, Brown, 1945), the progressive historians viewed Jackson's election in 1828 as the triumph of the common man in politics. Oversimplified as this interpretation may be, there is little doubt that a major change was taking place in our political system during these years. The death of both Thomas Jefferson and John Adams on July 4, 1826, the fiftieth anniversary of the U.S. Declaration of Independence from England, signified the end of the revolutionary generation's control over American politics. The first six presidents had been leaders or descendants of leaders in the revolutionary movement. At the Constitutional Convention in 1787, most of the time was spent discussing the powers of the presidency. Because of their experiences with the British king, the Founding Fathers were fearful of strong executive authority. Therefore, the presidency was entrusted only to those individuals whose loyalty remained unquestioned. Jackson was the first president of the United States who did not come from either Virginia or Massachusetts. Though Jackson was only a teenager at the time of the American Revolution, his career was similar to those of the early Founding Fathers. Like Washington and Jefferson, Jackson became a living legend before he was fifty years old. His exploits as an Indian fighter and the military hero of the Battle of New Orleans in the War of 1812 were more important than his western background in making him presidential material.

During the past two decades, a number of historians have studied the effects of presidential elections on the development and maintenance of our two-party system. Borrowing concepts and analytical techniques from political scientists and sociologists, the "new political" historians have demonstrated the effectiveness of our parties in selecting candidates, running campaigns, developing legislation, and legitimizing conflicts within our democratic system. By 1815, the first-party system of competition between the Federalists and the Republican-Democrats had broken down, in part because the Federalists had refused to become a legitimate opposition party. A second-party system developed during the Jackson era between Old Hickory's Democratic party and his Whig opponents. It lasted until the 1850s when the slavery issue led to the formation of a new system of party competition between Republicans and Democrats.

The following selections disagree on the significance of the 1828 presidential race as a critical election in the development of the second-party system. Professor Robert Remini agues that the 1828 presidential election symbolized the people's arrival at full political responsibility and began a genuine, nationally organized, two-party system that matured in the 1830s. But historian Richard McCormick revises the traditional interpretation. His analysis of the voting statistics demonstrates that a genuine political revolution did not take place until the presidential election of 1840 when fairly well-balanced parties had been organized in virtually every state.

YES

Robert V. Remini

JACKSON, CALHOUN, AND LIBERTY

Jackson's appearance on the national scene in larger-than-life size was indeed fortuitous. He arrived just as the country was undergoing profound economic and political changes, when a new generation of men was coming forward to seize leadership from an older social and political elite. These men saw in Jackson a symbol of their own ambitions; they also saw in him a living example of the self-made man. Surely if an orphan boy from the backwoods could make good, there was no reason why they too could not aspire to wealth and social status by relying on their own talents to get what they wanted.

Furthermore, this was an age of developing professionalism in all fields—including politics. In the 1820s, men were hard at work perfecting the techniques of winning elections. They built machines to manage the popular vote; they believed in organization; and they were determined to rule. As sharp-nosed professionals, like Van Buren, they were quick to sense the response the General's popularity produced among the "rising" classes of Americans and to realize that association with Jackson might be crucial to their future position in politics, both nationally and locally. Small wonder, then, that Van Buren decided in the winter of 1826-27 to move into the Jackson camp and to bring with him as many of the Old Republicans as he could influence. "If Gen Jackson & his friends will put his election on old party grounds," Van Buren wrote to one Radical, "preserve the old systems, avoid if not condemn the practices of the last campaign we can by adding his personal popularity to the yet remaining force of old party feeling, not only succeed in electing him but our success when achieved will be worth something."

Since Jackson had resigned his Senate seat after his House defeat and was therefore not in Washington, Van Buren went to Vice-President Calhoun, who was now openly allied to the General, and offered him Radical support for the election of Jackson in 1828. Van Buren promised to swing over the Richmond Junto, the Virginia political machine, through his influence with

From *The Coming to Power*, ed. Arthur Schlesinger, Jr. (New York: McGraw-Hill, 1972). Reprinted by permission.

Thomas Ritchie, editor of the Richmond *Enquirer* and a leader of the Junto. He also promised to tour the South and do everything possible to bring the entire Old Republican faction into the new coalition, even to the extent of seeing Crawford and winning his support. During their conversation about this alliance, Calhoun and Van Buren also discussed the possibility of holding a national nominating convention to replace the outmoded caucus system, but nothing definite was decided at this time.

In a subsequent letter to Ritchie, Van Buren clearly stated that his concern for the political scene went further than a single election. He urged the Radicals to join him in this new coalition, not simply to defeat Adams but to achieve "what is of still greater importance, the substantial reorganization of the Old Republican party." He called for a revival of the two-party system and for a renewal of Jefferson's old North-South alliance, between what he termed the "planters of the South and the plain Republicans of the North." For Van Buren, like many other politicians of the day, recognized that the political system of the 1820s had failed to respond to a changing society and that unless something were done right away it might collapse altogether.

Because of the efforts of many men to restructure the system, the election of 1828 witnessed the reemergence of the two-party system, in American politics. The Jackson-Calhoun-Van Buren coalition eventually became known as the "Democratic" Republican party, or simply the Democratic party, while the Adams-Clay combination was called the "National" Republican party. With respect to party principles—not that they were much discussed in the campaign of 1828—the Democrats tended, when prodded, to restate the doctrines of Jefferson, particularly those emphasizing the rights of the states and the importance of the ordinary citizen. The National Republicans, on the other hand, affirmed the need for a strong central government in advancing the material well-being of the nation. Although there continued to be personal factions and cliques operating within the system, and while party organization did not advance in every state with equal rapidity, still in 1828 there was the beginning of a genuine, nationally organized, two-party system, a system that came of age in the 1830s. . . .

Balloting in the election extended from September to November. In most states, voting occurred over a period of several days. The states did not provide an official ballot; instead, the parties printed their own ballots, distributing them to friends and employing high-pressure party hacks at the polls to get the voter to accept the ticket. It was not unusual for a person to be accosted by several hawkers at once and threatened with bodily harm unless he accepted the proffered ballot.

The procedures for voting varied considerably throughout the twenty-four states. Delaware and South Carolina were the only states whose legislatures chose the electors. In all other states, they were chosen from a general or district ticket by an electorate that was roughly equivalent—except in Louisiana, Virginia, and Rhode Island—to the adult, white male population. Maryland, Maine, Illinois, Tennessee, and New York were the states using the district system, which meant that their electoral votes could be split between the candidates on a proportional basis. In all other states where the general ticket was employed, the candidate with the highest popular vote received all the electoral votes. Only

Rhode Island and Virginia continued to restrict suffrage with property qualifications, and Louisiana maintained tax payments as a voting requirement.

When the election ended and the ballots were counted, it was clear that Jackson had won a stupendous victory. Out of a total of 1,155,022 popular votes cast, John Quincy Adams received 507,730; Andrew Jackson won 647,292 or just a little better than 56 per cent of the entire vote. This was an extraordinary achievement by Jackson, a veritable landslide. In percentages it was unequalled in any presidential election during the nineteenth century. And his total represented substantial support from all sections of this country, including New England.

The total popular vote in the election represented an increase of nearly eight hundred thousand over the previous election in 1824. In Pennsylvania alone, the number rose from forty-seven thousand to 152,000 four years later. There were several reasons for this spectacular rise. In the first place, the two-party system had been reestablished, if unevenly, and where in 1824 there were several candidates running for the Presidency there were only two in 1828. Second, there was considerable interest in the election generated to a large extent by an exciting, if not scurrilous, campaign initiated by both the Democratic and National Republican parties. Third, there was a concerted effort on the part of many politicians to get out the vote at election time; and finally, four states, representing a considerable electorate, changed their laws and transferred the selection of electors from the legislature to the people.

In the Electoral College, Jackson's victory was even more impressive. He won a total of 178 electoral votes to 83 for Adams. He swept everything south of the Potomac River and west of New Jersey. Adams carried New England (except for a single electoral vote in Maine), Delaware, New Jersey, and most of Maryland. Adams and Jackson shared New York, with the General taking 20 of the state's 36 electoral votes. All the remaining states went to Old Hickory. The election was relatively close in New Hampshire, New York, New Jersey, Maryland, Kentucky, Louisiana, Ohio, and Indiana. In the final analysis, what made the difference in virtually every one of these states was superior party organization.

In the Vice-Presidential race, Calhoun won an easy reelection over Richard Rush, but received 7 fewer electoral votes than Jackson, because Georgia, which resented Calhoun's treatment of William H. Crawford when they sat in Monroe's Cabinet together, awarded 7 votes to Senator William C. Smith of South Carolina.

Aside from the importance of party in producing Jackson's triumph there was also his own popularity and charisma. He was a living, authentic legend, the victor of New Orleans, the man who won over the British, the greatest feat of arms in American history. Moreover, there was a dignity and bearing about him that bespoke leadership and authority. He was "presidential-looking," more so than any other public figure of the day. He inspired confidence among the largest mass of voters despite his lack of education and his reputation as an untamed westerner. In that sense Jackson himself was the essential issue in the campaign, just as he would be again in 1832, and the people in "vast numbers" crowded to his side.

Recently, however, some historians have questioned the vastness of the 1828 victory.

Comparing the statistics of this election with previous state elections and future presidential elections, one historian has raised serious doubts as to whether the people poured out to the polls to express their confidence in Jackson. Perhaps it is possible to make meaningful comparisons between a presidential election and a state election for local officers held at different times or two presidential elections separated by a dozen or more years. And perhaps not. But in any event the fact remains that no matter how the statistics are analyzed or interpreted the people themselves who lived at the time believed that Jackson's election represented a great surge of popular support for the General. They believed that the ordinary citizen, the so-called "common man," who were farmers, workers, frontiersmen, and the like, had seized the opportunity to express their political opinion by voting for Jackson. And what is believed by the electorate is frequently more important than the objective reality. Many Democratic politicians, of course, saw the contest as one between "farmers & mechanics of the country" on one hand and the "rich and well born" on the other, "between the *aristocracy* and democracy of America." Thus when they read the returns from such states as Pennsylvania, Virginia, North Carolina, Ohio, and elsewhere they were astounded by the figures and therefore convinced of the truth of their own propaganda.

Not only did the Democrats see the election as a victory produced by the "vast numbers" of American people, but the National Republicans thought so too. That is what is even more astonishing. "Well," sighed one of them, "a great revolution has taken place. . . . This is what I all along feared but to a much

greater extent." "It was the howl of raving Democracy" wrote another, "that tiped /sic/ Pennsylvania & New York & Ohio—and this will be kept up here after to promote the ends of the /Democratic party./" "All our efforts," said one of Clay's friends, "have not withstood the Torrent." Hezekiah Niles in his newspaper credited Jackson's "triumphant victory" to the "ardor of thousands." And Edward Everett of Massachusetts, one of Adams' most dedicated supporters in Congress, explained to his brother that the General won "by a majority of more than *two* to *one*, an event astounding to the friends of the Administration and unexpected by the General himself and his friends. . . . /They/ are embarrassed with the vastness of their triumph and the numbers of their party."

Generations of historians, therefore, have interpreted Jackson's election in 1828 as the beginning of the "rise of the common man" in American history. Of course, such an easy and sweeping generalization does not take into consideration the fact that the "common man" had been rising for generations, and had made notable political advances long before Jackson appeared on the scene. Yet this election seemed to symbolize the people's arrival to political responsibility. Whether or not this was objectively true hardly mattered; what mattered was an expressed sense of participation in the electoral process experienced by ordinary citizens and that because of it a true "man of the people" had at last been elected President of the United States.

The notion of a popular "uprising" in Jackson's favor was strengthened by the scenes that occurred during his inauguration as President on March 4, 1829. Some twenty thousand people from all parts of the country converged on Washington to witness the triumph of their candidate. It was "like the inundation of the northern barbarians into Rome," wrote one, "save that the tumultuous tide came in from a different point of the compass." Daniel Webster was dumbfounded at the scene. "I never saw such a crowd here before," he said. "Persons have come five hundred miles to see General Jackson, *and they really seem to think that the country is rescued from some dreadful danger."*

NO

Richard P. McCormick

NEW PERSPECTIVES
ON JACKSONIAN POLITICS

The historical phenomenon that we have come to call Jacksonian democracy has long engaged the attention of American political historians, and never more insistently than in the past decade. From the time of Parton and Bancroft to the present day, scholars have recognized that a profoundly significant change took place in the climate of politics simultaneously with the appearance of Andrew Jackson on the presidential scene. They have sensed that a full understanding of the nature of that change might enable them to dissolve some of the mysteries that envelop the operation of the American democratic process. With such a challenging goal before them, they have pursued their investigations with uncommon intensity and with a keen awareness of the contemporary relevance of their findings. . . .

That a "new democracy, ignorant, impulsive, irrational" entered the arena of politics in the Jackson era has become one of the few unchallenged "facts" in an otherwise controversial field. Differences of opinion occur only when attempts are made to account for the remarkable increase in the size of the active electorate. The commonest explanations have emphasized the assertion by the common man of his newly won political privileges, the democratic influences that arose out of the western frontier, or the magnetic attractiveness of Jackson as a candidate capable of appealing with singular effectiveness to the backwoods hunter, the plain farmer, the urban working-man, and the southern planter.

Probably because the image of "mighty democratic uprising" has been so universally agreed upon, there has been virtually no effort made to describe precisely the dimensions of the "uprising." Inquiry into this aspect of Jacksonian democracy has been discouraged by a common misconception regarding voter behavior before 1824. As the authors of one of our most recent and best textbooks put it: "In the years from the beginning of the government to 1824, a period for which we have no reliable election statistics, only small numbers of citizens seemed to have bothered to go to the polls."

From the *American Historical Review* (January 1960). Reprinted by permission.

Actually, abundant data on pre-1824 elections is available, and it indicates a far higher rate of voting than has been realized. Only by taking this data into consideration can voting behavior after 1824 be placed in proper perspective.

The question of whether there was indeed a "mighty democratic uprising" during the Jackson era is certainly crucial in any analysis of the political character of Jacksonian democracy. More broadly, however, we need to know the degree to which potential voters participated in elections before, during, and after the period of Jackson's presidency as well as the conditions that apparently influenced the rate of voting. Only when such factors have been analyzed can we arrive at firm conclusions with respect to the dimensions of the political changes that we associate with Jacksonian democracy. Obviously in studying voter participation we are dealing with but one aspect of a large problem, and the limitations imposed by such a restrictive focus should be apparent.

In measuring the magnitude of the vote in the Jackson elections it is hardly significant to use the total popular vote cast throughout the nation. A comparison of the total vote cast in 1812, for example, when in eight of the seventeen states electors were chosen by the legislature, with the vote in 1832, when every state except South Carolina chose its electors by popular vote, has limited meaning. Neither is it revealing to compare the total vote in 1824 with that in 1832 without taking into consideration the population increase during the interval. The shift from the legislative choice of electors to their election by popular vote, together with the steady population growth, obviously swelled the presidential vote. But the problem to be investigated is whether the Jackson elections brought voters to the polls in such enlarged or unprecedented proportions as to indicate that a "new democracy" had burst upon the political scene.

The most practicable method for measuring the degree to which voters participated in elections over a period of time is to relate the number of votes cast to the number of potential voters. Although there is no way of calculating precisely how many eligible voters there were in any state at a given time, the evidence at hand demonstrates that with the exception of Rhode Island, Virginia, and Louisiana the potential electorate after 1824 was roughly equivalent to the adult white male population. A meaningful way of expressing the rate of voter participation, then, is to state it in terms of the percentage of the adult white males actually voting. This index can be employed to measure the variations that occurred in voter participation over a period of time and in both national and state elections. Consequently a basis is provided for comparing the rate of voting in the Jackson elections with other presidential elections before and after his regime as well as with state elections.

Using this approach it is possible, first of all, to ascertain whether or not voter participation rose markedly in the three presidential elections in which Jackson was a candidate. Did voter participation in these elections so far exceed the peek participation in the pre-1824 elections so as to suggest that a mighty democratic uprising was taking place? . . .

In the 1824 election not a single one of the eighteen states in which the electors were chosen by popular vote attained the percentage of voter participation that had been reached before 1824. Prior to that critical election, fifteen of those eighteen states had recorded votes in excess of 50 per cent of their adult white male population, but in 1824 only two states—Maryland and Alabama—exceeded this modest mark. The average rate of voter participation in the election was 26.5 per cent. This hardly fits the image of the "roaring flood of the new democracy . . . foaming perilously near the crest. . . ."

There would seem to be persuasive evidence that in 1828 the common man flocked to the polls in unprecedented numbers, for the proportion of adult white males voting soared to 56.3 per cent, more than double the 1824 figure. But this outpouring shrinks in magnitude when we observe that in only six of the twenty-two states involved were new highs in voter participation established. In three of these—Maryland, Virginia, and Louisiana—the recorded gain was inconsiderable, and in a fourth—New York—the bulk of the increase might be attributed to changes that had been made in suffrage qualifications as recently as 1821 and 1826. Six states went over the 70 per cent mark, whereas ten had bettered that performance before 1824. Instead of a "mighty democratic uprising" there was in 1828 a voter turnout that approached—but in only a few instances matched or exceeded—the maximum levels that had been attained before the Jackson era.

The advance that was registered in 1828 did not carry forward to 1832. Despite the fact that Jackson was probably at the peak of his personal popularity, that he was engaged in a campaign that was presumably to decide issues of great magnitude, and that in the opinion of some authorities a "well-developed two-party system on a national scale" had been established, there was a slight de-

cline in voter participation. The average for the twenty-three states participating in the presidential contest was 54.9 per cent. In fifteen states a smaller percentage of the adult white males went to the polls in 1832 than in 1828. Only five states bettered their pre-1824 highs. Again the conclusion would be that it was essentially the pre-1824 electorate—diminished in most states and augmented in a few—that voted in 1832. Thus, after three Jackson elections, sixteen states had not achieved the proportions of voter participation that they had reached before 1824. The "new democracy" had not yet made its appearance. . . .

When an examination is made of voting in other than presidential elections prior to 1824, the inaccuracy of the impression that "only small numbers of citizens" went to the polls becomes apparent. Because of the almost automatic succession of the members of the "Virginia dynasty" and the early deterioration of the national two-party system that had seemed to be developing around 1800, presidential elections did not arouse voter interest as much as did those for governor, state legislators, or even members of Congress. In such elections at the state level the "common man" was stimulated by local factors to cast his vote, and he frequently responded in higher proportions than he did to the later stimulus provided by Jackson.

The average voter participation for all states in 1828 was 56.3 per cent. Before 1824 fifteen of the twenty-two states had surpassed that percentage. Among other things, this means that the 1828 election failed to bring to the polls the proportion of the electorate that had voted on occasion in previous elections. There was, in other words, a high potential vote that was frequently realized in state elections but which did not materialize in presidential elections. The unsupported assumption that the common man was either apathetic or debarred from voting by suffrage barriers before 1824 is untenable in the light of this evidence. . . .

Down to this point the voter turnout in the Jackson elections has been compared with that in elections held prior to 1824. Now it becomes appropriate to inquire whether during the period 1824 through 1832 voters turned out in greater proportions for the three presidential contests than they did for the contemporary state elections. If, indeed, this "new democracy" bore some special relationship to Andrew Jackson or to his policies, it might be anticipated that interest in the elections in which he was the central figure would stimulate greater voter participation than gubernatorial contests, in which he was at most a remote factor.

Actually, the election returns show fairly conclusively that throughout the eight-year period the electorate continued to participate more extensively in state elections than in those involving the presidency. Between 1824 and 1832 there were fifty regular gubernatorial elections in the states that chose their electors by popular vote. In only sixteen of these fifty instances did the vote for President surpass the corresponding vote for governor. In Rhode Island, Delaware, Tennessee, Kentucky, Illinois, Mississippi, Missouri, and Georgia the vote for governor consistently exceeded that for President. Only in Connecticut was the reverse true. Viewed from this perspective, too, the remarkable feature of the vote in the Jackson elections is not its immensity but rather its smallness.

Finally, the Jackson elections may be compared with subsequent presidential elections. Once Jackson had retired to the Hermitage, and figures of less dramatic proportions took up the contest for the presidency, did voter participation rise or fall? This question can be answered by observing the percentage of adult white males who voted in each state in the presidential elections of 1836 through 1844. . . . Voter participation in the 1836 election remained near the level that had been established in 1828 and 1832, with 55.2 per cent of the adult white males voting. Only five states registered percentages in excess of their pre-1824 highs. But in 1840 the "new democracy" made its appearance with explosive suddenness.

In a surge to the polls that has rarely, if ever, been exceeded in any presidential election, four out of five (78.0 per cent) of the adult white males cast their votes for Harrison or Van Buren. This new electorate was greater than that of the Jackson period by more than 40 per cent. In all but five states—Vermont, Massachusetts, Rhode Island, Kentucky, and Alabama—the peaks of voter participation reached before 1824 were passed. Fourteen of the twenty-five states involved set record highs for voting that were not to be broken throughout the remainder of the ante bellum period. Now, at last, the common man—or at least the man who previously had not been sufficiently aroused to vote in presidential elections—cast his weight into the political balance. This "Tippecanoe democracy," if such a label is permissible, was of a different order of magnitude from the Jacksonian democracy. The elections in which Jackson figured brought to the polls only those men who were accustomed to voting in state or national elections, except in a very few states. The Tippecanoe canvass witnessed an extraordinary expansion of the size of the presidential electorate far beyond previous dimensions. It was in 1840, then, that the "roaring flood of the new democracy" reached its crest. And it engulfed the Jacksonians.

The flood receded only slightly in 1844, when 74.9 per cent of the estimated potential electorate went to the polls. Indeed, nine states attained their record highs for the period. In 1848 and 1852 there was a general downward trend in voter participation, followed by a modest upswing in 1856 and 1860. But the level of voter activity remained well above that of the Jackson elections. The conclusion to be drawn is that the "mighty democratic uprising" came after the period of Jackson's presidency. . . .

There remains to be considered the factor of Jackson's personal popularity. Did Jackson, the popular hero, attract voters to the polls in unprecedented proportions? The comparisons that have already been made between the Jackson elections and other elections—state and national—before, during, and after his presidency would suggest a negative answer to the question. Granted that a majority of the voters in 1828 favored Jackson, it is not evident that his partisans stormed the polls any more enthusiastically than did the Adams men. Of the six highest states in voter participation in 1828, three favored Adams and three were for Jackson, which could be interpreted to mean that the convinced Adams supporters turned out no less zealously for their man than did the ardent Jacksonians. When Van Buren replaced Jackson in 1836, the voting average increased slightly over 1832. And, as has been demonstrated, the real manifestation of the "new democracy" came not in 1828 but in 1840.

The most satisfactory explanation for the increase in voter participation between 1824 and 1828 is a simple and obvious one. During the long reign of the Virginia dynasty, interest in presidential elections dwindled. In 1816 and 1820 there had been no contest. The somewhat fortuitous termination of the Virginia succession in 1824 and the failure of the congressional caucus to solve the problem of leadership succession threw the choice of a President upon the electorate. But popular interest was dampened by the confusion of choice presented by the multiplicity of candidates, by the disintegration of the old national parties, by the fact that in most states one or another of the candidates was so overwhelmingly popular as to forestall any semblance of a contest, and possibly by the realization that the election would ultimately be decided by the House of Representatives. By 1828 the situation had altered. There were but two candidates in the field, each of whom had substantial sectional backing. A clear-cut contest impended, and the voters became sufficiently aroused to go to the polls in moderate numbers.

One final question remains. Why was the vote in the Jackson elections relatively low when compared with previous and contemporary state elections and with presidential votes after 1804? The answer, in brief, is that in most states either Jackson or his opponent had such a one-sided advantage that the result was a foregone conclusion. Consequently there was little incentive for the voters to go to the polls.

This factor can be evaluated in fairly specific quantitative terms. If the percentage of the total vote secured by each candidate in each state in the election of 1828 is calculated, the difference between the percentages can be used as an index of the closeness, or one-sidedness, of the contest. In Illinois, for example, Jackson received 67 per cent of the total vote and Adams, 33; the difference—thirty-four points—represents the margin between the candidates. The average difference between the candidates, taking all the states together, was thirty-six points. Expressed another way this would mean that in the average state the winning candidate received more than twice the vote of the loser. Actually, this was the case in thirteen of the twenty-two states. . . . Such a wide margin virtually placed these states in the "no contest" category. . . .

When Jacksonian democracy is viewed from the perspectives employed in this analysis, its political dimensions insofar as they relate to the behavior of the electorate can be described with some precision. None of the Jackson elections involved a "mighty democratic uprising" in the sense that voters were drawn to the polls in unprecedented proportions. When compared with the peak participation recorded for each state before 1824, or with contemporaneous gubernatorial elections, or most particularly with the vast outpouring of the electorate in 1840, voter participation in the Jackson elections was unimpressive. The key to the relatively low presidential vote would seem to be the extreme political imbalance that existed in most states as between the Jacksonians and their opponents. Associated with this imbalance was the immature development of national parties in connection with the Jackson elections. As balanced, organized parties subsequently made their appearance from state to state, and voters were stimulated by the prospect of a genuine contest, a marked rise in voter participation occurred. Such conditions did not prevail generally across the nation until 1840, and then at last the "mighty democratic uprising" took place.

POSTSCRIPT

Did the Election of 1828 Represent a Democratic Revolt of the People?

The two essays in this issue discuss the presidential election of 1828 from different approaches. The portion of Professor Remini's essay which is reprinted here is an example of good, solid narrative history sprinkled with interpretations. Though a full-fledged, two-party system was not yet in effect in all parts of the country, Remini demonstrates that a well-organized coalition of supporters for Andrew Jackson existed in Congress and in a number of states in various sections of the country. Often holding different ideological perspectives, these politicians united around one common goal: the election of Andrew Jackson to the presidency. Remini's description of the staged rallies, the name calling, the fudging of the issues, and the importance of organization over ideology, bears strong resemblance to our most recent presidential campaign.

Professor Richard McCormick, a veteran analyzer of nineteenth-century politics, views the 1828 election through the lens of quantitative history. He uses statistics to break down a number of generalizations about the significance of Jackson's election. The Rutgers University professor discounts the removal of property qualifications for voting, the influence of the western states, and the charisma of Jackson as the major reasons why twice as many voters turned out in the 1828 presidential race than they did four years earlier. He argues that in spite of such statistics, a higher percentage of voters had turned out for earlier gubernatorial and legislative elections in most states than for the 1828 presidential election. In McCormick's view, the key election was 1840, not 1828. Why? Because by this time, the two parties— Whigs and Democrats—were equally balanced in all sections of the country, and voters turn out in larger numbers when they perceive a closely contested presidential race.

McCormick's article raises a number of questions. Is he comparing apples and oranges, as Remini seems to imply? Using McCormick's data, is it possible for other historians to reach different conclusions? How does one explain a fifty-percent increase in voter turnout between 1824 and 1828?

For more information, see Richard P. McCormick, "Political Development and the Second Party System" as well as the other essays in William Nesbet Chambers and Walter Dean Burnham, eds., *The American Party Systems: Stages of Political Development* (New York, 1967).

ISSUE 11

Was Antebellum Reform Motivated Primarily by Humanitarian Goals?

YES: Alice Felt Tyler, from *Freedom's Ferment: Phases of American Social History from the Colonial Period to the Outbreak of the Civil War* (University of Minnesota Press, 1944)

NO: Michael B. Katz, from "Poorhouses and the Origins of the Public Old Age Home," *Milbank Memorial Fund Quarterly* (Winter 1984)

ISSUE SUMMARY

YES: Tyler argues that American reformers in the antebellum period were products of frontier democracy and evangelical religion who accepted a mission of perfecting human institutions.

NO: Katz contends that poorhouses were established not only to provide a refuge for the helpless but also to encourage the Protestant work ethic by deterring members of the working class from seeking poor relief.

The era following the War of 1812 witnessed several dramatic changes in the United States. Andrew Jackson's military triumph over the British at the Battle of New Orleans generated a wave of nationalistic sentiment in the country, even though the victory occurred two weeks *after* the Treaty of Ghent officially ended the conflict with England. The republic experienced important territorial expansion with the admission of new states in each of the half-dozen years following the end of the war. A "transportation revolution" produced a turnpike, canal, and railroad network that brought Americans closer together and enhanced the opportunities for economic growth. In politics, the demise of the nation's first two-party system, following the decline of the Federalists, was succeeded by the rise to prominence of the Democratic and, later, the Whig parties.

Although some historians have characterized this period as the "era of good feelings," it is important to remember that many Americans were aware that the United States was not without its problems. Drawing upon intellectual precepts unleashed by the Enlightenment, there were those who believed in the necessity and potential for perfecting American society. Ralph Waldo Emerson captured the sense of mission of many nineteenth-century men and women when he wrote: "What is man for but to be a Reformer, a Re-maker of what man has made; a renouncer of lies; a restorer of truth and good, imitating that great Nature which embosoms us all, and which sleeps no moment on an old past, but every hour repairs herself, yielding to us every morning a new day, and with every pulsation a new life?" These ideas were reinforced by the encouragement for moral and spiritual perfection produced by the Second Great Awakening. Significantly, revivalists like Charles G. Finney combined a desire to promote salvation through faith and spiritual conversion with an active interest in social change.

This "age of reform" was a multifaceted and often interrelated movement. Reformers, most of whom were from the middle and upper classes, hoped to improve the condition of inmates in the country's prisons and asylums or to encourage temperance or even total abstinence. Some emphasized the necessity of maintaining peace in the world, while others hoped to improve the educational system for the masses. Still others directed their energies into movements emphasizing dietary reform or clothing reform for women. Finally, large numbers of Americans sought to improve American society though campaigns to elevate the status of women and to eliminate slavery.

Thousands of Americans belonged to one or more of these antebellum reform societies, but some controversy exists as to the motivations of these reformers. Were they driven by humanitarian impulses which surfaced in the reinvigorated American republic after 1815? Or was it merely self-interest that encouraged middle- and upper-class Americans to attempt to order society in such a way as to preserve their positions of power?

Alice Felt Tyler's essay represents the traditional thesis that antebellum reformers were motivated largely by humanitarian ideals and desired primarily to perfect American society. These impulses, Tyler believed, stemmed from America's democratic spirit and the evangelical impulses produced by the Second Great Awakening.

Michael Katz, however, concludes that reformers had something else in mind. By focusing upon programs for impoverished citizens, Katz asserts that middle-class reformers sought to impose their system of order on the lower-class poor. The poorhouse, then, was established as a form of social policy to inculcate the Protestant work ethic as well as to rehabilitate and educate the pauper. Ultimately, Katz argues, reformers sought to instill a fear of the poorhouse that would induce the masses to adopt the work ethic, thereby preserving social and moral order in the United States.

YES

Alice Felt Tyler

FREEDOM'S FERMENT

THE FAITH OF THE YOUNG REPUBLIC

The time has come when the experiment is to be made whether the world is to be emancipated and rendered happy, or whether the whole creation shall groan and travail together in pain. . . . If it had been the design of Heaven to establish a powerful nation in the full enjoyment of civil and religious liberty, where all the energies of man might find full scope and excitement, on purpose to show the world by one great successful experiment of what man is capable . . . where should such an experiment have been made but in this country! . . . The light of such a hemisphere shall go up to Heaven, it will throw its beams beyond the waves; it will shine into the darkness there, and be comprehended—it will awaken desire, and hope, and effort, and produce revolutions and overturnings until the world is free. . . . Floods have been poured upon the rising flame, but they can no more extinguish it than they can extinguish the flames of Aetna. Still it burns, and still the mountain murmurs; and soon it will explode with voices and thunderings, and great earthquakes. . . . Then will the trumpet of jubilee sound, and earth's debased millions will leap from the dust, and shake off their chains, and cry, "Hosanna to the Son of David!"

With this vision of the future as a new and glorious epoch Lyman Beecher a hundred years ago voiced the exuberant optimism of the young American republic in which he lived. In that time, if ever in American history, the spirit of man seemed free and the individual could assert his independence of choice in matters of faith and theory. The militant democracy of the period was a declaration of faith in man and in the perfectibility of his institutions. The idea of progress so inherent in the American way of life and so much a part of the philosophy of the age was at the same time a challenge to traditional beliefs and institutions and an impetus to experimentation with new theories and humanitarian reforms.

The period was one of restless ferment. An expanding West was beckoning the hungry and dissatisfied to an endless search for the pot of gold.

From *Freedom's Ferment: Phases of America's Social History from the Colonial Period to the Outbreak of the Civil War* by Alice Felt Tyler (Minneapolis: University of Minnesota Press, 1944). Reprinted by permission.

Growing industrialization and urbanization in the East, new means of communication and transportation, new marvels of invention and science, and advance in the mechanization of industry, all were dislocating influences of mounting importance. And increasing immigration was bringing into the country thousands of Europeans who were dissatisfied with the difficult conditions of life in their native lands. Nor did religion place any restraint on the unrest; recurring revivals, emphasis on individual conversion and personal salvation, and the multiplicity of sects, all made religion responsive to the restlessness of the time rather than a calming influence upon it. The pious editors of the writings of a Shaker seeress asserted in their preface to her revelations.

Let any candid people, endowed with a common share of discernment seriously examine the signs of the times, and view the many wonderful events and extraordinary changes that are constantly taking place in the moral religious and political world, as well as in the natural elements, through the operations of Providence, and they cannot but consider the present age as commencing the most extraordinary and momentous era that ever took place on earth.

Each in his own way the citizens of the young republic recognized the ferment of the era and made answer to its challenge. Itinerant revivalists and the most orthodox of clergymen alike responded with missionary zeal. For an influential few transcendentalism proved to be a satisfying reconciliation between the rationalism of their training and the romanticism of the age, while among the less intellectual, adventism, spiritualism, Mormonism, and perfectionism each won adherents who founded churches and preached their creeds with fervor. To these sects were added the cults and communities transplanted from abroad. The combination of religious toleration, overflowing optimism, and cheap lands caused Europeans of unorthodox faith or unusual social ideas to seek asylum in America. Each such sect, each isolated religious community, each social utopia, was an evidence of the tolerant, eclectic spirit of the young republic, and each made its contribution to the culture of the land that gave it sanctuary.

The desire to perfect human institutions was the basic cause for each sect and community, and this same desire lay at the roots of all the many social reform movements of the period. The American reformer was the product of evangelical religion, which presented to every person the necessity for positive action to save his own soul, and dynamic frontier democracy, which was rooted deep in a belief in the worth of the individual. Born of this combination, the reformer considered reform at once his duty and his right, and he did not limit his activities to one phase of social betterment. Education, temperance, universal peace, prison reform, the rights of women, the evils of slavery, the dangers of Catholicism, all were legitimate fields for his efforts.

The American reformer knew that he did not work alone. He recognized that each cause he espoused was a part of a world of progress and aspiration, but peculiarly his was the freedom to experiment, for in his homeland there was room and hospitality for adventure. Happy in his privilege, he acknowledged his duty and accepted for his age the sign of his crusade. . . .

DYNAMIC DEMOCRACY

It was a long process of democratization, begun before the signing of the Declaration of Independence, accelerated by the Revolution, and continued through the influence of the frontier, that made American society, in the words of the French traveler, Michel Chevalier, in 1834, "essentially and radically a democracy, not in name merely but in deed." . . .

Frederick Jackson Turner, the historian whose name is identified with the frontier, has wisely said that the West is at bottom a form of society, rather than an area. From the beginning each colony had its frontier, its West: areas in which men of courage and vigor won new opportunities, where land was cheap or free and the struggle for existence, although severe, brought rewards commensurate with the effort expended. There the "cake of custom" was broken, old standards were discarded, new ideals and new institutions were set up. The back country was relatively near the Atlantic Coast in the early days, but it was pushed farther west, north, or south decade by decade. In 1790 one hundred thousand had reached the Mississippi Valley. The census of 1810 showed a Western population of a million, that of 1830 gave the West more than three and a half millions, and that of 1840 made the total six millions. . . .

From whatever background they came, no matter how diverse their motives or their equipment, the frontier shaped these settlers into its own pattern. And the type of American developed under frontier conditions set his mark upon the life of his nation so unmistakably that the philosophy of the frontier came to color the activities of the entire United States. Equality of condition was a fact, not a theory, on the frontier; station, education, refinement, and even wealth mattered little. All must face the same perils and hardships, the same grueling labor in clearing the land, the same isolation, the same grueling labor in clearing the land, the same isolation, the same lack of the refinement of civilization. The weaklings move on, dropped back, or died of their failures, while the vigorous and self-reliant remained to become the leaders and the models of frontier achievement.

The same conditions produced the paradox of the frontier—a belief in equality so profound that the American almost confounded equality of opportunity with equality of ability, together with an intense, militant individualism that resented all restrictions and was restless, buoyant, self-assertive, and optimistic. The frontiersman had the utmost confidence in himself, his region, and hs country, and he both craved and resented comparisons and criticisms. Acknowledging no debt to the past, he believed in progress and accepted change as the natural order. Hopeful and idealistic, he yet could not forget the necessity for commons sense and a realistic attitude, for the conquest of the wilderness was an arduous task, exacting, monotonous, and burdensome. . . .

The frontier's faith in democracy and freedom soon took on an element of crusading zeal as Americans became convinced of the glorious future ahead of them and came to consider themselves entrusted with the mission of portraying democracy to less favored nations. A magazine article in 1821, perhaps with some sense of humor, illustrated this confidence in the future with the statement:

Other nations boast of what they are or have been, but the true citizen of the United States exalts his head to the skies in the contemplation of what the grandeur of his country is going to be. Others claim respect and honor because of the things done by a long line of ancestors; an American appeals to prophecy, and with Malthus in one hand and a map of the back country in the other he defies us to a comparison with America as she is to be, and chuckles his delight over the splendors the geometrical ratio is to shed over her story. This appeal to the future is his never-failing resource. . . .

Francis Grund, writing in 1836 for an English public, made the same sort of comment in his statement that Americans loved their country not for what it then was, but for what it was to be—not the land of their fathers, but the land their children were destined to inherit. The Scotsman, Alexander Mackay, heard the same idea from a South Carolina farmer in response to a question about genealogy: "We don't vally those things in this country. It's what's above ground, not what's under, that we think on." Whether or not the visiting Europeans approved of American democracy, and many did not, they all were agreed that Americans themselves were content with their institutions and believed them better than those of Europe.

This American solidarity was noted by the most famous foreign visitor of the period, Alexis de Tocqueville, in a letter from the United States in June 1831. After stating that he envied Americans the comfort of their common opinion, he went on to enumerate them: All the people believe that a republic is the best possible government and do not question that the people have a right to govern themselves. This belief is almost a *faith*, which is at basis a faith in the good sense of human beings and in the perfectibility of human institutions. In order that those institutions may constantly improve, education and enlightenment must become as universal as suffrage. De Tocqueville found no evidence of ancient traditions and little effect of old customs or memories. Americans were a new people. He felt that the reason there was so great a respect for law was that the people made it themselves and could change it themselves. "It is really an incredible thing . . . to see how this people keeps itself in order through the single conviction that its only safeguard against itself lies in itself." Somewhat reluctantly, apparently, the young Frenchman admitted that on the whole the country presented "an admirable spectacle!" His great work published some years later, *Democracy in America*, reaffirmed this first impression, saying,

> In America, the principle of the sovereignty of the people is not either barren or concealed . . . it is recognized by the customs and proclaimed by the laws. . . . If there be a country in the world where the doctrine of the sovereignty of the people can be fairly appreciated, where it can be studied in its application to the affairs of society, and where its dangers and its advantages may be foreseen, that country is assuredly America.

The American's own view of his achievement in democracy was usually optimistic, sometimes complacent, but occasionally tempered by analysis and criticism. The novelist, James Fenimore Cooper, although professing belief in democracy, was a caustic critic of American life, attacking what he thought were its abuses and faults with a vehemence that won him many enemies. In his *America and the Americans: Notions Picked up by a Travelling Bachelor,* published in 1836, he endeavored to explain his country to the outside world and to express his own faith. But in *The American Democrat,* designed for his own countrymen, he warned of the danger of the rise of a "vulgar tyrant" and repeatedly asserted that the leading principle of a republic must be that political power is a trust to be guarded with "ceaseless vigilance." Feeling that imperfect as popular government was, it was less dangerous than any other, Cooper came to the conclusion that men of intelligence and wealth, of education and station, must take their proper place in democratic society and aid in directing national policies.

The self-conscious democracy of the West, in conjunction with the laboring classes of the seaboard states, exercised its newly acquired manhood suffrage in 1828 to bring about the Jacksonian Revolution and install "Old Hickory," the hero of the land-speculating, Indian-fighting West, in the White house. . . .

With the election of Andrew Jackson the creed of the frontier won its victory in the arena of national affairs, and the Western interest in politics became national with the rise of the common man to political importance. While officeholders trembled and Washington official and social circles paled with anticipatory anguish, the President-elect prepared to act in accordance with a creed that summarizes well the essential faith of the young republic:

> I believe man can be elevated; man can become more and more endowed with divinity; and as he does he becomes more God-like in his character and capable of governing himself. Let us go on elevating our people, perfecting our institutions, until democracy shall

reach such a point of perfection that we can acclaim with truth that the voice of the people is the voice of God.

EVANGELICAL RELIGION

The religious heritage of the young republic was as important in the development of nineteenth-century ideas as were the liberties won in the struggle with civil authorities. "When the common man has freed himself from political absolutism, he will become dissatisfied with theological absolutism." The cold and repressive doctrines of Calvinism could not win the hearts of those who escaped from its control when its dictatorial governmental power came to an end. Moreover, the rationalism of John Locke and the French philosophes had the same dislocating effect on religious thinking as on political ideas. Calvin's doctrine of total depravity might have sufficed an older generation as an explanation of the presence of evil in human society, but man's reason found other causes, and his common sense rejected the idea that he and his neighbor were utterly depraved. The idea of progress and of the importance of the individual undermined the old doctrines of election and predestination. The consequent dissatisfaction with Genevan dogma, coupled with the aridity and dullness of New England cultural life, caused the people to turn with eagerness to evangelical Protestantism. . . .

The frank and open adoption of emotionalism in religion and the sensational methods of revivalists did not go unnoticed by American and European contemporary commentators. Margaret Bayard Smith in describing a revival in Washington in 1822 stated that the preachers were introducing all the habits and hymns of the Methodists into our Presbyterian churches . . . that they were going through the highways and hedges, to invite guests . . . into every house exhorting the people, particularly into all the taverns, grog-shops, and other resorts of dissipation and vice. Whether all these excessive efforts will produce a permanent reformation I know not; but there is something very repugnant to my feelings in the public way in which they discuss the conversions and convictions of people and in which young ladies and children display their feelings and talk of their convictions and experiences. Dr. May calls the peculiar fever, the *night* fever, and he says almost all cases were produced by night meetings, crowded rooms, excited feelings, and exposure to night air.

A somewhat less naïve explanation of revivalistic phenomena was made by Bishop Hopkins of Vermont, who stated that revivalists secured conversions solely because of the terror induced by their exhortations. Disapproval of such tactics seems to have been prevalent among the Episcopalian clergy, one of whom Captain Marryat quoted as saying that revivals were

those startling and astounding shocks which are constantly invented, artfully and habitually applied, under all the power of sympathy, and of a studied and enthusiastic elocution, by a large class of preachers among us. To startle and to shock is their great secret power.

But the American clergy in general probably felt that the revival had come to stay and could be made a valuable part of the religious program of the Protestant churches.

European travelers almost invariably were taken to camp meetings, especially in the West, and reacted to the experience in accord with their own temperaments. Captain Marryat drew back in disgust from the preacher who began his prayer with the words "Almighty and diabolical God," and depreciated all the excesses and extravagances of evangelical religion. Frances Trollope made many caustic comments about both revivals and preachers. Always suspecting the worst, she felt sure that such sessions must turn at times into sex orgies, although the only ocular evidence she had was the sight of a preacher whispering consolation into the ear of a sobbing and distraught young feminine convert.

James Stuart was much impressed by the perfect decorum of the audience, the "faultless" sermons, and the magnificent singing. The revival he attended, however, was on Long Island; he was not exposed to the crudities of a genuine frontier camp meeting. It is more surprising to find the usually censorious Thomas Hamilton commending the camp meeting as an agency of civilization.

In a free community [he wrote] the follies of the fanatic are harmless. The points on which he differs from those around him are rarely of a nature to produce injurious effects on his conduct as a citizen. But the man without religion acknowledges no restraint but human laws; and the dungeon and the gibbet are necessary to secure the rights and interests of his fellow-citizens from violation. There can be no doubt, therefore, that in a newly settled country the strong effect produced by these camp-meetings and revivals is on the whole beneficial. The restraints of public opinion and penal legislation are little felt in the wilderness; and, in such circumstances, the higher principle of action, communicated by religion, is a new and additional security to society.

Two of the most detailed descriptions of camp-meeting revivals are those of Francis Lieber and Fredrika Bremer, written nearly twenty years apart and published in 1835 and 1853. Lieber was repelled by the emotionalism of the camp meeting he attended and was shocked by the "scenes of unrestrained excitement," but the Swedish traveler, Fredrika Bremer, was much impressed by the immense crowd of both white and colored people at the Georgia camp meeting she witnessed in the early 1850's. The grandeur of the night meeting in the forest, the eight fine altars, the campfires of resinous wood, the superb singing of the thousands of Negroes, the wails of the penitent, the thunder and lightning of an approaching storm—all, she said, combined to make the night one never to be forgotten.

The effects of the absence of state control and the consequent multiplicity of sects seemed to interest all foreign observers. Many of them mention the lack of religious intolerance in the United States and the easy "live and let live" philosophy apparent in the attitude of most men. Alexander Mackay, who traveled extensively in America in the 1840's, was so impressed that he wrote:

It is true that the insulting term "toleration" is but seldom heard in America in connexion with the religious system of the country. To say that one tolerates another's creed, implies some right to disallow it, a right that happens to be suspended or in abeyance for the time being. The only mode in which the American manifests any intolerance in reference to religion is that they will not tolerate that the independence of the individual should in any degree, be called in question in connexion with it.

On the more fundamental question of the connection between the American democratic faith and the emotional perfectionistic religion that had swept over the United States the observers seemed in agreement. Again and again missionaries and patriots identified democratic with religious faith and asserted that neither could stand alone, that combined they furnished an invincible bulwark for American freedom. Timothy Flint, writer and missionary preacher of the first decade of the century, emphasize always that missionary enterprise in the West was for the good of the whole country; the West must not fall into Godless anarchy, for the representative institutions of the East would then also perish. As the Western missionary told De Tocqueville, "It is, therefore, our interest that the New States should be religious, in order that they may permit us to remain free."

In an essay published in 1851, Mark Hopkins, president of Williams College, expressed the same feeling that democracy must be linked with Christianity:

Man himself is the highest product of this lower world, those institutions would seem to be the best which show, not the most imposing results of aggregated labor, but humanity itself, in its most general cultivation and highest forms. This idea finds its origin and support in the value which Christianity places upon the individual, and, fully carried out, must overthrow all systems of darkness and mere authority. Individual liberty and responsibility involve the right of private judgment; this involves the right to all the light necessary to form a correct judgment; and this again must involve the education of the people, and the overthrow of everything, civil and religious, which will not stand the ordeal of the most scrutinizing examination and of the freest discussion.

Regardless of their differences as to details, European and American observers alike were insistent upon the prominence of the part played by religion in the Western World. They saw that the same intensity of faith vivified both the democracy and the religious experience of many Americans, and they realized the potentialities of that combination. The mind and heart quickened by the "lively joy" of a vital religious experience were easily turned toward social reforms, and the spirit of inquiry and soul-searching that animated the revival had a dynamic social significance. The American faith in democratic institutions found its alter ego in the romantic evangelical spirit of American religious life. Together they gave to the Americans of the first half century of the republic their conviction that their institutions could be perfected and their national destiny be fulfilled.

NO

Michael B. Katz

POORHOUSES AND THE ORIGINS OF THE PUBLIC OLD AGE HOME

Public welfare is as old as the thirteen colonies. Its origins lie not in the New Deal but in attitudes and practices interwoven with American social experience over the last three centuries. Welfare is not a rational creation, a set of clear and consistent policies; it is a drafty, crazy, ungainly structure constructed over long periods of time. Throughout the century before the New Deal, the poorhouse dominated the structure of welfare (or, as it was called, relief). Despised, dreaded, and often attacked, the poorhouse nonetheless endured as the great central arch of public welfare policy. Even in the twentieth century it did not disappear. Instead, through a gradual transformation it slid into a new identity: the public old age home. This essay is an overview of its story.

INSTITUTIONS AND POVERTY

There were few formal, specialized institutions in colonial America. Criminals, for instance, were not punished by long periods of incarceration. Rather, they were held in jail only until trial; if found guilty, they were punished by fines, whipping, or execution. The mentally ill were cared for by their families or dumped in the few large almshouses that had been built in the eighteenth century. The poor were cared for largely through some form of outdoor relief, or were auctioned off to local farmers. Poor strangers were warned out of town. Children learned to read in a variety of ways: at home; in tiny, private schools; or in town schools that they attended irregularly.

By 1850 all of this had changed. Specialized institutions had been founded to care for the mentally ill, to rehabilitate juvenile delinquents, to educate the blind, deaf, and dumb, and to eradicate ignorance. New penitentiaries had been constructed on novel principles, and hundreds of almshouses had been built to implement new policies for the relief of the poor.

All of the new institutions rested on optimistic assumptions about the possibilities of reform, rehabilitation, and education. Their sponsors believed

From the *Milbank Memorial Fund Quarterly* 62 (Winter 1984). Reprinted by permission.

that institutions could improve society through their impact on individual personalities. Because of their environmental sources, crime, poverty, ignorance, and mental illness could be eradicated. Even intemperance could be treated in institutions because it originated in causes extrinsic to individual character, most often a faulty family life in childhood and an absence of religious and secular education. Institutions would seal off individuals from the corrupting, tempting and distracting influences of the world long enough for a kind but firm regimen to transform their behavior and reorder their personalities. Even poorhouses shared in this rehabilitative vision; they would suppress intemperance, the primary cause of pauperism, and inculcate the habit of steady work.

The institutional explosion that included the almshouse burst forth from both voluntary and state sponsorship, dotted the landscape with both residential asylums and nonresidential schools, and eventually encompassed almost everyone. Given its broad, inclusive quality and its shared goals, the institutional development of the early and mid-nineteenth century should be defined as the creation of formal organizations with specialized clienteles and reformist or character-building purposes. It was this use of secular institutions as deliberate agencies of social policy, their specialization, and their emphasis on the formation or reformation of character that represented a new and momentous development in modern history.

Despite their general role in social and personal transformation, each institution responded to a particular set of issues. In the case of poorhouses, it was the way in which the great economic, social, and demographic transformations of the late eighteenth and early nineteenth centuries made poverty a major American problem. Poverty was not unusual among the American working class in the early nineteenth century. In fact, working-class people often were poor at some point in their lives. Thus, no clear line demarcated ordinary working people from those in need of relief. This periodic poverty was a structural consequence of the great transformation of American life after about the mid-eighteenth century: the emergence of capitalist social relations, or, to put it another way, the creation of a class of highly mobile wage laborers subject to irregular, seasonal, dangerous, unhealthy, often badly compensated work. Those in need of relief were destitute immigrants, young men thrown out of apprenticeships or looking for work, unemployed household heads with families, widows without children, and those sick and elderly people without kin who could care for them. Crises were built into the very fabric of working-class experience, and periods of dependency were normal. They were part of the very structure of social and economic life. With luck, some people pulled themselves out. They got well or found work. Others were not so fortunate. For there was no provision for the periodic unemployment endemic to the emerging system, no provision for the women left widows, or for the elderly without families. Working-class experience was a continuum; no clear line separated the respectable poor from paupers. This is why all attempts to divide the poor into classes and all policies based upon those divisions—including the creation of poorhouses—ultimately failed. It is one reason why poorhouses so rarely matched the ideal of their founders.

EARLY POOR RELIEF PRACTICE AND THE ORIGINS OF POORHOUSES

Poorhouse advocates had high expectations. They viewed themselves as reformers, promoting the best alternative among existing poor relief practices, which varied widely even within the same state. Of these practices, the most important were: auction, contract, outdoor relief, and poorhouses. In the late eighteenth century, some larger towns and cities had established poorhouses while smaller towns and villages usually auctioned (that is, assigned the care of) individual poor people to the lowest bidder, contracted with one person to care for the town poor, or aided the poor in their homes. In the early decades of the nineteenth century, most states passed legislation enabling counties to establish poorhouses; only New York made them mandatory. Nonetheless, even without coercion, the poorhouse became a familiar American institution during the first decades of the nineteenth century, and by the Civil War poorhouses had spread from the outskirts of cities and the more densely populated seaboard to rural towns and counties throughout most of the settled regions of the country.

Early American relief for the poor, it is important to stress, drew heavily on English precedents. In fact, four principles inherited from England underlay the dazzling variety of local practice. First, relief of the poor was a public responsibility, usually assigned to officials called overseers of the poor. Second, it was profoundly local. Each parish in England or each town or county in America orga-

nized its own system of relief and retained responsibility for its own people, even when they had temporarily moved away. This made the question of legal residence, or settlement, the most contentious practical problem in aid to the poor. Kin responsibility, the third principle, denied public aid to individuals with parents, grandparents, adult children, or grandchildren who could take them into their homes. Finally, concerns about children and about work were combined in legislation that authorized overseers to apprentice the children of paupers to farmers and artisans who agreed to train and care for them in their homes.

Poorhouses did not replace all existing relief practices, and any attempt to write a general history confronts a bewildering array of local variations. Still, there were certain main themes. Chief among these were the objectives of reform, of which the first was to reduce the expense of caring for paupers. In the early decades of the nineteenth century, state and local officials everywhere claimed that pauperism was rising at an alarming rate, especially in cities. Unlike some social fears—such as moral decay, lax family discipline, a decline in civility, or, even, to some extent the safety of the streets—the increase in the number and expense of paupers was tangible. Relief expenses were not nebulous or largely a product of perception. Rather, they were concrete, measurable, translated into tax dollars. Indeed, poor rates (taxes for relief of the poor) often were billed separately from other taxes, making taxpayers immediately aware of every increase in public relief expenses.

Early nineteenth-century observers developed a clear explanation for the increase in pauperism. They placed some blame on the growth of cities and immigration. Even more, they stressed the role of intemperance. But the real villain was existing relief practice, including its legal basis, its administration, and the practices of private charity. None of the poor law critics, it must be stressed, proposed to eliminate poverty. To most people of the time, the idea would have been preposterous. Even in America, the vast majority would have to scrabble hard for a living. Nor was the issue redistributing wealth. Rather, it was this: How to keep the genuinely needy from starving without breeding a class of paupers who chose to live off public and private bounty rather than to work? These were the goals that contemporary relief practice defeated.

As the Quincy Report in Massachusetts made clear, there were two classes of paupers:

> 1. The impotent poor; in which denomination are included all, who are wholly incapable of work, through old age, infancy, sickness or corporeal debility. 2. the able poor; in which denomination are included all, who are capable of work, of some nature, or other; but differing in the degree of their capacity, and in the kind of work, of which they are capable.

There was no question about relieving the first class of poor. Christian charity and ordinary human compassion made their care a clear duty, although it was not so clear where and by whom they should be aided. The real issue concerned the able-bodied poor. According to the Quincy Report, all the "evils" attributed to the current system of poor relief could be traced to the same root: "the difficulty of discriminating between the able poor and the impotent poor and of apportioning the degree of public provision to the degree of actual impotency."

Underlying this assertion—which, with somewhat different language, could have been made at any point in the last 150 years—was the assumption that the able-bodied poor should fend for themselves. Indeed, the core of most welfare reform in America since the early nineteenth century has been a war on the able-bodied poor: an attempt to define, locate, and purge them from the rolls of relief.

According to poor relief critics, private charity and outdoor relief (assisting people outside of institutions) encouraged idleness by undermining the relation between work and survival. Indiscriminate charity and outdoor relief eroded the will to work and destroyed character, while generous public aid through taxation had begun to teach the poor that relief was a right. Thus, public relief of the poor promoted militancy and eroded the deference that should govern class relations. The problem of pauperism, therefore, extended beyond increased taxes. By draining the working class of its incentive, relief for the poor interfered with the supply of energy available for productive labor. Paupers were living proof that a modestly comfortable life could be had without hard labor. Their dissipation was a cancer, demoralizing the poor and eroding the independence of the working class.

It was, of course, a question of perception. The tiny amount of relief available from public or private sources could do little more than prevent starvation. Relief never approximated the wages that an employed laborer could earn, and, by themselves, without supplements from wives and children, even these were too low to support a family. Compassion, moreover, was an essential component of Christian charity, and no one advocated allowing needy people to starve or freeze to death. How to reconcile compassion with the need to deter people from relying on public and private relief was the great and irreconcilable dilemma at the core of relief for the poor.

Beside the expense of pauperism and the impact of outdoor relief and private charity on the character of the poor, critics attacked two other major features of relief: the practice of auctioning off the poor, and settlement laws. The case against the former had two sides. One was its brutality. In New York the Yates report (1824) concluded: "The poor, when farmed out, or sold, are frequently treated with barbarity and neglect by their keepers." The other side was the way the poor sometimes apparently turned the system of auction or sale to their own advantage. Families bid for the care of their own relatives, and they often put in the low bid because they were willing or able to care for them with very little additional money. In these instances, public funds subsidized a modestly comfortable life for dependent people with their kin. To poor law critics, these subsidies were an outrageous abuse of the taxpayers. But it was an abuse that was hard to eradicate because of the resistance posed by coalitions of poor people, their relatives, friends, and neighbors, and even local professionals and merchants who profited from their business, and justices of the peace and overseers of the poor who earned at least some of their living from the unreformed system.

Here is a hint that the substitution of poorhouses for other methods of relief met popular resistance. Indeed, in England, as British historians have shown, opposition to poorhouses was widespread. Although American historians have not studied resistance to poorhouses, there is every reason to believe that American working people in the early nineteenth century understood the meaning of reformed poor laws as well as their British counterparts. Poorhouses were designed to enforce discipline and help regulate labor markets and wages. Their advocates wanted to remove people too poor, sick, or old to care for themselves from their friends and families and put them into a harsh, degrading institution. In these circumstances, resistance was neither venal nor unreasonable.

The other great problem with the poor laws was settlement. Towns often spent more money ridding themselves of paupers than they would have in supporting them. Aside from the trouble and expense of endless litigation, the system often was cruel, for old and sick paupers frequently were shipped from town to town in the middle of winter. The Yates report estimated that one-ninth of all the taxes raised for relief were spent "in the payment of fees of justices, overseers, lawyers and constables" involved with the determination and administration of settlement. Part of the problem was the obscure nature of the laws themselves, which were "so technical, numerous, and complicated, if not obscure, that even eminent counsel" were "often at a loss to determine questions arising upon this branch of our pauper system." What, then, could be expected from the decisions of local officials "unlearned in our laws?"

The mix of outdoor relief, the auction of paupers, and their transport from town to town, although unsatisfactory for everyone, appeared especially harsh on children. Although the further demoralization of the adult poor was a serious danger, many of them were thought to be already beyond redemption. It was quite another matter with their children. By failing to intervene in pauper families, the state had abandoned the opportunity to break the mechanism through which pauperism and its allies, crime and ignorance, perpetuated each other. This inability to break the cycle of pauperism was one result of the poor laws that added urgency to appeals for reform.

POORHOUSE GOALS

Both the Quincy Report in Massachusetts and the Yates report in New York rejected the views of British political economists who advocated the total abolition of all relief to the poor. They found such a draconian solution offensive and contrary to American sentiment. But they did echo the sentiments of British writers who advocated replacing most forms of outdoor relief, the auction, and the contract system with a network of poorhouses (or almshouses). Within the almshouses, work—especially farm labor—would be mandatory for all inmates neither too sick nor too feeble, and both idleness and alcohol would be strictly prohibited. Able-bodied men would be rigorously pruned from the relief rolls; begging would be barred and punished; children would be schooled; and settlement laws would be greatly simplified. To their sponsors, poorhouses were partly an attempt to mitigate the harshness of contemporary relief practice by ending the auctioning of the poor to the lowest bidder and stopping the shunting of the poor from town to town regardless of their health or their weather. Thus, they seemed an ideal way to accomplish

a broad array of economic, disciplinary, rehabilitative, and humanitarian goals.

The state reports advocating poorhouses believed they had good reason to be optimistic. Although poorhouses were novel institutions in America, there were enough of them there and in England to provide an accumulating body of evidence about their virtues. And the verdict appeared unanimous. Every town or city with a poorhouse reported a reduction in the cost of poor relief and an improved moral climate. Clearly, in their early years, it was at least plausible to think of almshouses optimistically, as humane, reformatory institutions, reducing expenditures for relief and checking the growth of a demoralized pauper class.

But it is difficult to believe that even in these early years the picture was quite as cheery as poor law reformers would have had their contemporaries believe. For one thing, recall the hints of opposition, the local resistance to poorhouses. From their inception, poorhouses were not popular with the working class. Nor were they supposed to be. And here is the heart of the issue. Built into the foundation of the almshouse were irreconcilable contradictions. The almshouse was to be at once a refuge for the helpless and a deterrent to the able-bodied. It was to care for the poor humanely and to discourage them from applying for relief. In the end, one of these poles would have to prevail. Asserting that poverty was not a crime, almshouse sponsors protested against the inhumanity of existing relief practices such as auctioning off the poor or shunting them around from town to town. At the same time their discussions of the poor and their administrative policies confounded crime and poverty. Not least, they expected institutions designed to house only the most helpless and infirm paupers to be hives of industry and productivity. If the almshouses worked, the aged and infirm would be casualties of the war on able-bodied paupers. In essence, social policy advocated institutionalizing the old and sick away from their friends and relatives in order to deter the working class from seeking relief. In this way, fear of the poorhouse became the key to sustaining the work ethic in nineteenth-century America.

THE FAILURE OF THE POORHOUSE

By the 1850s almost every major institution founded in the early nineteenth century had lost its original promise. For a short time, mental hospitals had reported astonishing rates of cure; reform schools apparently were transforming young delinquents; and poorhouses were slowing the growth of pauperism and sheltering the helpless. But within several years the early optimism of institutional promoters had faded. Mental hospitals did not cure; prisons and reform schools did not rehabilitate; public schools did not educate very well; and poorhouses did not check the growth of outdoor relief or promote industry and temperance. A preoccupation with order, routine, and cost had replaced the founders' concern with the transformation of character and social reform. Everywhere, reform gave way to custody as the basis of institutional life.

The situation in poorhouses was especially bad. Most investigations found them filthy and badly ventilated, their inmates unclassified, largely idle, and lacking adequate medical care, their management negligent, corrupt, and often brutal. Poorhouses had not even managed to reduce the expense of caring for paupers. Despite the confident predictions of their founders in the 1820s, it proved more expensive to support someone in a poorhouse than on outdoor relief.

One reason was the contradiction between deterrence and compassion: the spread of fear and the kindly treatment of decent poverty. One or the other always had to prevail, and in the end deterrence won. Another reason was public indifference. Critics who blamed public apathy and neglect for some of the hideous conditions in poorhouses reflected a growing fear that the well-to-do had abandoned their civic responsibilities. Not only the corruption of politics but the decay of public institutions and the emergence of a militant and undeferential working class, so it was argued, resulted from the withdrawal of educated, well-off citizens from their role as "moral policeman," that is, from active participation in local government, the oversight of public institutions, and their former close and personal contact with the poor.

The reassertion of the citizen as "moral policeman," a major theme of late nineteenth-century history, affected the history of poorhouses through the creation of local visiting committees (usually consisting of affluent women), which tried to monitor conditions in poorhouses and stimulate improvements. Most notable of these was the New York State Charities Aid Association, a coalition of local committees founded in the early 1870s, which, as might be expected, had a stormy relation with the superintendents or poorhouses whose work they scrutinized and sometimes attacked. In fact, the Westchester County visitors (the nucleus of the organization) at first were denied entrance to the local poorhouse. Using their influence, however, they turned to the state legislature and, within a year, had sponsored a bill granting them access to poorhouses. Their success revealed both the power and influence of their membership, and the close, complex relations between the state and voluntarism, the indistinct boundaries between public and private that always have been a feature of American life.

A third reason why poorhouses failed to meet the expectations of their founders was the difficulty of providing work for inmates. In Philadelphia, for example, almshouse managers repeatedly tried to make inmates run factories that would produce an income. They never succeeded. Only a minority of inmates were well enough or strong enough to work; often goods were produced more cheaply outside the almshouse; and inmates had few skills. Nonetheless, managers clung to the importance of work for its moral as well as its economic returns. No clearer example exists than in the 1820s when they sold the poorhouse horses and constructed tread wheels instead, which, according to Priscilla Clement, they used to punish men and women inmates. When there were too few paupers who needed punishment because they were lazy or had contracted venereal disease, the managers used mentally ill inmates to work the tread wheels. Despite their inefficiency and a committee's recommendation to replace them with steam-driven machinery, most officials wanted to retain the tread wheels to deter the poor from seeking public relief.

In 1855 a New York critic of relief praised the success of the Providence, Rhode Island, poorhouse which, he claimed, utilized pauper labor so effi-ciently that it operated much more cheaply than almost any other urban almshouse. Even if the almshouse managers had no "profitable work," they set inmates to work at some task, however pointless. During his last visit, he "saw a party of men carrying wood from one corner of the yard to another and piling it there; when it was all removed it was brought back again and piled in the old place." This sort of practice rid "Providence of all lazy drones, such as infest our poor houses to a great degree." This critic had begun his argument by stressing the need to increase the profitability of pauper labor, but he slipped without transition into the virtues of labor, any hard labor, for its own sake. In the end, it was deterrence, not profitability, that mattered.

It is not surprising that satisfactory work arrangements rarely existed. Work's deterrent, educational, and money-making purposes contradicted each other, and the large share of inmates who were old, sick, and disabled left only a minority able to labor. The most successful form of work was farming. Poorhouses often were built in the country with farms attached to them. Indeed, in many states they were called poor farms rather than poorhouses. In some instances, superintendents who were both good managers and good farmers ran productive farms that provided a large share of the inmates' food. However, in many instances, farms, like manufacturing operations, were failures. One reason was the seasonal relation between their population and work. Farms needed able-bodied labor in the summer; but it was in the summer that able-bodied men left poorhouses because they could find paid work. Indeed, poorhouses were most crowded in winter when they could offer their inmates little outdoor labor. Thus, even in the country most poorhouses failed to employ their inmates usefully.

Another set of reasons for the failure of poorhouses reflected weaknesses in poorhouse management and organization. Managerial problems in relief began with the office of overseer of the poor. So unpopular was the job that fines sometimes were necessary to force men to serve. Because superintendents or overseers of the poor often used their offices as sources of graft, petty corruption infected the administration of relief. Poorhouse keepers often were men of limited ability. With "dreary work, small pay, and practically no general recognition" for their services, whatever their quality, "a sensitive, high-minded, ambitious man" was not likely to take the job, and, "almost of necessity," the typical keeper was "a tolerably stolid, unsympathetic person, and one who has not been very successful in other lines. . . ." Unfortunately, the job usually exceeded his abilities.

Like the other new service professions that developed during the nineteenth century, poorhouse administrators had to forge an occupational identity over the course of several decades. The first school systems, penitentiaries, reform schools, mental hospitals, and poorhouses could not draw on a pool of trained administrators or a body of technical and managerial knowledge. In each case, as officials accumulated practical experience, they developed their own organizations, journals, and, eventually, training procedures. By the early twentieth century, all of them had generated new professions: school superintendent, penologist, psychiatrist, social worker, public welfare official. In New York State,

the Annual Convention of the County Superintendents of the Poor, which met first in 1870, was a loosely knit organization that held annual conventions, published its proceedings, and sometimes lobbied the state legislature. Over the years, its proceedings show the gradual emergence of a sense of occupational identity, fostered, especially late in the nineteenth century, by attacks on county poorhouses and attempts to remove the insane to state institutions. A few superintendents, who held their jobs for many years, obviously were well read in contemporary literature about pauperism and relief of the poor, and they tried to run their own institutions professionally and to stimulate their colleagues throughout the state to higher standards. Indeed, by 1913 the professionalization of poorhouse administration had reached the point where the country convention changed its name to the New York Association of Public Welfare Officials.

Nonetheless, probably no more than a few poorhouses were very well administered. In small county poorhouses there were few staff besides the keeper or superintendent and his wife. Cities such as Philadelphia or New York developed elaborate hierarchies for administering their large poorhouses, but these, too, were understaffed. Medical care, always insufficient, sometimes was the responsibility of local doctors for whom the poorhouse was a lucrative and steady source of income (and a source of contention among local physicians who sometimes underbid one another for the contract). Occasionally, as in Philadelphia, medical students provided much of the medical care. Professional nurses were almost nonexistent. Most of the nursing, in fact, was done by other patients.

Indeed, patients did a great deal of the routine work around poorhouses. They not only nursed other patients and gardened but also often cooked, cleaned, sewed, and did other domestic jobs. In fact, in some ways the patients ran the larger poorhouses, as in Philadelphia, where they greatly outnumbered the paid staff. With inmates serving as attendants, officials had little control over life on the wards. As a consequence, large poorhouses were rowdy, noisy places in which discipline was almost impossible. According to Clement, in Philadelphia some of the inmates formed their own organizations; others fought with each other; and the city's ethnic tensions erupted into conflicts within the almshouse. Even liquor was fairly easily available. Doctors failed to conceal the keys to the liquor cabinet; the inmates managed to steal liquor from the managers' private supply; employees smuggled in liquor which they sold; and doctors prescribed a great deal of liquor as medicine.

The ease with which inmates could enter or leave almshouses exacerbated discipline problems. Despite the rule requiring inmates to work off the cost of their care, in Philadelphia it was a simple matter to leave the almshouse permanently. Inmates went to an official who checked the records and, in most cases, finding nothing wrong, handed them their clothes and allowed them to leave. (Inside the almshouse all the inmates had to wear the same uniform.) One expert complained of the "laxness" of admission and discharge policies. Because everyone was "entitled to be saved from starvation and death from exposure," anyone could enter the almshouse. However, because it was "not a penal institution" and it was "in the interest of no one to have persons stay

there who can support themselves outside," inmates could discharge themselves at will. "The average almshouse official regards the justification of our laxness indicated above as entirely conclusive." Thus, "the door swings . . . outward or inward with the greatest of ease." As a result, the almshouse became a temporary refuge for the degenerate poor. It was "a winter resort for tramps, and a place where the drunkard and the prostitute" recuperated "between debauches." The open door policy had spawned a class of almshouse recidivists.

A failure to classify inmates underlay the administrative problems of poorhouses. According to critics throughout the century, many poorhouses did not separate paupers by age and condition, allowed moral inmates to mingle with the degraded, and failed to send the insane or other handicapped inmates to special institutions. "Probably a majority of the grave evils which could be charged at the present time to the American almshouse," asserted an authority, "have their origin in a lack of proper classification." There were two aspects to classification. One stressed that some categories of people (children, the insane) should be taken out of almshouses altogether. The other dealt with the inmates who remained. Wherever possible, classification should be based on color, "the separation of the sexes," "isolation of defectives," "special provision for the sick," "age," and "the character . . ." of inmates.

One other administrative problem made classification impossible and prevented the poorhouse from reaching any of its goals except deterrence. That, of course, was the cheapness that governed poor relief, or, as one critic said, the "culpable stinginess on the part of the appropriating power, resulting in inadequate or unhealthful food, lack of proper building, heating apparatus, clothing and so forth." Everywhere, the real concern of public officials was to keep the expense of poor relief as low as possible. In the end, all of the various goals of poor law reform throughout the century could be sacrificed, as long as the poor tax went down.

POSTSCRIPT

Was Antebellum Reform Motivated Primarily by Humanitarian Goals?

The social-control school of thought, into which Katz's essay could be placed, draws upon the works of Michel Foucault, Erving Goffman, Howard Becker, Thomas Szasz, and others and contends that American reformers were more interested in serving their own interests than in providing assistance to mankind. As a result, middle- and upper-class reformers, responding to momentous changes within their society, imposed their standards of morality and order on the lower classes and, thus, denied the latter group freedom to act as a diverse set of individuals.

Ronald G. Walters, in *American Reformers, 1815–1860* (Hill and Wang, 1978), attempts to balance these opposing schools of interpretation. Walters concludes that although many nineteenth-century reformers expressed sentiments that were self-serving and bigoted, their motivations were not based entirely upon a desire to control the lower classes. Rather, reformers were convinced that improvements could and should be made to help people.

The scholarly literature on the "age of reform" is extensive. Interested students should consult Timothy L. Smith, *Revivalism and Social Reform: American Protestantism on the Eve of the Civil War* (Harper & Row, 1957); Whitney R. Cross, *The Burned-Over District: The Social and Intellectual History of Enthusiastic Religion in Western New York, 1800–1850* (Cornell University Press, 1950); and Clifford S. Griffin, *Their Brothers' Keepers: Moral Stewardship in the United States, 1800–1865* (Rutgers University Press, 1960). David Brion Davis, ed., *Ante-Bellum Reform* (Harper & Row, 1967) is an excellent collection of readings. The social-control thesis can be traced for various reform endeavors in Joseph R. Gusfield, *Symbolic Crusade: Status Politics and the American Temperance Movement* (University of Illinois Press, 1966); Michael B. Katz, *The Irony of Early School Reform: Education and Innovation in Mid-Nineteenth Century Massachusetts* (Beacon Press, 1968); Joseph M. Harris, *Children in Urban Society: Juvenile Delinquency in Nineteenth-Century America* (Oxford University Press, 1971); David J. Rothman, *The Discovery of the Asylum: Social Order and Disorder in the New Republic* (Little, Brown, 1971); and Gerald Grob, *Mental Institutions in America: Social Policy to 1875* (Free Press, 1973). For some of the aspects of American reform generally dismissed by Tyler as "fads," see John D. Davies, *Phrenology, Fad and Science: A Nineteenth-Century American Crusade* (Yale University Press, 1955), and Ronald L. Numbers, *Prophetess of Health: A Study of Ellen G. White* (Harper & Row, 1976).

ISSUE 12

Was U.S. Foreign Policy in the Early Nineteenth Century Imperialistic?

YES: Ramon Edwardo Ruiz, from "Manifest Destiny and the Mexican War," Quint et al., eds., *Major Problems in American History, vol. 1,* 5th ed. (Dorsey Press, 1988)

NO: Robert Hugh Ferrell, from *American Diplomacy, A History,* 2d ed. (W. W. Norton, 1969)

ISSUE SUMMARY

YES: Professor Ramon E. Ruiz argues that for the purpose of conquering Mexico's northern territories, the United States waged an aggressive war against Mexico from which she never recovered.

NO: Diplomatic historian Robert Ferrell, however, believes that although the American government waged an aggressive war in Mexico, it remained the manifest destiny of the United States to possess Texas, New Mexico, and California.

The American government in the early 1800s greatly benefited from the fact that European nations generally considered what was going on in North America of secondary importance to what was happening in their own countries. In 1801, President Jefferson became alarmed when he learned that France had acquired the Louisiana territory from Spain. He realized that western states might revolt if the government did not control the city of New Orleans as a seaport for shipping their goods. Jefferson dispatched negotiators to buy the port. He pulled off the real estate coup of the nineteenth century when his diplomats caught Napoleon in a moment of despair. With a stroke of the pen and $15 million, the Louisiana Purchase of 1803 nearly doubled the size of the country. The exact northern, western, and southeastern boundaries were not clearly defined. "But," as diplomatic historian Thomas Bailey has pointed out, "the American negotiators knew that they had bought the western half of perhaps the most valuable river valley on the face of the globe, stretching between the Rockies and the Mississippi, and bounded somewhere on the north by British North America."

After England fought an indecisive war with the United States in the years 1812–1815, she realized that it was to her advantage to maintain peaceful relations with her former colony. In 1817, the Great Lakes which bordered on the United States and Canada were mutually disarmed. Over the next half-century, the principle of demilitarization was extended to the land, resulting in an undefended frontier line which stretched for more than 3,000 miles. The Convention of 1818 clarified the northern boundary of the Louisiana Purchase and ran a line along the forty-ninth parallel from Lake of the Woods in Minnesota to the Rocky Mountains. Beyond that point there was to be a ten-year joint occupancy in the Oregon Territory. In 1819, Spain sold Florida to the United States after Secretary of State John Quincy Adams sent a note telling the Spanish government to keep the Indians on their side of the border or else to get out of Florida. A few years later, the Spanish Empire crumbled in the New World and a series of Latin American republics emerged.

Afraid that the European powers might attack the newly independent Latin American republics and that Russia might expand south into the Oregon Territory, Secretary of State John Quincy Adams convinced President James Monroe to reject a British suggestion for a joint declaration and to issue instead a unilateral policy statement. The Monroe Doctrine, as it was called by a later generation, had three parts. First, it closed the western hemisphere to any future colonization. Second, it forbade "any interposition" by the European monarchs which would "extend their system to any portion of this hemisphere as dangerous to our peace and safety." And third, the United States pledged to abstain from any involvement in the political affairs of Europe. Viewed in the context of 1823, it is clear that President Monroe was merely restating the principles of unilateralism and nonintervention. Both of these were at the heart of American isolationism.

While President Monroe renounced the possibility of American intervention in European affairs, he made no such disclaimer toward Latin America, as was originally suggested by Great Britain. It would be difficult to colonize in South America. But the transportation revolution, the land hunger which created political turmoil in Texas, and the need for ports on the Pacific to increase our trade in Asia encouraged the acquisition of new lands contiguous to the southwestern boundaries. In the 1840s journalists and politicians furnished an ideological rationale for this expansion and referred to the Manifest Destiny of Americans to spread democracy, freedom, and white American settlers across the entire North American continent. Blacks and Indians were excluded in this expansion and so was Canada because it was a possession of Great Britain.

In the first selection Professor Ramon E. Ruiz argues that the United States waged a racist and aggressive war against Mexico for the purpose of conquering what became the American southwest. In his view Manifest Destiny was strictly an ideological rationale to provide noble motives for what were really acts of aggression against a neighboring country. In the second selection diplomatic historian Robert Ferrell justifies the United States government's expansionist policies in the 1840s in terms of the ideology of Manifest Destiny. Admitting that the American government started the war against Mexico, Ferrell still argues that it was inevitable for the United States to possess Texas, New Mexico, and California.

YES

Ramon Eduardo Ruiz

MANIFEST DESTINY
AND THE MEXICAN WAR

All nations have a sense of destiny. Spaniards braved the perils of unknown seas and the dangers of savage tribes to explore and conquer a New World for Catholicism. Napoleon's armies overran Europe on behalf of equality, liberty, and fraternity. Communism dictates the future of China and the Soviet Union. Arab expansionists speak of Islam. In the United States, Manifest Destiny in the nineteenth century was the equivalent of these ideologies or beliefs. Next-door neighbor Mexico first felt the brunt of its impact and suffered the most from it.

What was Manifest Destiny? The term was coined in December 1845 by John L. O'Sullivan, then editor and cofounder of the *New York Morning News*. Superpatriot, expansionist, war hawk, and propagandist, O'Sullivan lived his doctrine of Manifest Destiny, for that slogan embodied what he believed. O'Sullivan spoke of America's special mission, frequently warned Europe to keep hands off the Western Hemisphere, later joined a filibustering expedition to Cuba, and had an honored place among the followers of President James K. Polk, Manifest Destiny's spokesman in the Mexican War.

Manifest Destiny voiced the expansionist sentiment that had gripped Americans almost from the day their ancestors had landed on the shores of the New World in the seventeenth century. Englishmen and their American offspring had looked westward since Jamestown and Plymouth—confident that time and fate would open the vast West that stretched out before them. Manifest Destiny, then, was first territorial expansion—American pretensions to lands held by Spain, France, and later Mexico; some even spoke of a United States with boundaries from pole to pole. But Manifest Destiny was greater than mere land hunger; much more was involved. A spirit of nationalism was pervasive—the belief that what Americans upheld was right and good, and that providence had designated them the chosen people. In a political framework, Manifest Destiny stood for democracy as Americans conceived it; to spread democracy and freedom was the goal. Also included were ideals of regeneration: the conquest of virgin lands for the sake of their

From *Main Problems in American History, Vol. 1,* pp. 254–260, by Quint et al., eds., "Manifest Destiny and the Mexican War," by Ramon Eduardo Ruiz. © 1972 by The Dorsey Press. Reprinted by permission of Wadsworth, Inc.

development, and concepts of Anglo-Saxon superiority. All these slogans and beliefs played a role in the Mexican question that culminated in hostilities in 1846.

Apostles of these slogans pointed out that Mexicans claimed lands from the Pacific to Texas but tilled only a fraction of them, and did so inefficiently. "No nation has the right to hold soil, virgin and rich, yet unproducing," stressed one U.S. representative. "No race but our own can either cultivate or rule the western hemisphere," acknowledged the *United States Magazine and Democratic Review*. The Indian, almost always a poor farmer in North America, was the initial victim of this concept of soil use; expansionists later included nearly everyone in the New World, and in particular, Mexicans. For, Caleb Cushing asked: "Is not the occupation of any portion of the earth by those competent to hold and till it, a providential law of national life?"

Oregon and Texas, and the Democratic Party platform of 1844, kindled the flames of territorial expansion in the roaring forties. Millions of Americans came to believe that God had willed them all of North America. Expansion symbolized the fulfillment of "America's providential mission or destiny"—a mission conceived in terms of the spread of democracy, which its exponents identified with freedom. Historian Albert K. Weinberg has written: "It was because of the association of expansion and freedom in a means-end relationship, that expansion now came to seem most manifestly a destiny."

Americans did not identify freedom with expansion until the forties. Then, fears of European designs on Texas, California, and Oregon, perhaps, prompted an identity of the two. Not only were strategic and economic interests at stake, but also democracy itself. The need to extend the area of freedom, therefore, rose partly from the necessity of keeping absolutistic European monarchs from limiting the area open to American democracy in the New World.

Other factors also impelled Americans to think expansion essential to their national life. Failure to expand imperiled the nation, for as historian William E. Dodd stated, Westerners especially believed "that the Union gained in stability as the number of states multiplied." Meanwhile, Southerners declared the annexation of Texas essential to their prosperity and to the survival of slavery, and for a congressional balance of power between North and South. Other persons insisted that expansion helped the individual states to preserve their liberties, for their numerical strength curtailed the authority of the central government—the enemy of local autonomy and especially autonomy of the South. Moreover, for Southerners extension of the area of freedom meant, by implication, expansion of the limits of slavery. Few planters found the two ideas incompatible. Religious doctrines and natural principles, in their opinion, had ruled the Negro ineligible for political equality. That expansion favored the liberties of the individual, both North and South agreed.

In the forties, the pioneer spirit received recognition as a fundamental tenet of American life. Individualism and expansion, the mark of the pioneer, were joined together in the spirit of Manifest Destiny. Expansion guaranteed not just the political liberty of the person, but the opportunity to improve himself economically as well, an article of faith for the democracy of the age. Furthermore, when antiexpansionists declared that the territorial limits of the United States in 1846 assured all Americans ample room for growth in the future, the expansionists-turned-ecologists replied that some 300 million Americans in 1946 would need more land, a prediction that overstated the case of the population-minded experts. And few Americans saw the extension of freedom in terms other than liberty for themselves—white, Anglo-Saxon, and Protestant. All these concepts, principles, and beliefs entered into the expansionist creed of Manifest Destiny.

None of these was a part of the Mexican heritage, the legacy of three centuries of Spanish rule and countless years of pre-Columbian civilization. Mexico and the United States could not have been more dissimilar in 1846. A comparison of colonial backgrounds helps to bring into focus the reasons that the two countries were destined to meet on the field of battle. One was weak and the other strong; Mexico had abolished slavery and the United States had not; Americans had their Manifest Destiny, but few Mexicans believed in themselves.

Daughter of a Spain whose colonial policy embraced the Indian, Mexico was a mestizo republic, a half-breed nation. Except for a small group of aristocrats, most Mexicans were descendants of both Spaniards and Indians. For Mexico had a colonial master eager and willing to assimilate pre-Columbian man. Since the days of the conqueror Hernán Cortés, Spaniards had mated with Indians, producing a Mexican both European and American in culture and race. Offspring of the Indian as well as the Spaniard, Mexican leaders, and even the society of the time, had come to accept the Indian, if not always as an equal, at least as a member of the republic. To have rejected

him would have been tantamount to the Mexican's self-denial of himself. Doctrines of racial supremacy were, if not impossible, highly unlikely, for few Mexicans could claim racial purity. To be Mexican implied a mongrel status that ruled out European views of race.

Spain bequeathed Mexico not merely a racial attitude but laws, religious beliefs, and practices that banned most forms of segregation and discrimination. For example, reservations for Indians were never a part of the Spanish heritage. Early in the 16th century, the Spaniards had formulated the celebrated Laws of the Indies—legislation that clearly spelled out the place of the Indian in colonial society. Nothing was left to chance, since the Spanish master included every aspect of life—labor, the family, religion, and even the personal relations between Spaniard and Indian. The ultimate aim was full citizenship for the Indian and his descendants. In the meantime, the Church ruled that the Indian possessed a soul; given Christian teachings, he was the equal of his European conqueror. "All of the people of the world are men," the Dominican Bartolomé de las Casas had announced in his justly famous 1550 debate with the scholar Sepúlveda.

Clearly, church and state and the individual Spaniard who arrived in America had more than charity in mind. Dreams of national and personal glory and wealth dominated their outlook. Yet, despite the worldly goals of most secular and clerical conquerors, they built a colonial empire on the principle that men of all colors were equal on earth. Of course, Spain required the labor of the Indian and therefore had to protect him from the avarice of many a conquistador. Spaniards, the English were wont to say, were notorious for their disdain of manual labor of any type. But Spain went beyond merely offering the Indian protection in order to insure his labor. It incorporated him into Hispanic-American society. The modern Mexican is proof that the Indian survived: all Mexicans are Indian to some extent. That the Indian suffered economic exploitation and frequently even social isolation is undoubtedly true, but such was the lot of the poor in the Indies—Indian, half-breed, and even Spaniard.

Spain's empire, as well as the Mexican republic that followed, embraced not just the land but the people who had tilled it for centuries before the European's arrival. From northern California to Central America, the boundaries of colonial New Spain, and later Mexico, the Spaniard had embraced the Indian or allowed him to live out his life. It was this half-breed population that in 1846 confronted and fell victim to the doctrine of Manifest Destiny.

America's historical past could not have been more dissimilar. The English master had no room for the Indian in his scheme of things. Nearly all Englishmen—Puritans, Quakers, or Anglicans—visualized the conquest and settlement of the New World in terms of the exclusive possession of the soil. All new lands conquered were for the immediate benefit of the new arrivals. From the days of the founding of Jamestown and Plymouth, the English had pushed the Indian westward, relentlessly driving him from his homeland. In this activity, the clergy clasped hands with lay authorities, neither offered the red man a haven. Except for a few hardy souls, invariably condemned by their peers, Englishmen of church and state gave little thought to the Indian. Heaven, hell, and the teach-ings of Christ were the exclusive domain of the conquerors.

Society in the thirteen colonies, and in the Union that followed, reflected English and European customs and ways of life. It was a transplanted society. Where the Indian survived, he found himself isolated from the currents of time. Unlike the Spaniards, whose ties with Africa and darker skinned peoples through seven centuries of Moorish domination had left an indelible imprint on them, most Englishmen had experienced only sporadic contact with people of dissimilar races and customs. Having lived a sheltered and essentially isolated existence, the English developed a fear and distrust of those whose ways were foreign to them. The Americans who walked in their footsteps retained this attitude.

Many American historians will reject this interpretation. They will probably allege that American willingness to accept millions of destitute immigrants in the nineteenth century obviously contradicts the view that the Anglo-Saxon conqueror and settler distrusted what was strange in others. Some truth is present here, but the weight of the evidence lies on the other side. What must be kept firmly in mind is that immigration to the English colonies and later to the United States—in particular, the tidal wave of humanity that engulfed the United States in the post-Civil War era—was European in origin. Whether Italians, Jews, or Greeks from the Mediterranean, Swedes, Scots, or Germans from the North, what they had in common far outweighed conflicting traits and cultural and physical differences. All were European, offspring of one body of traditions and beliefs. Whether Catholics, Protestants, or Jews, they professed adherence to Western religious practices and beliefs. The so-called melting pot was scarcely a melting pot at all; the ingredients were European in origin. All spices that would have given the stew an entirely different flavor were carefully kept out—namely, the Black and the Indian.

It was logical that Manifest Destiny, that American belief in a Providence of special design, should have racial overtones. Having meticulously kept out the infidel, Americans could rightly claim a racial doctrine of purity and supremacy in the world of 1846. Had not the nation of Polk's era developed free of those races not a part of the European heritage? Had the nation not progressed rapidly? Most assuredly, the answer was yes. When American development was compared to that of the former Spanish-American colonies, the reply was even more emphatically in the affirmative. After all, the latin republics to the south had little to boast about. All were backward, illiterate, and badly governed states. Americans had just cause for satisfaction with what they had accomplished.

Unfortunately for Latin America, and especially Mexico, American pride had dire implications for the future. Convinced of the innate racial supremacy which the slogan of Manifest Destiny proclaimed throughout the world, many Americans came to believe that the New World was theirs to develop. Only their industry, their ingenuity, and their intelligence could cope fully with the continental challenge. Why should half-breed Mexico—backward, politically a wasteland, and hopelessly split by nature and man's failures—hold Texas, New Mexico, and California? In Mexico's possession, all those lands would lie virgin, offering a home to a few thousand savage Indians, and here and there a Mexican pueblo of people scarcely different from their heathen neighbors. Manifest Destiny proclaimed what most Americans firmly believed—the right of Anglo-Saxons and others of similar racial origin to develop what Providence had promised them. Weak Mexico, prey of its own cupidity and mistakes, was the victim of this belief.

Manifest Destiny, writes Mexican historian Carlos Bosch García, also contradicts an old American view that means are as important as ends. He stresses that the key to the history of the United States, as the doctrine of Manifest Destiny illustrates, lies in the willingness of Americans to accept as good the ultimate result of whatever they have undertaken. That the red man was driven from his homeland is accepted as inevitable and thus justifiable. American scholars might condemn the maltreatment of the Indian, but few question the final verdict.

Equally ambivalent, says Bosch García, is the American interpretation of the Mexican War. Though some American scholars of the post-Civil War period severely censured the South for what they called its responsibility for the Mexican War, their views reflected a criticism of the slavocracy rather than a heartfelt conviction that Mexico had been wronged. Obviously, there were exceptions. Hubert H. Bancroft, a California scholar and book collector, emphatically denounced Polk and his cohorts in his voluminous *History of Mexico* (1883–88). Among the politicians of the era, Abraham Lincoln won notoriety—and probably lost his seat in the House of Representatives—for his condemnation of Polk's declaration of war against Mexico. There were others, mostly members of the Whig Party, which officially opposed the war; but the majority, to repeat, was more involved with the problem of the South than with the question of war guilt.

Most Americans have discovered ways and means to justify Manifest Destiny's war on Mexico. That country's chronic political instability, its unwillingness to meet international obligations, its false pride in its military establishment—all, say scholars, led Mexican leaders to plunge their people into a hopeless war. Had Mexico been willing to sell California, one historian declares, no conflict would have occurred. To paraphrase Samuel F. Bemis, distinguished Yale University diplomatic scholar, no American today would undo the results of Polk's war. Put differently, to fall back on Bosch García, American writers have justified the means because of the ends. Manifest Destiny has not only been explained but has been vindicated on the grounds of what has been accomplished in California and New Mexico since 1848. Or, to cite Hermann Eduard von Holst, a late nineteenth-century German scholar whose writings on American history won him a professorship at the University of Chicago, the conflict between Mexico and the Untied States was bound to arise. A virile and ambitious people whose cause advanced that of world civilization could not avoid battle with a decadent, puerile people. Moral judgments that applied to individuals might find Americans guilty of aggression, but the standards by which nations survive and prosper upheld the cause of the United States. Might makes right? Walt Whitman, then editor of the *Brooklyn Daily Eagle*, put down his answer succinctly:

We love to indulge in thoughts of the future extent and power of this Republic—because with its increase is the increase in human happiness and liberty. . . . What has miserable Mexico—with her superstition, her burlesque upon freedom, her actual tyranny by the few over the many— what has she to do with the great mission of peopling the New World with a noble race? Be it ours, to achieve that mission! Be it ours to roll down all of the upstart leaven of the old despotism, that comes our way.

The conflict with Mexico was an offensive war without moral pretensions, according to Texas scholar Otis A. Singletary. It was no lofty crusade, no noble battle to right the wrongs of the past or to free a subjugated people, but a war of conquest waged by one neighbor against another. President Polk and his allies had to pay conscience money to justify a "greedy land-grab from a neighbor too weak to defend herself." American indifference to the Mexican War, Singletary concludes, "lies rooted in the guilt that we as a nation have come to feel about it."

American racial attitudes, the product of a unique colonial background in the New World, may also have dictated the scope of territorial conquest in 1848 and, ironically, saved Mexico from total annexation. Until the clash with Mexico, the American experience had been limited to the conquest, occupation, and annexation of empty to sparsely settled territories, or lands already colonized by citizens of the United States, such as Oregon and Texas. American pioneers had been reincorporated into the Union with the annexation of Oregon and Texas and even with the purchase of Louisiana in 1803. The alien population proved small and of little importance in all three territories. White planters, farmers, and pioneers mastered the small Mexican population in Texas and easily disposed of the Indians and half-breeds in the Louisiana territory.

Expansionists and their foes had long considered both Indian and Black unfit for regeneration; both were looked on as inferior and doomed races. On this point, most Americans were in agree-ment. While not entirely in keeping with this view, American opinions of Latin Americans, and of Mexicans in particular, were hardly flattering. Purchase and annexation of Louisiana and Florida, and of Texas and Oregon, had been debated and postponed partly out of fear of what many believed would be the detrimental effect on American democracy resulting from the amalgamation of the half-breed and mongrel peoples of these lands. Driven by a sense of national aggran-dizement, the expansionists preferred to conquer lands free of alien populations. Manifest Destiny had no place for the assimilation of strange and exotic peo-ples. Freedom for Americans—this was the cry, regardless of what befell the conquered natives. The location of sparsely held territory had dictated the course of empire.

James K. Polk's hunger for California reflected national opinion on races as well as desire for land. Both that territory and New Mexico, nearly to the same extent, were almost barren of native pop-ulations. Of sparsely settled California, in 1845, the *Hartford Times* eloquently declared that Americans could "redeem from unhallowed hands a land, above all others of heaven, and hold it for the use of a people who know how to obey heaven's behests." Thus, it was that the

tide of conquest—the fruits of the confer-ence table at Guadalupe Hidalgo—stopped on the border of Mexico's inhab-ited lands, where the villages of a people alien in race and culture confronted the invaders. American concepts of race, the belief in the regeneration of virgin lands—these logically ordered annexa-tion of both California and New Mexico, but left Mexico's settled territory alone.

Many Americans, it is true, gave much thought to the conquest and regenera-tion of all Mexico, but the peace of 1848 came before a sufficiently large number of them had abandoned traditional thoughts on race and color to embrace the new gospel. Apparently, most Amer-icans were not yet willing to accept dark-skinned people as the burden of the white man.

Manifest Destiny, that mid-nineteenth-century slogan, is now merely a histori-cal question for most Americans. Despite the spectacular plums garnered from the conference table, the war is forgotten by political orators, seldom discussed in classrooms, and only infrequently recal-led by historians and scholars.

But Mexicans, whether scholars or not, have not forgotten the war; their country suffered most from Manifest Destiny's claims to California. The war of 1846–48 represents one of the supreme tragedies of their history. Mexicans are intimately involved with it, unlike their late adver-saries who have forgotten it. Fundamen-tal reasons explain this paradox. The victorious United States went to a post-Civil War success story unequaled in the annals of Western civilization. Mexico emerged from the peace of Guadalupe Hidalgo bereft of half of its territory, a beaten, discouraged, and divided coun-try. Mexico never completely recovered from the debacle.

Mexicans had known tragedy and defeat before, but their conquest by General Zachary Taylor and Winfield Scott represented not only a territorial loss of immense proportions, but also a cataclysmic blow to their morale as a nation and as a people. From the Mexican point of view, pride in what they believed they had mastered best—the science of warfare—was exposed as a myth. Mexicans could not even fight successfully, and they had little else to recall with pride, for their political development had enshrined bitter civil strife and callous betrayal of principle. Plagued by hordes of scheming politicians, hungry military men, and a backward and reactionary clergy, they had watched their economy stagnate. Guadalupe Hidalgo clearly outlined the scope of their defeat. There was no success story to write about, only tragedy. Mexicans of all classes are still engrossed in what might have been *if* General Antonio López de Santa Anna had repelled the invaders from the North.

Polk's war message to Congress and Lincoln's famous reply in the House cover some dimensions of the historical problem. Up for discussion are Polk's role in the affair, the responsibility of the Untied States and Mexico, and the question of war guilt—a question raised by the victorious Americans and their allies at Nuremberg after World War II. For if Polk felt "the blood of this war, like the blood of Abel, is crying to Heaven against him," as Lincoln charged, then both the war and Manifest Destiny stand condemned.

SUGGESTED READINGS

Bill, A. H. *Rehearsal for Conflict: The War with Mexico, 1846–1848*. New York: Alfred A. Knopf, 1947.

Billington, Ray A. *Westward Expansion: A History of the American Frontier*. New York: Macmillan, 1949.

Bulnes, Francisco. *Las Grandes Mentiras de Nuestra Historia*. Mexico: Editorial Nacional, 1969.

Castañeda, Carolos E., ed. *The Mexican Side of the Texas Revolution*. Dallas: P. L. Turner, 1928.

DeVoto, Bernard. *The Year of Decision, 1846*. Boston: Little, Brown, 1946.

Fuentes Mares, José. *Poinsett. La Historia de una Intriga*. Mexico: Editorial Jus, 1964.

Graebner, Norman A. *Empire on the Pacific*. New York: Ronald Press, 1955.

Merk, Frederick. *Manifest Destiny and Mission in American History: A Reinterpretation*. New York: Alfred A. Knopf, 1963.

Price, Glenn W. *Origins of the War with Mexico: the Polk-Stockton Intrigue*. Austin: University of Texas, 1967.

Ramirez, Jose Fernando. *Mexico during the War with the United States*. Columbia, MO.: University of Missouri Press, 1950.

Roa Barcena, José María. *Recuerdos de la Invasión Norteamericana, 1846–1848*. 3 vols., Mexico: Editorial Porrúa, 1947.

Santa Anna, Antonio López de. *Mi Historia Militar y Política, 1810–1874*. Mexico: Editorial Nacional, 1958.

Singletary, Otis A. *The Mexican War*. Chicago: University of Chicago Press, 1960.

Smith, Justin H. *The War with Mexico*. 2 vols. New York: Macmillan, 1919.

Stephenson, Nathaniel W. *Texas and the Mexican War*. New Haven, Conn.: Yale University Press, 1921.

Valades, Jose C. *Santa Anna y la Guerra de Texas*. Mexico: Imprenta Mundial, 1935.

Vasconcelos, José. *Breve Historia de México*. Mexico: Editorial Continental, 1980.

Vázquez, Josefina. *Mexicanos y Norteamericanos Ante la Guerra Del 47*. Mexico: Secretaría de Educación Pública, 1972.

Weinberg, Albert K. *Manifest Destiny: A Study of Nationalist Expansion in American History*. Baltimore: Johns Hopkins Press, 1935.

NO

Robert Hugh Ferrell

MANIFEST DESTINY

In the history of American diplomacy few ideas have been more important than "manifest destiny"—the belief of the people of the United States that the North American continent, despite prior claims by France, Spain, Russia, Great Britain, and Mexico, was destined to become American territory. This mystic conviction translated itself into reality in the years from the beginning of the nineteenth century to the end of the Civil War. It was the presiding force behind the Mexican War of 1846–1848, the subject of the present chapter. French claims to North America vanished with the Louisiana Purchase of 1803. Spanish claims received settlement in the Adams-Onís Transcontinental Treaty of 1819, after which Spain's lands contiguous to the United States passed under control of the new government of Mexico. Russia's claims to Pacific territory withdrew northward to Alaska in a Russian-American agreement of 1824. British claims to Oregon territory disappeared in a treaty signed in 1846. And by 1848 Mexico's claims to Texas, New Mexico, and California were no more. "Away, away with all those cobweb tissues of rights of discovery, exploration, settlement, continuity, etc.," cried the New York editor, John L. O'Sullivan, who in the year 1845 coined the phrase "manifest destiny." It was, O'Sullivan claimed, "the right of our manifest destiny to overspread and to possess the whole of the continent which Providence has given us for the development of the great experiment in liberty and federative self-government entrusted to us."

Some exponents of manifest destiny believed that the United States should not confine its territorial ambitions to the continent of North America. According to one writer "Its floor shall be as a hemisphere, its roof the firmament of the star-studded heavens, and its congregation a Union of many Republics, comprising hundreds of happy millions . . . governed by God's natural and moral law of equality." Such hopes, of course, were never to be realized, and manifest destiny in its more practical vision limited itself to North America.

"Manifest Destiny" has been edited with the permission of the author and is reprinted by permission of the author and W. W. Norton & Company, Inc. Copyright © 1959 by W. W. Norton & Company, Inc. Copyright renewed 1987 by Robert H. Ferrell.

Two questions might arise at this point, the first of which can be stated as follows: Was manifest destiny nothing but imperialism, an American brand of a well-known nineteenth-century European practice? The nineteenth century was the age of imperialism in Europe, and although European nations undertook their vast colonial conquests in the latter part of the century, whereas the United States pursued its manifest destiny and continental ambition in earlier years, still it might well seem that there was little difference between imperialism and manifest destiny.

In actual fact there was a considerable difference. Manifest destiny was not imperialism if the latter term is properly defined as "rule over alien peoples." There were few Indians in the American West, hardly any at all if compared to the millions of inhabitants of Africa and the hundreds of millions of Asians. It is true that American policy toward the Indians frequently adhered to the frontier maxim that the only good Indians were dead Indians, and it is true that new diseases brought by the settlers decimated the Indians. But in view of the few indians in the United States one must say that only in an extremely legalistic sense was the American nation imperialist during the early nineteenth century.

A second question in connection with manifest destiny concerns specifically the Mexican War: Was not this war, one of the most important chapters in American territorial expansion, a war of aggression—did not Americans pick a quarrel in 1846 with a weak and divided Mexico for the purpose of despoiling the Mexicans of New Mexico and California, and could not one therefore say that manifest destiny, at least as avowed in 1846–1848, was only an excuse for a war of conquest? . . .

MEXICO AND THE TEXAS REVOLUTION

At the turn of the nineteenth century the lands of Mexico belonged to Spain, and it was only after some years of uncertainty during the Napoleonic wars, after reconquest of Mexico by Spain at the end of the wars, that Mexico in 1821 became an independent nation. Twenty-five years of independence followed before the government in Mexico City had to face war with the United States.

The tasks of the Mexican government in its early years were, by any standard, large. The lands of Mexico began in Central America at the border of Guatemala. Mexican territory reached eastward through Yucatán, northward through the isthmus of Tehuantepec to spread like a gigantic fan across twelve hundred miles of virgin territory from the Sabine River in the east to California in the west. Over these distances the government in Mexico City had to exert its authority, distances that in the early nineteenth century rendered them much more remote from the Mexican capital than mid-twentieth century Fairbanks or Honolulu from Washington, D.C. The task of administering the territory of Mexico from the capital in Mexico City was therefore almost impossible. The northern Mexican provinces of Texas, New Mexico, and California were distinctly separated by geography from the populous region about Mexico City, and were oriented economically to the United States. From the Nueces River to the Rio Grande was a desert tract. South of the Rio Grande for hundreds of miles there was almost no cultivation. Westward for hundreds of miles stretched sheer wilderness and desert.

Was there any chance that with time Mexico might have peopled its northern empire? Not unless time were reckoned in terms of several decades, perhaps a century or more, and even this might not have sufficed. Some six million Indians and half-castes lived in Mexico—no one knows, of course, just what the population really was—and controlling this ignorant and poverty-stricken mass were only some 60,000 Spanish-speaking and Spanish-descended persons who were the government officials and landholders and priests and army officers. Nearly all of the 60,000 Spanish lived in the area now embraced within the republic of Mexico. They had little desire to migrate to the northern provinces, Texas and New Mexico and California. They remained in their comfortable towns and ranches, and only a trickle of people from Mexico proper entered the upper territories. This trickle could do little when the Yankee flood began coming across the Sabine shortly after signature of the Transcontinental Treaty in 1819.

One cannot stress sufficiently the point that Texas and the other northern territories of Mexico were virtually empty lands, lacking Mexican settlers, and because of distance lacking almost any control from Mexico City.

Mexican establishments in California, like those in Texas, were pitiful in their poverty and unimportance. If in Texas there were only about three thousand Mexicans of Spanish origin in the 1830s, there were little more than four thousand in California, a mere handful consisting chiefly of priests and monks about the missions, soldiers employed to keep the Indians submissive, and a few large landowners and cattle raisers. In California the area of Mexican control never extended north of San Francisco, nor inland beyond the coastal area. The first Mexican settlers had come at about the time of the American revolution, and few settlers followed them. Certainly there could be no comparison between the Mexican attempt to settle California and the effort by Englishmen a hundred and fifty years earlier to settle the province of New England, for in the Great Migration of 1630–142 some 16,000 Englishmen from the Old World came there, to say nothing of simultaneous English migrations to other parts of America.

Aside from the difficulty of holding the northern territories there was the more serious problem of the debility and incompetence of the Mexican government. The revolution against Spain had broken out in 1810, and the Mexicans triumphed conclusively over the forces of their mother country in 1821. In the next year a military adventurer, Augustín de Iturbide, made himself emperor of Mexico with the title of Augustus I. After a short time he fell from power, went abroad, returned, and was shot. The Mexicans in 1824 established a federal constitution on the United States model, and this constitution managed to stay in effect for five years, after which another military leader, Bustamante, subverted it and took office for three years. He was displaced by Antonio López de Santa Anna, the prince of Mexican adverturers, who was in and out of power several times in the next two decades. There was no peace in Mexico before 1877 when General Porfirio Díaz took the reins of government and held them with absolute authority until 1911, after which came a new time of trouble for government in Mexico.

It was nominally the effort of Santa Anna in 1835 to centralize the Mexican government that led to a revolt in Texas in 1835–1836, but behind the constitutional issue lay the weakness of Mexican control in Texas, the thinness of Mexican settlement, and—above all—the fact that in the fifteen years preceding the Texas revolution some thirty thousand Americans had moved into the Mexican province.

Land hunger had drawn American settlers to Texas during the years after the first group arrived in 1821 under the guidance of the *empresario* Stephen F. Austin. Austin had contracted with the Mexican government for many thousands of acres of land in return for bringing in families of settlers. The families paid about ten cents an acre for their land, with liberal arrangements of credit, at a time when inferior land was selling in the United States for $1.25 cash. The United States government, following a financial panic in 1819, had tightened its land policy, and the Bank of the United States, then the principal bank of credit in the country, had drastically reduced its loans and raised its rates of interest, so that settlers seeking cheap lands were driven by force of circumstance to accept the propositions of such men as Stephen Austin. Few of these early American settlers in Texas stopped to inquire as to the type of government they would encounter in their new country. Even the demand of Mexican authorities that they become converts to Catholicism did not disturb their consciences, and they accepted the forms of Catholicism as easily as they accepted other Mexican laws exercised through the Texas organs of the Mexican government—always provided that government, law, and religion did not interfere with their wholehearted search for cheap land.

Naturally the carefree attitude and abandon with which settlers moved into Texas changed when, after a few years, prosperity permitted leisure for thought and consideration. What in early days had proved acceptable began to irk. Especially the effects of frontier religious revivals must be considered, for as Methodist and Baptist preachers took up superintendence over the souls of American frontiersmen, there came advice from the new ministers that it was blasphemous for the settlers to participate in any way in the forms of the Catholic Church. By the latter 1820s, when signs of civilization were appearing at every hand and settlers were becoming annoyed by increased numbers of Mexican government officials, a new spirit of discontent swept the scattered communities of Texas. Settlers remembered their old allegiance to the United States. When General Andrew Jackson took office as president of the United States in 1829, a wave of enthusiasm and hope rose in the American West. No frontier settlement, even in Mexican Texas, could forget that the "Ginral" was a man of the people. Meanwhile life kept improving. "Within four miles of me," wrote one Texan settler in the mid-1830s, "there are more than one thousand inhabitants, chiefly new emigrants, and within the same distance we have four small stores, two blacksmith shops and two schools. We have a dancing frolick every week and preaching allmost [*sic*] every Sunday."

In a bare decade and a half more settlers came to Texas than in centuries of Spanish administration. This was the inescapable statistic of the Texas situation by the time of the Texas revolution. By the early 1830s the American settlers outnumbered the Spanish-Mexican population by ten to one. Mexican administrators in Mexico City and Texas took alarm. The Americans had been fairly happy under the short-lived constitution of 1824, the easy requirements of which were laxly enforced. The processes of Mexican government had not touched them to any important extent. But when the government of Santa Anna sought in 1835 to tighten the administration in Texas, trouble began, which might have been foreseen from the moment the first American immigrants entered Texas in 1821. It was not foreseen, and by 1835 time had run out on Mexican claims to Texas. There followed during the winter and early spring of 1835–1836 the chief events of the Texas revolution.

Some settlers in Texas had risen in November 1835 and in an unorganized but effective fashion had expelled the few Mexican soldiers and administrators then present on Texas soil. To quell this rebellion, Santa Anna led a large army of 3,000 men into Texas and began his assault with the famous attack on the Alamo. There the rapacious Mexican leader isolated 188 Americans under Colonel William B. Travis and raised from the cathedral the black flag of No Quarter. For seven or eight days the Texas held out, issuing a defiant call for help to "all Americans in the world." but no help arrived, and the Mexican troops closed in on the defenders and slaughtered them to the last man. The Alamo, to indulge in an understatement, incited Texans to fury. "Thermopylae had her messenger of defeat—the Alamo had none," roared General Edward Burleson when he heard the news of the tragedy. Foolishly Santa Anna followed up this slaughter by an even larger carnival at Goliad, where he shot down more than 300 American prisoners in cold blood. News of these massacres spread terror among thousands of the Texas settlers, and as Santa Anna advanced there began a wild flight to the border of the United States, the Sabine River. A long, suffering procession of refugees, women and children and Negro slaves, struggled to reach American territory. The exodus took place in cold weather, with incessant rain. Fortunately Santa Anna shortly thereafter met his downfall when General Sam Houston caught him encamped in a trap. Houston had only to attack. This the Texan leader vigorously did, to the embarrassment of the Head of the Mexican State, who at the crucial moment was taking a siesta. With the Battle of San Jacinto on April 21, 1836, the capture of Santa Anna and dispersal of his army, Texas became independent. . . .

The Texan revolution of 1835–1836 made no change in American policy. Andrew Jackson, consummate politician that he was, refused during his second administration to sponsor admission of Texas to the union. Desiring annexation, he refrained from making political capital of it, for fear that the Texas question if propelled into politics would reopen the slavery question, uneasily adjourned by the Compromise of 1820. Northern congressional leaders were certain that Texas upon admission to the union would be a slave state, and this would raise the inconvenient issue of balance of slave versus free states in the Senate, which then was exactly even, thirteen slave and thirteen free. Especially they thought of what might happen if Texas upon annexation should split itself into five or ten slave states, for this would ruin any hope of maintaining the sectional balance. Jackson was aware of Northern feeling on this matter. The most obtuse states-man—which Jackson assuredly was not—could hardly remain ignorant of the rising feeling between North and South. Jackson moved gingerly and with complete impartiality of action, if not of feeling, when the Texans in 1836 declared their independence. . . . Giving as excuse for his inaction the existence of a treaty between his country and Mexico, and the proprieties of international intercourse, Jackson had in mind the delicate political situation in the United States.

With the refusal of the Jackson administration to annex Texas after San Jacinto, relations between the two sovereign English-speaking states of North America settled down to a brief and quiet interlude. Jackson recognized Texan independence eleven months after San Jacinto, four months longer than the American government had waited to recognize Mexico after its successful revolution against Spain in 1821. The Mexicans nonetheless protested American recognition of Texas, and refused themselves to recognize Texan independence, a policy in which they persisted to the bitter end. Events continued in this course—Texan independence, American recognition, Mexican nonrecognition—until President John Tyler in 1844 sponsored in the Senate a treaty of annexation, and failing in that effort resorted early in 1845 to a joint resolution of annexation. . . .

To no avail were the antislavery arguments against annexation. The feeling of manifest destiny was too strong and too popular in 1845, antislavery sentiment not yet strong enough. Tyler's joint resolution passed Congress with a whoop. "You might as well attempt to turn the current of the Mississippi," Old Hickory declared in a letter given to the press at the crucial political moment, "as to turn the democracy from the annexation of Texas to the United States . . . obtain it the U. States must—peaceably if we can, but forcibly if we must."

All but forgotten in the uproar were the pretensions of the Mexican government. Texas, Mexican diplomats had been claiming, was still part of Mexico, and annexation by the United States would be tantamount to a declaration of war. Upon passage of the joint resolution of March 1, 1845, the Mexican minister in Washington asked for and received his passports.

THE MEXICAN WAR

A year elapsed after the annexation of Texas before the war with Mexico began. There followed after Tyler's resolution of March 1845 a period of maneuvering and uncertainty during which President Polk waited to see what the Mexicans would do. The president was not averse to war. Still, he did not wish war if he could get its fruits without any fighting. He therefore sent a representative to Mexico City, John Slidell, in the hope of obtaining Mexican recognition of a Texas boundary at the Rio Grande, in exchange for which the United States would assume payments of claims of its nationals against the Mexican government. (Because Mexico had been in turmoil for thirty years and more, many Americans had found their properties confiscated and sometimes their lives endangered by the various revolutionary troubles; these claims had been settled by a mixed claims commission for approximately two million dollars, but the Mexicans had refused to pay the claims.) This was Slidell's minimum proposal: recognition of the Rio Grande boundary in return for American assumption of the claims payments. In addition the emissary was empowered to purchase New Mexico and California for $25,000,000. Polk would have gone as high as $40,000,000. He especially desired California with its fine harbor of San Francisco.

The president's representative, Slidell, unfortunately for Mexico, met with rebuff. Before Slidell's journey to Mexico City Polk had received a stately in writing from the Mexican foreign minister to the effect that an American commissioner would find a friendly reception. The Mexican government upon Slidells arrival refused to treat with him, on the technicality that his credentials were those of a minister plenipotentiary rather than a special *ad hoc* representative. What happened was that the Mexican government of the moment, led by General Mariano Paredes, was in imminent peril of being thrown from office, and could not face the hostility of popular opinion in the capital city, should it undertake to negotiate with the Americans. The Mexican people—when one spoke of a "people" of Mexico in the nineteenth century he meant little more than the literate inhabitants of the capital—were determined that annexation of Texas would be tantamount to war.

Whatever sort of government was in control, it was a fatuous act in 1846 to turn down an overture from the government of the United States. Mexico was in the position of refusing to sell territories that she could not keep anyway. Napoleon in 1803, seeing that he could not hold Louisiana, had sold it. There were no Napoleons in Mexico in 1846 but only factional politicians who found momentary power too sweet to relinquish, be the responsibilities of their decisions ever so serious for the future of their country.

And so John Slidell went away, and President Polk, tired of the irresolution of his adversary, disposed American troops under Brigadier General Zachary ("Old Zach") Taylor in the disputed border area of Texas between the Nueces River and the Rio Grande. The local Mexican commander on April 25, 1846 surprised a company of American soldiers, killing or wounding sixteen and capturing the remainder, and the war was on. This even before news had reached the Mexican commander that the government in Mexico City had declared a "defensive war" against the United States. In Washington, Polk was preparing a war message to Congress when the welcome news arrived of the Mexican attack. War, Polk then could assert, had been forced upon the United States by act of Mexico. Congress declared on May 13, 1846 that "by the act of the Republic of Mexico, a state of war exists between the Government and the United States."

That this war with Mexico in the mid-nineteenth century was not a popular conflict soon became obvious to everyone. The war with Mexico of 1846–1848 never evoked the popularity that surrounded the first or second World Wars or the war with Spain in 1898. Not merely was there grumbling and disgruntledness in New England, but outright speeches against the war by such Western opponents as Congressman Abraham Lincoln of Illinois. The issue on which opposition arose was, of course, the extension of slavery. Northern opposition to the war found expression everywhere from pulpits, rostrums, and "stump" platforms. No sooner had the war begun than it received a name indicating its alleged origin—President Polk's War. . . .

President Polk in taking the country to war against Mexico did not, incidentally, act from proslavery motives. Polk was dismayed at the debates over the slavery issue, and became embittered after the war began by the reintroduction into Congress in January 1847 of the Wilmot Proviso to prevent the expansion of slavery into new territory. Slavery as an institution, the president always maintained, had no connection with the war or the peace. "Its introduction in connection with the Mexican War," he recorded in his diary, "is not only mischievous but wicked." Although a citizen of Tennessee and a slaverholder, like his predecessor Andrew Jackson, he had in mind first and foremost the territory and Pacific ports of California, and only after this goal was achieved would he concern himself over the slavery question. Economic interests, but of a territorial sort, moved Polk in his actions, peaceful and otherwise, toward Mexico. . . .

The Treaty of Guadalupe Hidalgo was concluded on February 2, 1848, and had a most interesting background. It was signed by Trist after his commission had expired. President Polk through Secretary of State James Buchanan had annulled Trist's commission, fearing that to have a negotiator accompanying Scott's army would seem to the Mexicans like a sign of American weakness. But Trist at this point began to fear that without an immediate peace there might develop a sentiment in the United States for taking all of Mexico. The Mexican government had been reconstituted through the efforts of General Scott, whose troops were billeted comfortably in the Mexican capital. The abject defeat of the Mexicans was so obvious that, as Trist knew, it might well encourage the more ambitious apostles of manifest destiny to stretch the American eagle's wings all the way to Guatemala. . . . Trist negotiated his treaty at the little village of Guadalupe Hidalgo just outside Mexico City and sent the treaty off to Washington to see what Polk would do with it.

Polk was furious. The president, an able, conscientious, sincere man, was intensely suspicious of political plots during his administration—and he saw a plot in Trist's treaty.

Polk, it seems altogether fair to say, had begun the Mexican War not out of partisan but for national reasons. The president believed that his country's future demanded a border of Texas at the Rio Grande, and in addition he wanted to acquire New Mexico and especially California. This was a broadly national purpose, but as Whig opposition to the war became more vehement Polk found that matters of politics plagued his every move, that he had to be circumspect in his every act to fend off the Whigs and keep the war going to a victorious conclusion. He managed to do this, but only with difficulty, and one of his worst problems in the conduct of the war was that the two leading military commanders, Generals Taylor and Scott, were both Whigs and likely to profit personally from the war by being nominated on the Whig ticket for the presidency. . . .

Trist's treaty, despite the improprieties of its conclusion, was not unwelcome, for Polk's agent had secured New Mexico and California plus Mexican acceptance of the Texan boundary at the Rio Grande, and the United States was to pay $15,000,000 and assume the adjusted claims of its citizens against the Mexican government. These terms, Polk realized, were virtually the maximum that Slidell had been empowered to negotiate in the abortive mission of 1846, and despite his intense disgust with Trist for acting without commission the president sent the treaty to the Senate, which gave its advice and consent on March 10, 1848. After ratification by Mexico, Polk proclaimed the treaty in effect on the anniversary of American independence, July 4, 1848. By this stroke of war, following upon the stroke of diplomacy which had gained Texas in 1845, the United States had added altogether (including Texas) 1,200,000 square miles to its domain, an increase of more than sixty-six percent.

What could one say about manifest destiny, as it had found fulfillment in the events of 1845–1848? The peaceful process by which the United States of America had been expanding across the enormously valuable North American continent had been punctuated by a short and sharp and altogether victorious war. At the time, people were asking whether political leaders from the Southern portion of the United States had not forced the war with Mexico for the enlargement of their slave domains, for the miserable purpose of obtaining "more pens to cram slaves in." This fear, so far as concerned the reasoning of President Polk himself and probably many of his supporters, was unfounded. Even so, in the twentieth century when war led to the near-destruction of Western civilization, many people were again going to ask if the Mexican War were not an unjust war of aggression. Was, then, the Mexican War a conflict that for this latter reason should have been avoided? Should not the United States in 1846–1848 have trusted to its diplomacy and restrained its pursuit of manifest destiny, if that were possible?

The answer to this question is not easy. No American today would like to give up the territories secured from Mexico. Those expanses so varied in their riches gave us first gold, then oil, now uranium, and have increased enormously the power of the United States. If one may be permitted the luxury of reading the present into the past—assuredly a most unhistorical operation—he can easily see that at a time in the mid-twentieth century when the power of the United States and the Union of Soviet Socialist Republics is so neatly balanced, any large subtraction from American power might have changed the course of history. This is no fanciful notion, pleasantly speculated upon in these pages, but an idea that bears some considerable possibilities for thought. What might have happened if the United States during the second World War had not had enough economic and military strength to throw the victory to the Allies? Or for that matter, what might have happened in the gray spring of 1918 when the German offensive came within an ace of success, if the morale of Allied troops had not been bucked up by the prospect, soon to be realized, of two million American soldiers in France? If the nation had stopped at the Sabine River, if such statesmen as John Tyler and James K. Polk had taken Mexican complaints and protests as insuperable obstacles to realization of manifest destiny, the American people might today find their personal and public circumstances altogether unenviable.

POSTSCRIPT

Was U.S. Foreign Policy in the Early Nineteenth Century Imperialistic?

Professor Ferrell presents an interesting defense of the United States' policy of Manifest Destiny towards Mexico in the 1840s. Admitting that the United States created conditions which pushed Mexico into starting the war, Ferrell nevertheless justifies the goals of the war, which were the acquisition of Texas, New Mexico, and California. Not everyone will agree with Professor Ferrell's acceptance of the ideology of Manifest Destiny. Some historians like Richard W. Van Alstyne in *The Rising American Empire* (Quadrangle, 1965) and William Appleman Williams in the very influential *The Tragedy of American Diplomacy*, 2d rev., enlarged edition (Delta, 1972) are critical of the narrow definition of imperialism employed by writers like Ferrell. These radical historians believe that America created an economic empire during the nation's formative years which has continued into the present day.

Professor Ruiz's essay offers a fresh approach when he considers the causes and effects of the war upon both sides. He rejects the ethnocentric approaches of earlier diplomatic historians like Justin Smith, Samuel F. Bemis and Robert Ferrell as well as the economic deterministic views of the radical historians. Ruiz tries to balance the North American and Latin American perspectives but in the end comes down hard upon the racist and aggressive policies of Polk's administration. Students who would like to see the Mexican perspective more fully developed should read the passionate account by Rodolfo Acuna in "Legacy of Hate: The Conquest of the Southwest," in *Occupied America: A History of Chicanos*, 2d ed. (Harper & Row, 1981).

Though somewhat dated, the most accessible collection of interpretations on *The Mexican War* was edited in 1963 by Ramon E. Ruiz. Ruiz's selections are well-balanced in terms of their interpretations and include two translated essays from Carlos Bosch Garcia and Justo Sierra. Recent writings from American diplomatic scholars are also less ethnocentric and paternalistic in tone. Norman A. Graebner has continually refined his interpretations about the Mexican War period in a number of essays which have been conveniently reprinted in *The Foundation of American Foreign Policy* (Scholarly Resources, 1985). Reginald Horseman updates Alfred K. Weinberg's classic treatment on *Manifest Destiny* (Johns Hopkins Press, 1935) with his emphasis on *Race and Manifest Destiny: The Origins of American Anglo-Saxonism* (Harvard University Press, 1981). Finally, in *The Diplomacy of Annexation* (University of Missouri Press, 1985), David M. Pletcher revives the needless war theory.

ISSUE 13

Did Slavery Destroy the Black Family?

YES: Kenneth M. Stampp, from *The Peculiar Institution: Slavery in the Ante-Bellum South* (Alfred A. Knopf, 1956)

NO: Leslie Howard Owens, from *This Species of Property: Slave Life and Culture in the Old South* (Oxford University Press, 1976)

ISSUE SUMMARY

YES: Stampp contends that the master's absolute power prevented slaves from establishing and maintaining stable family units.
NO: Owens recognizes the threats to family stability among slaves but emphasizes the relentless efforts of fathers, mothers, and children to achieve family unity within the slave quarters.

Since the mid-1950s, few issues in American history have generated more interest among scholars than the institution of slavery. Books and articles analyzing the treatment of slaves, comparative slave systems, the profitability of slavery, slave rebelliousness (or lack thereof), urban slavery, slave religion, and the slave family have abounded. This proliferation of scholarship, stimulated in part by the civil rights movement, contrasts sharply with slavery historiography between the two world wars, which was monopolized by a single book—Ulrich B. Phillips's apologetic and blatantly racist *American Negro Slavery* (1918).

Phillips, a native Georgian who taught for most of his career at Yale, based his sweeping view of the Southern slave system upon plantation records left by some of the wealthiest slaveowners. He concluded that American slavery was a benign institution controlled by paternalistic masters. These owners, Phillips insisted, rarely treated their bondservants cruelly but, instead, provided their childlike, acquiescent human property with food, clothing, housing, and other necessities of life.

Although black historians such as George Washington Williams, W. E. B. Du Bois, Carter G. Woodson, and John Hope Franklin produced scholarly works which emphasized the brutal impact of slavery, their views received almost no consideration from the wider academic community. Consequently, recognition of a "revisionist" interpretation of slavery was delayed until the post–World War II era when, in the wake of the *Brown* desegregation case, Kenneth Stampp, a white Northern historian, published *The Peculiar Institution* (1956). Stampp also focused primarily upon antebellum plantation records, but his conclusions were literally a point-by-point rebuttal of

Phillips's thesis. The institution of slavery, he said, was a harsh, oppressive system in which slaveowners controlled their servants through fear of the lash. Further, in contrast to the image of the passive, happy-go-lucky "Sambo" described by Phillips, Stampp argued that slaves were "a troublesome property" who resisted their enslavement in subtle as well as overt ways.

In 1959, Stanley Elkins synthesized these seemingly contradictory interpretations in his controversial study *Slavery: A Problem in American Institutional and Intellectual Life*. Elkins clearly accepted Stampp's emphasis on the harshness of the slave system by hypothesizing that slavery was a "closed" system in which masters dominated their slaves in the same way that Nazi concentration camp guards in World War II had controlled the lives of their prisoners. Such an environment, he insisted, generated severe psychological dysfunctions which produced the personality traits of Phillips's "Sambo" character type.

As the debate over the nature of slavery moved into the 1960s and 1970s, several scholars, seeking to provide a history of the institution "from the bottom up," began to focus upon the slaves themselves as a contributing force in the slave system. Interviews with ex-slaves had been conducted in the 1920s and 1930s under the auspices of Southern University in Louisiana, Fisk University in Tennessee, and the Federal Writers Project of the Works Progress Administration. Drawing upon these interviews and previously ignored slave autobiographies, sociologist George Rawick and historians John Blassingame and Eugene D. Genovese, among others, portrayed a multifaceted community life over which slaves held a significant degree of influence. This community, operating beyond the view of the "Big House," was, in Genovese's phrase, "the world the slaves made."

These contrasting interpretive currents are reflected in the following essays on the nature of the black family in slavery. In the first selection, Kenneth Stampp emphasizes the ways in which slavery destroyed the family life of its black victims. By selling off fathers, mothers, and children without consideration to blood ties, he argues, masters prevented slaves from establishing and maintaining stable family units. In addition, owners supplanted their male bondservants as decision makers for the slave family. Stripped of familial status as well as patriarchal authority, male slaves were psychologically emasculated. Under these circumstances, Stampp concludes, a matriarchal family structure came to typify life in the quarters.

Leslie Howard Owens challenges Stampp's "neo-abolitionist" view by insisting that slaves played a significant role in establishing and protecting the family unit within the quarters. Despite the many threats to the stability of the black family in bondage, slaves took their marriage vows seriously and devoted most of their evenings and weekends to family affairs. Parents worked hard to protect their children from the harshest realities of slavery. In fact, Owens concludes, the slave family sustained itself against great odds because the slaves themselves were committed to its survival.

YES

Kenneth M. Stampp

THE BLACK FAMILY
IN THE PECULIAR INSTITUTION

When slaves protested against bondage . . . by flight . . . they normally had a clear personal grievance or an obvious objective. One of their most common grievances was being arbitrarily separated from families and friends. Hired slaves often became fugitives as they attempted to get back to their homes. Many of the runaways had recently been carried from an eastern state to the Southwest; torn by loneliness they tried frantically to find their ways back to Virginia or to one of the Carolinas. Sometimes a timid slave had never before attempted escape until he was uprooted by sale to a trader or to another master.

The advertisements for runaways were filled with personal tragedies such as the following: "I think it quite probable that this fellow has succeeded in getting to his wife, who was carried away last Spring out of my neighborhood." Lawrence, aged fourteen, was trying to make his way from Florida to Atlanta where "his mother is supposed to be." Mary "is no doubt lurking about in the vicinity of Goose Creek, where she has children." Will, aged fifty, "has recently been owned in Savannah, where he has a wife and children." Items such as these appeared regularly in the southern press.

Since slaves, as chattels, could not make contracts, marriages between them were not legally binding. "The relation between slaves is essentially different from that of man and wife joined in lawful wedlock," ruled the North Carolina Supreme Court, for "with slaves it amy be dissolved at the pleasure of either party, or by the sale of one or both, depending upon the caprice or necessity of the owners," Their condition was compatible only with a form of concubinage, "voluntary on the part of the slaves, and permissive on that of the master." In law there was no such thing as fornication or adultery between slaves; nor was there bastardy, for, as a Kentucky judge noted, the father of a slave was "unknown" to the law. No state legislature ever seriously entertained the thought of encroaching upon the master's rights by legalizing slave marriages.

There were virtually no restrictions upon the owner's right to deed his bondsmen to others. Normally the courts nullified such transfers only if the seller fraudulently warranted a slave to be "free from defects" or "vices" such as the "habit of running away." In devising his chattels a testator had the power to divide them among his heirs in any way he saw fit—including the power to dissolve families for the purpose of making an equitable distribution. If a master died intestate, the division was made in accordance with the states's laws of inheritance.

Sometimes the division provided by a will, or the claims of heirs of a master who died intestate, could not be realized without the sale of slaves. In such cases the southern courts seldom tried to prevent the breaking up of slave families. The executor of an estate was expected to dispose of human chattels, like other property, in the way that was most profitable to the heirs. It may be "harsh" to separate members of families, said the North Carolina Supreme Court, Yet "it mush be done, if the executor discovers that the interest of the estate requires it; for he is not to indulge his charities at the expense of others."

If most slaveholders condoned slave trading under conditions they accepted as unavoidable, few had a good word to say for the slavemongers themselves. Daniel R. Hundley reflected the attitude of most articulate Southerners when he wrote a defense of his section's institutions. The "hard-hearted Negro Trader" was "preeminent in villainy and a greedy love of filthy lucre." This "Southern Shylock," Hundley claimed, was usually "a coarse illbred person, provincial in speech and manners, with a cross-looking phiz, a whisky-tinctured nose, cold hard-looking eyes, a dirty tobacco-stained mouth, and shabby dress."

Many speculators . . . often purchased slaves in family groups and promised not to divide them, or pretended to buy them for personal use or for some kindly planter who wanted whole families. They made these promises to win good will or to quiet the consciences of the sellers. But a Louisianian observed that it was a "daily occurrence" for these slaves to be sold individually upon reaching the Deep South. For example, the sheriff of Chicot County, Arkansas, advertised that he had in his jail two fugitives, husband and wife, who had been "purchased by . . . a negro trader . . . in the State of Virginia, and taken to New Orleans." There the husband had been sold separately "to a gentleman whose name he does not know, as he runaway immediately on learning that he was sold from his wife." Traders frequently gave public notice that they had children under ten for sale apart from their mothers. . . .

If the dissolution of families was one of the cardinal sins of the traffic, masters merited some of the opprobrium that was heaped upon the traders. They frequently sold their slaves knowing full well that families would be broken whenever the traders found it to their advantage to do so. Sometimes the masters themselves agreed to dissolve families. A Kentuckian advertised a slave woman and her four children whom he would sell "together or separately"; a Virginian agreed to sell a slave woman "with one or more Children, to suit the purchaser"; and another Virginian offered a reward for his runaway Nat who was "no doubt attempting to follow his wife, who was lately sold to a speculator." A mistress in Nelson County, Virginia, sent a female slave to an agent in Lynchburg with instructions "to see her sold." After being sold to a trader, this slave twice escaped and returned to her husband at her former home. These were not isolated cases.

Purchasers in the Deep South selected from the trader's supply whatever slaves best satisfied their needs, occasionally whole families but usually not. For instance, an Arkansas planter visited the slave market in Memphis and bought five women with their children but not a single husband. In fact, when a trader or purchaser spoke of a "family" of slaves he was ordinarily referring only to a mother and her children. Thus a planter who thought of buying some slaves from a trader noted that the lot included "a family" consisting of "a woman 27 years old, five children and another hourly expected." The mother was "stout and healthy"; the children were "very likely, sprightly and smart" and seemed to be "all one man's children"; but the father was not part of the trader's stock.

In Africa the Negroes had been accustomed to a strictly regulated family life and a rigidly enforced moral code. But in America the disintegration of their social organization removed the traditional sanctions which had encouraged them to respect their old customs. Here they found the whites organized into families having real social and economic importance but regulated by different laws. In the quarters they were usually more or less encouraged to live as families and to accept white standards of morality.

But it was only outwardly that the family life of the mass of southern slaves resembled that of their masters. Inwardly, in many crucial ways, the domestic regimes of the slave cabin and of the "big house" were quite different. Be-

cause the slaves failed to conform to the white pattern, the master class found the explanation, as usual, in the Negro's innate racial traits. Actually, the differences resulted from the fact that slavery inevitably made much of the white caste's family pattern meaningless and unintelligible—and in some ways impossible—for the average bondsman. Here, as at so many other points, the slaves had lost their native culture without being able to find a workable substitute and therefore lived in a kind of cultural chaos.

The most obvious difference between the slave family and the white family was the legal foundation upon which each rested. In every state white marriages were recognized as civil contracts which imposed obligations on both parties and provided penalties for their violation. Slave marriages had no such recognition in the state codes; instead, they were regulated by whatever laws the owners saw fit to enforce.

A few masters arbitrarily assigned husbands to women who had reached the "breeding age"; but ordinarily they permitted slaves to pick their own mates and only required them to ask permission to marry. On the plantations most owners refused to allow slaves to marry away from home and preferred to make additional purchases when the sexes were out of balance. Thus an Alabama overseer informed his employer that one slave was without a wife and that he had promised to "indever to git you to Bey a nother woman sow he might have a wife at home." Still, it did frequently happen on both large and small estates that husbands and wives were owned by different masters. Sometimes when a slave wished to marry the slave of another owner, a sale was made in order to unite them.

Have obtained their master's consent, the couple might begin living together without further formality; or their master might hastily pronounce them man and wife in a perfunctory ceremony. But more solemn ceremonies, conducted by slave preachers or white clergymen, were not uncommon even for the field-hands, and they were customary for the domestics. The importance of the occasion was sometimes emphasized by a wedding feast and gifts to the bride.

After a marriage many masters ignored the behavior of the couple so long as neither husband nor wife caused any loud or violent disturbances. Others insisted that they not only live together but respect their obligations to each other. A Louisianian made it a rule that adultery was to be "invariably punished." On a Mississippi plantation, the husband was required to provide firewood for his family and "wait on his wife"; the wife was to do the family's cooking, washing, and mending. Failure to perform these duties was "corrected by words first but if not reformed . . . by the whip." According to a Georgian, "I never permit a husband to abuse, strike or whip his wife. . . . If the wife teases and provokes him . . . she is punished, but it sometimes happens that the husband petitions for her pardon, which I make it a rule not to refuse, as it imposes a strong obligation on the wife to . . . be more conciliating in her behavior." Some masters apparently ran domestic relations courts and served as family counselors.

Divorce, like marriage, was within the master's jurisdiction. He might permit his slaves to change spouses as often and whenever they wished, or he might establish more or less severe rules. A Louisiana master granted a divorce only after a month's notice and prohibited remar-riage unless a divorcee agreed to receive twenty-five lashes. James H. Hammond inflicted one hundred lashes upon partners who dissolved their marriage and forced them to live singly for three years. One day in 1840, Hammond noted in his diary: "Had a trial of Divorce and Adultery cases. Flogged Joe Goodwyn and ordered him to go back to his wife. Dito Gabriel and Molly and ordered them to come together again. Separated Moses and Anny finally. And flogged Tom Kollock . . . [for] interfering with Maggy Campbell, Sullivan's wife." While one master might enforce divorce laws as rigid as these, his neighbor might tolerate a veritable regime of free love—of casual alliances and easy separations. Inevitably the rules on a given estate affected the family life of its slaves.

Not only did the slave family lack the protection and the external pressure of state law, it also lacked most of the centripetal forces that gave the white family its cohesiveness. In the life of the slave, the family had nothing like the social significance that it had in the life of the white man. The slave woman was first a full-time worker for her owner, and only incidentally a wife, mother, and home-maker. She spent a small fraction of her time in the house; she often did no cooking or clothes making; and she was not usually nurse to her husband or children during illness. Parents frequently had little to do with the raising of their children; and children soon learned that their parents were neither the fount of wisdom nor the seat of authority. Thus a child on a Louisiana farm saw his mother receive twenty-five lashes for countermanding an order his mistress had given him. Lacking autonomy, the slave family could not offer the child shelter or security from the frightening creatures in the outside world.

The family had no greater importance as an economic unit. Parents and children might spend some spare hours together in their garden plots, but, unlike rural whites, slaves labored most of the time for their masters in groups that had no relationship to the family. The husband was not the director of an agricultural enterprise; he was not the head of the family, the holder of property, the provider, or the protector. If his wife or child was disrobed and whipped by master or overseer, he stood by in helpless humiliation. In an age of partriarchal families, the male slaves's only crucial function within the family was that of siring offspring.

Indeed, the typical slave family was matriarchal in form, for the mother's role was far more important that the father's. In so far as the family did have significance it involved responsibilities which traditionally belonged to women, such as cleaning house, preparing food, making clothes, and raising children. The husband was at most his wife's assistant, her companion, and her sex partner. He was often thought of as her possession ("Mary's Tom"), as was the cabin in which they lived. It was common for a mother and her children to be considered a family without reference to the father.

Given these conditions - the absence of legal marriages, the family's minor social and economic significance, and the father's limited role—it is hardly surprising to find that slave families were unstable. Lacking both outer pressures and inner pulls, they were also exposed to the threat of forced separations through sales. How dispersed a slave family could be as a result of one or more of these factors was indicated by an advertise-ment for a North Carolina fugitive who was presumed to be "lurking in the neighborhood of E. D. Walker's, at Moore's Creek, who owns most of his relations, or Nathan Bonham's who owns his mother; or, perhaps, near Fletcher Bell's, at Long Creek, who owns his father." A slave preacher in Kentucky united couples in wedlock "until death or distance do you part." When Joshua and Bush asked for permission to marry, their Virginia master read them, "so Joshua must not then say I have taken his wife from him." Thus every slave family had about it an air of impermanence, for no master could promise that his debts would not force sales, or guarantee that his death would not cause division.

If the state did not recognize slave marriages, the churches of the Protestant South might have supplied a salutary influence, since they emphasized the sanctity of the home and family. The churches did try to persuade their own slave members to respect the marriage sacrament and sometimes even disciplined those who did not. But they were quite tolerant of masters who were forced by "necessity" to separate husbands, wives, and children. For example, in 1856, a committee of the Charleston Baptist Association agreed that slave marriages had "certain limitations" and had to be "the subject of special rules." Hence, though calling these marriages "sacred and binding" and urging that they be solemnized by a religious ceremony, the committee raised no objection to the separation of couples against their wills. Apparently the only sinful separation was one initiated by the slaves themselves.

The general instability of slave families had certain logical consequences. One was the casual attitude of many bondsmen toward marriage; another was the failure of any deep and enduring affection to develop between some husbands and wives. The South abounded in stories of slaves who elected to migrate with kind masters even when it meant separation from their spouses. "Ef you got a good marster, foller him," was the saying Virginia, according to an ex-slave. An equally common story, which was often true, was that chattels were not severely disturbed by forced separation and soon found new husbands or wives in their new homes. All who were familiar with the Negro, wrote a South Carolina, understood how difficult it was "to educate even the best and most intelligently moral of the race to a true view and estimation of marriage." Here, presumably, was proof that separations through the slave trade caused no real hardship.

Still another consequence was the indifference with which most fathers and even some mothers regarded their children. An angry Virginian attributed the death of a slave infant to "the unnatural neglect of his infamous mother"; he charged that another infant was "murdered right out by his mother's neglect and barbarous cruelty." Fanny Kemble observed the stolid reaction of slave parents to the death of their children. "I've lost a many; they all goes so," was the only comment of one mother when another child died; and the father, "without word or comment, went out to his enforced labor." Many slaveholders complained that mothers could not be trusted to nurse their sick children, that some showed no affection for them and treated them cruelly. This, of course, was not a manifestation of Negro "character" as masters seemed to think. How these calloused mothers could have produced the affectionate slave "mammies" of tra-

dition was never explained. But one master spoke volumes when he advocated separating children from their parents, because it was "far more humane not to cherish domestic ties among slaves."

The final consequence of family instability was widespread sexual promiscuity among both men and women. The case of a Kentucky slave woman who had each of her seven children by a different father was by no means unique. This was a condition which some masters tried to control but which most of them accepted with resignation, or indifference, or amusement. As to the slave's moral habits, wrote one discourage owner, "I know of no means whereby to regulate them, or to restrain them; I attempted it for many years by preaching virtue and decency, . . . but it was all in vain." Olmsted cited numerous instances of masters who regarded the whole matter with complete unconcern; and masters themselves rarely gave any sign of displeasure when an unmarried slave woman became pregnant. A Virginia planter kept a record of the fathers of his slave children when he knew who the fathers were, but often he could only guess—and sometimes he suggested that the child was sired "by the Commonwealth," or "by the Universe," or "God knows who by." Overseers were generally even less concerned; as one overseer explained, the morals of the slaves were "no business of his, and he did no care what they did." Nor was the law concerned. In Mississippi, when a male slave was indicted for the rape of a female slave, the state Supreme Court dismissed the case on the ground that this was not an offense known to common or statute law.

If most slaves regarded the white man's moral code as unduly severe, many whites did too. Indeed, the number of bastardy cases in southern court records seems to confirm the conclusion that women of the poor-white class "carried about the same reputation for easy virtue as their sable sisters." Marriage, insisted Frederick Douglass, had no existence among slaves, "except in such hearts as are purer and higher than the standard morality around them." His consolation was that at least some slaves "maintained their honor, where all around was corrupt."

That numerous slaves did manage somehow to surmount the corrupting influences everywhere about them, their masters freely admitted. A South Carolinian admired the slave mother's "natural and often ardent and endearing affection for her offspring"; and another declared that "sound policy" as well as humanity required that everything be done "to reconcile these unhappy beings to their lot, by keeping mothers and children together." The majority of slave women were devoted to their children, regardless of whether they had been sired by one or by several fathers. Nor was sexual promiscuity a universal trait of southern Negroes even in bondage. Many slave couples, affirmed a Georgian, displayed toward each other a high degree of "faithfulness, fidelity, and affection."

Seldom, when slave families were broken to satisfy creditors or settle estates, was a distinction made between those who were indifferent to the matter and those who suffered deeply as a consequence. The "agony at parting," an ex-slave reminded skeptics, "must be seen and felt to be fully understood." A slave woman who had been taken from her children in Virginia and sent to the Southwest "cried many a night about it; and went 'bout mazin' sorry-like all day,

a wishing I was dead and buried!" Sometimes the "derangement" or sudden rebelliousness of a slave mother was attributed to "grief at being separated from her children." Often mothers fought desperately to prevent traders from carrying off their children, and often husbands and wives struggled against separation when they were torn apart.

But the most eloquent evidence of the affection and devotion that bound many slave families together appeared in the advertisements for fugitives. A Virginian sought a runaway whose wife had been transported to Mississippi, "and I understand from some of my servants, that he had been speaking of following her." A Maryland master was convinced that a female fugitive would attempt to get back to Georgia "where she came from, and left her husband and two children." Even when fugitives hoped to reach the free states, husbands often took their wives and parents their children, though this obviously lessened their chance of a successful escape. Clearly, to many bondsmen the fellowship of the family, in spite of its instability, was exceedingly important.

Some of the problems that troubled slave families, of course, had nothing to do with slavery—they were the tragically human problems which have ever disturbed marital tranquility. One such domestic dilemma involved a slave whose wife did not return his devotion. "He says he loves his wife and does not want to leave her," noted the master. "She says she does not love him and wont live with him. Yet he says he thinks he can over come her scruples and live happily with her." For this slavery was not the cause nor freedom the cure.

But other kinds of family tragedies were uniquely a part of life in bondage. A poignant example was the scene that transpired when an overseer tied and whipped a slave mother in the presence of her children. The frightened children pelted the overseer with stones, and one of them ran up and bit him in the leg. During the ruction the cries of the mother were mingled with the screams of the children, "Let my mammy go—let my mammy go."

NO

Leslie Howard Owens

A FAMILY FOLK

Few aspects of the slave's bondage have come in for as much speculative writing as the impact of slavery upon the slave family. Researchers in many disciplines have argued that bondage rent asunder this most basic of American institutions, injured black identity, and left scars to haunt black Americans down to our day. But all this needs further examination. . . .

The primacy of one's family relationships in shaping one's character is axiomatic among today's social theorists. Family members gain personal strength from being loved and trusted by one another, and the family unit serves as a shield against outside attacks and the feeling of emptiness that often comes from being alone. The principles are easy to understand, but the elusive nature of the slave family makes them difficult to apply. Even the concept "family" as it applies to slaves needs reconsideration. With regard to them we might view it as several overlapping concepts. Slavery made it essential that the slave family be a great deal more inclusive than its white counterpart. Its ranks included not only blood relatives but also "adopted" relatives. Few slaves seemed lacking in aunts or uncles, real or otherwise.

The odds against survival of the slave family intact were formidable. To begin with, marriage was not legally binding between slaves in any of the southern states. As late as 1855 there was a petition before the North Carolina Legislature requesting "that the parental relation . . . be acknowledged and protected by law; and that the separation of parents from their young children, say of twelve years and under, be strictly forbidden, under heavy pains and penalties." Though such memorials were frequent, legislators never heeded them, for their implementation would merely have served to increase the moral questions that bothered many slaveholders, as well as greatly restrict the domestic slave trade. In the main, masters dictated the rules governing slave unions. What they were not able to dictate, however, was the seriousness with which bondsmen took their vows. These a sizeable majority stood by steadfastly . . .

At the center of the controversy over the slave family is the bondswoman. Her image usually stands in direct contrast to that of the plantation mistress.

From Leslie Howard Owens, "A Family Folk," in *This Species of Property: Slave Life and Culture in the Old South* (New York: Oxford University Press, 1976). Reprinted by permission.

While her mistress was pure and digni-fied, she was tainted and uncouth. The mistress was ethereal and supposedly "begins from the earliest years to think herself a lady" whereas the slave woman was all too earthy. One mistress listed desired behavior for southern women in "A marriage Platform." Rule two called for virtue and discreetness, and rule seven emphasized "setting a right exam-ple of the cardinal virtues—meekness, temperance, faith, and love with an eye to Heavens reward her *chief end.*" All this and more—except heaven's reward—seemed lacking in work-weary female slaves. Capping the entire contrast was the sensuality supposedly characteristic of slaves. Mysterious in its workings, it was thought to make them excellent breeders.

I have tried to capture an argument presented all too frequently, trusting it is clear that the portrayal misrepresents both mistress and slave. The image of slave women as somewhat less than what a woman should be immediately puts in doubt their role as effective mem-bers of a family. In fact, the entire slave marriage relationship calls into question the interaction of wife and husband and parent and child in slave culture.

Many past and present researchers have assumed that the slave family was a very loosely organized group whose pri-mary cohesion was provided by women. The black sociologist E. Franklin Frazier capsulized this interpretation in his 1939 study when he characterized the slave mother "as the mistress of the cabin and as the head of the family." Frazier also mentioned that the mother had a "more fundamental interest in her children" and was able to develop "a spirit of independence and a keen sense of her personal rights." His canonization of

slave women catapulted them to the fore-front of modern discussions about the slave family. Was he correct in his conclu-sion about the matriarchal structure of the family? His picture seems somehow too inflexible, for the slave family devel-oped in ways which Frazier seems not to have imagined.

Under some conditions—when slave children were infants—southern laws provided that masters could not divide slave families. What these laws sought primarily to prevent was the separation of child from mother; the father might still be sold. Indeed, when planters spoke of slave families they often re-ferred to husbandless women and their children. The logic rings familiar even today, in that when a husband and wife legally separate the wife normally ob-tains custody of the children. We seldom assume, however, that the husband has been a passive agent in the family. Why then should we assume this to be so in the case of the slave, when there is no significant precedent for such an as-sumption in the slave's African past or in many of his American associations? Of course, this is not to deny that a slave father was a great deal more helpless than a free father today. . . .

Slavery struck most directly at bonds of affection joining husband and wife. The slave trade occasionally separated slaves married only a few weeks. We may suppose that some slaves were reluctant to love anyone deeply under these cir-cumstances. Yet most spent several years with one owner and one husband or wife, and came to know their fellow bondsmen well. Thus when slaves mar-ried it was often the consequence of courtship extending over some time. The resultant marriage was steeped in emo-tional attachment. "Our affection for each other was strong," wrote a slave of his marriage, "and this made us always apprehensive of a cruel parting." The slave Sam, like so many others, ran away from his Virginia master because he thought "it a hard case to be separated from his wife. . . ."

Planters understood such affections. "You have a woman hired in the neighborhood whose husband we own," began a letter to Colonel Barksdale of Virginia. His "name is Israel, he is our Blacksmith, and he seems to be so much attached to her we [would] like very much for her to be hired near him . . . would you sell the woman?" A sound marriage meant a better worker for the planter and often a sense of purpose for the slave.

But slavery compelled an uneven husband-wife relationship. A master could physically discipline either while the other stood by helpless, at least for the moment. Slaveowners worked both hard, and they often had little time left to enjoy each other's company in the evening. The relationship nonetheless had many interesting potentials. "A slave possessing nothing . . . except a wife and children, has all his affections concentrated upon them," wrote Francis Fedric. Occasionally, the marriage partners focused so much attention on each other that the slightest change in the routine of one tended to disrupt the other's habits. Sickness is a good example. Wives and husbands often insisted that they nurse each other back to health, fighting bitterly against efforts to force them into the fields when the possibility of a loved one dying existed. Slaveholders severely punished many and accused them of merely trying to escape duties—but discipline was seldom an effective deterrent. A planter could, of course, make arrangements for such times; expecting that wives and husbands might be off work briefly or difficult to manage during days when important personal matters came up. Sometimes a sick husband would prolong his sickness by refusing to take medicine from any but the hands of his wife, whom he could also trust to find out if someone had "hexed" him.

The marriage and family bond endured an additional hardship when masters hired out either partner, though often slaves saw being hired out as a means of bettering the quality of their lives. The slave Noah Davis was a preacher in Virginia. His master allowed him to travel and deliver sermons to raise money for his freedom. Davis' initial reaction was, "how can I leave my wife and seven children, to go to Baltimore . . . I thought my children would need my watchful care . . ." Other slaves hired their time to earn money for purchasing additional clothing and articles for the home.

The arrival of children served in large measure to solidify the slave marriage. Yet some parents feared that slaveholders would mistreat offspring or sell them away. A few adults also refused to assume parental responsibilities. They married and had children, but declined or allowed others to take care of them, and were occasionally abusive parents. Still, most assumed parental ties eagerly and were, according to a Mississippi mistress, "all so proud of showing their children." While discussing the possible sale of a slave to an Annapolis slaveholder, Charles Ridgely wrote that she "is married in the neighborhood and has a family of young children, and would I think now be extremely unwilling to be separated from them. . . ."

In Africa "tribal customs and taboos tended to fix the mother's attitude toward her child before it was born," making children greatly appreciated, and such tendencies were not absent in American slaves. Few women probably did not want children, though they were aware they might not be able to devote the attention to them that would be required. The emotional outbursts of mothers following the deaths of infants, and their resistance to being parted from offspring, indicate that female slave attitudes in this regard were not markedly distinct from those of mothers worldwide.

In fact, many disruptions of the workday stemmed from slave parents' requests to tend their children. Masters set aside a period during the day for the nursing of babies, but there was also frequent disciplining of bondswomen when they failed to return to their duties on schedule. Yet mothers repeatedly risked the lash in order to allow their body temperatures to cool down enough for effective milk nourishment. Still Moses Grandy observed that overseers forced many to work in the field carrying full breasts of milk. "They therefore could not keep up with the other hands," and when this happened overseers whipped them "so that blood and milk flew mingled from their breasts." It does not appear that he was merely trying to achieve literary effect with this dramatic statement. But often mothers got their way, for it was difficult for a master to justify, either to his conscience of his hands, children found dead from want of care. The slave's human increase was also an owner's most valuable form of property. On many plantations masters periodically assigned one or two slaves to furnish the nursing needs of all infants.

They also hired slaves to nurse their own offspring.

Most planters were probably never able to solve the problems of mothers working during the day while their children languished back at the quarters or under nearby trees, or crawled and kicked "in the filthy cabins or on the broiling sand which surrounds them." A similar dilemma, though lesser in degree, confronted their own wives, especially on small farms where everyone had chores to perform. Many small slaveholding farmers were perhaps better able to understand the immediate problems confronting motherhood in bondage. They needed only to look at their own wives' workload for several months during the suckling period. Some permitted mothers to finish their duties in the early afternoon so they might spend the remainder of the day with their children. They also permitted, sometimes insisted, that husbands work overtime to make up the slack caused by their wives' partial absence from the work force. Usually men did the extra work rather than see their women suffer, though not without complaint. Adolescents also served in this capacity, taking up their mother's tasks in the afternoon, while learning one further example of family cooperation. Thus in the midst of this swirl of life's events, slaves improvised the conditions of the family as best they could.

In bondage, the varieties of adult family behavior served as the most significant models after which slave children patterned their own actions. We know that "where a variety of behavior or models is available, selection can be influenced either by affection and rewards, by punishment, or by awareness of what is appropriate." All these factors operated with peculiar force within and upon the slave family. J. W. C. Pennington, the fugitive blacksmith, experienced what he called a "want of parental care and attention." By way of explanation he added, "my parents were not able to give any attention to their children during the day." While this was not unusual, many parents did devote their evenings and weekends to family affairs—a first duty of which was to teach children the limits placed on their conduct. This was no simple task.

Pressures from within and outside the slave family further encouraged its members to identify with one another. Planters sometimes tried to compel the association. Beginning in January, 1847, William Ervin of North Carolina ruled for his bondsmen that "each family [was] to live in their own house." This was the same suggestion advanced by several writers in De Bow's Review. But Ervin enumerated some minimal duties: "The husband to provide firewood . . . The wife to cook and wash for the husband and her children . . ." Slaves who failed to carry out these chores were subject to immediate correction. But actually bondsmen needed little prompting in this regard. They realized that a division of labors was essential to a family's survival.

Contributing to family unity on plantations was the absence of the condescending glances that shadowed the daily lives of urban bondsmen. In contact chiefly with other slaves, there was no need for them continually to compare their family life to that of whites. Charles Ball observed of his bondage that despite the equality of slaves as slaves, "there was in fact a very great difference in the manner of living, in the several families." The ways parents viewed their roles could affect this difference. Many husbands hunted in the evening to furnish additional meat for the family's diet. Ball "understood various methods of entrapping raccoons, and other wild animals . . . and besides the skins, which were worth something for their furs, I generally procured as many raccoons, opossums, and rabbits, as afforded us two or three meals in a week." This type of activity identified the male as the "bread-winner" in the household. His wife and children tended to trust his abilities to provide for them, and to appreciate the risks—such as leaving the plantation without a pass—he took in their behalf. But Charles Ball notes too that not all slave families were as fortunate as his; many lacked motivation for the kinds of activities the Balls engaged in. "Many of the families in the quarter caught no game . . ."

Sometimes children accompanied their fathers on a hunting expedition. J. W. C. Pennington tells us as well that he assisted his "father at night in making strawhats and willow-baskets, by which means we supplied our family with little articles of food, clothing and luxury . . ." The impact of these minor activities was telling. Some families began to think of themselves as better than their neighbors, though their members worked daily at the same jobs. They might think of families less "affluent" as lazy. Children picked up these prejudices and, at the behest of their parents, were sometimes very selective in their playmates. Feuds between families of a mild nature could result and ironically serve to link husband, wife, and children in a family closer together, though disrupting the quarters. . . .

To a great extent, children learned to shape their behavior to the expectations of other slaves. A beginning lesson was to respect slave elders, particularly the aged. Tradition shaped this differential treatment. The child was, moreover, at the bottom of the hierarchy of both blacks and whites, while old slaves were in a manner the domestics of the slave quarters. . . .

The slave child's early experiences helped to hone him into readiness for but not acceptance of bondage. He might start his work life by picking up a few sticks that cluttered the slave yard, advance to carrying his youthful master's books to school, and eventually merge into the adolescent "slave gangs" that went about the plantation doing odd jobs mixed with "funning." Children repeatedly slowed down the daily operations of the plantation. They naturally wanted to go to the fields to be near parents and friends, who doled out stories of spirits and connivance interrupted by orders to run the bucket to fetch some water or into the woods to examine opossum traps. . . .

For reasons of safety, many parents tried to get work assignments for their children paralleling their own duties. In this way they could assume some of the work load during a particularly difficult day and thereby shield children from abuse. They were not always successful in this, although when a child failed at his tasks or violated plantation rules masters usually left it to parents to administer the appropriate discipline. Mothers and fathers accepted the responsibility willingly, for they could give the child a well-intentioned talking to. Parental assumption of childhood discipline also strengthened the primary identification young slaves had with their parents as symbols of authority.

Some parents also saw initial work responsibilities, if properly performed, as an opportunity for their sons and daughters to escape the rigors of field labor. They encouraged their children to learn a trade if possible. A skill meant an opportunity to obtain preferred duties in later life. Masters wanted at least a few trained hands, chiefly as carpenters, for they increased the efficiency of the plantation as well as their own monetary value. John McDonogh of New Orleans hired a slave brickmason and later recommended him to a neighbor, suggesting that he might teach bricklaying to "two or three of your black boys" and "with two boys of 10 or 12 years of age to work with him in laying brick he will do all your buildings."

Occasionally, children's jobs required that they go through a prolonged or permanent separation from their families; but a determined parent was willing to accept this if it promised ultimately to provide an easier life for a son or daughter. The slave Julianna, age twelve, was the subject of a contract that engaged her services for six years. Her contractual master guaranteed "to teach her to sew, & bring her up to be a good seamstress, and a useful servant." The arrangement continued on a partially personal note; "In addition to the above I agree to allow the said girl Julianna to go to Shirley [Plantation] . . . once each year to see her relations, & remain with them one week each year. . . ."

Bondsman Henry Bibb was especially aware of the shortened childhood of the slave. "I was taken away from my mother," he wrote, "and hired out to labor for various persons, eight or ten years in succession . . ." Other hired-out children were more fortunate than Bibb. Employed as families, as were "Great

Jenny & her 3 youngest children," they partially escaped the emotional turmoil that accompanied separations.

Beyond the duties children had as plantation "hands," parents urged them to assume a full role in family affairs by doing small chores during the day. A slave born in 1844 recalled, "My father had some very fine dogs; we hunted coons, rabbits and opossum." Parents expected each child to contribute his share to the family's welfare. Some children spent part of their time fishing or checking the animal traps set by their fathers. Henry C. Bruce wrote, "We often brought home as much as five pounds of fish in a day." They would bring the catch in and reap the reward of an extra helping at dinner and much affection. Parents seldom hesitated to brag about such accomplishments. During the sickly season, if both parents became ill, total responsibility for taking care of the family garden and checking traps fell to children. Thus, as soon as young ones came of age they confronted a variety of role alternatives. They saw their parents as providers, loved ones, and disciplinarians. Moses Grandy's claim of "no lasting ties to bind relations together" seems questionable at this point.

Despite the potential of bondage to disrupt the slave family, its members—for example, brothers and sisters—often tried desperately to nurture familial affections. When no separation occurred they naturally spent much of their time together, playing and fighting. Parents told older ones to look after youngsters and to protect them from the bands of little ruffians who often roamed plantations. An ex-slave observed, "Some of us children that were too small to go to the field had to stay around and take care of the slave babies. This was my job at times. Whenever the babies got to crying too much I would go and call their mothers from the field to come and suckle them." There was also occasion to shield brothers and sisters from the "tyranny" of the master's children.

When the terms of bondage necessitated the division of families, parents often sought the aid of masters to reunite them. Lucinda, who served as a washwoman for a planter "nearly twelve years," asked him to hire her daughter Mary Jane from a nearby planter. "To oblige her," wrote her owner to Mary Jane's master, "I will become responsible for the amount, if you will let her have her daughter for the sum of Thirty dollars," which Lucinda was apparently willing to repay by her earnings during the remainder of the year. In another case, the slave George approached his master R. Carter about his daughter Betty—"7 years old, motherless, now at Colespoint-plantation —." In a letter to his overseer, Carter noted that "George wishes Betty live at Aires, with his Wife who lives there." As if not to appear overly accommodating to George's wishes Carter continued, "If Betty is not useful where She now lives—I desire to indulge George . . . you will accordingly permit him to take his daughter." At other times, slaves acted on their own to reunite themselves with loved ones. One runaway was persistent in this way: "She has a husband, I think, at his [a neighbor's] house & tho' taken up by him the first time came straight back to his house. . . ."

On weekends and holidays families spent many of their hours together, resting and joining in various festivities. Remembering that his father "could read a little," an ex-slave observed that his "custom on those Sabbaths when we remained at home, was to spend his time in instructing his children, or neighboring servants out of a New Testament. . . ." Such activities enhanced his prestige in his son's eyes.

Parents also carted children to slave gatherings dressed in their cleanest clothes, little girls adorned with bright ribbons in their hair. On these occasions parents warned them in advance to watch their manners so as not to embarrass the family. They were also to be especially careful that they were not rude to their elders. Parents would rush them from group to group, making sure that slaves on other plantations saw how intelligent and well-behaved they were. Adults told children to run races and throw rocks in competition with other boys and girls. Some of the old slaves would catch them by the ears and just hold them there "looking 'em over." Slaves paid much attention to presenting the family's best "side" wherever they appeared together. Often they seemed overly concerned that they not shame themselves in any way, for it reflected poorly on one's upbringing.

When a master abused or humiliated one member of a family, the rebuff reverberated throughout the slave household and beyond. An example appears in the opening pages of the fugitive blacksmith's narrative. Following the whipping of his father, J. W. C. Pennington remembered, "an open rupture" developed in his family [against their master]. Each member felt deeply offended by the deed, for they had always believed their conduct and faithfulness was exemplary. They talked of their humiliation in the "nightly gatherings, and showed it in . . . daily melancholy aspect."

Planters' ill-handling of slaves was only one of many factors that brought out family consciousness. Bondsmen's misdeeds against other bondsmen sometimes marked families for harassment and shame. A serious offense, such as stealing another's hunting catches, might lead to brief periods of social isolation, with members of the offending family finding themselves excluded from slave gatherings or nightly ramblings. Bondsmen saw themselves as having their primary identification with a distinct family unit to which they had responsibility and which had responsibility to them.

However, the slave family was a unit with extensions. Quite frequently it seems to have consisted of more than just parents and their natural children. It could include a number of blood or adopted relations—uncles, aunts, and cousins—who lived on the same plantation or on nearby estates. Adults "claimed" parentless children, and the slave community seldom neglected old slaves. Local bondsmen usually absorbed new arrivals on a plantation into a family setting and expected them to make a full contribution immediately. But can such a group really be called a family? Slaves considered it as such and treated adopted relatives with real affection.

The extended slave family frequently arose to augment or replace the regular family unit split up by slavery's misfortunes. There were deaths resulting from disease, accidents, and natural causes that left wives husbandless and children without parents. Then there were the family breakups caused by the slave trade. In an important, though not typical, exception, however, Robert Carter of Virginia agreed to sell his slaves to the Baltimore Company only " . . . if the Company will purchase men their wives & children [ten families]. . . ."

In slave families wives seldom possessed greater financial stability than husbands, a circumstance that often gives rise to psychological problems in men of minority households in our day. Both worked at tasks that the slave culture did not stigmatize as menial, so there was no need for the male to feel a lack of importance in his family on that score. The power of masters to disrupt families at any time weakened male slaves' sense of responsibility and dignity, but they did not invariably see this as a slight to their manhood. Yet for the slave who experienced the breakup of his household there remained that indelible hurt, as perhaps exemplified by Charles Ball's father, who "never recovered from the effects of the shock" of losing a portion of his family and became "gloomy and morose." Whenever the slave family—natural or extended—was intact, however, and slave males were reliably performing their duties, they most likely did symbolize authority within the family structure.

Except for sales of its members, much of the time slaveholders left the slave family to its own devices. And though the slave trade drove blood relatives apart, bondsmen's common persecution brought many of them back together in extended family groupings which provided for many of the emotional needs whose satisfaction the regular family, had it remained untouched, might have rendered less vexatious. Under these conditions the personalities of bondsmen were certain to gain much strength.

POSTSCRIPT

Did Slavery Destroy the Black Family?

Although W. E. B. Du Bois's *The Negro American Family* (Atlanta University Press, 1908) marked the first scholarly treatment of the black family in the United States, the works of E. Franklin Frazier and Melville J. Herskovits stimulated far more interest in this topic by addressing the origins of matriarchal family patterns among Afro-Americans.

Frazier, a black sociologist, initiated the debate in a series of studies, foremost of which was *The Negro Family in the United States* (The University of Chicago Press, 1939). In this work, Frazier contended that matricentric family patterns predominated among slaves and created a model for lower-class blacks after emancipation. Herskovits, a white anthropologist who specialized in African culture, accepted the existence of black matriarchal patterns but argued in *The Myth of the Negro Past* (Harper & Bros., 1941) that this structure was a product of African cultural survivals rather than of slavery. In many West African tribes, he asserted, women assumed important roles in the socioeconomic lives of their villages. The prominent position of women in many black American families, then, simply marked an extension of one aspect of African culture to the New World.

The Frazier thesis influenced many studies of black family life in the United States, including Daniel Patrick Moynihan's *The Negro Family: The Case for National Action* (United States Department of Labor, 1965). Moynihan's highly controversial report identified black matriarchy as a symptom of what he labeled the "tangle of pathologies" within the twentieth-century black community.

Other scholars have painted a different portrait of the typical slave family. George P. Rawick, *From Sundown to Sunup: The Making of the Black Community* (Greenwood Press, 1972); John W. Blassingame, *The Slave Community: Plantation Life in the Antebellum South* (Oxford University Press, 1972, 1979); Eugene D. Genovese in *Roll, Jordon, Roll: The World the Slaves Made* (Pantheon, 1974); and Herbert G. Gutman in *The Black Family in Slavery and Freedom, 1750–1925* (Pantheon, 1976) describe a slave culture striving to maintain traditional family units. Gutman, in particular, offers substantial data to support his argument that slaves developed a stable network of two-parent households which extended into the post–Civil War era.

Other important issues related to the structure of the black family in slavery and freedom are treated in Elmer P. Martin and Joanne Mitchell Martin, *The Black Extended Family* (University of Chicago Press, 1978) and Bell Hooks, *Ain't I a Woman: Black Women and Feminism* (South End Press, 1981).

PART 4

Conflict and Resolution

The changing nature of the American nation and the demands of its own principles finally erupted into violent conflict. Perhaps it was an inevitable step in the process of building a coherent nation from a number of distinct and diverse groups. The leaders, attitudes, and resources that were available to the North and the South were to determine the course of the war itself, as well as the national healing process that followed.

Were the Abolitionists "Unrestrained Fanatics"?

Was the Antebellum South a Unique Section in American History?

Was Abraham Lincoln America's Greatest President?

Was Reconstruction a Total Failure?

ISSUE 14

Were the Abolitionists "Unrestrained Fanatics"?

YES: Avery Craven, from *The Coming of the Civil War*, 2d ed. (University of Chicago Press, 1957)

NO: Irving H. Bartlett, from "The Persistence of Wendell Phillips," Martin Duberman, ed., *The Antislavery Vanguard: New Essays on the Abolitionists* (Princeton University Press, 1965)

ISSUE SUMMARY

YES: Avery Craven believes that the fanaticism of the abolitionist crusade created an atmosphere of crisis that resulted in the outbreak of the Civil War.
NO: Irving Bartlett differentiates between agitation and fanaticism and claims that abolitionists like Wendell Phillips were deeply committed to improving the quality of life for all Americans, including those blacks held as slaves.

Opposition to slavery in the American colonies dates back to the seventeenth and eighteenth centuries, when Puritan leaders, like Samuel Sewall, and Quakers, such as John Woolman and Anthony Benezet, published a number of pamphlets condemning the existence of the slave system. The connection between religion and antislavery sentiment also is evident in the decision of the Society of Friends in 1688 to prohibit members from owning bondservants because slavery was contrary to Christian principles. These attacks, however, did little to diminish the institution. In fact, efforts to force emancipation gained little headway in the colonies until the outbreak of the American Revolution. Complaints that the English government had instituted a series of measures that "enslaved" the colonies in British North America also raised thorny questions about the presence of *real* slavery in those colonies. How could Americans demand their freedom from King George III, who was cast in the role of oppressive master, and at the same time deny freedom and liberty to black bondsmen in their midst? Such a contradiction inspired a gradual emancipation movement in the North, which often was accompanied by compensation for the former owners.

In addition, antislavery societies sprang up throughout the nation to continue the crusade against bondage. Interestingly, the majority were located in the South. Prior to the 1830s, the most prominent antislavery organization was the American Colonization Society which offered a two-fold program: (1) gradual, compensated emancipation of slaves; and (2) exportation of the new freedmen to colonies outside the boundaries of the United States, especially to Africa.

In the 1830s, antislavery activity underwent an important transformation. As the colonizationists proved unable to eliminate either slavery or blacks from the country, a new strain of antislavery sentiment expressed itself in the abolitionist movement. Drawing momentum from both the Second Great Awakening and the example set by England (which prohibited slavery in its imperial holdings in 1833), abolitionists called for an immediate end to slavery without compensation to masters for the loss of their property. Abolitionists viewed slavery not so much as a practical problem to be resolved but rather as a moral offense incapable of being resolved through traditional channels of political compromise. In January 1831, William Lloyd Garrison, who came to symbolize the abolitionist crusade, published the first issue of *The Liberator*, a newspaper dedicated to the immediate end to slavery. In his first editorial, Garrison expressed the self-righteous indignation of many in the abolitionist movement when he warned slaveholders and their supporters to "urge me not to use moderation in a cause like the present. I am in earnest—I will not equivocate—I will not excuse—I will not retreat a single inch—AND I WILL BE HEARD. . . ."

Unfortunately for Garrison, relatively few Americans were inclined to respond positively to his call. His newspaper generated little interest outside Boston, New York, Philadelphia, and other major urban centers of the North. This situation, however, changed within a matter of months. In August 1831, a slave preacher named Nat Turner led a rebellion of slaves in Southampton County, Virginia, resulting in the death of some sixty whites. Although the revolt was quickly suppressed and Turner and his supporters (along with many slaves not involved in the uprising) were executed, the incident spread fear throughout the South. Governor John B. Floyd of Virginia turned an accusatory finger toward the abolitionists when he concluded that the Turner revolt was "undoubtedly designed and matured by unrestrained fanatics in some of the neighboring states." The message was clear: Garrison and other abolitionist "fanatics" were responsible for generating discontent among slaves and attempting to undermine traditional Southern institutions. Moreover, it would be charged, these radicals contributed to a crisis environment that degenerated over the next generation and ultimately produced civil war.

Many historians have accepted this view that abolitionist fanaticism, expressed through irresponsible attacks on Southern slavery, led to political deterioration in the United States which culminated in secession and war. Avery Craven, for example, blames abolitionists for inciting volatile emotions by characterizing slaveholders as sinful aristocrats willing to distort the American dream of freedom to preserve their peculiar institution.

Irving Bartlett, in contrast, surveys the abolitionist career of Wendell Phillips and concludes that he was not a fanatic but rather a practical agitator, an intellectual, and a committed philosopher of reform who clearly understood the difference between agitation and demagoguery.

YES   Avery Craven

THE NORTHERN ATTACK ON SLAVERY

The abolition movement . . . was part of the drive to unseat aristocrats and re-establish American democracy according to the Declaration of Independence. It was a clear-cut effort to apply Christianity to the American social order.

The anti-slavery effort was at first merely one among many. It rose to dominance only gradually. Fortunate from the beginning in leadership, it was always more fortunate in appeal. Human slavery more obviously violated democratic institutions than any other evil of the day; it was close enough to irritate and to inflame sensitive minds, yet far enough removed that reformers need have few personal relations with those whose interests were affected. It rasped most severely upon the moral senses of a people whose ideas of sin were comprehended largely in terms of self-indulgence and whose religious doctrines laid emphasis on social usefulness as the proper manifestation of salvation. And, what was more important, slavery was now confined to a section whose economic interests, and hence political attitudes, conflicted sharply with those of the Northeast and upper Northwest.

Almost from the beginning of the new anti-slavery movement, two distinct centers of action appeared, each with its distinct and individual approach to the problem. One developed in the industrial areas of New England. Its most important spokesman was William Lloyd Garrison, founder and editor of a Boston abolition paper called the *Liberator*. Garrison at first accepted the old idea that slavery was an *evil* to be pointed out and gradually eradicated by those among whom it existed, but he shifted his position in the early 1830's and denounced slavery as a damning crime to be unremittingly assailed and immediately destroyed. The first issue of his paper announced a program from which he never deviated: " . . . *I do not wish to think or speak or write with moderation. I will not retreat a single inch, and I will be heard.*" The problem, as Garrison saw it, was one of abstract right and wrong. The Scriptures and the Declaration of Independence had already settled the issue. Slavery could have no legal status in a Christian democracy. If the Constitution recognized it, then the Constitution should be destroyed. Slaveholders were both

From Avery Craven, *The Coming of the Civil War* (Chicago: University of Chicago Press, 1957). Copyright © 1957 by Avery Craven. All rights reserved. Reprinted by permission.

sinners and criminals. They could lay no claim to immunity from any mode of attack. . . .

The extreme and impractical nature of the Garrison anti-slavery drive served to attract attention and arouse antagonism rather than to solve the problem. It did, however, show how profoundly the conditions of the time had stirred the reform spirit and how wide the door had been opened to the professional reformers— men to whom the question was not so much "how shall we abolish slavery, as how shall we best discharge our duty . . . to ourselves." Garrison may be taken as typical of the group. His temperament and experiences had combined to set him in most relationships against the accepted order of things. His life would probably have been spent in protesting even if slavery had never existed. From childhood he had waged a bitter fight *against* obstacles and *for* a due recognition of his abilities. A drunken father had abandoned the family to extreme poverty before William was three years old, and the boy, denied all but the rudiments of an education, had first been placed under the care of Deacon Bartlett, and then apprenticed for seven years to one Ephraim Allen to learn the printing trade. His first venture after his apprenticeship was over failed. His second gave him the opportunity to strike back at an unfair world. He became an editor of the *National Philanthropist*, a paper devoted to the suppression of "intemperance and its Kindred vices." This publication served also as a medium through which to attack lotteries, Sabbath-breaking, and war. A new Garrison began to emerge. His personality, given opportunity for expression, asserted itself. . . .

Anti-slavery efforts entered the Garrison program when Benjamin Lundy, the pioneer abolitionist, invited him to help edit the *Genius of Universal Emancipation* in Baltimore. Hostile treatment there, climaxed by imprisonment for libel, together with the influence of extreme British opinion, changed a moderate attitude which admitted "that immediate and complete emancipation is not desirable . . . no rational man cherishes so wild a vision," into the extreme and uncompromising fanaticism expressed only two years later in the *Liberator*. From that time on Garrison was bothered only by the fact that the English language was inadequate for the expression of his violent opinions. Southerners in Congress were desperados.

> We would sooner trust the honor of the country . . . in the hands of the inmates of our penitentiaries and prisons than in their hands . . . they are the meanest of thieves and the worst of robbers. . . . We do not acknowledge them to be within the pale of Christianity, or republicanism, or humanity!

Hatred of the South had supplanted love for the Negro!

In such an approach as this, there could be no delay, no moderation. Right was right, and wrong was wrong. The Slaveholder could not be spared or given time to learn the evil of his ways. Action immediate and untempered was demanded. . . .

The second center of anti-slavery effort was in upper New York and the farther Northwest. Influences from this center included in their sweep, however, much of rural New England and the Middle States and the movement found liberal financial help in New York City. Benjamin Lundy and other Quaker leaders started the crusade, but it did not come to full and wide expression until Theodore Weld, already the ablest temperance orator in the Northwest, set about cultivating the great field prepared for social reform by the Finney revivals.

Weld was, like Garrison, unusual both in abilities and in personal characteristics. He was much given to "anti-meat, -butter, -tea, and -coffee, etc. -ism[s]." He indulged in excessive self-effacement and in extravagant confessions of selfishness, pride, impatience of contradiction, personal recklessness, and "a bad, unlovely temper." . . .

He wrote also of his contempt of opponents—"one of the *trade* winds of my nature [which] very often . . . *blows a hurricane*," and he listed by name those "who strangely and stupidly idolize me . . . and yield themselves to my sway in all confidence and love." He boasted of his daring and told of how as a child a tremendous thunderstorm would send him whooping and hallooing through the fields like a wild Indian. He had the Puritan's love of enduring; the saint's "right" to intolerance. He was, in fact, always a revivalist—a man with a mission to perform in the great West—"the battlefield of the World."

The campaign which he launched was but an expansion of the benevolence crusade already a part of the Western revival effort. As W. C. Preston said: "Weld's agents made the anti-slavery cause 'identical with religion,' and urged men, by all they esteem[ed] holy, by all the high and exciting obligations of duty to man and God . . . to join the pious work of purging the sin of slavery from the land." The movement, as it developed, was generally temperate in tone, and tended to function through the existing agencies of religion and politics. Lane Theological Seminary, founded in Cincinnati to train leaders in the Finney tradition, became the center from which Weld worked. Here, in a series of debates, he shaped the doctrine of gradual immediatism which by insisting that *gradual emancipation* begin *at once*, saved the movement from Garrison'S extremes; from here he went out to win a group of converts which included James G. Birney, Joshua Giddings, Edwin M. Stanton, Elizur Wright, and Beriah Green; and here he adapted the revival technique to the abolition crusade and prepared the way for his loyal band of Seventy to carry that crusade throughout the whole Northwest.

There was, however, another aspect to the movement in this region—a very hard-headed practical aspect. Its leaders believed in action as well as agitation. And action here meant political action. Western men had a way of viewing evil as something there ought to be a law against. They thought it was the business of government to secure morality as well as prosperity. They were even inclined to regard the absence of prosperity as the result of the existence of evil. Naturally, therefore, in spite of the revival-meeting procedure used to spread the gospel of abolition, action against slavery followed political precedent. This action began with petitions to Congress for such a practical end as the abolition of slavery in the District of Columbia. When Southern resentment of such a measure brought the adoption of gag rule methods, the contest was broadened into a fight on the floors of Congress for the constitutional rights of petition and free speech. This proved to be an excellent way to keep the slavery question before the public and to force slaveholders to reveal their undemocratic attitudes. Petitions arrived in such quantities as to clog the work of Congress. A Washington organization for agitation and lobbying became necessary. Weld himself went to Washington to advise with John Quincy Adams and his fellow workers. Slavery thus again entered national politics, this time by way of the Northwest. Anti-slavery politicians, such as Joshua Giddings and Salmon P. Chase of Ohio, quickly proved the value of the cause as a stepping-stone to public office. . . .

With the new growth and importance of the movement, the technique of its propaganda also reached new efficiency. Never before or since has a cause been urged upon the American people with such consummate skill and such lasting effects. Every agency possible in that day was brought into use; even now the predominating opinions of most of the American people regarding the antebellum South and its ways are the product of that campaign of education.

Indoctrination began with the child's A B C's which were learned from booklets containing verses like the following:

A is an Abolitionist
A man who wants to free
The wretched slave, and give to all
An equal liberty.
B is a Brother with a skin
Of somewhat darker hue,
But in our Heavenly Father's sight,
He is as dear as you.
C is the Cotton field, to which
This injured brother's driven,
When, as the white man's *slave*, he toils
From early morn till even.
D is the Driver, cold and stern,
Who follows, whip in hand,
To punish those who dare to rest,
Or disobey command.
• • •
I is the Infant, from the arms

Of its fond mother torn,
And at a public auction sold
With horses, cows, and corn.
• • •
Q is the Quarter, where the slave
On coarsest food is fed
And where, with toil and sorrow worn
He seeks his wretched bed.
• • •
W is the Whipping post,
To which the slave is bound,
While on his naked back, the lash
Makes many a bleeding wound.
• • •
Z is a Zealous man, sincere,
Faithful, and just, and true;
An earnest pleader for the slave—
Will you not be so too?

For children able to read, a wider variety of literature was written. One volume in verse urged "little children" to "plead with men, that they buy not slaves again." . . .

Juvenile story books, with some parts written in verse and printed in large and bold type and the rest written in prose and set in smaller type, were issued with the explanation that the verses were adapted to the capacity of the youngest reader, while the prose was well suited for being read aloud in the family circle. "It is presumed," said the preface, "that [with the prose] our younger friends will claim the assistance of their older brothers and sisters, or appeal to the ready aid of their mamma." Such volumes might contain pictures and stories from *Uncle Tom's Cabin* or they might consist of equally appealing tales of slave children cruelly torn from their parents or tortured by ingenious methods.

For adults the appeal was widened. No approach was neglected. Hymn books offered abolition songs set to familiar tunes. To the strains of "Old Hundred" eager voices invited "ye Yeomen brave" to rescue "the bleeding slave," or, to the "Missionary Hymn," asked them to consider

The frantic mother
Lamenting for her child,
Till falling lashes smother
Her cries of anguish wild!

Almanacs, carrying the usual information about weather and crops, filled their other pages with abolition propaganda. In one of these, readers found the story of Liburn Lewis, who, for a trifling offense, bound his slave, George, to a meat block and then, while all the other slaves looked on, proceeded slowly to chop him to pieces with a broad ax, and to cast the parts into a fire. Local, state, and national societies were organized for more efficient action in petitioning, presenting public speakers, distributing tracts, and publishing anti-slavery periodicals. The American Anti-Slavery Society "in the year 1837-38, published 7,877 bound volumes, 47,256 tracts and pamphlets, 4,100 circulars, and 10,490 prints. Its quarterly *Anti-Slavery Magazine* had an annual circulation of 9,000; the *Slave Friend*, for children, had 131,050; the monthly *Human Rights*, 189,400, and the weekly *Emancipator*, 217,000." From 1854 to 1858 it spent $3281 on a series of tracts discussing every phase of slavery, under such suggestive titles as "Disunion, our Wisdom and our Duty," "Relations of Anti-Slavery to Religion," and "To Mothers in the Free States." Its "several corps of lecturers of the highest ability and worth . . . occupied the field" every year in different states. Its Annual Reports, with their stories of atrocities and their biased discussion of issues, constituted a veritable arsenal from which weapons of attack could be drawn. Like other anti-slavery societies, it maintained an official organ, issued weekly, and held its regular conventions for the generation of greater force.

Where argument and appeal to reason failed, the abolitionists tried entertainment and appeal to emotion. *Uncle Tom's Cabin* was written because its author, "as a woman, as a mother," was "oppressed and broken hearted, with the sorrows & injustice" seen, and "because as a Christian" she "felt the dishonor to Christianity—because as a lover of [her] country, [she] trembled at the coming day of wrath." It became a best seller in the most complete sense. Only the Bible exceeded it in numbers sold and in the thoroughness with which it was read in England and America. Editions were adapted to every pocketbook, and translations carried it throughout the world. Dramatized and put on the stage, it did more to make the theatre respectable in rural America than any other single influence. The fictitious Uncle Tom became the stereotype of all American Negro slaves; Simon Legree became the typical slaveholder. A generation and more formed its ideas of Southern life and labor from the pages of this novel. A romantic South, of planter-gentlemen and poor whites, of chivalry and dissipation, of "sweet but worthless" women, was given an imaginative reality so wide and so gripping that no amount of patient research and sane history writing could alter it. Other novels, such as *Our World: or the Slaveholder's Daughter*, built their plots about the love affairs of Southern planters with their Negro slaves. Jealousies between wives and mistresses, struggles between brothers for the possession of some particularly desirable wench, or the inner conflict of a master over his obligation to his mulatto bastards, constituted the main appeal in such works. The object was always the same: to reveal the licentious character of Southern men, the unhappy status of Southern homes, and the horrible violation of Negro chastity everywhere existing under slavery.

Reformed slaveholders and escaped slaves were especially valuable in the crusade. Under the warming influence of sympathetic audiences their stories of cruelty and depravity grew apace. Persecution and contempt from old friends increased their zeal. Birney, the Grimké sisters, Frederick Douglass, and many others influenced the movement and were influenced by it in a way comparable only to the relation of reformed drunkards to the temperance cause.

By means of such agencies and methods a well-defined picture of the South and slavery became slowly fixed in Northern minds. The Southern people were divided into two distinct classes—slaveholders and poor whites. The former constituted an aristocracy, living in great white-pillared houses on extended plantations. The latter, ignorant and impotent, made up a rural slum which clung hopelessly to the pine barrens or the worn-out acres on the fringes of the plantations. Planters, who lived by the theft of Negro labor, completely dominated the section. They alone were educated; they alone held office. Nonslaveholders were too poor to "buy an education for themselves and their children," and the planters, not wishing to "endanger their supremacy," refused to establish public schools. Few poor whites could either read or write. They gained their opinions and their principles from "stump speeches and tavern conversations." They were "absolutely in the slaveholder's power." He sent "them to the polls to vote him into office and in so doing to vote down their own rights and interests. . . ." They knew "no more what they [were] about, than so many children or so many Russian serfs. . . ."

Social-economic conditions in the South were described as tumble-down and backward. The slave, lacking the incentive of personal gain, was inefficient. The master, ruined by power, self-indulgence, and laziness, was incapable of sound management. . . . Others went so far as to charge the panic of 1837 to Southern profligacy. "The existence of Slavery," resolved the American Anti-Slavery Society in 1840, "is the grand cause of the pecuniary embarrassments of the country; and . . . no real or permanent relief is to be expected . . . until the total abolition of that execrable system." Joshua Leavitt called the slave system "a bottomless gulf of extravagance and thriftlessness." Another explained its "withering and impoverishing effect by the fact that it was the "rule of violence and arbitrary will. . . . It would be quite in character with its theory and practice," he said, "if slave-drivers should refuse to pay their debts and meet the sheriff with dirk and pistol." Leavitt estimated that the South had "taken from the North, within five years, more than $100,000,000, by notes which will never be paid," and quoted an English writer to the effect that "planters are always in debt. The system of society in a slaveholding community is such as to lead to the contraction of debt, which the system itself does not furnish the means of paying. . . ."

Nor did the Southern shortcomings, according to the anti-slavery view, end with things material. Moral weaknesses were even more offensive. Sexual virtue was scarcely known. "The Slave States," wrote an abolitionist, "are Sodoms, and almost every village family is a brothel." Another writer declared that "in the slaveholding settlements of Middle and Southern Mississippi . . . there [was] not a virtuous young man of twenty years of age." "To send a lad to a male academy in Mississippi," he said, "is moral murder." An anti-slavery pamphlet told of "a million and a half of slave women, some of them without even the tinge of African blood . . . given up a lawful prey to the unbridled lusts of their masters." Another widely circulated tract described a slave market in which one dealer "devoted himself exclusively to the sale of young mulatto women." The author pictured the sale of "the most beautiful woman I ever saw," without "*a single trace of the African about her features*" and with "a pair of eyes that pierced one through and through" to "one of the most lecherous-looking old brutes" that he had ever seen. The narrative closed with the shrieking appeal: "God shield the helpless victim of that bad man's power—it may be, ere now, that bad man's lust!" The conclusion was inescapable. Slavery and unrestrained sexual indulgence at Negro expense were inseparable.

In such a section and in the hands of such men, abolitionists assumed that slavery realized its most vicious possibilities. Anti-slavery men early set themselves to the task of collecting stories of cruelty. These were passed about from one to another, often gaining in ferocity as they travelled. Weld gathered them together in a volume entitled *American Slavery As It Is* and scattered them broadcast over the North. The annual reports of the anti-slavery societies, their tracts and periodicals, also revelled in atrocities, asking no more proof of their absolute truth than the word of a fellow fanatic.

The attempt to picture slavery "as it was," therefore, came to consist almost entirely of a recital of brutalities. Now and then a kind master and seemingly contented slaves were introduced for the purpose of contrast—as a device to deepen shadows. But, as a rule, Southerners, according to these tracts, spent their time in idleness broken only by brutal cock-fights, gander pullings, and horse races so barbarous that "the blood of the tortured animal drips from the lash and flies at every leap from the stroke of the rowel." Slavery was one continual round of abuse. The killing of a slave was a matter of no consequence. Even respectable ladies might cause "several to be *whipped to death*." Brandings, ear cropping, and body-maiming were the rule. David L. Child honestly declared: "From all that I have read and heard upon the subject of whipping done by masters and overseers to slaves . . . I have come to the conclusion that some hundreds of *cart whips* and cowskin instruments, which I am told make the skin fly like feathers, and cut frequently to the bone, are in *perpetual daily motion* in the slave states." John Rankin told of Negroes stripped, hung up and stretched and then "whipped until their bodies [were] covered with blood and mangled flesh," some dying "under the lash, others linger[ing] about for a time, and at length die[ing] of their *wounds.* . . ." The recital was indeed one of "*groans, tears, and blood.*"

To abuse was added other great wrongs. Everywhere slaves were overworked, underfed, and insufficiently clothed and sheltered. Family ties were cut without the slightest regard for Negro feelings—infants were torn from the mother's breast, husbands separated from their wives and families. Marriage was unknown among slaves, and the right to worship God generally denied. Strangely enough, little was said of slave-breeding for market. That charge was largely left to the politicians of the next decades and to the historians of a later day.

Two principal assumptions stood out in this anti-slavery indictment of the slaveholder. He was, in the first place, the arch-aristocrat. He was the great enemy of democracy. He was un-American, the oppressor of his fellow men, the exploiter of a weaker brother. Against him could be directed all the complaints and fears engendered by industrial captains and land speculators. He, more than any other aristocrat, threatened to destroy the American democratic dream.

In the second place, he was a flagrant sinner. His self-indulgence was unmatched. His licentious conduct with Negro women, his intemperance in the use of intoxicating liquors, his mad dueling, and his passion for war against the weak were enough to mark him as the nation's moral enemy number one! The time for dealing moderately had passed. Immediate reform was imperative.

Thus it was that the slaveholder began to do scapegoat service for all aristocrats and all sinners. To him were transferred resentments and fears born out of local conditions. Because it combined in itself both the moral and the democratic appeal, and because it coincided with sectional rivalry, the abolition movement gradually swallowed up all other reforms. The South became the great object of all efforts to remake American society. Against early indifference and later persecution, a handful of deadly-in-earnest men and women slowly built into a section's consciousness the belief in a Slave Power. To the normal strength of sectional ignorance and distrust they added all the force of Calvinistic morality and American democracy and thereby surrounded every Northern interest and contention with holy sanction and reduced all opposition to abject depravity. When the politician, playing his risky game, linked expansion and slavery, Christian common folk by the thousands, with no great personal urge for reforming, accepted the Abolition attitudes toward both the South and slavery. Civil war was then in the making.

NO

Irving H. Bartlett

THE PERSISTENCE OF WENDELL PHILLIPS

Wherever Wendell Phillips walked on the Harvard campus he carried the aura of Beacon Hill with him. He was as well born as any Winthrop or Saltonstall and had been brought up in an imposing brick mansion on Beacon Hill only a few steps from the State House. The son of Boston's first mayor, a man universally respected for sound conservative principles, young Phillips seemed intent on following in his father's footsteps. He gained a reputation as being "the pet of the aristocracy," and in orations at the college exhibitions went out of his way to attack reformers and defend the standing order. One of his friends later recalled that Phillips would probably have been chosen by his classmates as the man "*least likely* to give the enthusiasm and labor of [his life] to the defense of popular rights."

Fifteen years after he left Harvard Phillips was asked by the secretary of the class of 1831 to fill out a questionnaire. He noted that he was in good health but growing bald. Under occupation he said he had prepared for the law "but grew honest and quitted what required an oath to the Constitution of the United States." Asked to note any other remarks that might be interesting to his classmates, he wrote: "My main business is to forward the abolition of slavery. I hold that the world is wrong side up and maintain the propriety of turning it upside down. I go for Disunion and have long since abjured that contemptible mockery, the Constitution of the United States."

To understand Phillips' career as an abolitionist and free-lance radical it is first necessary to account for his transformation from gentility to "fanaticism." Certainly it was not a natural development. After graduating from Harvard College Phillips entered the Harvard Law School. His career there and later as a practicing attorney was uneventful. Like most of the other sons of the old Federalists, he was happy to follow Daniel Webster into the Whig party which continued to serve the bulwarked conservatism of Massachusetts. He shared an office at this time with a man who later led a mob against abolitionists, and most of his social contacts were with the old aristocratic families who, if they knew anything about William Lloyd Garrison, naturally "supposed him to be a man who ought to be hung," and were unanimously determined to outlaw

From *Antislavery Vanguard: New Essays on The Abolitionists*, ed. Martin Duberman. Copyright © 1965, Princeton University Press. Excerpts, pp. 102–122, reprinted with permission of Princeton University Press.

288

anyone, even the saintly William Ellery Channing, for expressing the slightest sympathy with his principles.

Phillip's first personal encounter with the antislavery movement came in October 1835, when he stood on a Boston street corner and watched a jeering mob drag Garrison through the street at the end of a rope. A few weeks later he met Ann Terry Greene, one of Garrison's disciples, and in less than a year, to the consternation of his mother and most of Boston society, married her. A few months later he made his first antislavery speech.

As with most of the early abolitionists, religion played a dominant role in making Phillips an abolitionist. We will never know how successful he might have been in law or politics, but his advantages in family background and education, his intelligence, and his remarkable oratorical talent suggest that the achievements of a Webster, Choate, or Sumner were not beyond his reach. The fact is, however, that between the time he graduated from college and met his wife, Phillips appears to have been in a melancholy state of mind largely because he lacked a sense of vocation. He had been brought up as a devout Calvinist, and it was a fundamental article in his belief that a man must make his life count for something. Like all new lawyers he found it slow going to get a practice started, but even more important he found no great satisfaction in the profession. He needed to find a calling. As it turned out he fell in love and found his calling at the same time. His bride introduced him to William Lloyd Garrison and other Boston abolitionists, and in the early days of their marriage, when her health permitted, accompanied him to antislavery meetings. Phillips had undergone religious conversion years before under the powerful preaching of Lyman Beecher. As he joined hands with the abolitionists he felt he was being born a third time. "None know what it is to live," he wrote in 1841, "till they redeem life from its seeming monotony by laying it a sacrifice on the altar of some great cause."

Phillips never forgot the importance of religion to the antislavery movement. "Our enterprise is eminently a religious one," he said, "dependent for success entirely on the religious sentiment of the people." When Phillips refused to take an oath to support the "proslavery constitution" of the United States, he thought of himself as following in the tradition of his forbear, the Reverend George Phillips, who had come to America in 1630 to put the Atlantic Ocean "between himself and a corrupt church." He did not think of himself as an ordinary lecturer or orator, but as a kind of minister to the public, preaching the gospel of reform. When he was called to fill Theodore Parker's pulpit in the Boston Music Hall in 1860, it was natural for him to begin a sermon by announcing that "Christ preached on the last political and social item of the hour; and no man follows in his footsteps who does not do exactly the same thing." Phillips' sermons before Parker's congregation were the same sermons that he preached in Faneuil Hall before antislavery meetings, and he was convinced that he did his duty to God in both places by flaying the public sinners of the day whether their names were Webster, Everett, Jefferson Davis, or Abraham Lincoln.

The idealism of the American revolutionary tradition also played a decisive role in shaping Phillips' career. When he was a boy, he remembered later, the Boston air still "trembled and burned with Otis and Sam Adams." He had been born practically next door to John Hancock's mansion, within site of Bunker Hill and only a few steps from the site of the Boston massacre. When he was thirteen years old and a student at the Boston Latin School he stood for hours in a crowd on the Common to catch a glimpse of Lafayette upon his visit to the city. Two years later, while poring over his lessons at the school, the sound of tolling bells came through the open windows announcing the deaths of Thomas Jefferson and John Adams.

Phillips never doubted that the revolutionary fathers were on his side. His first antislavery speech was given to support John Quincy Adams in his fight to get the Congress to hear petitions attacking slavery. Phillips argued that the right of petition was a traditional right for free men and that in attacking it the South threatened the freedom of all men. "This is the reason we render to those who ask us why we are contending against southern slavery," he said, *"that it may not result in northern slavery . . .* it is our own rights which are at issue."

The speech which made Phillips famous in Boston was given at a Faneuil Hall meeting to honor the memory of Elijah Lovejoy who had been killed by a mob in Alton, Illinois. The meeting was called to pay tribute to Lovejoy, but the abolitionists almost lost control of it when James Austin, the Attorney General for Massachusetts, stood up and made a violent speach attacking Lovejoy for having published an incendiary antislavery newspaper. Austin likened the mob which destroyed Lovejoy and his press to the patriots responsible for the Boston Tea Party. Phillips was able to get the floor after Austin, and overcome the hooting and jeering of the proslavery faction in the audience with an eloquent defense of

Lovejoy. Again Phillips was defending a traditional American right, freedom of the press, and he insisted that the spirit of the American revolution supported him. . . .

In his reliance on religion and the spirit of the Declaration of Independence, Phillips was like most other abolitionists. As an orator, however, despite the fact that he was part of a movement full of celebrated speakers, his uniqueness is unchallenged. . . .

By far the most sensational characteristic of Phillips as a speaker was the contrast between his perfectly controlled, poised, almost dispassionate manner, and the inflammatory language he employed. It was the apparent effortlessness of his delivery that impressed many listeners most. "Staples said the other day that he heard Phillips speak at the State House," wrote Thoreau in his *Journal*. "By thunder! he never heard a man that could speak like him. His words come so easy. It was just like picking up chips." In an effort to explain how the speaker remained somehow detached from his own eloquence, another observer compared him to "a cold but mysteriously animated statue of marble." Time and time again when Phillips was on tour, talking before new audiences, the reporter would register the audience's surprise. "They had conceived him to be a ferocious ranter and blustering man of words. They found him to be a quiet, dignified and polished gentleman and scholar, calm and logical in his argument."

One of the reasons why abolitionist meetings in the middle and later 1850's began to draw impressively large crowds, as the critics of the abolitionists pointed out, was that for many people an antislavery meeting had all the elements of a theatrical performance. The star performer was usually Wendell Phillips, and his stock in trade, according to the unconverted, was "personal abuse." To the abolitionists themselves he was, as his publisher remarked, the greatest "master of invective" in the nineteenth century. With sublime confidence, almost as if he were reading from a sheaf of statistics or reciting a series of scientific facts, Phillips would take the platform to announce that Daniel Webster was "a great mass of dough," Edward Everett "a whining spaniel," Massachusetts Senator Robert C. Winthrop "a bastard who had stolen the name of Winthrop," and the New England churches an ecclesiastical machine to manufacture hypocrisy "just as really as Lowell manufactures cotton." It was the way Phillips uttered his epithets that fascinated most critics. The shrewd Scottish traveler David Macrae who had been led "from the ferocity of his onslaughts on public men and public measures . . . to form a false conception of his delivery" noted with surprise that vehemence and declamation were replaced by sarcasm, "cold, keen, withering." Macrae was impressed by the relentless manner in which Phillips pursued his opponents. "He follows an enemy like an Indian upon the trail. . . . When he comes to strike, his strokes are like galvanic shocks; there is neither noise nor flash but their force is terrible."

A writer for an English paper who was contrasting Phillips' speeches with "the rounded periods of Mr. Seward" and "the finished artistic rhetoric of the patriotic Mr. Everett" noted one quality which grated on European ears, and that was "the concentrated bitterness, the intense spirit of hatred with which they are frequently suffused." Because Phillips did not like to talk in general terms about issues, because he always took dead aim on personalities and heaped "the concentrated bitterness" of his rhetoric upon the heads of men prominent in public life, and because the people turned out in droves to hear him, Robert C. Winthrop believed that Phillips had "gradually educated our people to relish nothing but the 'eloquence of abuse.' "

A good many later critics have been much harsher than Winthrop in criticizing Phillips. Theodore Roosevelt called him a wild-eyed fanatic and Professor Randall has dismissed his speeches as "a kind of grandiloquent, self-righteous raving." A careful reading of his career shows these estimates to be incorrect. What distinguishes Phillips from the other abolitionists more significantly than anything else is that he was an intellectual, a philosopher of reform as well as a practical agitator. It is impossible to understand him, therefore, without knowing more about his political ideas and his conception of the role of the reformer in America.

Like other abolitionists Phillips believed in the Higher Law and judged every public question from an absolute moral standard. He believed that a man's first duty was to God, and that men should do their duty at whatever cost. He was convinced that anything right in principle had to be right in practice. He accepted Garrison's demand for immediate emancipation without question. Phillips' Calvinism, his belief in Divine Providence, made it possible for him to dismiss whatever doubts he might have had about the practicality of this radical solution. "No matter if the charter of emancipation was written in blood," he said in one of his early speeches, "and anarchy stalk abroad with giant strides—if God commanded, it was right." Phillips' Calvinism reinforced his radicalism. He did not have to worry about the consequences of his agitation. A man could only do his duty and let God do the rest.

As the most eloquent and intellectual of all the radicals, Phillips was called upon to defend the position that abolitionists should not support a constitution or government which supported slavery. Although the refusal of the radical abolitionists to vote or hold office, and their continued agitation to get the North to secede from the union seemed incomprehensible to most people, the position was perfectly consistent with Phillips' principles. Slavery was evil and this evil was supported by a Federal government which protected slave states from insurrection, undertook to return their fugitives and gave them special representation in Congress. Therefore anything voluntarily done in support of this government (i.e. taking an oath to support the Constitution or voting for a candidate who would be required to take such an oath), supported slavery also and was evil.

Despite the fact that his position was condemned in the public mind from the beginning, Phillips, through pamphlets and lectures, did as much as anyone could do to persuade people of its worth. He never once doubted its soundness. When friends like Charles Sumner argued that the course he advocated would impede the struggle for emancipation, he replied that "honesty and truth are more important than even freeing slaves." When Sumner asked how he could consistently pay taxes or even remain in the country, he reminded him that a man's choices were always limited by the social and historical situation in which God placed him. A man had to live in the world, but he did not have to collaborate with the devil, which is what Sumner and all other "loyal citizens" were doing. "To live

where God sent you and protest against your neighbor—this is certainly different from *joining him* in sinning, which the office holder of this country does."

Phillips' moralism supplied the ballast for his career. His solutions to difficult problems were both "right" and simple. When he continued to badger the government long after Garrison and other abolitionists had retired from the field after the war, it was because he sought *"justice—* absolute, immediate, unmixed justice to the negroe." He did not, however, live by shibboleths alone, and his tactics as a reformer were based on a surprisingly sophisticated conception of American politics and society.

Phillips recognized that slavery was a threat to the freedom of all Americans. This conviction developed gradually out of his early experiences. He had the grisly reminiscences of the Grimké sisters to remind him of the evils of slavery in the south—the whippings and mutilations, the ruthless separation of husband and wife, of parent and child. Closer to his personal experience was what slavery had done to supposedly free American citizens. It had jailed Prudence Crandall for opening a school for Negro girls. It had publicly whipped Amos Dresser for daring to distribute antislavery literature. It had tried to gag John Quincy Adams in Congress, had mobbed Garrison within the shadow of Faneuil Hall, and had finally killed Lovejoy. The pattern seemed always to be the same; principle was overcome by power. For the first time Phillips sensed the demonic possibilities of a slave power supported by public opinion in America. . . .

Having recognized the importance of public opinion in America Phillips began to examine American institutions more closely. He distinguished a fundamental tension between the American ideal, a society based on the rights of man, and an American political system based on numbers. "The majority rules, and law rests on numbers, not on intellect or virtue," thus "while theoretically holding that no vote of the majority can authorize injustice, we practically consider public opinion the real test of what is true and what is false; and hence, as a result, the fact which Tocqueville has noticed, that practically our institutions protect, not the interest of the whole community but the interests of the majority." . . .

Although Phillips knew that in some nations public opinion was shaped by political leaders, he could find nothing to show that this was true in the American experience. Theoretically every American male citizen was supposed to be eligible for office, but in practice, "with a race like ours, fired with the love of material wealth," the best brains were drawn into commerce. As a result politics took up with small men, "men without grasp enough for large business . . . men popular because they have no positive opinions." Even if an occasional man of the first rank (a Charles Sumner for example), did emerge in politics, he would be lost to the reformer because the whole art of politics in America was based on the ability to compromise. "The politician must conceal half his principles to carry forward the other half," Phillips said, "must regard, not rigid principle and strict right, but only such a degree of right as will allow him at the same time to secure *numbers.*"

These considerations led Phillips to conclude that the reformer in America had to confront the people directly. "Our aim," he said in his lecture *The Philosophy of Abolitionism*, "is to alter public opinion." Slavery endured and abolitionists were mobbed because a majority of Americans refused to face the moral issues involved. Phillips was too much of a realist to believe that he could suddenly convert the nation, but he did feel that he could force the issue and change the public attitude toward slavery.

Phillips knew that most people in the North disliked slavery, but he also knew that it was to their self-interest to leave it alone. To stir up controversy was dangerous: no one wanted to be known as a troublemaker; mill owners were concerned for their capital; mill hands were concerned for their jobs; the respectable middle class was concerned for its reputation. The easy thing for everyone was to turn away from the problem. The abolitionist's job was to scatter thorns on the easy road by dramatizing the moral issue and insisting that every man who did not throw his whole influence into the scales against slavery was as guilty as the slaveholder. . . .

Phillips was not a fanatic. He used the most violent language dispassionately as a surgeon uses the sharpest steel. He could not actually cut away the diseased tissue with his rhetoric, but he could expose it. Thus when he called Lincoln a "slave hound" he was reminding his listeners and readers that as a Congressman Lincoln had supported a bill which would have enforced the return of fugitive slaves escaping into the District of Columbia. This was the man who expected to get the antislavery vote. Phillips' intention in attacking Lincoln so savagely was simply to dramatize the rottenness of the American conscience by showing that only a "slave hound" could be elected President. His reply to those who accused him of extravagance and distortion was that "there are far more dead hearts to be quickened, than confused intellects to be cleared up—

more dumb dogs to be made to speak than doubting consciences to be enlightened. We have use, then, for something beside argument."

The easiest way to treat nettlesome reformers like the abolitionists is to dismiss them as cranks. Nothing irritated Phillips more than the attempts of his opponents to thrust him outside the mainstream of American life. The antislavery agitation, he insisted, was "an essential part of the machinery of the state . . . not a disease nor a medicine . . . the normal state of the nation."

The preceding statement takes us to the heart of Phillips' philosophy of reform. He recognized that American ideals could ultimately be translated into practice only through politics. At the same time he knew that the American politician's ability to gain and hold power was largely determined by his ability to effect compromises that appealed to numbers rather than to principle. He added to these corruptive tendencies the fact that people in a democracy always tend to have as high an opinion of themselves as possible—always tremble on the edge of national idolatry. . . . A democratic society that trusted to constitutions and political machinery to secure its liberties never would have any. "The people must be waked to a new effort," he said, "just as the church has to be regenerated in each age." In the middle of the nineteenth century the abolitionist was the agency of national regeneration, but even after he had vanished his function in the American system would still remain. . . .

It should be clear now that Phillips believed the radical abolitionist to be justified as much by his radicalism as by his abolitionism. Phillips preferred the word agitator to radical, and since he himself was frequently accused of demagoguery,

he took pains to point out the difference between the demagogue and agitator. A demagogue (he used Robespierre as an example), "rides the storm; he has never really the ability to create one. He uses it narrowly, ignorantly, and for selfish ends. If not crushed by the force which, without his will, has flung him into power, he leads it with ridiculous miscalculation against some insurmountable obstacle that scattters it forever. Dying, he leaves no mark on the elements with which he has been mixed." Quoting Sir Robert Peel, Phillips defined agitation as "the marshalling of the conscience of a nation to mould its laws." Daniel O'Connell who, after thirty years of "patient and sagacious labor," succeeded in creating a public opinion and unity of purpose to free Ireland from British tyranny was one of Phillips' models as a successful agitator.

It was because Phillips thought of himself primarily as an agitator and Garrison thought of himself primarily as an abolitionist that the two came to a parting of the ways in 1865. With the war over and slavery prohibited by the passage of the thirteenth amendment, Garrison felt that the "covenant with death" had been annulled. The American nation had become "successor to the abolitionists," and the American Anti-Slavery Society had lost its excuse for being. Phillips did not agree. He argued that the nation needed "the constant, incessant discriminating criticism of the abolitionists as much as ever." The debate grew rancorous and resulted in Garrison's quitting the Society. Phillips was elected President in his place, and for the next five years continued to agitate as fiercely for Negro suffrage as he had for emancipation. Only after the fifteenth amendment was passed did he allow the organization to be dissolved.

Even then Phillips did not relax his efforts. He denounced the decision to remove Federal troops from the South as vehemently as he had the Fugitive Slave Law, and predicted that a " 'solid south'— the slave power under a new name" would soon control national politics. Most of the other surviving abolitionists had long since gone over to the Republican party lock, stock, and barrel, but Phillips saw through the moral pretensions of the Republicans as clearly as anyone in the country. They had waved the bloody flag with regularity, but had been unwilling to make the sacrifices and the long-term commitments in reconstruction that were necessary if the moral legacy of the war was not to be squandered away. Accusing the Republicans of "a heartless and merciless calculation" to exploit war memories and Ku Klux Klan atrocities for party purposes, Phillips claimed that no party in history had ever "fallen from such a height to such a depth of disgrace."

The rhetoric was the same but the response was not. The people had grown tired of the war, and newspapers that would have praised him in the sixties now wrote about "Mr. Phillips' Last Frenzy" and called him "the apostle of unforgiving and relentless hate."

Meanwhile, even as he decried the growing popularity of the illusion that the Negro might be safe in the hands of his old master, Phillips turned his attention to the struggle of free labor in the North. "While this delusion of peace without purity persists," he was saying in 1878, "labor claims every ear and every hand." And so, in the declining years of his life, Wendell Phillips, true to his belief that agitation was "an essential part of the machinery of the state," poured his whole influence into the struggle for social justice in an industrial society. His solutions were still simple—passage of an eight-hour law—the unlimited issuance of Greenbacks. His tactics were the same. "The only way to accomplish our object," he said, "is to shame greedy men into humanity. Poison their wealth with the tears and curses of widows and orphans. In speaking of them call things by their right names. Let men shrink from them as from slave dealers and pirates." And the response was the same he had received during the hard, bitter years before the war. If anything Phillips was even more of an outsider now than he had been then. His support of unions, the right to strike, shorter hours of work, a graduated income tax, and his derision of laissez-faire ("the bubble and chaff of 'supply and demand' ") offended even the old abolitionists. If Phillips had acted "with ordinary common sense and good temper when slavery was abolished and had gone into politics," Edmund Quincy thought, "he might have been the next Senator . . . but he is 'played out' as we say, and will be merely a popular lecturer and a small demagogue for the rest of his life."

Quincy was a retired reformer. Like most of his contemporaries and most of the American historians who have followed, he could not appreciate Wendell Phillips, a gentleman who understood the difference between agitation and demagoguery, and knew that the radical in America could never retire.

POSTSCRIPT

Were the Abolitionists "Unrestrained Fanatics"?

One of the weaknesses of most studies of abolitionism, which is reflected in both of the preceding essays, is that they are generally written from a monochromatic perspective. In other words, historians typically discuss whites within the abolitionist crusade and give little, if any, attention to the roles blacks themselves played in the movement. Instead, whites are the active agents of reform while blacks are the passive recipients of humanitarian efforts to eliminate the scourge of slavery. Students should be aware that Afro-Americans, slave and free, also rebelled against the peculiar institution both directly and indirectly.

Benjamin Quarles in *Black Abolitionists* (Oxford University Press, 1969) describes a wide range of roles played by blacks in the abolitionist movement. For example, as Garrison's *Liberator* struggled to survive in the early months of 1831, black subscribers in the North kept the paper afloat. In addition, black Americans organized themselves into local antislavery societies, became members of the national abolitionist organizations (especially the American Anti-Slavery Society and the American and Foreign Anti-Slavery Society), contributed funds to the operations of those societies, made black churches available for abolitionist meetings, and promoted abolitionism through pamphlet-writing and speaking engagements. Between 1830 and 1835, the Negro Convention Movement sponsored annual meetings of blacks in which protests against slavery were a central feature.

David Walker, a free black from North Carolina who resided in Boston, published his famous *Appeal* in 1828. In vitriolic language rivaling that of Garrison, Walker urged slaves to rebel against their bondage. Frederick Douglas, who had escaped from slavery in Maryland, became one of the most popular speakers on the abolitionist circuit.

The black challenge to the slave system is also evident in the network known as the underground railroad. Traditionally, the heroes of this means of abetting black fugitives from Southern bondage are the white abolitionists who "conducted" runaways to freedom in the Northern United States or Canada. Larry Gara, however, in *The Liberty Line: The Legend of the Underground Railroad* (University of Kentucky Press, 1961), concludes that the real heroes of the underground railroad were not white abolitionists but the slaves themselves who depended primarily upon their own resources or assistance they received from other blacks, slave and free.

Other studies treating the role of black abolitionists in the antislavery movement include Jane H. and William H. Pease, *They Who Would Be Free: Blacks' Search for Freedom, 1830–1861* (Atheneum, 1974), and James M. McPherson, *The Struggle For Equality: Abolitionists and the Negro in the Civil War and Reconstruction* (Princeton University Press, 1964). Walker's pamphlet can be read in Charles M. Wiltse, ed., *David Walker's Appeal* (Hill and Wang, 1965). Frederick Douglass's contributions are evaluated in Benjamin Quarles, *Frederick Douglass* (Atheneum, 1968; originally published 1948); Nathan Irvin Huggins, *Slave and Citizen: The Life of Frederick Douglass* (Little, Brown, 1980); and Waldo E. Martin, Jr., *The Mind of Frederick Douglass* (University of North Carolina Press, 1984).

Conflicting views of the abolitionists are presented in Richard O. Curry, ed., *The Abolitionists: Reformers or Fanatics?* (Holt, Rinehart and Winston, 1965). For general discussions of the abolitionist movement, see Merton L. Dillon, *The Abolitionists: The Growth of a Dissenting Minority* (Northern Illinois Press, 1974); Gerald Sorin, *Abolitionism: A New Perspective* (Praeger, 1972); and Lawrence J. Friedman, *Gregarious Saints: Self and Community in American Abolitionism, 1830–1870* (Cambridge University Press, 1982). The lives of individual participants in the abolitionist movement are discussed in Russell B. Nye, *William Lloyd Garrison and the Humanitarian Reformers* (Little, Brown, 1955); Gerda Lerner, *The Grimke Sisters from South Carolina: Pioneers for Woman's Rights and Abolition* (Schocken Books, 1967); and Stephen B. Oates, *To Purge This Land With Blood: A Biography of John Brown* (Harper & Row, 1970).

ISSUE 15

Was the Antebellum South a Unique Section in American History?

YES: Eugene D. Genovese, from *The Political Economy of Slavery* (Pantheon Books, 1965)

NO: Edward Pessen, from "How Different From Each Other Were the Antebellum North and South?" *American Historical Review* (December 1980)

ISSUE SUMMARY

YES: Marxist historian Eugene D. Genovese believes "that slavery gave the South a social system and a civilization with a distinct class structure, political community, economy, ideology and set of psychological patterns."
NO: Social historian Edward Pessen argues that a comparison of Northern and Southern states in the three decades before the Civil War reveals common political, economic, and social practices.

"The South is not quite a nation within a nation but it is the next thing to it," began the North Carolinian journalist Wilbur J. Cash in his classic statement on *The Mind of the South* (Knopf, 1941). Cash wrote his book on the eve of World War II, shortly before he committed suicide (some say because he dared to tell the truth about the South). Cash's death created a myth within a myth and helped solidify the popular image of the "tragic" South.

Since *The Mind of the South* first appeared, novelists, journalists, and historians from all sections of the country and of various political persuasions have tried to explain the myths and realities of the American South. When the reader cuts through the multitude of adjectives used to describe the South, he concludes that there are actually only two types—positive and negative.

An earlier generation of Southern historians—Louis Wright, Clement Eaton, and Rollin G. Osterweis—have taken the myths of the plantation South seriously enough to claim that with an addition of small doses of realism, such a place did in fact exist before the Civil War. Louis Wright claims the first gentlemen of Virginia had established an aristocracy of large land-owing farmers who developed great wealth from the profits on their tobacco estates. Although they were not descendants of British nobility, these planters lived in considerable splendor and developed a pattern of life modeled after the mother country's gentry. Dominating the colony's assemblies from its earliest years, the Virginia planter produced generations of leaders who, in the late eighteenth century, would be in the forefront of the American Revolution. Clement Eaton describes how the descendants of the coastal aristocrats carried the ideal of the country gentlemen with them as they migrated to other portions of the southwest in the early nineteenth century. Rollin G. Osterweis argues that the cult of chivalry permeated the South's romantic image of itself in the plantation system and that the institution of slavery shaped Southern nationalism, eventually leading to secession and civil war.

Howard Zinn, a white radical historian who spent many years teaching at a black Southern college in Atlanta while actively participating in the civil rights movement in the 1960s, has turned these epithets on their heads. In his book *The Southern Mystique* (Knopf, 1964), he defines "southernism" as merely being an extension of the nation's worst qualities. There is no distinct South, he argues. Non-Southerners have merely projected onto the South those qualities which they least like about the American nation. Professor Zinn points out that more violence occurred in clashes between settlers and Indians on our western frontier than between masters and slaves in the antebellum South.

In the first selection Professor Eugene D. Genovese, author of the best modern study of slavery, disagrees with Howard Zinn. Employing a sophisticated Marxian class analysis, Genovese argues that the antebellum South was a unique pre-capitalist society dominated by "quasi-aristocratic landowners who had to adjust their economy and ways of thinking to a capitalist world market." Paradoxically, Genovese's interpretation is in partial agreement with the views of the older traditional racist interpretation of the South put forth sixty years ago by Ulrich B. Phillips in his classic *Life and Labor in the Old South* (Little, Brown, 1929, 1957). "The essential features of Southern particularity," maintains Genovese in words Phillips would have approved, "as well as of Southern backwardness, can be traced to the relationship of master and slave."

In the second selection, Professor Edward Pessen, from the City University of New York, contends that the similarities between the Northern and Southern sections in the three decades before the Civil War were more important than their differences. Pessen performs yeoman service in summarizing much of the recent scholarly literature on the pre–Civil War political, social, and economic structures of both North and South. Socially he finds that an unequal distribution of wealth between the upper and lower classes continued to widen during the three decades before the Civil War in both sections. At the same time, planter-aristocrats and urban merchants dominated the economies and the two major political parties in their respective sections as well.

YES
Eugene D. Genovese

THE POLITICAL ECONOMY OF SLAVERY

The premodern quality of the Southern world was imparted to it by its dominant slaveholding class. Slavery has existed in many places, side by side with other labor systems, without producing anything like the civilization of the South. Slavery gave the South a special way of life because it provided the basis for a regional social order in which the slave labor system could dominate all others. Southern slavery was not "mere slavery"—to recall Louis Hartz's luckless term—but the foundation on which rose a powerful and remarkable social class: a class constituting only a tiny portion of the white population and yet so powerful and remarkable as to try, with more success than our neo-abolitionists care to see, to build a new, or rather to rebuild an old, civilization.

. . . "The Slave South: An Interpretation," sketches the main features of antebellum Southern civilization, which it describes as having been moving steadily into a general crisis of society as a whole and especially of its dominant slaveholding class.[1] The slaveholders' economic and political interests, as well as ideological and psychological commitments, clashed at many points with those of Northern and European capitalists, farmers, and laborers. The successful defense of slavery presupposed an adequate rate of material growth, but the South could not keep pace with an increasingly hostile North in population growth, manufacturing, transportation, or even agricultural development. The weaknesses of Southern agriculture were especially dangerous and galling to the regime—dangerous because without adequate agricultural progress other kinds of material progress were difficult to effect; galling because Southerners prided themselves on their rural society and its alleged virtues. . . .

THE PROBLEM

The uniqueness of the antebellum South continues to challenge the imagination of Americans, who, despite persistent attempts, cannot divert their attention from slavery. Nor should they, for slavery provided the foundation on which the South rose and grew. The master-slave relationship permeated Southern life and influenced relationships among free men. A full history would have to treat the impact of the Negro slave and of slaveless as well as slaveholding whites, but a first approximation, necessarily concerned with essentials, must focus on the slaveholders, who most directly exercised power over men and events. The hegemony of the slaveholders, presupposing the social and economic preponderance of great slave plantations, determined the character of the South. These men rose to power in a region embedded in a capitalistic country, and their social system emerged as part of a capitalistic world. Yet, a nonslaveholding European past and a shared experience in a new republic notwithstanding, they imparted to Southern life a special social, economic, political, ideological, and psychological content.

To dissolve that special content into an ill-defined agrarianism or an elusive planter capitalism would mean to sacrifice concern with the essential for concern with the transitional and peripheral. Neither of the two leading interpretations, which for many years have contended in a hazy and unreal battle, offers consistent and plausible answers to recurring questions, especially those bearing on the origins of the War for Southern Independence. The first of these interpretations considers the antebellum South an agrarian society fighting against the encroachments of industrial capitalism; the second considers the slave plantation merely a form of capitalistic enterprise and suggests that the material differences between Northern and Southern capitalism were more apparent than real. These two views, which one would think contradictory, sometimes combine in the thesis that the agrarian nature of planter capitalism, for some reason, made coexistence with industrial capitalism difficult.

The first view cannot explain why some agrarian societies give rise to industrialization and some do not. A prosperous agricultural hinterland has generally served as a basis for industrial development by providing a home market for manufactures and a source of capital accumulation, and the prosperity of farmers has largely depended on the growth of industrial centers as markets for foodstuffs. In a capitalist society agriculture is one industry, or one set of industries, among many, and its conflict with manufacturing is one of many competitive rivalries. There must have been something unusual about an agriculture that generated violent opposition to the agrarian West as well as the industrial Northeast.

The second view, which is the more widely held, emphasizes that the plantation system produced for a distant market, responded to supply and demand, invested capital in land and slaves, and operated with funds borrowed from banks and factors. This, the more sophisticated of the two interpretations, cannot begin to explain the origins of the conflict with the North and does violence to elementary facts of antebellum Southern history.

SLAVERY AND THE EXPANSION OF CAPITALISM

The proponents of the idea of planter capitalism draw heavily, wittingly or not, on Lewis C. Gray's theory of the genesis of the plantation system. Gray defines the plantation as a "capitalistic type of agricultural organization in which a considerable number of unfree laborers were employed under a unified direction and control in the production of a staple crop." Gray considers the plantation system inseparably linked with the international development of capitalism. He notes the plantation's need for large outlays of capital, its strong tendency toward specialization in a single crop, and its commercialism and argues that these appeared with the industrial revolution.

In modern times the plantation often rose under bourgeois auspices to provide industry with cheap raw materials, but the consequences were not always harmonious with bourgeois society. Colonial expansion produced three sometimes overlapping patterns: (1) the capitalists of the advanced country simply invested in colonial land—as illustrated even today by the practice of the United Fruit Company in the Caribbean; (2) the colonial planters were largely subservient to the advanced countries—as illustrated by the British West Indies before the abolition of slavery; and (3) the planters were able to win independence and build a society under their own direction—as illustrated by the Southern United States.

In alliance with the North, the planter-dominated South broke away from England, and political conditions in the new republic allowed it considerable freedom for self-development. The plantation society that had begun as an appendage of British capitalism ended as a powerful, largely autonomous civilization with aristocratic pretensions and possibilities, although it remained tied to the capitalist world by bonds of commodity production. The essential element in this distinct civilization was the slaveholders' domination, made possible by their command of labor. Slavery provided the basis for a special Southern economic and social life, special problems and tensions, and special laws of development.

THE RATIONALITY AND IRRATIONALITY OF SLAVE SOCIETY

Slave economies normally manifest irrational tendencies that inhibit economic development and endanger social stability. Max Weber, among the many scholars who have discussed the problem, has noted four important irrational features. First, the master cannot adjust the size of his labor force in accordance with business fluctuations. In particular, efficiency cannot readily be attained through the manipulation of the labor force if sentiment, custom, or community pressure makes separation of families difficult. Second, the capital outlay is much greater and riskier for slave labor than for free.[4] Third, the domination of society by a planter class increases the risk of political influence in the market. Fourth, the sources of cheap labor usually dry up rather quickly, and beyond a certain point costs become excessively burdensome. Weber's remarks could be extended. Planters, for example, have little opportunity to select specifically trained workers for special tasks as they arise.

There are other telling features of this irrationality. Under capitalism the pressure of the competitive struggle and the bourgeois spirit of accumulation direct the greater part of profits back into production. The competitive side of Southern slavery produced a similar result, but one that was modified by the pronounced tendency to heavy consumption. Economic historians and sociologists have long noted the high propensity to consume among landed aristocracies. No doubt this difference has been one of degree. The greater part of slavery's profits also find their way back into production, but the method of reinvestment in the two systems is substantially different. Capitalism largely directs its profits into an expansion of plant and equipment, not labor; that is, economic progress is qualitative. Slavery, for economic reasons as well as for those of social prestige, directs its reinvestments along the same lines as the original investment—in slaves and land; that is, economic progress is quantitative.

In the South this weakness proved fatal for the slaveholders. They found themselves engaged in a growing conflict with Northern farmers and businessmen over such issues as tariffs, homesteads, internal improvements, and the decisive question of the balance of political power in the Union. The slow pace of their economic progress, in contrast to the long strides of their rivals to the north, threatened to undermine their political parity and result in a Southern defeat on all major issues of the day. The qualitative leaps in the Northern economy manifested themselves in a rapidly increasing population, an expanding productive plant, and growing political, ideological, and social boldness. The slaveholders' voice grew shriller and harsher as they contemplated impending disaster and sought solace in complaints of Northern aggression and exploitation.

Just as Southern slavery directed reinvestment along a path that led to economic stagnation, so too did it limit the volume of capital accumulated for investment of any kind. We need not reopen the tedious argument about the chronology of the plantation, the one-crop system, and slavery. While slavery existed, the South had to be bound to a plantation system and an agricultural economy based on a few crops. As a result, the South depended on Northern facilities, with inevitably mounting middlemen's charges. Less obvious was the capital drain occasioned by the importation of industrial goods. While the home market remained backward, Southern manufacturers had difficulty producing in sufficient quantities to keep costs and prices at levels competitive with Northerners. The attendant dependence on Northern and British imports intensified the outward flow of badly needed funds.

Most of the elements of irrationality were irrational only from a capitalist standpoint. The high propensity to consume luxuries, for example, has always been functional (socially if not economically rational) in aristocratic societies, for it has provided the ruling class with the facade necessary to control the middle and lower classes. Thomas R. Dew knew what he was doing when he defended the high personal expenditures of Southerners as proof of the superiority of the slave system.[5] Few Southerners, even few slaveholders, could afford to spend lavishly and effect an aristocratic standard of living, but those few set the social tone for society. One wealthy planter with a great house and a reputation for living and entertaining on a grand scale could impress a whole community and keep before its humbler men the shining ideal of plantation magnificence. Consider Pascal's observation that the habit of seeing the king accompanied by guards, pomp, and all the paraphernalia designed to command respect and inspire awe will produce those reactions even when he appears alone and informally. In the popular mind he is assumed to be naturally an awe-inspiring being.[6]

In this manner, every dollar spent by the planters for elegant clothes, a college education for their children, or a lavish barbecue contributed to the political and social domination of their class. We may speak of the slave system's irrationality only in a strictly economic sense and then only to indicate the inability of the South to compete with Northern capitalism on the latter's grounds. The slaveholders, fighting for political power in an essentially capitalist Union, had to do just that.

CAPITALIST AND PSEUDO-CAPITALIST FEATURES OF THE SLAVE ECONOMY

The slave economy developed within, and was in a sense exploited by, the capitalist world market; consequently, slavery developed many ostensibly capitalist features, such as banking, commerce, and credit. These played a fundamentally different role in the South than in the North. Capitalism has absorbed and even encouraged many kinds of precapitalist social systems: serfdom, slavery, Oriental state enterprises, and others. It has introduced credit, finance, banking, and similar institutions where they did not previously exist. It is pointless to suggest that therefore nineteenth-century India and twentieth-century Saudi Arabia should be classified as capitalist countries. We need to analyze a few of the more important capitalist and pseudo-capitalist features of Southern slavery and especially to review the barriers to industrialization in order to appreciate the peculiar qualities of this remarkable and anachronistic society.

The defenders of the "planter-capitalism" thesis have noted the extensive commercial links between the plantation and the world market and the modest commercial bourgeoisie in the South and have concluded that there is no reason to predicate an antagonism between cotton producers and cotton merchants. However valid as a reply to the naive arguments of the proponents of the agrarianism-versus-industrialism thesis, this criticism has unjustifiably been twisted to suggest that the presence of commercial activity proves the predominance of capitalism in the South. Many precapitalist economic systems have had well-developed commercial relations, but if every commercial society is to be considered capitalist, the word loses all meaning. In general, commercial classes have supported the existing system of production. As Maurice Dobb observes, their fortunes are bound up with those of the dominant producers, and merchants are more likely to seek an extension of their middlemen's profits than to try to reshape the economic order.

We must concern ourselves primarily with capitalism as a social system, not merely with evidence of typically capitalistic economic practices. In the South extensive and complicated commercial relations with the world market permitted the growth of a small commercial bourgeoisie. The resultant fortunes flowed into slaveholding, which offered prestige and economic and social security in a planter-dominated society. Independent merchants found their businesses dependent on the patronage of the slaveholders. The merchants either became planters themselves or assumed a servile attitude toward the planters. The commercial bourgeoisie, such as it was, remained tied to the slaveholding interest, had little desire or opportunity to invest capital in industrial expansion, and adopted the prevailing aristocratic attitudes.

The Southern industrialists were in an analogous position, although one that was potentially subversive of the political power and ideological unity of the planters. The preponderance of planters and slaves on the countryside retarded the home market. The Southern yeomanry, unlike the Western, lacked the purchasing power to sustain rapid industrial development. The planters spent much of their money abroad for luxuries. The plantation market consisted primarily of the demand for cheap slave clothing and cheap agricultural implements for use or misuse by the slaves. Southern industrialism needed a sweeping agrarian revolution to provide it with cheap labor and a substantial rural market, but the Southern industrialists depended on the existing, limited, plantation market. Leading industrialists like William Gregg and Daniel Pratt were plantation-oriented and proslavery. They could hardly have been other.

The banking system of the South serves as an excellent illustration of an ostensibly capitalist institution that worked to augment the power of the planters and retard the development of the bourgeoisie. Southern banks functioned much as did those which the British introduced into Latin America, India, and Egypt during the nineteenth century. Although the British banks fostered dependence on British capital, they did not directly and willingly generate internal capitalist development. They were not sources of industrial capital but "large-scale clearing houses of mercantile finance vying in their interest charges with the local usurers."

The difference between the banking practices of the South and those of the West reflects the difference between slavery and agrarian capitalism. In the West, as in the Northeast, banks and credit facilities promoted a vigorous economic expansion. During the period of loose Western banking (1830-1844) credit flowed liberally into industrial development as well as into land purchases and internal improvements. Manufacturers and merchants dominated the boards of directors of Western banks, and landowners played a minor role. Undoubtedly, many urban businessmen speculated in land and had special interests in underwriting agricultural exports, but they gave attention to building up agricultural processing industries and urban enterprises, which guaranteed the region a many-sided economy.

The slave states paid considerable attention to the development of a conservative, stable banking system, which could guarantee the movement of staple crops and the extension of credit to the planters. Southern banks were primarily designed to lend the planters money for outlays that were economically feasible and socially acceptable in a slave society: the movement of crops, the purchase of land and slaves, and little else.

Whenever Southerners pursued easy-credit policies, the damage done outweighed the advantages of increased production. This imbalance probably did not occur in the West, for easy credit made possible agricultural and industrial expansion of a diverse nature and, despite acute crises, established a firm basis for long-range prosperity. Easy credit in the South led to expansion of cotton production with concomitant overproduction and low prices; simultaneously, it increased the price of slaves.

Planters wanted their banks only to facilitate cotton shipments and maintain sound money. They purchased large quantities of foodstuffs from the West and, since they shipped little in return, had to pay in bank notes. For five years following the bank failures of 1837 the bank notes of New Orleans moved at a discount of from 10 to 25 percent. This disaster could not be allowed to recur. Sound money and sound banking became the cries of the slaveholders as a class.

Southern banking tied the planters to the banks, but more important, tied the bankers to the plantations. The banks often found it necessary to add prominent planters to their boards of directors and were closely supervised by the planter-dominated state legislatures. In this relationship the bankers could not emerge as a middle-class counterweight to the planters but could merely serve as their auxiliaries.

The bankers of the free states also allied themselves closely with the dominant producers, but society and economy took on a bourgeois quality provided by the rising industrialists, the urban middle classes, and the farmers who increasingly depended on urban markets. The expansion of credit, which in the West financed manufacturing, mining, transportation, agricultural diversification, and the numerous branches of a capitalist economy, in the South bolstered the economic position of the planters, inhibited the rise of alternative industries, and guaranteed the extension and consolidation of the plantation system.

If for a moment we accept the designation of the planters as capitalists and the slave system as a form of capitalism, we are then confronted by a capitalist society that impeded the development of every normal feature of capitalism. The planters were not mere capitalists; they were precapitalist, quasi-aristocratic landowners who had to adjust their economy and ways of thinking to a capitalist world market. Their society, in its spirit and fundamental direction, represented the antithesis of capitalism, however many compromises it had to make. The fact of slave ownership is central to our problem. This seemingly formal question of whether the owners of the means of production command labor or purchase the labor power of free workers contains in itself the content of Southern life. The essential features of Southern particularity, as well as of Southern backwardness, can be traced to the relationship of master to slave.

THE BARRIERS TO INDUSTRIALIZATION

If the planters were losing their economic and political cold war with Northern capitalism, the failure of the South to develop sufficient industry provided the most striking immediate cause. Its inability to develop adequate manufactures is usually attributed to the inefficiency of its labor force. No doubt slaves did not easily adjust to industrial employment, and the indirect effects of the slave system impeded the employment of whites. Slaves did work effectively in hemp, tobacco, iron, and cotton factories but only under socially dangerous conditions. They received a wide variety of privileges and approached an elite status. Planters generally appreciated the potentially subversive quality of these arrangements and looked askance at their extension.

Slavery concentrated economic and political power in the hands of a slaveholding class hostile to industrialism.

The slaveholders feared a strong urban bourgeoisie, which might make common cause with its Northern counterpart. They feared a white urban working class of unpredictable social tendencies. In general, they distrusted the city and saw in it something incongruous with their local power and status arrangements. The small slaveholders, as well as the planters, resisted the assumption of a heavy tax burden to assist manufacturers, and as the South fell further behind the North in industrial development more state aid was required to help industry offset the Northern advantages of scale, efficiency, credit relations, and business reputation.

Slavery led to the rapid concentration of land and wealth and prevented the expansion of a Southern home market. Instead of providing a basis for industrial growth, the Southern countryside, economically dominated by a few large estates, provided only a limited market for industry. Data on the cotton textile factories almost always reveal that Southern producers aimed at supplying slaves with the cheapest and coarsest kind of cotton goods. Even so, local industry had to compete with Northern firms, which sometimes shipped direct and sometimes established Southern branches.

William Gregg, the South's foremost industrialist, understood the modest proportions of the Southern market and warned manufacturers against trying to produce exclusively for their local areas. His own company at Graniteville, South Carolina, produce fine cotton goods that sold much better in the North than in the South. Gregg was an unusually able man, and his success in selling to the North was a personal triumph. When he had to evaluate the general position of Southern manufacturers, he asserted that he was willing to stake his reputation on their ability to compete with Northerners in the production of *"coarse cotton fabrics."*

Some Southern businessmen, especially those in the border states, did good business in the North. Louisville tobacco and hemp manufacturers sold much of their output in Ohio. Some producers of iron and agricultural implements sold in nearby Northern cities. This kind of market was precarious. As Northern competitors rose and the market shrank, Southern producers had to rely on the narrow and undependable Southern market.[16] Well before the 1840 iron-manufacturing establishments in the Northwest provided local farmers with excellent markets for grain, vegetables, molasses, and work animals. During the antebellum period and after, the grain growers of America found their market at home. America's rapid industrial development offered farmers a magnificently expanding urban market, and not until much later did they come to depend to any important extent on exports.

To a small degree the South benefited in this way. By 1840 the tobacco-manufacturing industry began to absorb more tobacco than was being exported, and the South's few industrial centers provided markets for local grain and vegetable growers. Since the South could not undertake a general industrialization, few urban centers rose to provide substantial markets for farmers and planters. Southern grain growers, except for those close to the cities of the free states, had to be content with the market offered by planters who preferred to specialize in cotton or sugar and buy foodstuffs. The restricted rations of the slaves limited this market, which inadequate transportation further narrowed. It did not pay the planters to appropriate state funds to build a transportation system into the back country, and any measure to increase the economic strength of the back-country farmers seemed politically dangerous to the aristocracy of the Black Belt. The farmers of the back country remained isolated, self-sufficient, and politically, economically, and socially backward. Those grain-growing farmers who could compete with producers in the Upper South and Northwest for the plantation market lived within the Black Belt. Since the planters did not have to buy from these local producers, the economic relationship greatly strengthened the political hand of the planters.

THE GENERAL FEATURES OF SOUTHERN AGRICULTURE

The South's greatest economic weakness was the low productivity of its labor force. The slaves worked indifferently. They could be made to work reasonably well under close supervision in the cotton fields, but the cost of supervising them in more than one or two operations at a time was prohibitive. Slavery prevented the significant technological progress that could have raised productivity substantially. Of greatest relevance, the impediments to technological progress damaged Southern agriculture, for improved implements and machines largely accounted for the big increases in crop yields per acre in the Northern states during the nineteenth century.

Slavery and the plantation system led to agricultural methods that depleted the soil. The frontier methods of the free states yielded similar results, but slavery forced the South into continued dependence upon exploitative methods after the frontier had passed further west. It prevented reclamation of worn-out lands. The plantations were much too large to fertilize easily. Lack of markets and poor care of animals by slaves made it impossible to accumulate sufficient manure. The low level of capital accumulation made the purchase of adequate quantities of commercial fertilizer unthinkable. Planters could not practice proper crop rotation, for the pressure of the credit system kept most available land in cotton, and the labor force could not easily be assigned to the required tasks without excessive costs of supervision. The general inefficiency of labor thwarted most attempts at improvement of agricultural methods.

The South, unable to feed itself, faced a series of dilemmas in its attempts to increase production of nonstaple crops and to improve its livestock. An inefficient labor force and the backward business practices of the dominant planters hurt. When planters did succeed in raising their own food, they also succeeded in depriving local livestock raisers and grain growers of their only markets. The planters had little capital with which to buy improved breeds and could not guarantee the care necessary to make such investments worth while. Livestock raisers also lacked the capital, and without adequate urban markets they could not make good use of the capital they had.

Thoughtful Southerners, deeply distressed by the condition of their agriculture, made a determined effort to remedy it. In Maryland and Virginia significant progress occurred in crop diversification and livestock improvement, but this progress was contingent on the sale of surplus slaves to the Lower South. These sales provided the income that offset agricultural losses and made possible investment in fertilizers, equipment, and livestock. The concomitant reduction in the size of the slave force facilitated supervision and increased labor productivity and versatility. Even so, the income from slave sales remained an important part of the gross income of the planters of the Upper South. The reform remained incomplete and could not free agriculture from the destructive effects of the continued reliance on slave labor.

The reform process had several contradictions, the most important of which was the dependence on slave sales. Surplus slaves could be sold only while gang-labor methods continued to be used in other areas. By the 1850s the deficiencies of slavery that had forced innovations in the Upper South were making themselves felt in the Lower South. Increasingly, planters in the Lower South explored the possibilities of reform. If the deterioration of agriculture in the Cotton Belt had proceeded much further, the planters would have had to stop buying slaves from Maryland and Virginia and look for markets for their own surplus slaves. Without the acquisition of fresh lands there could be no general reform of Southern agriculture. The Southern economy was moving steadily into an insoluble crisis.

THE IDEOLOGY OF THE MASTER CLASS

The planters commanded Southern politics and set the tone of social life. Theirs was an aristocratic, antibourgeois spirit with values and mores emphasizing family and status, a strong code of honor, and aspirations to luxury, ease, and accomplishment. In the planters' community, paternalism provided the standard of human relationships, and politics and statecraft were the duties and responsibilities of gentlemen. The gentleman lived for politics, not, like the bourgeois politician, off politics.

The planter typically recoiled at the notions that profit should be the goal of life; that the approach to production and exchange should be internally rational and uncomplicated by social values; that thrift and hard work should be the great virtues; and that the test of the wholesomeness of a community should be the vigor with which its citizens expand the economy. The planter was no less acquisitive than the bourgeois, but an acquisitive spirit is compatible with value antithetical to capitalism. The aristocratic spirit of the planters absorbed acquisitiveness and directed it into channels that were socially desirable to a slave society: the accumulation of slaves and land and the achievement of military and political honors. Whereas in the North people followed the lure of business and money for their own sake, in the South specific forms of property carried the badges of honor, prestige, and power. Even the rough parvenu planters of the Southwestern frontier—the "Southern Yankees"—strove to accumulate wealth in the modes acceptable to plantation society. Only in their crudeness and naked avarice did they differ from the Virginia gentlemen. They were a generation removed from the refinement that follows accumulation.

Slavery established the basis of the planter's position and power. It measured his affluence, marked his status, and supplied leisure for social graces and aristocratic duties. The older bourgeoisie of New England in its own way struck an aristocratic pose, but its wealth was rooted in commercial and industrial enterprises that were being pushed into the background by the newer heavy industries arising in the West, where upstarts took advantage of the more lucrative ventures like the iron industry. In the South few such opportunities were opening. The parvenu differed from the established planter only in being cruder and perhaps sharper in his business dealings. The road to power lay through the plantation. The older aristocracy kept its leadership or made room for men following the same road. An aristocratic stance was no mere compensation for a decline in power; it was the soul and content of a rising power.

Many travelers commented on the difference in material conditions from one side of the Ohio River to the other, but the difference in sentiment was seen most clearly by Tocqueville. Writing before the slavery issue had inflamed the nation, he remarked that slavery was attacking the Union "indirectly in its manners." The Ohioan "was tormented by wealth," and would turn to any kind of enterprise or endeavor to make a fortune. The Kentuckian coveted wealth "much less than pleasure or excitement," and money had "lost a portion of its value in his eyes."

Achille Murat joined Tocqueville in admiration for Southern ways. Compared with Northerners, Southerners were frank, clever, charming, generous, and liberal. They paid a price for these advantages. As one Southerner put it, the North led the South in almost everything because the Yankees had quiet perseverance over the long haul, whereas the Southerners had talent and brilliance but no taste for sustained labor. Southern projects came with a flash and died just as suddenly.[19] Despite such criticisms from within the ranks, the leaders of the South clung to their ideals, their faults,

and their conviction of superiority. Farmers, said Edmund Ruffin, could not expect to achieve a cultural level above that of the "boors who reap rich harvests from the fat soil of Belgium." In the Northern states, he added with some justification, a farmer could rarely achieve the ease, culture, intellect, and refinement that slavery made possible. The prevailing attitude of the aristocratic South toward itself and its Northern rival was ably summed up by William Henry Holcombe of Natchez: "The Northerner loves to make money, the Southerner to spend it."

At their best, Southern ideals constituted a rejection of the crass, vulgar, inhumane elements of capitalist society. The slaveholders simply could not accept the idea that the case nexus offered a permissible basis for human relations. Even the vulgar parvenu of the Southwest embraced the plantation myth and refused to make a virtue of necessity by glorifying the competitive side of slavery as civilization's highest achievement. The slaveholders generally, and the planters in particular, did identify their own ideals with the essence of civilization and, given their sense of honor, were prepared to defend them at any cost.

This civilization and its ideals were antinational in a double sense. The plantation offered virtually the only market for the small nonstaple-producing farmers and provided the center of necessary services for the small cotton growers. Thus, the paternalism of the planters toward their slaves was reinforced by the semipaternal relationship between planters and their neighbors. The planters, in truth, grew into the closest thing to feudal lords imaginable in a nineteenth-century bourgeois republic. The planters' protestations of love for the

Union were not so much a desire to use the Union to protect slavery as a strong commitment to localism as the highest form of liberty. They genuinely loved the Union so long as it alone among the great states of the world recognized that localism had a wide variety of rights. The Southerners' source of price was not the Union, nor the nonexistent Southern nation; it was the plantation, which they raised to a political principle.

THE INNER REALITY OF SLAVEHOLDING

The Southern slaveholder had "extraordinary force." In the eyes of an admirer his independence was "not as at the North, the effect of a conflict with the too stern pressure of society, but the legitimate outgrowth of a sturdy love of liberty." This independence, so distinctive in the slaveholders' psychology, divided them politically from agrarian Westerners as well as from urban Easterners. Commonly, both friendly and hostile contemporaries agreed that the Southerner appeared rash, unstable, often irrational, and that he turned away from bourgeois habits toward an aristocratic pose.

Americans, with a pronounced Jeffersonian bias, often attribute this spirit to agrarians of all types, although their judgment seems almost bizarre. A farmer may be called "independent" because he works for himself and owns property; like any grocer or tailor he functions as a petty bourgeois. In Jefferson's time, when agriculture had not yet been wholly subjected to the commanding influences of the market, the American farmer perhaps had a considerable amount of independence, if we choose to call self-sufficient isolation by that name,

but in subsequent days he has had to depend on the market like any manufacturer, if not more so. Whereas manufacturers combine to protect their economic interests, such arrangements have proved much more difficult, and until recently almost impossible, to effect among farmers. In general, if we contrast farmers with urban capitalists, the latter emerge as relatively more independent. The farmer yields constantly to the primacy of nature, to a direct, external force acting on him regardless of his personal worth; his independence is therefore rigorously circumscribed. The capitalist is limited by the force of the market, which operates indirectly and selectively. Many capitalists go under in a crisis, but some emerge strong and surer of their own excellence. Those who survive the catastrophe do so (or so it seems) because of superior ability, strength, and management, not because of an Act of God.

The slaveholder, as distinct from the farmer, had a private source of character making and mythmaking—his slave. Most obviously, he had the habit of command, but there was more than despotic authority in this master-slave relationship. The slave stood interposed between his master and the object his master desired (that which was produced); thus, the master related to the object only mediately, through the slave. The slaveholder commanded the products of another's labor, but by the same process was forced into dependence upon this other.

Thoughtful Southerners such as Ruffin, Fitzhugh, and Hammond understood this dependence and saw it as arising from the general relationship of labor to capital, rather than from the specific relationship of master to slave. They did not grasp that the capitalist's dependence upon his laborers remains obscured by the process of exchange in the capitalist market. Although all commodities are products of social relationships and contain human labor, they face each other in the market not as the embodiment of human qualities but as things with a seemingly independent existence. Similarly, the laborer sells his labor-power in the way in which the capitalist sells his goods—by bringing it to market, where it is subject of the fluctuations of supply and demand. A "commodity fetishism" clouds the social relationship of labor to capital, and the worker and capitalist appear as mere observers of a process over which they have little control. Southerners correctly viewed the relationship as a general one of labor to capital but failed to realize that the capitalist's dependence on his laborers is hidden, whereas that of master on slave is naked. As a Mississippi planter noted:

> I intend to be henceforth stingy as far as unnecessary expenditure—as a many should not squander what another accumulates with the exposure of health and the wearing out of the physical powers, and is not that the case with the man who needlessly parts with that which the negro by the hardest labor and often undergoing what we in like situation would call the greatest deprivation . . .

This simultaneous dependence and independence contributed to that peculiar combination of the admirable and the frightening in the slaveholder's nature: his strength, graciousness, and gentility; his impulsiveness, violence, and unsteadiness. The sense of independence and the habit of command developed his poise, grace, and dignity, but the less obvious sense of dependence on a despised other made him violently intolerant of anyone and anything threatening to expose the full nature of his relationship to his slave. Thus, he had a far deeper conservatism than that usually attributed to agrarians. His independence stood out as his most prized possession, but the instability of its based produced personal rashness and directed that rashness against any alteration in the status quo. Any attempt, no matter how well meaning, indirect, or harmless, to question the slave system appeared not only as an attack on his material interests but as an attack on his self-esteem at its most vulnerable point. To question either the morality or the practicality of slavery meant to expose the root of the slaveholder's dependence in independence.

THE GENERAL CRISIS OF THE SLAVE SOUTH

The South's slave civilization could not forever coexist with an increasingly hostile, powerful, and aggressive Northern capitalism. On the one hand, the special economic conditions arising from the dependence on slave labor bound the South, in a colonial manner, to the world market. The concentration of landholding and slaveholding prevented the rise of a prosperous yeomanry and of urban centers. The inability to build urban centers restricted the market for agricultural produce, weakened the rural producers, and dimmed hopes for agricultural diversification. On the other hand, the same concentration of wealth, the isolated, rural nature of the plantation system, the special psychology engendered by slave ownership, and the political opportunity presented by the separation from England, converged to give the

South considerable political and social independence. This independence was primarily the contribution of the slave-holding class, and especially of the planters. Slavery, while it bound the South economically, granted it the privilege of developing an aristocratic tradition, a disciplined and cohesive ruling class, and a mythology of its own.

Aristocratic tradition and ideology intensified the South's attachment to economic backwardness. Paternalism and the habit of command made the slaveholders tough stock, determined to defend their Southern heritage. The more economically debilitating their way of life, the more they clung to it. It was this side of things—the political hegemony and aristocratic ideology for the ruling class—rather than economic factors that prevented the South from relinquishing slavery voluntarily.

As the free states stepped up their industrialization and as the westward movement assumed its remarkable momentum, the South's economic and political allies in the North were steadily isolated. Years of abolitionist and free-soil agitation bore fruit as the South's opposition to homesteads, tariffs, and internal improvements clashed more and more dangerously with the North's economic needs. To protect their institutions and to try to lessen their economic bondage, the slaveholders slid into violent collision with Northern interests and sentiments. The economic deficiencies of slavery threatened to undermine the planters' wealth and power. Such relief measures as cheap labor and more land for slave states (reopening the slave trade and territorial expansion) conflicted with Northern material needs, aspirations, and morality. The planters faced a steady deterioration of their political and social power. Even if the relative prosperity of the 1850s had continued indefinitely, the slave states would have been at the mercy of the free, which steadily forged ahead in population growth, capital accumulation, and economic development. Any economic slump threatened to bring with it an internal political disaster, for the slaveholders could not rely on their middle and lower classes to remain permanently loyal.

When we understand that the slave South developed neither a strange form of capitalism nor an undefinable agrarianism but a special civilization built on the relationship of master to slave, we expose the root of its conflict with the North. The internal contradictions in the South and the external conflict with the North placed the slaveholders hopelessly on the defensive with little to look forward to except slow strangulation. Their only hope lay in a bold stroke to complete their political independence and to use it to provide an expansionist solution for their economic and social problems. The ideology and psychology of the proud slaveholding class made surrender or resignation to gradual defeat unthinkable, for its fate, in its own eyes at least, was the fate of everything worth while in Western civilization.

NO

Edward Pessen

HOW DIFFERENT FROM EACH OTHER WERE THE ANTEBELLUM NORTH AND SOUTH?

How different from each other were the North and South before the Civil War? Recent work by historians of antebellum America throws interesting new light on this old question. Since some of these studies deal with individual communities, others with single themes of antebellum life, they are in a sense Pirandelloan pieces of evidence in search of an overarching synthesis that will relate them to one another and to earlier findings and interpretations. My modest hope is that the discussion that follows will be useful to historians in pursuit of such a synthesis.

The terms "North" and "South" are, of course, figures of speech that distort and oversimplify a complex reality, implying homogeneity in geographical sections that, in fact, were highly variegated. Each section embraced a variety of regions and communities that were dissimilar in climatic, topographical, demographic, and social characteristics. If, as Bennett H. Wall has written, "there never has been the 'one' South described by many historians," neither has there been the one North. Historians who have compared the antebellum South and North without referring to the diversity of each have not necessarily been unaware of this diversity. Their premise, in speaking of the North and South, is that the Mason-Dixon line divided two distinctive civilizations, the basic similarities within each of which transcended its internal differences. . . .

Here were two sections containing roughly equal areas for human settlement. Yet on the eve of the Civil War the population of the North was more than 50 percent greater than that of the South. The most dramatic disparity concerned racial balance: roughly one-quarter of a million Northern blacks comprised slightly more than 1 percent of the Northern population; the more than four million blacks in the South constituted one-third of the Southern population. And almost 95 percent of Southern blacks were slaves. Although the value of agricultural products in the two sections was almost equal,

From the *American Historical Review* (December 1980). Reprinted with permission.

Northern superiority in manufactures, railroad mileage, and commercial profits was overwhelming, far surpassing the Northern advantage in population. Similarly, Northern urban development outdistanced Southern, whether measured by the number of cities or by the size and proportions of the population within them. What did these and other, harder to measure, differences signify? To what extent were they balanced out by important sectional similarities? These are among the questions this essay will consider. . . .

A comprehensive comparison of the two sections would overlook nothing, not even the weather, which, according to Phillips, "has been the chief agency in making the South distinctive." In the space available here I shall focus on what our sociological friends might call three social indicators: (1) the economy, (2) the social structure, and (3) politics and power. In selecting these matters for examination, I do not mean to suggest that they are more important than values, ideals, the life of the mind, or any number of other features of antebellum life. Tangible phenomena may be easier to measure than intangible, but they offer no better clue to the essential character of a place and a people. I emphasize economic, social, and political themes because all of them are clearly important, the evidence on them is substantial, and each has recently been re-examined to interesting effect.

The economic practices of each section—one hesitates to call them economic "systems" in the face of the contradictory and largely planless if not improvisatory nature of these practices—were similarly complex. Northerners and Southerners alike made their living primarily in agriculture. Guided by the unique weather and the unequal length of the growing seasons in their sections, Northern and Southern farmers increasingly specialized, but in dissimilar crops. Tobacco and, above all, rice, sugar, and cotton were largely unknown to the North. Yet in the South, as in the North, farmers—whether large or small—sought and, for the most part achieved, self-sufficiency. They produced more grains and corn than anything else and in both sections raised and kept domestic animals roughly equal in quantity and, it has recently been claimed, comparable in quality. In view of the regularity with which Northern farmers brushed aside the lonely voices in their midst who urged subordination of profits to the "long-range needs of the soil," their money-mindedness in planting wheat (their own great dollar earner) year after year, and their unsentimental readiness to dispose of "family land" so long as the price was right, what Stanley L. Engerman had said about Southern planters seems to apply equally well to Northern agriculturists: they were certainly not "non-calculating individuals not concerned with money." . . .

The most distinctive feature of the antebellum Southern economy, as of Southern life as a whole, was, of course, its "peculiar institution." Slavery had not been unknown in the North, flourishing through much of the seventeenth and eighteenth centuries and persisting in New Jersey until 1846. But it had involved relatively few blacks and had had slight effect on Northern life and thought. Northern public opinion, better represented by the authors of the Federal Constitution in 1787 and the Missouri Compromise in 1820 than by the abolitionists of the antebellum decades, accepted slavery, approved of doing business with those who controlled it, abhorred its black victims, and loathed Northern whites who agitated against it. Northern acquiescence in Southern slavery does not erase this most crucial difference between the sections, but it does argue for the complementarity and economic interdependence of North and South. . . .

Several trade unionists in the antebellum North agreed with slavery's apologists that not only the working and living conditions but in some respects the "liberty" enjoyed by Northern hirelings compared unfavorably with the situation of slaves. These were patently self-serving arguments, designed to put the lot of the Northern worker in the worst possible light. The fact remains that the economic gap between enslaved black and free white workers in antebellum South and North was narrower than historians once thought. Evidence bearing on the conditions of white Northern as well as black Southern labor demonstrates that during the middle decades of the nineteenth century the real wages of Northern workingmen declined and their living conditions remained bleak, their job security was reduced, their skills were increasingly devalued, and in many respects their lives became more insecure and precarious.

At mid-century industrial workers in the South as in the North worked primarily in small shops and households rather than in factories. Trade unionists in Baltimore, Louisville, St. Louis, and New Orleans were with few exceptions skilled and semi-skilled white artisans, precisely as they were in Philadelphia, New York, Boston, and Pittsburgh. In Southern as in Northern towns and cities, the least skilled and prestigious jobs were those done preponderantly by Catholic immigrants rather than by older Protestant, ethnic groups. Significantly, the South attracted far fewer of the antebellum era's "new immigrants"—that is, Germans and Irish—than did the North. For all of their smaller numbers in the South, European immigrants played an economic and social role there that was not dissimilar to what it was in the North. Diverse measurable evidence indicates that the pattern of immigrant life in the United States was national, rather than distinctly regional, in character. A similar point can be made about Southern urbanism and manufacturing— namely, quantitative distinctiveness (or deficiency), qualitative similarity to the North. Although the value of Southern manufactured products was usually less than one-fifth of the national total during the antebellum decades, the South was hardly a region devoid of industrial production. Articulate Southerners "crusade[d] to bring the cotton mills to the cotton fields," and, whether due to their exhortations or to the play of market forces, the amount of capital the slave states invested in cotton manufacturing doubled between 1840 and 1860, surpassing their rate of population growth. Because the South nevertheless lagged far behind the Northeast in manufacturing, one influential school of historians has described the antebellum economy— and, for that matter, Southern society as a whole—as noncapitalist, prebourgeois, or "seigneurial."

Some historians have criticized Southern deficiences in commerce, finance, transportation, and manufacturing as manifestations of economic wrongheadedness and irrationality and have attributed to these deficiencies the South's defeat in the Civil War. A number of modern economic historians, cliometricians for the most part, have interpreted the evidence somewhat differently. Invoking the old argument of "comparative advantage," they have noted that heavy investment in cotton, the nation's great dollar earner in international trade, was hardly irrational, since it enabled the South to equal the national rate of profit during the era. Southerners who did invest in Southern factories got a return that compared favorably with industrial profits elsewhere. (Why, ask the critics, didn't they invest more of their capital that way?) If Southern manufacturing was outdistanced by that in the Northeast, it compared favorably with industrial production in the Northwest and, for that matter, in Continental Europe in the mid-nineteenth century. If the South suffered inordinately in the wake of the financial panics of 1837 and 1839, it was, as Reginald C. McGrane noted long ago, precisely because the South had speculated excessively in transportation projects and land acquisition as well as other investments. The South's "unusually favorable system of navigable streams and rivers" has been cited to explain its lag in railroads. Yet in the 1840s Southern railroads "equalled or exceeded the national average capitalization per mile." The views of many scholars are expressed in Gavin Wright's recent observation that "before the War the South was wealthy, prosperous, expanding geographically, and gaining economically at rates that compared favorably to those of the rest of the country.

Antebellum Northern investors, like their counterparts in the South and in Europe, put their money into American products, industrial and agricultural, solid and flimsy, drawn almost entirely by the profit margin likely to result from their investment. Investors in all latitudes appear to have been indifferent to possible long-range consequences of their financial transactions, acting rather on the principle that the "rational" investment was the one likely to pay off. That the railroads, the diversified industry, and the commercial superiority of the North turned out to have important military implications in the 1860s could hardly have been anticipated by earlier profit-seekers. . . .

Historians have long known that a society's social structure offers an important clue to its character. The kind of social classes that exist, the gulf between them, their roles in society, the ease or difficulty of access to higher from lower rungs on the social ladder, and the relationships between the classes tell as much about a civilization as do any other phenomena. What distinguishes modern from earlier historians in their treatment of social class is the extent to which they have borrowed from social scientists both in theorizing about class and in the methodology used for measurement. Employing these new approaches, historians have drastically modified earlier notions of antebellum society.

The ancient belief that the white antebellum South consisted of two classes, wealthy planters at the top and a great mass of poor whites below, may continue to command some popular acceptance. That belief has been so long dead among historians, however, that as early as 1946 Fabian Linden could remark that "the debunking of the 'two class' fallacy" had "become the tedious cliché." For, beginning in 1940 and continuing steadily thereafter, Frank L. Owsley and a group of scholars influenced by his work utilized hitherto neglected primary sources to reveal that the most typical white Southerners by far were small farmers working the modest acreage they owned with few, if any, slaves.

The too neat portrait that the Owsley school drew of the white Southern social structure was quite similar to the picture of *Northern* society accepted by historians less than a generation ago. The white population was ostensibly composed primarily of the great "middling orders," hard-working, proud, and not unprosperous farmers for the most part, whose chance to rise even higher socially matched the opportunities an increasingly democratic society gave them to exert political influence and power. Small groups of rich men—great planters in the one clime and merchants and industrialists in the other—occupied the highest social plateau; professionals who served the rich were slightly above the middle, which was occupied by small business people and independent farmers, skilled artisans, and clerks; and below them stood industrial and landless agricultural laborers. Since class is determined not by bread alone, blacks—whether slave or free and regardless of how much individuals among them had managed to accumulate—were universally relegated to the lowest levels of the social structure, scorned even by white vagrants and frequently unemployed workers, urban and rural, who constituted America's equivalent of a propertyless proletariat.

The achievement of recent research is its transformation of what was a rather blurred image of social groups, whose membership and possessions were both unclear, into a more sharply focused picture. By digging deeper, particularly in nineteenth-century data on wealth and property, historians have come close to knowing the numbers of families belonging to different wealth strata and the amount of wealth these families owned. The beauty of the new evidence on who and how many owned what and how much is that in the antebellum era wealth appears to have been the surest sign of social, as well as economic, position. Antebellum wealth was almost invariably made in socially acceptable ways. Modern scholars have found that "the social divisions of antebellum America were essentially wealth-holding categories." The upper class did not comprise so much the families who "controlled the means of production" as it did the families who "controlled the vast wealth created largely through the exchange of goods produced." Degree of wealth was the surest sign of the quality of housing, furnishings, and household goods a family could afford, of its style of living and uses of leisure, and of the social circle within which it moved and its individual members married. Gathering from the manuscript census schedules, probate inventories, and tax assessors' reports statistically valid samples or, in some cases, evidence on every family in the community under study, modern scholars have been able to arrange the antebellum Southern and Northern populations on a wealth-holding scale. While it is close to a statistical inevitability that the distribution of wealth in the South and North would not be precisely the same, the most striking feature of the evidence is how similarly wealth was distributed—or maldistributed—in the two sections.

On the eve of the Civil War one-half of the free adult males in both the South and the North held less than 1 percent of the real and personal property. In contrast, the richest 1 percent owned 27 percent of the wealth. Turning from the remarkable similarity in sectional patterns of wealthholding at the bottom and the very top, the richest 5 to 10 percent of propertyowners controlled a somewhat greater share of the South's wealth, while what might be called the upper middle deciles (those below the top tenth) held a slightly smaller share in the North. The South also came close to monopolizing wealthy counties, the per capita wealth of which was $4,000 or more and, despite its smaller population, the South, according to the 1860 census, contained almost two-thirds of those persons in the nation whose worth was at least $110,000. According to Lee Soltow, the leading student of this evidence, these sectional disparities "could be attributed almost entirely to slave values. . . . If one could eliminate slave market value from the distribution of wealth in 1860 . . . , the inequality levels in the North and South were similar."

In view of the centrality of slavery to the antebellum South, it is idle to speak of "eliminating the market value" of slaves from the sectional comparison. Northern free labor, rural and industrial, also represented a form of "sectional wealth," if a much overlooked form. Although as individual human beings they did not add to their own private wealth or to the wealth of the employers they served, their labor created wealth for themselves and for these same capitalists at rates of productivity that, I believe, even Robert W. Fogel and Stanley L. Engerman would concede compared favorably with the rates of the most efficient slaves. In other words, the North had access to a form of wealth, free labor, that was roughly as valuable per capita as was slave wealth, however absent this Northern wealth was from the reports prepared by census takers and assessors.

Given the known habits of these officials to overlook small property holdings—precisely the kind of holdings that would have been owned by Northern working people—and to accept as true the lies people swore to as to their worth, it is likely that the fairly substantial cumulative wealth owned by small farmers and modest wage earners was almost entirely omitted from the wealth equation. Such groups were far more numerous in the North than in the South. Had slaves been treated as part of the potential property-owning Southern population to which they actually belonged, instead of being treated as property pure and simple, the total wealth of the antebellum South would have been diminished by several billion dollars: the product of multiplying the number of slaves by the average market price of almost $1,000 per slave. The addition of nearly four million very poor black people to the number of potential propertyowners in the South would have increased its rate of inequality (and the Gini coefficient of concentration that measures it), although not everywhere to the same extent.

Wealth in both sections was distributed more equally—perhaps the more apt phrase is less unequally—in the countryside than in towns and cities. While the rural North has been less intensively investigated than its Southern counterpart, enough research has been completed to disclose that the North was hardly a haven of egalitarian distribution of property. Rural Wisconsin (which had a Gini coefficient of inequality as high as that of antebellum Texas), the Michigan frontier, and northwestern New York State were centers of inequality and poverty. At mid-century, the proportion of white men who owned land in any amount was substantially lower in the

Northwest than in the South. The percentage of free males owning land in the North as a whole was slightly smaller than in the South. Owing to the absence of slaves and to the relative paucity of very large farms, wealth was somewhat less unequally distributed in the rural North than in the South.

In investigating the distribution of wealth in the antebellum rural South, scholars have probed data on different states, counties, and regions. The patterns throughout are remarkably similar, whether for wealth in general, land and real estate, or personal and slave property. Accentuating the maldistribution of landed wealth—whether in Alabama, Mississippi, Louisiana, Texas, the "cotton South," or the agricultural South as a whole—was a fact of life that the Owsley school neglected: the dollar value per acre of large farms owned by slave-owning planters was substantially greater than the value per acre of the small farm. And yet, regardless of the nature of the soil or the proportion of large farms in a given region, the rates of wealth concentration were remarkably similar as well as constant during the decades before the war. Paralleling the recent finding that in antebellum Texas, no matter what the differences were "in climate, soil, and extent of settlement, the most striking fact is . . . the high degree of concentration in wealthholding across all the regions," another recent study reports no great differences in "the degree of inequality" between the cotton South and the other "major agricultural regions" of grain, tobacco, sugar, and rice production in 1860.

The distribution of slave wealth closely followed the pattern of other forms of Southern wealth. During the decade before the war, slaveownership was con-fined to between 20 and 25 percent of white families, and maldistribution of this form of property was the rule within the slave-owning population. Half of all slaveowners owned five or fewer slaves, with only one-tenth owning the twenty or more slaves that by Ulrich B. Phillips's definition made them "planters." Less than one-half of 1 percent owned one hundred or more slaves. As with other forms of wealth, the concentration of slave wealth increased slightly between 1850 and 1860.

While the South had long lagged behind the North in urban development, recent scholarship has unearthed evidence that Southern cities grew at a remarkable rate during the antebellum decades. If the Southern rate of urban expansion still did not match the Northern quantitatively, Southern cities, old and new, were qualitatively not unlike their Northern counterparts. Antebellum cities in all latitudes were amazingly similar in the roles they played in the political, administrative, financial, economic, artistic, and intellectual affairs of their regions. Antebellum cities were also alike in the types of men who ran them, in the underlying social philosophies guiding those men, and in their "social configurations." Not the least of the similarities of cities in both great sections was in their distribution of wealth.

Three things can be said about the distribution of wealth in the towns and cities of the Old South. Property ownership was even more concentrated there than in rural areas. Riches became more unequally distributed with the passage of time, with the proportion of the propertyless increasing sharply between 1850 and 1860. There was an increase too in the proportion of urban wealth owned by the largest wealthholders—at least for the dozen communities measured to date. And the patterns of wealth distribution in Southern cities were very much like those that were obtained in the North. . . .

Throwing important, if indirect, light on the relatively slight opportunities for upward social and economic movement antebellum America offered to poor or economically marginal men is the era's high rate of physical or geographical mobility. In rural as well as urban communities, in large cities and small, and on both sides of the Mason-Dixon line, armies of footloose Americans were on the move, following trails never dreamed of in the Turner thesis. One-half of the residents, primarily the poorer and propertyless, left those communities from one decade to another in their search for a more acceptable living. I have no doubt that future research will yet disclose that, during what was a period of economic expansion in both sections, significant numbers of Americans improved their lot, even if modestly. To date, however, the data reveal equally slight rates of social mobility and high rates of geographical mobility on both sides of the Mason-Dixon line.

Carl Degler has recently observed that Southern society "differed from northern in that the social hierarchy culminated in the planter, not the industrialist." At mid-century, great Northern fortunes, in fact, owned more to commerce and finance than to manufacturing. What is perhaps more important is that a sharply differentiated social hierarchy obtained in both sections. In Degler's phrase, planter status was "the ideal to which other white southerners aspired." A good case can be made for the equally magnetic attraction that exalted merchant status had for Northerners. If the

fragmentary evidence on Virginia, Georgia, and the Carolinas, which Jane H. Pease has so effectively exploited, is any indication, then great planters lived less sybaritically and consumed less conspicuously than historians had previously thought. If Philip Hone's marvelous diary—two dozen full-to-the-brim volumes of life among the swells during the antebellum decades—had broader implication, then the Northeastern social and economic elite commanded a lifestyle of an elegance and costliness that, among other things, proved irresistably attractive to the aristocratic Southerners who graced Hone's table, pursued diversion with other members of Hone's set, and married into its families—the Gardiners, Coolidges, Coldens, Bayards, Gouverneurs, and Kortrights. . . .

Influence, power, and, above all, politics in antebellum America have been the subjects of massive recent research. Most discussions of antebellum politics have stressed differences between the major parties. The literature takes on new meaning peculiarly germane to this discussion when it is recast and its focus shifted to a comparison of politics in the North and South. . . .

By mid-century the American political system was everywhere formally democratic. Notorious exceptions to and limitations on democracy persisted, but they persisted in both North and South and for largely the same reasons. If blacks could not vote in the Old South, with rare exceptions neither could they vote in the Old North, where they were barred by statute, subterfuge, custom, and intimidation. The South initiated the movement to limit the powers and terms of office of the judiciary and substitute popular elections for the appointment of judges. When Fletcher M. Green reminded us a generation ago that ante-bellum Southern states created new, and modified old, constitutions that were fully as democratic as those in Northern states, he concluded that by this "progressive expansion in the application of the doctrine of political equality . . . , the aristocratic planter class had been shorn of its political power." Power, he claimed, had now been transferred to "the great mass of whites." As Green's critics were quick to point out, popular suffrage and theoretical rights to hold office are not synonomous with popular power. Yet these are not empty or hollow rights. That they have often been made so testifies not to their insignificance but rather to the importance of the larger context in which democratic political gains are registered. It remains neither a small matter nor a small similarity that on the constitutional level the antebellum North and South were similarly democratic and republican.

At least as important as society's system for selecting political officeholders is the kind of men who are regularly selected and their characteristic performance in office. . . .

Abundant data have been accumulated on the occupations, wealth and property ownership, church affiliations, education, and other social indicators not only of antebellum officeholders in several dozen cities equally divided between South and North and in counties in every Southern state but also of state officials in all of the Southern and most of the Northern states and of Congressmen from most of the states in the Union. The resultant picture inevitably is not uniform. Humble county and town officials, for example, were less likely to be drawn from the highest levels of wealth and from the most prestigious occupations

than were men who occupied more exalted state and federal positions. Aldermen and councilmen usually did not match the mayor either in wealth or in family prestige. But the relatively slight social and economic differences found between men at different levels of government or between men nominated by the parties that dominated American politics from the 1830s to the 1850s were not differences between the North and South. In the South as in the North, men similar in their dissimilarity to their constituencies held office and exercised behind-the-scenes influence. In contrast to the small farmers, indigents, laborers, artisans, clerks, and shopkeepers—the men of little or no property who constituted the great majority of the ante-bellum population—the men who held office and controlled the affairs of the major parties were everywhere lawyers, merchants, businessmen, and relatively large property owners. In the South they were inordinately men who owned slaves and owned them in unusually large numbers. It may well be that a society that is stratified economically and socially will confer leadership on those who have what Robert A. Dahl has called substantial material "advantages." It is not clear that this is an iron law. What is clear is that the Old South and the North awarded leadership to precisely such men.

More important than the social and economic backgrounds of political leaders are their public behavior and the ideologies or "world views" underlying this behavior. Not that the thinking or action of powerful men is totally unaffected by their material circumstances. But, in view of the complexity of any individual's ideology and of the diverse elements that help shape it, the effect of these circumstances cannot be assumed and is likely to vary from one individual to another. Although the political philosophies of men do not lend themselves to quantitative or precise measurement, the burden of recent scholarship is that most Southern and Northern political activists were similarly ambitious for worldly success, opportunistic, materialistic, and disinclined to disturb their societies' social arrangements. Men with values such as these were ideally suited to lead the great pragmatic parties that dominated antebellum politics.[1]

Many parties flashed across the American political horizon during the antebellum decades. That the Antimasonic Party, the Liberty Party, and the Free Soil Party almost entirely bypassed the South is an important difference between the sections. The South was not hospitable to organized political dissent, particularly dissent hostile to the expansion of slavery. . . .

The Democrats and Whigs were national parties drawing their leaders and followers from both sections. They could usually count on intersectional support for the national tickets they presented quadrennially to the nation at large. Interestingly, the presidency—whether occupied by Southerners Jackson, Tyler, Polk, and Taylor and the Southern-born Harrison or Northerners Van Buren, Fillmore, Pierce, and Buchanan—was in the 1830s, 1840s, and 1850s in the hands of Whigs and Democrats who displayed great sensitivity toward the political and economic interests of the slave-owning South In the 1840s Congressmen voted not by region as Northerners or Southerners but primarily as Whigs and Democrats. Party rather than sectional interest prevailed in the roll calls on most issues reaching the national political

agenda. In the 1850s, as Thomas B. Alexander has reported, "forces greater than party discipline . . . were evidently at work . . . , forcing party to yield to section on a definable number of issues." Yet, even in the 1950s, "both major parties maintained a high level of cohesion of intersectional comity" with regard to the range of issues not bearing on slavery and its right to expansion.

The great national issues of antebellum politics, culminating as they did in Sumter and the ensuing war, were of transcendant importance to Americans. A good case can nonetheless be made that local and state politics touched the lives of people more often and more directly than did national politics, particularly during an era when the men in the nation's capital were inclined to treat laissez faire as an article of faith. State governments in North and South, by contrast, engaged in vigorous regulation of a wide range of economic activities. Local governments taxed citizens and, if with limited effectiveness, sought to provide for their safety, regulate their markets and many of their business activities, look after the poor, maintain public health, improve local thoroughfares, dispose of waste, pump in water, light up the dark, and furnish some minimal cultural amenities though the exercise of powers that characteristically had been granted by state government. States chartered banks, transportation companies, and other forms of business enterprise, determined the scope of such charters, themselves engaged in business, disposed of land, and regulated local communities. The great question is how did the actual operations of local and state governments in the North and South compare during the antebellum decades.

Antebellum state government was almost invariably controlled by either Whigs or Democrats. The major parties were essentially state parties, bound together in the most loosely organized national confederations. Citizens divided not by geographical section but by party preference within each state. The parties were in all latitudes characteristically controlled by tight groups of insiders that sometimes monopolized power, sometimes shared it with rival factions, in the one case as in other controlling nominations and conventions, hammering out policy, disseminating and publicizing the party line, organizing the faithful to support it, enforcing strict discipline, and punishing those who dared challenge either the policies or the tactics pursued by the leadership. While party policies could conceivably have been infused with the noble principles proclaimed in party rhetoric, such infusion rarely appears to have been the case. The "Albany Regency," the "Richmond Junto," the "Bourbon Dynasty" of Arkansas, and similar cliques in control elsewhere have been described as realists rather than idealists.

In towns and cities, unlike the states, party counted for little. Candidates for the mayor's office and the local council or board of aldermen did not fail to remind voters of the moral superiority of their own parties. But, as students of antebellum urban politics have noted, it mattered little whether this major party or that won the election or whether the town was located north or south of the Mason-Dixon line. . . .

Perhaps in no other milieu was governmental policy so permeated with class bias. Whether it was Natchez or Springfield, Charleston or Brooklyn, New Orleans or Boston, the lawyers, merchants, and large propertyowners who occupied city hall ran things in the interests of the "wealthier inhabitants." Tax rates were everywhere miniscule and property flagrantly underassessed, at the insistence of large taxpayers. Valuable lots were leased to rich men at ridiculously low rates, if not sold to them for a song. Funds provided by the niggardly budgets typical of the time were spent most freely to improve or widen streets used by businessmen rather than to clean streets in the neighborhoods of the poor. Improved public facilities for disposing of waste or carrying fresh water into the city were usually introduced first in upper-class residential districts. The "indisputable connection between the policies of the city council and the interests of the wealthier inhabitants" that Richard Wade discerned in Cincinnati early in the era could be found in most other cities.

Power is not, of course, confined to control of government. Control over banks, credit, capital, communications, and voluntary associations, which in an era of laissez faire often exercised more influence than did public authorities over education and culture, crime and punishment, social welfare and poverty, gave to those who had it a power that was barely matched by those who held the reins of government. The burden of recent research is that small social and economic elites exercised a degree of control over the most important institutions in the antebellum North that bears close resemblance to the great power attributed to the great planter-slaveowners by William E. Dodd a half century ago and by Eugene D. Genovese more recently. Influential voluntary associations and financial institutions appear to have been run by similarly atypical sorts on both sides of the Mason-Dixon line.

Shortly after secession, Governor Joseph E. Brown told the Georgia legislature that in the South the "whole social system is one of perfect homogeneity of interest, where every class is interested in sustaining the interest of every other class." Numerous Southerners agreed with him, and many scholars concur. In their failure to challenge planter supremacy, small farmers—slaveowners and nonslaveowners alike—ostensibly demonstrated the unique identity of interest that was said to bind all whites together in the antebellum South. The interest of a group is a normative term, known only to God (and perhaps to Rousseau in his capacity as authority on the General Will), in contrast to its perceived interests, as stated in its words and implicit in its actions. There are, therefore, as many interpretations of the "true interests" of Southern—or, for that matter, of Northern—small farmers as there are historians writing on the subject. The South's large enslaved black population doubtless affected the perceptions of all Southern whites, if in complex and unmeasurable ways. Recent research indicates that poorer and nonslave-owning Southern whites were, nevertheless, sensitive enough to their own social and economic deprivation to oppose their social superiors on secession and other important matters. Whether the acquiescence of the mass of antebellum Northerners in their inferior social and economic condition was in their own interest will be decided differently by conservative, reformist, and radical historians. Our admittedly insubstantial evidence on the issue suggests that the degree of social harmony coexisting with subtle underlying social tensions was,

racial matters apart, not much different in the North and the South.

Limitations of space permit no more than a swift allusion to a number of other matters that are fascinating either because, like religiosity and values, they are intangible or, like crime and violence, they resist precise measurement. Scholars of a revisionist bent can have a field day with these themes, for the growing literature on them yields tantalizing evidence that appears to overturn the traditional view of a distinctive antebellum South. Legal briefs can thus be written attesting the near similarity of the South and North in their achievements in science, medicine, public health, and other aspects of intellectual and cultural life, in their ideals of womanhood, in their racial attitudes, in their violence and attitudes toward violence, in their materialism as in other values, in aspects of humanitarian reform, and in religion, particularly in the roles played by evangelicalism and the Benevolent Empire in the Protestant denominations that were predominant in both sections. Much of this literature implicitly promotes the concept of sectional convergence either by upgrading Southern or by downgrading Northern achievements. But, since historians—unlike embattled attorneys—cannot content themselves with evidence that is both insubstantial and contradicted by evidence pointing in an opposite direction, they are best advised to reserve judgment. Wisdom consists in re-examining and re-evaluating the earlier literature on these themes, weighing carefully the merits of the recent contributions, and, above all, probing for additional evidence.

Having examined economic developments, social structure, and politics and power in the antebellum sections, let me now return to the question of capitalism in the Old South. Several historians have recently argued that Southern planters constituted a "seigneurial" class presiding over a "pseudocapitalistic" society, a class whose "world view" ostensibly set them "apart from the mainstream of capitalistic civilization." By this analysis, the Old South, though influenced by modern capitalism, belonged (as do early modern India and Saudi Arabia, among others) to the category of "premodern" societies that have been the economic and political dependencies of the dynamic industrial world that exploits them. The antebellum South's banking, commercial, and credit institutions did not in this view manifest the section's own capitalistic development so much as they served to facilitate the South's exploitation by the "capitalistic world market." This argument can be accepted uncritically only be accepting Eugene D. Genovese, Barrington Moore, Jr., and Raimondi Luraghi as the arbiters and interpreters of what represents "every normal feature of capitalism."

Capitalism is not a rigid system governed by uniform economic practices, let alone inflexible definitions. The economy of the antebellum United States, like capitalistic economies in Victorian England and other nations, was composed of diverse elements, each playing a part in a geographical and functional division of labor within the larger society. As Lewis C. Gray and Thomas P. Govan long ago and other scholars more recently have observed, Southern planters had the attitudes and goals and were guided by the classic practices of capitalistic businessmen. The antiurbanism and antimaterialism that Genovese has attributed to the great planters is unconvincing because thinly documented and contradicted by much other evidence. Some people, including planters themselves, may have likened the planter class to a seigneurial aristocracy. Unlike the lords of the textbook manor, however, Southern planters depended heavily on outside trade, participated enthusiastically in a money economy, and sought continuously to expand their operations and their capital. Marx once said that the limits of the serf's exploitation were determined by the walls of the lord's stomach. The limits of the slave's exploitation were determined by the expanding walls of the world cotton market.

That slavery is not the classic labor system associated with a Marxist definition of capitalism is, of course, true. The problem with Marx as Pundit of capitalism, for all the undeniable brilliance of his interpretation, is that he was, as he conceded, more interested in changing the system than in explaining it. Those of us content with merely understanding so complex a phenomenon as capitalism know that, whether in its labor system or in other respects, it is a flexible and constantly shifting order, susceptible of diverse definitions. The Southern economy did differ in important respects from the Northern, developing special interests of its own. Yet, far from being in any sense members of a colony or dependency of the North, the Southern upper classes enjoyed close ties with the Northern capitalists who were, in a sense, their business partners. The South was an integral component of a wealthy and dynamic national economy, no part of which conformed perfectly to a textbook definition of pure capitalism. In part because of the central place in that economy of its great export crop, cotton, the South from the 1820s to the 1860s exerted a degree of influence over the nation's domestic and foreign policies that was barely equalled by the antebellum North. India within the Empire indeed! The South's political system of republicanism and limited democracy, like its hierarchical social structure, conformed closely to the prevailing arrangements in the North, as they also did to the classic features of a capitalistic order.

The striking similarities of the two antebellum sections of the nation neither erase their equally striking dissimilarities nor detract from the significance of these dissimilarities. Whether in climate, diet, work habits, uses of leisure, speech and diction, health and disease, mood, habits, ideals, self-image, or labor systems, profound differences separated the antebellum North and South. One suspects that antebellum Americans regarded these matters as the vital stuff of life. The point need not be labored that a society, one-third of whose members were slaves (and slaves of a distinctive "race"), is most unlike a society of free men and women. An essay focusing on these rather than on the themes emphasized here would highlight the vital disparities between the antebellum South and North. And yet the striking dissimilarities of the two antebellum sections do not erase their equally striking similarities, nor do they detract from the significance of these similarities.

The antebellum North and South were far more alike than the conventional scholarly wisdom has led us to believe. Beguiled by the charming version of Northern society and politics composed by Tocqueville, the young Marx, and other influential antebellum commentators, historians have until recently believed that the Northern social structure was far more egalitarian and offered far greater opportunity for upward social movement than did its Southern counterpart and that white men of humble position had far more power in the Old North than they did in the Old South. In disclosing that the reality of the antebellum North fell far short of the egalitarian ideal, modern studies of social structure sharply narrow the gulf between the antebellum North and South. Without being replicas of one another, both sections were relatively rich, powerful, aggressive, and assertive communities, socially stratified and governed equally—and disconcertingly—oligarchic internal arrangements. That they were drawn into the most terrible of all American wars may have been due, as is often the case when great powers fight, as much to their similarities as to their differences. The war owed more, I believe, to the inevitably opposed but similarly selfish interests—or perceived interests—of North and South than to differences in their cultures and institutions.

Late in the Civil War, William King of Cobb County, Georgia, reported that invading Union officers had told him, "We are one people, [with] the same language, habits, and religion, and ought to be one people." The officers might have added that on the spiritual plane Southerners shared with Northerners many ideals and aspirations and had contributed heavily to those historical experiences the memory and symbols of which tie a people together as a nation. For all of their distinctiveness, the Old South and North were complementary elements in an American society that was everywhere primarily rural, capitalistic, materialistic, and socially stratified, racially, ethnically, and religiously heterogeneous, and stridently chauvinistic and expansionist — a society whose practice fell far short of, when it was not totally in conflict with, its lofty theory.

NOTES

1.-By pragmatic parties I mean, as do most historians and political scientists who have used the term, parties largely but not solely concerned with electoral success, parties not devoid of principles so much as parties of flexible or shifting principles.

POSTSCRIPT

Was the Antebellum South a Unique Section in American History?

Traditional Southern historians like Ulrich B. Phillips and Frank Owsley as well as Southern novelists like Thomas Wolfe and William Faulkner would have accepted that portion of Genovese's argument which views the South as a distinct section in pre–Civil War America. More recently Pulitzer Prize-winning historian Carl N. Degler accepts the unique Southern identity argument in *Place Over Time: The Continuity of Southern Distinctiveness* (LSU Press, 1977). If the reader wishes to pursue Genovese's approach further, two books should be read: *Roll Jordan Roll* (Pantheon, 1974), the best full-scale account of nineteenth-century slavery, and *In Red and Black: Marxian Explorations in Southern and Afro-American History* (Pantheon Books, 1971).

Professor Pessen has presented the reader with a synthesis of pre–Civil War American society. He has based his findings on a number of local mobility studies employing quantitative evidence of census data including his own works about New York City during the Jacksonian era.

Books continue to proliferate about the American South. The starting point is Williams Cash's poetic *The Mind of the South* (Knopf, 1941). An updated version of Cash's thesis can be found in the more scholarly but still interesting work on *Southern Honor: Ethics and Behavior in the Old South* (Oxford, 1982), by Bertram Wyatt Brown. Cash's thesis about a unique South has been challenged by C. Van Woodward. Worth reading are selections from *The Burden of Southern History*, rev. ed. (LSU Press, 1968); *American Counterpoint: Slavery and Racism in the North-South Dialogue* (Little, Brown, 1971); and in its entirety the classic statement about *The Strange Career of Jim Crow*, 2d rev. ed. (Oxford, 1966).

The University of South Carolina has produced a wonderful 14-part television series *The American South Comes of Age*. Jack Bass and Thomas E. Terrill have edited the anthology which accompanies this series (Knopf, 1987). Students who wish to understand why the "newest" South votes Republican in presidential elections have an excellent guide in Earl and Merle Black's *Politics and Society in the South* (Harvard, 1987).

Those who wish to ponder the issue of the new South's emulation of the North should read Richard N. Current's delightful *Northernizing the South* (University of Georgia, 1983) and sociologist John Shelton Reed's "Up From Segregation," *Virginia Quarterly Review* (Summer 1984).

ISSUE 16

Was Abraham Lincoln America's Greatest President?

YES: Stephen B. Oates, from *Abraham Lincoln: The Man Behind the Myths* (Harper & Row, 1984)

NO: M. E. Bradford, from *Remembering Who We Are: Observations of a Southern Conservative* (University of Georgia Press, 1985)

ISSUE SUMMARY

YES: Oates insists that Abraham Lincoln's greatness as president of the United States stemmed from a moral vision that had as its goal the protection and expansion of popular government.

NO: Bradford characterizes Lincoln as a cynical politician whose abuse of authority as president and commander-in-chief during the Civil War marked a serious departure from the republican goals of the Founding Fathers and established the prototype for the "imperial presidency" of the twentieth century.

The American Civil War (1861–1865) produced what historian Arthur Schlesinger, Jr., has called "our greatest national trauma." To be sure, the War Between the States was a searing event that etched itself on the collective memory of the American people and inspired an interest that has made it the most thoroughly studied episode in American history. During the last century and a quarter, scholars have identified a variety of factors (including slavery, economic sectionalism, cultural distinctions between North and South, the doctrine of states' rights, and the irresponsibility of abolitionists and proslavery advocates) that contributed to sectional tensions and, ultimately, war. Although often presented as "sole causes," these factors are complicated, interconnected, and controversial. Consequently, historians must consider as many of them as possible in their evaluations of the war, even if they choose to spotlight one or another as a major explanation.

Most historians, however, agree that the war would not have occurred had eleven Southern states not seceded from the Union to form the Confederate States of America following Abraham Lincoln's election to the presidency in 1860. Why was Lincoln viewed as a threat to the South? A Southerner by birth, Lincoln's career in national politics (as a congressman representing his adopted state of Illinois) apparently had been short-circuited by his unpopular opposition to the Mexican War. His attempt to emerge from political obscurity a decade later failed when he was defeated by Stephen Douglas in a bid for an Illinois Senate seat. This campaign, however, gained for Lincoln a reputation as a powerful orator, and in 1860 Republican party managers passed over some of their more well-known leaders, such as William Henry Seward, and nominated the moderate Mr. Lincoln for the presidency. His victory was guaranteed by factionalism within Democratic ranks, but the election results revealed that the new president received only thirty-nine percent of the popular vote. This fact, however, provided little solace for Southerners, who mistook the new president's opposition to the extension of slavery into the territories for evidence that he supported the abolitionist wing of the Republican party. Despite assurances during the campaign that he would not tamper with slavery where it already existed, Lincoln could not prevent the splintering of the Union.

Given such an inauspicious beginning, few observers at the time could have predicted that future generations would view Lincoln as our nation's greatest president. What factors have contributed to this assessment? The answer would appear to lie in his role as commander-in-chief during the Civil War. Is this reputation deserved? The essays that follow assess Lincoln's presidency from dramatically different perspectives.

Stephen B. Oates, a recent biographer of Lincoln, presents the views of historians who see greatness in the leadership of the nation's sixteenth chief executive. Lincoln, writes Oates, possessed a moral vision that served as his inspiration for ending oppression and enlarging the rights of the people. His reputation as "the Great Emancipator" is deserved, Oates claims, because he issued the Emancipation Proclamation and supported the Thirteenth Amendment. Oates's Lincoln is a practical politician who held the Union together and played a prominent role in formulating the strategy for the North's military victory.

M. E. Bradford offers a sharp critique of the conclusions reached by Oates. By pursuing an anti-Southern strategy, Bradford argues, President Lincoln perverted the republican goals advanced by the Founding Fathers and destroyed the Democratic majority which was essential to the preservation of the Union. Furthermore, Bradford's Lincoln abused his executive authority by cynically expanding the scope of presidential powers to an unhealthy extent. Finally, in contrast to Oates's interpretation, Bradford charges that Lincoln was uncommitted to the cause of black Americans.

YES

Stephen B. Oates

THE MAN BEHIND THE MYTHS

THE BEACON LIGHT OF LIBERTY

In presidential polls taken by *Life* Magazine in 1948, the *New York Times Magazine* in 1962, and the *Chicago Tribune Magazine* in 1982, historians and political scholars ranked Lincoln as the best chief executive in American history. They were not trying to mythologize the man, for they realized that errors, vacillations, and human flaws marred his record. Their rankings indicate, however, that the icon of mythology did rise out of a powerful historical figure, a man who learned from his mistakes and made a difference. Indeed, Lincoln led the lists because he had a moral vision of where his country must go to preserve and enlarge the rights of all her people. He led the lists because he had an acute sense of history—an ability to identify himself with a historical turning point in his time and to articulate the promise that held for the liberation of oppressed humanity the world over. He led the lists because he perceived the truth of his age and embodied it in his words and deeds. He led the lists because, in his interaction with the spirit and events of his day, he made momentous *moral* decisions that affected the course of humankind. . . .

THE CENTRAL IDEA

In the flames of civil war, Lincoln underwent seemingly endless crises that might have shattered a weaker man. Here he was—a President who lacked administrative experience, suffered from chronic depression, hated to fire inept subordinates and bungling generals (he had never liked personal confrontations anyway)—thrust into the center of a fratricidal conflict. Here he was, forced to make awesome decisions in a war that had no precedent in all American history, a war without constitutional or political guidelines for him to follow. At the same time, Lincoln had to live with the knowledge that he was the most unpopular President the Republic had known up to that time. . . .

From all directions came cries that Lincoln was unfit to be President, that he was too inexperienced, too inept, too stupid and imbecilic, to reunite the country. Even some of his Cabinet secretaries, even some of his friends, feared that the war was too much for him.

Melancholy and inexperienced though he was, unsure of himself and savagely criticized though he was, Lincoln managed nevertheless to see this huge and confusing conflict in a world dimension. He defined and fought it according to his core of unshakable convictions about America's experiment and historic mission in the progress of human liberty. The central issue of the war, he told Congress on Independence Day, 1861, was whether a constitutional republic—a system of popular government—could preserve itself. There were Europeans who argued that anarchy and rebellion were inherent weaknesses of a republic and that a monarchy was the more stable form of government. Now, in the Civil War, popular government was going through a fiery trial for its very survival. If it failed in America, if it succumbed to the forces of reaction represented by the slave-based Confederacy, it might indeed perish from the earth. The beacon of hope for oppressed humanity the world over would be destroyed. . . .

In short, the war and Lincoln's response to it defined him as a President. Here is a classic illustration of how the interaction of people and events shapes the course of history. As the war grew and changed, so Lincoln grew and changed. At first, he warned that the conflict must not turn into a "remorseless revolutionary struggle," lest that cause wide-scale social and political wreckage. As a consequence, his initial war strategies were cautious and limited.

But when the conflict ground on with no end in sight, Lincoln resorted to one harsh war measure after another to subdue the rebellion and save popular government: he embraced martial law, property confiscation, emancipation, Negro troops, conscription, and scorched-earth warfare. These turned the war into the very thing he had cautioned against: a remorseless revolutionary struggle whose concussions are still being felt.

And it became such a struggle because of Lincoln's unswerving commitment to the war's central idea.

DEATH WARRANT FOR SLAVERY

Nowhere was the struggle more evident than in the nagging problem of slavery. How Lincoln approached that problem—and what he did about it—is one of the most written about and least understood facets of his presidency. As we examine this dramatic and complicated story, recall that what guided Lincoln in the matter of emancipation was his commitment, not just to the Union, but to what it represented and symbolized. Here, as in all war-related issues, Lincoln's devotion to the war's central idea—to preserving a system that guaranteed to all the right of self-government—dictated his course of action. . . .

At first, Lincoln rejected a presidential move against slavery. "I think Sumner and the rest of you would upset our applecart altogether if you had your way," he told some advanced Republicans one day. "We didn't go into the war to put down slavery, but to put the flag back; and to act differently at this moment would, I have no doubt, not only weaken our cause, but smack of bad faith. . . . This thunderbolt will keep."

In short, as President he was accountable to the entire country, or what remained of it in the North and West, and the vast majority of whites there remained adamantly opposed to emancipation.

Still, Lincoln was sympathetic to the entire range of arguments Sumner and his associates rehearsed for him. Personally, Lincoln hated slavery as much as they did, and many of their points had already occurred to him. On certain days he could be seen like them in the lecture hall of the Smithsonian Institution, listening quietly and intently as antislavery orators damned slavery for the evil that it was. Under the combined and incessant demands that he act, Lincoln began wavering in his hands-off policy about slavery; as early as November and December, 1861, he began searching about for some compromise—something short of a sweeping emancipation decree, which he still regarded as "too big a lick." Again he seemed caught in an impossible dilemma: how to remove the cause of war, keep Britain out of the conflict, solve the refugee problem, cripple the Confederacy, and suppress the rebellion, and yet retain the allegiance of northern Democrats and the critical border. . . .

On July 22, 1862, Lincoln summoned his Cabinet members and read them a draft of a preliminary Emancipation Proclamation. Come January 1, 1863, in his capacity as Commander-in-Chief of the armed forces in time of war, Lincoln would free all the slaves everywhere in the rebel states. He would thus make it a Union objective to annihilate slavery as an institution in the Confederate South.

Contrary to what many historians have said, Lincoln's projected Proclamation went further than anything Congress had done. True, Congress had just enacted (and Lincoln had just signed) the second confiscation act, which provided for the seizure and liberation of all slaves of people who supported or participated in the rebellion. Still, most slaves would be freed only after protracted case-by-case litigation in the federal courts. Another section of the act did liberate certain categories of slaves without court action, but the bill exempted loyal slaveowners in the rebel South, allowing them to keep their slaves and other property. Far short of a genuine emancipation measure, the act was about as far as Congress could go in attacking slavery, for most Republicans still acknowledged that Congress had no constitutional authority to remove bondage as a state institution. Only the President with his war powers—or a constitutional amendment—could do that. Nevertheless, the measure seemed a clear invitation for the President to exercise his constitutional powers and abolish slavery in the rebellious states. And Stevens, Sumner, and others repeatedly told Lincoln that most congressional Republicans now favored this.

In contrast to the confiscation act, Lincoln's Proclamation was a sweeping blow against slavery as an institution in the rebel states, a blow that would free *all* slaves there—those of secessionists and loyalists alike. Thus Lincoln would handle emancipation himself (as congressional Republicans wanted him to do), avoid judicial red tape, and use the military to vanquish the cornerstone of the Confederacy. Again, he justified this as a military necessity to save the Union—and with it America's experiment in popular government. . . .

THE MAN OF OUR REDEMPTION

When he won the election of 1864, Lincoln interpreted it as a popular mandate for him and his emancipation policy. But in reality the election provided no clear referendum on slavery, since Republican campaigners had played down emancipation and concentrated on the folly of the Democrats in running General George McClellan on a peace plank in the midst of civil war. Nevertheless, Lincoln used his reelection to promote a constitutional amendment that would guarantee the freedom of all slaves, those in the loyal border states as well as those in the rebel South. Even before issuing his Proclamation, Lincoln had worried that it might be nullified in the courts or thrown out by a later Congress or a subsequent administration. Consequently he wanted a constitutional amendment that would safeguard his Proclamation and prevent emancipation from ever being overturned.

Back in December, 1862, Lincoln himself had called on Congress to adopt an emancipation amendment, and advanced Republicans had introduced one in the Senate and guided it through, reminding their colleagues that nobody could deny that all the death and destruction of the war stemmed from slavery and that it was their duty to support this amendment. In April, 1864, the Senate adopted it by a vote of thirty-eight to six, but it failed to muster the required two-thirds majority in the House.

After that Lincoln had insisted that the Republican platform endorse the measure. And now, over the winter of 1864 and 1865, he put tremendous pressure on the House to approve the amendment, using all his powers of persuasion and patronage to get it through. He buttonholed conservative Republicans and opposition Democrats and exhorted them to support the amendment. He singled out "sinners" among the Democrats who were "on praying ground," and informed them that they had a lot better chance for the federal jobs they desired if they voted for the measure. Soon two Democrats swung over in favor of it. In the House debates, meanwhile, Republican James Ashley quoted Lincoln himself that "if slavery is not wrong, nothing is wrong," and Thaddeus Stevens, still tall and imposing at seventy-two, asserted that he had never hesitated, even when threatened with violence, "to stand here and denounce this infamous institution." With the outcome much in doubt, Lincoln and congressional Republicans participated in secret negotiations never made public—negotiations that allegedly involved patronage, a New Jersey railroad monopoly, and the release of rebels related to congressional Democrats—to bring wavering opponents into line. "The greatest measure of the nineteenth century," Stevens claimed, "was passed by corruption, aided and abetted by the purest man in America."

On January 31, 1865, the House adopted the present Thirteenth Amendment by just three votes more than the required two-thirds majority. At once a storm of cheers broke over House Republicans, who danced around, embraced one another, and waved their hats and canes. "It seemed to me I had been born into a new life," recalled one advanced Republican, "and that the world was overflowing with beauty and joy."

Lincoln, too, pronounced the amendment "a great moral victory" and "a King's cure" for the evils of slavery.

When ratified by the states, the amendment would end human bondage everywhere in America. Lincoln pointed across the Potomac. "If the people over the river had behaved themselves, I could not have done what I have." . . .

He had come a long distance from the harassed political candidate of 1858, opposed to emancipation lest his political career be jeopardized, convinced that only the distant future could remove slavery from his troubled land, certain that only colonization could solve the ensuing problem of racial adjustment. He had also come a long way in the matter of Negro social and political rights, . . . The Proclamation had indeed liberated Abraham Lincoln, enabling him to act more consistently with his moral convictions.

He had none of the racial prejudice that infected so many whites of that time, even advanced Republicans like Benjamin Wade. Frederick Douglass, who interviewed Lincoln in 1863, said he was "the first great man that I talked with in the United States freely who in no single instance reminded me of the difference between himself and myself, of the difference of color." Other blacks also testified that the President treated them as they wanted to be treated—as human beings with feelings. He did not tell dialect jokes in their presence, did not condescend to them, did not spell out his thoughts in imbecilic one-syllable language, as did many other whites when speaking to Negroes. He opened the White House doors to black visitors as no other President had ever done before and as few would do after. At his New Year's reception in 1865, he shook hands with a parade of Negro men and women, some in their Sunday finest, others in patched overalls, who had come to pay their respects to the man who signed "the Freedom bill."

During his inaugural reception that March, the President learned that Frederick Douglass was at the front door of the executive mansion, but was having trouble getting past the police because he was a Negro. Lincoln had him shown in at once, hailed him as "my friend Douglass," and asked what he thought of the Inaugural Address. "There is no man in the country whose opinion I value more than yours," Lincoln said. Douglass replied that he was impressed, that he thought it "a sacred effort." "I am glad you liked it!" Lincoln said. In truth, he strongly identified with this proud black man, referring to "the similarity with which I had fought my way up, we both starting off at the lowest round of the ladder."

Douglass, reflecting back on Lincoln's presidency, recalled how in the first year and a half of the war, Lincoln "was ready and willing" to sacrifice black people for the benefit and welfare of whites. But since the preliminary Emancipation Proclamation, Douglass said, American blacks had taken Lincoln's measure and had come to admire and some to love this complicated man. Though Lincoln had taxed Negroes to the limit, they had decided, in the roll and tumble of events, that "the how and the man of our redemption had somehow met in the person of Abraham Lincoln."

NECESSITY KNOWS NO LAW

Lincoln became a tough wartime President, flexing his executive muscles and expanding his war powers whenever necessity demanded. "Necessity," he argued, "knows no law." In the exigency of domestic insurrection, he would do whatever he thought imperative to save the country and all it represented. Yet he did not intend to establish a precedent for an "imperial presidency," one that would allow subsequent chief executives to meddle in the internal affairs of other nations, under the pretext of saving the world. In short, we cannot blame Lincoln for Lyndon Johnson's disastrous policy in Vietnam. Except for emancipation, Lincoln regarded all of his severe war measures as temporary necessities to end the rebellion and preserve the American experiment, the central idea of the war.

Consider his emergency measures during the eighty days between the outbreak of war and the convening of Congress on Independence Day, 1861. Since rebel forces were threatening to occupy Washington and the nation was on the brink of disintegration, Lincoln met with his Cabinet, and they all decided that they must assume broad emergency powers or let the government fall. Accordingly, Lincoln directed that Secretary of the Navy Gideon Welles empower several individuals—among them his own brother-in-law—to forward troops and supplies to embattled Washington. The President allowed his Secretary of War to authorize the governor of New York and one Alexander Cummings to transport troops and acquire supplies for the public defense. Since Lincoln believed that government departments brimmed with traitors, he himself chose private citizens known for "their ability, loyalty, and patriotism" to spend public money for arms and military preparations. Perhaps these emergency measures were "without authority of law," Lincoln told Congress later, but he deemed them absolutely necessary to save popular government itself. And his Cabinet unanimously agreed.

With Cabinet approval, Lincoln also declared a blockade of the southern coast, added 22,000 men to the regular army and 18,000 to the navy, called for 42,000 three-year volunteers, and put national armories into full production. As Lincoln subsequently informed Congress, "These measures, whether strictly legal or not, were ventured upon, under what appeared to be a popular demand, and public necessity; trusting, then as now, that Congress would readily ratify them." When Congress convened in July, it did indeed ratify "all the acts, proclamations, and orders of the President" relating to the army and navy and the volunteers, "as if they had been issued and done under the previous express authority and direction of Congress." In short, if Lincoln went beyond the letter of the law to save the government, Congress sanctioned his actions.

Generally Congress did the same in the area of martial law and military arrests. From the outset, Lincoln dealt harshly with "the enemy in the rear"— with what he called "a most efficient corps of spies, informers, suppliers, and aiders and abettors" of the rebellion who took advantage of "Liberty of speech, Liberty of the press and *Habeas corpus*" to disrupt the Union war effort. Consequently, he suspended the writ of habeas corpus—which required that a citizen be told why he was being held—and authorized army commanders to declare martial law in various areas behind the lines and to try civilians in military courts without juries. Lincoln openly defended such an invasion of civil liberties, contending that strict measures were essential if the laws of the Union—and liberty itself—were to survive the war.

Lincoln's suspension of the writ of habeas corpus infuriated Roger B. Taney,

Chief Justice of the U.S. Supreme Court, who accused the President of usurping power. Taney argued that only Congress could legally suspend the writ, and he admonished Lincoln not to violate the very laws he had sworn to defend. "Are all the laws, but one, to go unexecuted," Lincoln asked Congress, in reference to habeas corpus, "and the government itself go to pieces lest that one be violated?" Moreover, the Constitution did not specify which branch of the government could suspend the writ, so that Lincoln did not think he had broken any laws or violated his oath of office.

Still, he invoked his presidential powers in heretofore undreamed-of-ways, as we have seen in the matter of emancipation. Recall, though, the novelty of the war. Nothing like this had ever occurred in America, and there were no guidelines in dealing with dissent and national security in the midst of a giant domestic insurrection that imperiled the nation itself. As in most war matters, Lincoln and his Cabinet found themselves in uncharted legal territory.

In 1862 the President centralized jurisdiction over internal-security matters in the War Department. To deal with such matters, the department created a corps of civilian provost marshals, but allowed them too much independence in policing and jailing alleged disloyalists. Their zealous, far-ranging operations led to widespread criticism of the Lincoln administration. At the same time, Lincoln's War Department empowered army officers to apprehend anybody who discouraged volunteering or otherwise helped the enemy. And the department got up dragnets in which state militia, home guards, police chiefs, and vigilantes all participated. In all, they seized and imprisoned at least 14,000 people—many of them antiwar Democrats—under Lincoln's authority. The outcry against arbitrary arrests became so strident that Lincoln tried to restrain excessive use of power whenever he could. He speedily ordered the release of people unwarrantedly arrested, especially political prisoners. Also, when General Ambrose E. Burnside suspended the Chicago *Times* for virulent outbursts against the administration, Lincoln promptly revoked the order. . . .

Lincoln admitted that internal security in the midst of civil war was a complex problem and that errors and excesses had occurred. It pained him that government agents often confused antiwar rhetoric with disloyal designs and that innocent people suffered. That was why he tempered military arrests with generous pardons and refused to suppress popular assemblies and antiwar newspapers. Yet throughout the conflict he maintained a severe line on disloyalty; and most Republicans supported him. Without military law, they all feared, the rebellion would rage into the North and consume the government from within.

Lincoln was a tough warrior in other ways, too. He fully endorsed military conscription—which Congress authorized in April, 1863—and saw to it that the War Department rigorously enforced the measure. No matter what some historians have claimed, the President also enforced the confiscation of enemy property, believing as he did that "the traitor against the general government" should forfeit his farms, plantations, and other property as just punishment for the crime of insurrection.

Still, Lincoln was no dictator—the very idea appalled him, for it violated everything he held sacred in government. In fact, one of the major reasons he remains our best President is that he shunned a dictatorship, even when some Americans thought it the only way to save the country. But what kind of country would remain if popular government itself were sacrificed? Was it not for this that the war was being fought? Consider Lincoln's stand on the presidential election of 1864. With Union fortunes still uncertain, some men urged Lincoln to cancel the contest lest it result in the victory of antiwar Democrats who would sell out the Union cause. Lincoln refused. "The election," he said later, "was a necessity." We can not have free government without elections; and if the rebellion could force us to forego, or postpone a national election, it might fairly claim to have already conquered us." So he ran against George B. McClellan and the peace plank of the Democratic party, and he won in a fair and open contest.

Later he told a group of White House serenaders what this meant to him. Above all, it meant that the American system still worked, that the people could still choose their leaders even in the middle of domestic rebellion. By holding the contest, Lincoln and the northern people had preserved their popular government and demonstrated how strong they were. And Lincoln was glad, he told the serenaders, that most voters had gone for him, the candidate most devoted to the Union and opposed to treason.

Harriet Beecher Stowe, who interviewed Lincoln in 1864, thought him the most trusted leader the country could have in war. "Surrounded by all sorts of conflicting claims," she wrote, "by traitors, by half-hearted, timid men, by Border States men, and Free States men, by radical Abolitionists and Conservatives, he has listened to all, weighed the words of all, waited, observed, yielded now here and now there, but in the main kept one inflexible, honest purpose, and drawn the national ship through." Had he been "a reckless, bold, theorizing, dashing man of genius," she said, he "might have wrecked our Constitution and ended us in a splendid military despotism."

THE WARRIOR

He was, then, a warrior for the American dream, prepared to do whatever was necessary to save it short of abandoning the dream itself. This ends-justifies-the-means philosophy was blazingly clear in Lincoln's approach to military strategy. Here he faced some perplexing questions: How could he utilize the Union's vast superiority in manpower and war materiel to stamp out the rebellion? Should he battle only the armies of the insurrectionists, or their institutions and resources as well?

At first, Lincoln elected to fight only the rebel military forces, a decision that would alter drastically as the war roared on and necessity demanded a harsher strategy. But almost from the start Lincoln had the whole military picture in mind, which was to be expected of a man who saw the struggle itself in a world dimension. Before any of his generals or advisers, Lincoln understood that the only way to whip the hard-fighting Confederates was to hit them with coordinated attacks in all theaters. Only that way could the Union bring to bear its tremendous advantage in manpower and war resources.

Yet it took Lincoln a long time to translate his strategic insights into action. He made mistakes. He gave too many important commands to "political" generals or to incompetent professionals who impressed him simply because they were generals. Who was he, a mere civilian, to question their military expertise? When his chosen commanders failed to fight as he wanted, he could lose his temper and cry "damn" or "hell" or even throw his stovepipe hat on the floor, as he did on one battlefront visit in 1862. Too many of his early generals, as he put it himself, had the "slows" when it came to fighting. Yet it was Lincoln who had chosen them. . . .

During the summer and autumn of 1863, Lincoln kept prodding his generals to fight in concert, to move against Confederate forces with coordinated attacks. He wanted to "hurt this enemy," to "whip these people." But it took Lincoln until 1864 before he found in Grant and William Tecumseh Sherman the right combination to implement his big-picture strategy. In the spring of that year, Lincoln made Sherman overall commander in the West and called Grant to the East as General-in-Chief of all Union armies. Now Lincoln had a command set-up that he hoped would produce victories. With Grant as General-in-Chief, Halleck functioned officially as chief of staff, integrating information and giving out advice. Grant, electing to travel with Meade and the Army of the Potomac, would coordinate its movements with those of armies in other theaters.

A terse, slight man who chewed cigars and walked with a lurch, Grant worked out with Lincoln a Grand Plan that called for simultaneous offensive movements on all battlefronts. In the East, Grant and Meade would attempt to obliterate Lee's force while Sherman's powerful army would punch into Georgia, seize Atlanta and its crucial railway nexus, and destroy rebel resources in the Atlanta area. In sum, the Union war machine would now utilize its vastly superior manpower and smash the Confederacy with concerted blows in all theaters.

Lincoln was delighted. The Grand Plan entailed exactly the kind of concerted action he had advocated since 1861. And though it was basically Grant's design, Lincoln helped forge it in weekly strategy sessions in the White House. So in May, 1864, Union armies on all fronts moved forward in the mightiest offensive of the war, battering the Confederacy from all directions and thrusting toward "a common center." Alas, in East and West alike, the offensive mired down and Union casualties, especially in Virginia, were staggering. Yet Lincoln never lost hope. Even when Lee escaped to the redoubts of Petersburg and Grant settled in for a protracted seige, Lincoln urged him to "hold on with bull-dog grip, and chew & choke, as much as possible."

The Grand Plan worked better in the western theater, where Sherman captured and burned Atlanta, and General George "Old Pap" Thomas smashed the Confederate Army of Tennessee, destroying it so completely that it could never fight again. What Lincoln had long desired had finally been accomplished.

In the late fall of 1864 red-haired Bill Sherman, a tall, lean man who spoke in picturesque phrases, proposed to take Lincoln's strategic notions a step further. Even more than Grant, Sherman realized that modern wars were won not simply by fighting enemy armies, but by destroying the very ability of the enemy to wage war—that is, by wrecking railroads, burning fields, and eradicating other economic resources. "We are not only fighting hostile armies," Sherman reasoned, "but a hostile people, and must make old and young, rich and poor, feel the hard hand of war."· "There is many a boy here who looks on war as all glory," Sherman later told his veterans, "but, boys, it is all hell."

Those were Lincoln's sentiments exactly. And since war was hell, it should be ended as swiftly as possible, by whatever means were necessary. Thus, when Sherman proposed to visit total war on the people of the Deep South, Lincoln approved. With ruthless efficiency, Sherman's army stormed through Georgia and the Carolinas, tearing up railroads, pulverizing corn and cotton fields, assassinating cows and chickens, wiping out all and anything that might sustain Lee's army and all other rebel forces. At the same time, Union calvary in Virginia's Shenandoah Valley burned a broad path of destruction clear to the Rapidan River.

The Union's scorched-earth warfare earned Lincoln and Sherman undying hatred in Dixie, but it paid off: within five months after Sherman started his march through Georgia, the war was over.

It cannot be stressed enough that Lincoln, then deeply involved in matters of reconstruction, fully endorsed Sherman's scorched-earth policy. If Sherman was "a total warrior," so was his Commander-in-Chief. Putting aside his own aversion to bloodshed and violence, Lincoln ended up pounding all his southern foes into submission—civilians and soldiers alike. And he did so because that was the surest way he knew to shorten the conflict, end the killing, and salvage his American dream.

NO

M. E. Bradford

THE LINCOLN LEGACY: A LONG VIEW

With the time and manner of his death Abraham Lincoln, as leader of a Puritan people who had just won a great victory over "the forces of evil," was placed beyond the reach of ordinary historical inquiry and assessment. Through Booth's bullet he became the one who had "died to make men free," who had perished that his country's "new birth" might occur: a "second founder" who, in Ford's theater, had been transformed into an American version of the "dying god." Our common life, according to this construction, owes its continuation to the shedding of the sacred blood. Now after over a century of devotion to the myth of the "political messiah," it is still impossible for most Americans to see through and beyond the magical events of April 1865. However, Lincoln's daily purchase upon the ongoing business of the nation requires that we devise a way of setting aside the martyrdom to look behind it at Lincoln's place in the total context of American history and discover in him a major source of our present confusion, our distance from the republicanism of the Fathers, the models of political conduct which we profess most to admire. . . .

Of course, nothing that we can identify as part of Lincoln's legacy belongs to him alone. In some respects the Emancipator was carried along with the tides. Yet a measure of his importance is that he was at the heart of the major political events of his era. Therefore what signifies in a final evaluation of this melancholy man is that many of these changes in the country would never have come to pass had Lincoln not pushed them forward. Or at least not come so quickly, or with such dreadful violence. I will emphasize only the events that he most certainly shaped according to his relentless will, alterations in the character of our country for which he was clearly responsible. For related developments touched by Lincoln's wand, I can have only a passing word. The major charges advanced here, if proved, are sufficient to impeach the most famous and respected of public men. More would only overdo.

The first and most obvious item in my bill of particulars for indictment concerns Lincoln's dishonesty and obfuscation with respect to the nation's

Reprinted from *Remembering Who We Are: Observations of a Southern Conservative* by M. E. Bradford. Copyright © 1985, the University of Georgia Press. Reprinted by permission of the University of Georgia Press.

future obligations to the Negro, slave and free. It was of course an essential ingredient of Lincoln's position that he make a success at being anti-Southern or antislavery without at the same time appearing to be significantly impious about the beginnings of the Republic (which was neither anti-Southern nor antislavery)—or significantly pro-Negro. He was the first Northern politician of any rank to combine these attitudes into a viable platform persona, the first to make his moral position on slavery in the South into a part of his national politics. It was a posture that enabled him to unite elements of the Northern electorate not ordinarily willing to cooperate in any political undertaking. And thus enabled him to destroy the old Democratic majority—a coalition necessary to preserving the union of the states. Then came the explosion. But this calculated posturing has had more durable consequences than secession and the Federal confiscation of property in slaves. . . .

In the nation as a whole what moves toward fruition is a train of events set in motion by the duplicitous rhetoric concerning the Negro that helped make Abraham Lincoln into our first "sectional" president. Central to this appeal is a claim to a kind of moral superiority that costs absolutely nothing in the way of conduct. Lincoln, in insisting that the Negro was included in the promise of the Declaration of Independence and that the Declaration bound his countrymen to fulfill a pledge hidden in that document, seemed clearly to point toward a radical transformation of American society. Carried within his rejection of Negro slavery as a continuing feature of the American regime, his assertion that the equality clause of the Declaration of Independence was "the father of all moral principle among us," were certain muted corollaries. By promising that the peculiar institution would be made to disappear if candidates for national office adopted the proper "moral attitude" on that subject, Lincoln recited as a litany the general terms of his regard for universal human rights. But at the same time he added certain modifications to this high doctrine: modifications required by those of his countrymen to whom he hoped to appeal, by the rigid racism of the Northern electorate, and by "what his own feelings would admit." The most important of these reservations was that none of his doctrine should apply significantly to the Negro in the North. Or, after freedom, to what he could expect in the South. It was a very broad, very general, and very abstract principle to which he made reference. By it he could divide the sheep from the goats, the wheat from the chaff, the patriot from the conspirator. But for the Negro it provided nothing more than a technical freedom, best to be enjoyed far away. Or the valuable opportunity to "root, hog, or die." For the sake of such vapid distinctions he urged his countrymen to wade through seas of blood.

To be sure, this position does not push the "feelings" of that moralist who was our sixteenth president too far from what was comfortable for him. And it goes without saying that a commitment to "natural rights" which will not challenge the Black Codes of Illinois, which promises something like them for the freedman in the South, or else offers him as alternative the proverbial "one-way-ticket to nowhere" is a commitment of empty words. It is only an accident of political history that the final Reconstruction settlement provided a bit more for the former slave—principally, the chance to vote Republican; and even that "right" didn't last, once a better deal was made available to his erstwhile protectors. But the point is that Lincoln's commitment was precisely of the sort that the North was ready to make—while passing legislation to restrict the flow of Negroes into its own territories, elaborating its own system of segregation by race, and exploiting black labor through its representatives in a conquered South. Lincoln's double talk left his part of the country with a durable heritage of pious self-congratulation,. . . .

The second heading in this "case against Lincoln" involves no complicated pleading. Neither will it confuse any reader who examines his record with care. For it has to do with Lincoln's political economy, his management of the commercial and business life of the part of the Republic under his authority. This material is obvious, even though it is not always connected with the presidency of Abraham Lincoln. Nevertheless, it must be developed at this point. For it leads directly into the more serious charges upon which this argument depends. It is customary to deplore the Gilded Age, the era of the Great Barbecue. It is true that many of the corruptions of the Republican Era came to a head after Lincoln lay at rest in Springfield. But it is a matter of fact that they began either under his direction or with his sponsorship. Military necessity, the "War for the Union," provided an excuse, an umbrella of sanction, under which the essential nature of the changes being made in the relation of government to commerce could be concealed. Of his total policy the Northern historian Robert Sharkey has written, "Human ingenuity would have had difficulty in contriving a more perfect engine for class and sectional exploration:

creditors finally obtaining the upper hand as opposed to debtors, and the developed East holding the whip over the underdeveloped West and South." Until the South left the Union, until a High Whig sat in the White House, none of this return to the "energetic government" of Hamilton's design was possible. Indeed, even in the heyday of the Federalists it had never been so simple a matter to translate power into wealth. Now Lincoln could try again the internal improvements of the early days in Illinois. The difference was that this time the funding would not be restrained by political reversal or a failure of credit. For if anything fell short, Mr. Salmon P. Chase, "the foreman" of his "green printing office," could be instructed "to give his paper mill another turn." And the inflationary policy of rewarding the friends of the government sustained. The euphemism of our time calls this "income redistribution." But it was theft in 1864, and is theft today.

A great increase in the tariff and the formation of a national banking network were, of course, the cornerstones of this great alteration in the posture of the Federal government toward the sponsorship of business. From the beginning of the Republican Party Lincoln warned his associates not to talk about their views on these subjects. Their alliance, he knew, was a negative thing: a league against the Slave Power and its Northern friends. But in private he made it clear that the hidden agenda of the Republicans would have its turn, once the stick was in their hand. In this he promised well. Between 1861 and 1865, the tariff rose from 18.84 percent to 47.56 percent. And it stayed above 40 percent in all but two years of the period concluded with the election of Woodrow Wilson. Writes the Virginia historian Ludwell H. Johnson, it would "facilitate a massive transfer of wealth, satisfying the dreariest predictions of John C. Calhoun." The new Republican system of banking (for which we should note Lincoln was directly accountable) was part of the same large design of "refounding." The National Banking Acts of 1863 and 1864, with the earlier Legal Tender Act, flooded the country with $480 million of fiat money that was soon depreciated by about two-thirds in relation to specie. Then all notes but the greenback dollar were taxed out of existence, excepting only United States Treasury bonds that all banks were required to purchase if they were to have a share in the war boom. The support for these special bonds was thus the debt itself—Hamilton's old standby. Specie disappeared. Moreover, the bank laws controlled the money supply, credit, and the balance of power. New banks and credit for farms, small businesses, or small town operations were discouraged. And the Federalist model, after four score and seven years, finally achieved.

As chief executive, Lincoln naturally supported heavy taxes. Plus a scheme of tax graduation. The war was a legitimate explanation for these measures. Lincoln's participation in huge subsidies or bounties for railroads and in other legislation granting economic favors is not so readily linked to "saving the Union." All of his life Lincoln was a friend of the big corporations. He had no moral problem in signing a bill which gifted the Union Pacific Railway with a huge strip of land running across the West and an almost unsecured loan of $16,000 to $48,000 per mile of track. The final result of this bill was the Credit Mobilier scandal. With other laws favoring land speculation it

helped to negate the seemingly noble promise of the Homestead Act of 1862—under which less than 19 percent of the open lands settled between 1860 and 1900 went to legitimate homesteaders. The Northern policy of importing immigrants with the promise of this land, only to force them into the ranks of General Grant's meatgrinder or into near slavery in the cities of the East, requires little comment. Nor need we belabor the rotten army contracts given to politically faithful crooks. Nor the massive thefts by law performed during the war in the South. More significant is Lincoln's openly disgraceful policy of allowing special cronies and favorites of his friends to trade in Southern cotton—even with "the enemy" across the line—and his calculated use of the patronage and the pork barrel. Between 1860 and 1880, the Republicans spent almost $10 million breathing life into state and local Republican organizations. Lincoln pointed them down that road. There can be no doubt of his responsibility for the depressing spectacle of greed and peculation concerning which so many loyal Northern men of the day spoke with sorrow, disappointment, and outrage. . . .

A large part of the complaint against Lincoln as a political precedent for later declensions from the example of the Fathers has to do with his expansion of the powers of the presidency and his alteration of the basis for the Federal Union. With reference to his role in changing the office of chief magistrate from what it had been under his predecessors, it is important to remember that he defined himself through the war powers that belonged to his post. In this way Lincoln could profess allegiance to the Whig ideal of the modest, self-effacing leader, the antitype of Andrew Jackson, and, in his capacity as Commander-in-Chief, do whatever he wished. That is, if he could do it in the name of preserving the Union. As Clinton Rossiter has stated, Lincoln believed there were "no limits" to his powers if he exercised them in that "holy cause." Gottfried Dietze compares Lincoln in this role to the Committee of Public Safety as it operated in the French Revolution. Except for the absence of mass executions, the results were similar. War is of course the occasion for concentration of power and the limitation of liberties within any nation. But an internal war, .. war between states in a union of states, is not like a war to repel invasion or to acquire territory. For it is an extension into violence of a domestic political difference. And it is thus subject to extraordinary abuses of authority—confusions or conflations of purpose which convert the effort to win the war into an effort to effect even larger, essentially political changes in the structure of government. War, in these terms, is not only an engine for preserving the Union; it is also an instrument for transforming its nature. But without overdeveloping this structure of theory, let us shore it up with specific instances of presidential misconduct by Lincoln: abuses that mark him as our first imperial president. Lincoln began his tenure as a dictator when between April 12 and July 4 of 1861, without interference from Congress, he summoned militia, spent millions, suspended law, authorized recruiting, decreed a blockade, defied the Supreme Court, and pledged the nation's credit. In the following months and years he created units of government not known to the Constitution and officers to rule over them in "conquered" sections of the South, seized property throughout both

sections, arrested upwards of twenty thousand of his political enemies and confined them without trial in a Northern "Gulag," closed over three hundred newspapers critical of his policy, imported an army of foreign mercenaries (of perhaps five hundred thousand men), interrupted the assembly of duly elected legislatures and employed the Federal hosts to secure his own reelection—in a contest where about thirty-eight thousand votes, if shifted, might have produced an armistice and a negotiated peace under a President McClellan. To the same end he created a state in West Virginia, arguing of this blatant violation of the explicit provisions of the Constitution that it was "expedient." But the worst of this bold and ruthless dealing (and I have given but a very selective list of Lincoln's "high crimes") has to do with his role as military leader per se: as the commander and selector of Northern generals, chief commissary of the Federal forces, and head of government in dealing with the leaders of an opposing power. In this role the image of Lincoln grows to be very dark—indeed, almost sinister.

The worst that we may say of Lincoln is that he led the North in war so as to put the domestic political priorities of his political machine ahead of the lives and the well-being of his soldiers in the field. The appointment of the venal Simon Cameron of Pennsylvania as his secretary of war, and of lesser hacks and rascals to direct the victualing of Federal armies, was part of this malfeasance. By breaking up their bodies, the locust hoard of contractors even found a profit in the Union dead. And better money still in the living. They made of Lincoln (who winked at their activities) an accessory to lost horses, rotten meat, and worthless guns. But all such mendacity was nothing in comparison to the price in blood paid for Lincoln's attempts to give the nation a genuine Republican hero. He had a problem with this project throughout the entire course of the war. That is, until Grant and Sherman "converted" to radicalism. Prior to their emergence all of Lincoln's "loyal" generals disapproved of either his politics or of his character. These, as with McClellan, he could use and discharge at will. Or demote to minor tasks. One thinks immediately of George G. Meade—who defeated Lee at Gettysburg, and yet made the mistake of defining himself as the defender of a separate Northern nation from whose soil he would drive a foreign Southern "invader." Or of Fitz John Porter, William B. Franklin, and Don Carlos Buell—all scapegoats thrown by Lincoln to the radical wolves. In place of these heterodox professionals, Lincoln assigned such champions of the "new freedom" as Nathaniel P. ("Commissary") Banks, Benjamin F. ("Beast") Butler, John C. Fremont, and John A. McClernand. Speaking in summary despair of these appointments (and adding to my list, Franz Sigel and Lew Wallace), General Henry Halleck, Lincoln's chief-of-staff, declared that they were "little better than murder." Yet in the East, with the Army of the Potomac, Lincoln make promotions even more difficult to defend, placing not special projects, divisions, and brigades but entire commands under the authority of such "right thinking" incompetents as John Pope (son of an old crony in Illinois) and "Fighting Joe" Hooker. Or with that "tame" Democrat and late favorite of the radicals, Ambrose E. Burnside. Thousands of Northern boys lost their lives in order that the Republican Party might experience rejuvenation, to serve its partisan goals. And those were "party supremacy within a Northern dominated Union." A Democratic "man-on-horseback" could not serve those ends, however faithful to "the Constitution as it is, and the Union as it was" (the motto of the Democrats) they might be. For neither of these commitments promised a Republican hegemony. To provide for his faction both security and continuity in office, Lincoln sounded out his commanders in correspondence (much of which still survives), suborned their military integrity, and employed their focus in purely political operation. Writes Johnson:

> Although extreme measures were most common in the border states, they were often used elsewhere too. By extreme measures is meant the arrest of anti-Republican candidates and voters, driving anti-Republican voters from the polls or forcing them to vote the Republican ticket, preventing opposition parties from holding meetings, removing names from ballots, and so forth. These methods were employed in national, state and local elections. Not only did the army interfere by force, it was used to supply votes. Soldiers whose states did not allow absentee voting were sent home by order of the President to swell the Republican totals. When voting in the field was used, Democratic commissioners carrying ballots to soldiers from their state were . . . unceremoniously thrown into prison, while Republican agents were offered every assistance. Votes of Democratic soldiers were sometimes discarded as defective, replaced by Republican ballots, or simply not counted.

All Lincoln asked of the ordinary Billy Yank was that he be prepared to give himself up to no real purpose—at least until Father Abraham found a general with the proper moral and political credentials to lead him on to Richmond. How this part of Lincoln's career can be reconciled to the myth of the "suffering savior" I cannot imagine.

We might dwell for some time on what injury Lincoln did to the dignity of his office through the methods he employed in prosecuting the war. It was no small thing to disavow the ancient Christian code of "limited war," as did his minions, acting in his name. However, it is enough in this connection to remember his policy of denying medicines to the South, even for the sake of Northern prisoners held behind the lines. We can imagine what a modern "war crimes" tribunal would do with that decision. There may have been practicality in such inhumane decisions. *Practicality* indeed! As Charles Francis Adams, Lincoln's ambassador to the Court of St. James and the scion of the most notable family in the North, wrote in his diary of his leader, the "President and his chief advisers are not without the spirit of the serpent mixed in with their wisdom." And he knew whereof he spoke. For practical politics, the necessities of the campaign of 1864, had led Lincoln and Seward to a decision far more serious than unethical practices against prisoners and civilians in the South. I speak of the rejection by the Lincoln administration of peace feelers authorized by the Confederate government in Richmond: feelers that met Lincoln's announced terms for an end to the Federal invasion of the South. The emissary in this negotiation was sponsored by Charles Francis Adams. He was a Tennessean living in France, one Thomas Yeatman. After arriving in the United States, he was swiftly deported by direct order of the government before he could properly explore the possibility of an armistice on the conditions of reunion and an end to slavery. Lincoln sought these goals, but only on his terms. And in his own time. He wanted total victory. And he needed a still-resisting, impenitent Confederacy to justify his re-election. We can only speculate as to why President Davis allowed the Yeatman mission. We know that he expected little of such peace feelers. (There were many in the last stages of the conflict.) He knew his enemy too well to expect anything but subjection, however benign the rhetoric used to disguise its rigor. Adam's peace plan was perhaps impossible, even if his superiors in Washington had behaved in good faith. The point is that none of the peace moves of 1864 was given any chance of success. Over one hundred thousand Americans may have died because of the Rail-Splitter's rejection of an inexpedient peace. Yet we have still not touched upon the most serious of Lincoln's violations of the Presidential responsibility. I speak, finally, of his role in bringing on the War Between the States.

There is, we should recall, a great body of scholarly argument concerning Lincoln's intentions in 1860 and early 1861. A respectable portion of this work comes to the conclusion that the first Republican president expected a "tug," a "crisis," to follow his election. And then, once secession had occurred, also expected to put it down swiftly with a combination of persuasion, force, and Southern loyalty to the Union. The last of these, it is agreed, he completely overestimated. In a similar fashion he exaggerated the force of Southern "realism," the region's capacity to act in its own pecuniary interest. The authority on Lincoln's political economy has remarked that the Illinois lawyer-politician and old line Whig always made the mistake of explaining in simple economic terms the South's hostile reaction to anti-slavery proposals. To that blunder he added the related mistake of attempting to end the "rebellion" with the same sort of simplistic appeals to the prospect of riches. Or with fear of a servile insurrection brought on by his greatest "war measure," the emancipation of slaves behind Southern lines, beyond his control. A full-scale Southern revolution, a revolution of all classes of men against the way he and some of his supporters thought, was beyond his imagination. There was no "policy" in such extravagant behavior, no human nature as he perceived it. Therefore, on the basis of my understanding of his overall career, I am compelled to agree with Charles W. Ramsdell concerning Lincoln and his war. Though he was no sadist and no war-monger, and though he got for his pains much more of a conflict than he had in mind, Lincoln hoped for an "insurrection" of some sort—an "uprising" he could use.

The "rational" transformation of our form of government which he had first predicted in the "Springfield Lyceum Speech" required some kind of passionate disorder to justify the enforcement of a new Federalism. And needed also for the voting representatives of the South to be out of their seats in the Congress. It is out of keeping with his total performance as a public man and in contradiction of his campaigning after 1854 not to believe that Lincoln hoped for a Southern attack on Fort Sumter. As he told his old friend Senator Orville H. Browning of Illinois: "The plan succeeded. They attacked Sumter—it fell, and thus did more service than it otherwise could." And to others he wrote or

spoke to the same effect. If the Confederacy's offer of money for Federal property were made known in the North and business relations of the sections remained unaffected, if the Mississippi remained open to Northern shipping, there would be no support for "restoring" the Union on a basis of force. Americans were in the habit of thinking of the unity of the nation as a reflex of their agreement in the Constitution, of law as limit on government and on the authority of temporary majorities, and of revisions in law as the product of the ordinary course of push and pull within a pluralistic society, not as a response to the extralegal authority of some admirable abstraction like equality. In other words, they thought of the country as being defined by the way in which we conducted our political business, not by where we were trying to go in body. Though once a disciple of Henry Clay, Lincoln changed the basis of our common bond away from the doctrine of his mentor, away from the patterns of compromise and dialectic of interests and values under a limited, Federal sovereignty with which we as a people began our adventure with the Great Compromise of 1787-1788. The nature of the Union left to us by Lincoln is thus always at stake in every major election, in every refinement in our civil theology; the Constitution is still to be defined by the latest wave of big ideas, the most recent mass emotion. Writes Dietze:

> Concentrations of power in the national and executive branches of government, brought about by Lincoln in the name of the people, were processes that conceivably complemented each other to the detriment of free government. Lincoln's administration thus opened the way for the development of

an omnipotent national executive who as a spokesman for the people might consider himself entitled to do whatever he felt was good for the Nation, irrespective of the interests and rights of states, Congress, the judiciary, and the individual. . . .

But in my opinion the capstone of this case against Lincoln . . . is what he had done to the language of American political discourse that makes it so difficult for us to reverse the ill effects of trends he set in motion with his executive fiat. When I say that Lincoln was our first Puritan president, I am chiefly referring to a distinction of style, to his habit of wrapping up his policy in the idiom of Holy Scripture, concealing within the Trojan horse of his gasconade and moral superiority an agenda that would never have been approved if presented in any other form. It is this rhetoric in particular, a rhetoric confirmed in its authority by his martyrdom, that is enshrined in the iconography of the Lincoln myth preserved against examination by monuments such as the Lincoln Memorial, where his oversized likeness is elevated above us like that of a deified Roman emperor.

POSTSCRIPT

Was Abraham Lincoln America's Greatest President?

As Oates reveals in his essay, Abraham Lincoln, at the time of his assassination, was perhaps the most hated president in history. Still, virtually no scholars in recent times have launched the type of assault exhibited by M. E. Bradford. Instead, since Arthur Schlesinger, Jr., first polled experts on the subject in 1948, historians consistently have rated Lincoln the nation's best chief executive. Another president, Harry Truman, also ranked Lincoln in the category of "great" chief executives. In words that are echoed by Oates, Truman wrote of Lincoln: "He was a strong executive who saved the government, saved the United States. He was a president who understood people, and when it came time to make decisions, he was willing to take the responsibility and make those decisions, no matter how difficult they were. He knew how to treat people and how to make a decision stick, and that's why his is regarded as such a great Administration."

Lincoln also is the most written-about president. Students should consult Carl Sandburg, *Abraham Lincoln* (6 vols., Harcourt, Brace and World, 1926–1939), a poetic panorama which focuses upon the mythic Lincoln. Benjamin Thomas, *Abraham Lincoln: A Biography* (Knopf, 1952) and Stephen B. Oates, *With Malice Toward None: The Life of Abraham Lincoln* (Harper & Row, 1977) are both excellent one-volume biographies. David Donald, *Lincoln Reconsidered: Essays on the Civil War Era* (Knopf, 1956) and Richard N. Current, *The Lincoln Nobody Knows* (McGraw-Hill, 1958) offer incisive interpretations of many aspects of Lincoln's political career and philosophy. Psychoanalytical approaches to Lincoln are offered by George B. Forgie, *Patricide in the House Divided: A Psychological Interpretation* (Norton, 1979) and Dwight G. Anderson, *Abraham Lincoln: The Quest for Immortality* (Knopf, 1982). The events leading up to the Civil War are presented best in David M. Potter, *The Impending Crisis, 1848–1861* (Harper & Row, 1976). Lincoln's responsibility for the precipitating event of the war is explored in Richard N. Current, *Lincoln and the First Shot* (Lippincott, 1963). T. Harry Williams, *Lincoln and His Generals* (Knopf, 1952) looks at Lincoln as commander-in-chief and remains one of the best Lincoln studies. Peyton McCrary, *Abraham Lincoln and Reconstruction: The Louisiana Experiment* (Princeton University Press, 1978) examines Lincoln's plan for restoring the Southern states to the Union. For his role as "the Great Emancipator" and his attitudes toward race and slavery, see Benjamin Quarles, *Lincoln and the Negro* (Oxford University Press, 1962) and LaWanda Cox, *A Study in Presidential Leadership* (University of South Carolina Press, 1981). Gabor S. Boritt, ed., *The Historian's Lincoln: Pseudohistory, Psychohistory, and History* (University of Illinois Press, 1988) is a valuable recent collection.

ISSUE 17

Was Reconstruction a Total Failure?

YES: J. G. Randall, from *The Civil War and Reconstruction** (D. C. Heath and Company, 1937)

NO: Eric Foner, from "The New View of Reconstruction," *American Heritage* (October/November 1983)

ISSUE SUMMARY

YES: Randall argues that Reconstruction failed because carpetbaggers and their "Negro" allies misgoverned the South and looted its treasuries.
NO: Professor Eric Foner believes that, although Reconstruction was nonrevolutionary and conservative, it was a splendid failure because it offered blacks a temporary vision of a free society.

The Reconstruction Era (1865–1877) contains a mythological history which has been impossible for professional historians to dislodge. While the Civil War has been portrayed as an heroic era for both sides, Reconstruction has been categorized as a tragedy for all Americans—Northerners, Southerners, whites, and blacks. According to the mythology a vengeful Congress, dominated by radical Republicans, imposed military rule upon the Southern states. Carpetbaggers from the North, along with traitorous white scalawags and their ignorant Negro accomplices, rewrote the state constitutions, disenfranchised former Confederate whites, controlled the legislature, passed laws which enabled them to raise taxes, looted the coffers of the government, and stole the possessions of the good white Northerners. This farce came to an end in 1877 when a deal was made to allow Rutherford B. Hayes to assume the office of the presidency. Hayes was given fifteen disputed electoral college votes (which enabled him to defeat his opponent Samuel J. Tilden by one vote). In return, Hayes agreed to end Reconstruction by withdrawing federal troops from the Southern states.

Between the years 1890 and 1930, this mythological portrait of Reconstruction dominated the historical profession. The reasons for this are obvious: White Southerners who wrote about this period made two basic assump-

*[*This textbook has been substantially revised by David Donald in the 1961 and 1985 editions in order to reflect recent changes in thought concerning this period.*—Eds.]

tions: (1) that the South was capable of solving its own problems without federal government inference, and (2) that blacks were intellectually inferior to whites and incapable of running a government (much less one in which whites would be their subordinates). Furthermore, the events of the times made this interpretation seem plausible. By the 1890s, most social scientists believed that white Anglo-Saxon Protestants (WASPs) were biologically superior to all other races and religions. Segregation was legalized by statutes in the Southern states and by the Supreme Court; and the rest of the nation wanted to heal the wounds of the Civil War and allowed the South to handle its own "problem." As a result of the Spanish American War in 1898, the United States acquired an empire in South America and the Pacific and forcibly ruled over non-white inhabitants.

Professional historians now reject this interpretation of the Reconstruction Era. The general public, however, still learns most of its history from fiction, movies, and the televised docudramas.

The traditional interpretation of Reconstruction has been under attack by historians for the past fifty years. Corruption, for example, existed in some Reconstruction states but it also existed in Northern states. (The Grant administration in Washington has been called the "era of good stealings.") Even after Reconstruction ended, many other Southern states became more corrupt than they had been during Reconstruction.

Progressive historians have painted a more positive picture of Reconstruction. New state constitutions were written during this era that outlasted the politicians who wrote them; improvements were made in local administrations; the court systems were revised; and state-supported public schools were established for both whites and blacks.

Revisionist historians sharply attacked the notion that blacks had dominated the politics of the Reconstruction South. They pointed out that there were no black governors, only two black senators, and fifteen black congressmen during this period. In no Southern state did blacks control both houses of the legislature. Black politicians were usually better educated than their constituents and, contrary to legend, generally followed moderate policies favoring black equality; through the adoption of the Fourteenth and Fifteenth Amendments blacks were granted citizenship and adult males were given the right to vote.

In a selection that represents the traditional view of Reconstruction, the late Lincoln scholar J. G. Randall argues that Reconstruction failed because the carpetbagger-Negro coalition of radical Republicans mismanaged the state governments and robbed its citizens. Searching for a new synthesis which moves beyond the negative post-revisionist studies, Professor Eric Foner concedes that Reconstruction was not very radical, much less revolutionary. Nevertheless, it was a splendid failure because it offered blacks a vision of what a free society should look like.

YES

J. G. Randall

RECONSTRUCTION DÉBÂCLE

I

For the seceded states the Grant period constituted the darkest days of "reconstruction." Coming south after the war to make money and seize political power, the Northern "carpetbagger" became the dominant figure in Southern politics for a decade. In collusion with the carpetbaggers were the "scalawags," native whites in the South who took advantage of the chance for aggrandizement which the postwar régime offered. Southern as they were, familiar with Negro characteristics and unembarrassed by the extravagance and gaucherie of the carpetbaggers, they obtained control of numerous offices and became a power in local politics. Aided by a system which gave the vote to the Negro while it disfranchised the more substantial element among the whites, these political adventurers improved upon the system and added extra-legal touches of their own.

Elections in the South became a byword and a travesty. Ignorant blacks by the thousands cast ballots without knowing even the names of men for whom they were voting.[1] Southern communities in their political, social, and economic interests were subjected to the misguided action of these irresponsible creatures directed by white bosses. Election laws were deliberately framed to open the way for manipulation and fraud. Ballots were inspected before going into the box, and Negroes seeking to cast Democratic ballots were held up by objections and by an effort to change their votes.[2] Registration lists showed Negroes in proportion to population at a much higher ratio than the actual fact. Vote-buying became so common that Negroes came to expect it; much of the bacon and ham mentioned as "relief" was distributed with an eye to election-day results.[3] To colored voters in Florida, acting under instructions from Radical leaders, the motto seemed to be "Vote early and often." Starting in early morning they moved along in groups, voting "at every precinct" on a long "line of march," each time under assumed names.[4] In advance of the voting hour ballots would be

From *The Civil War and Reconstruction* by J. G. Randall. Copyright © 1937. Reprinted by permission of D. C. Heath, Inc. Publishers.

fraudulently deposited in the box. Party conventions were manipulated by Radical leaders, and nominations were forced by the bosses (sometimes military officers) in control. Reporting on the election of 1872 in Louisiana a committee of Congress stated that in their determination to have a legislature of their own party, the Republican returning board juggled election returns, accepted false affidavits, and in some cases merely estimated "what the vote ought to have been." The whole proceeding was characterized as a "comedy by blunders and frauds."[5]

In 1867 the Union League had become strongly intrenched in the South; and it proved an effective instrument in the organization of the Radical Republican party among the blacks. It was stated in October, 1867, that the League had eighty-eight chapters in South Carolina, and that almost every Negro in the state was enrolled in the order.[6] According to a statement of a Leaguer, every member was oath-bound to vote for those nominated by the order. The league, he said, existed "for no other purpose than to carry the elections. . . ."[7] Ritual, ceremony, high-flown phrases about freedom and equal rights, sententious references to the Constitution and the Declaration of Independence, accompanied by song, prayer, and oratory had a compelling effect upon Negro emotions, while the black man's instinctive dependence upon whites made conquest easy; so that the sanctimonious League functioned with remarkable success in capturing and delivering the Negro vote. The Leagues "voted the Negroes like 'herds of senseless cattle' " is the statement of competent observers, borne out by numerous instances similiar to that of a South Carolina black who explained his vote by saying that the League was the "place

where we learn the law." Another typical case was that of a Negro who was asked why he voted Republican and replied, "I can't read, and I can't write. . . . We go by instructions. We don't know nothing much."[8]

As the processes of carpetbag rule unfolded, honest men in the South felt increasing disgust. Conservative editors referred to the fancy state conventions as "black and tan" gatherings, "ring-streaked and speckled" conventions, or as assemblies of "baboons," "ragamuffins," or "jailbirds."[9] "The maddest, most . . . infamous revolution in history," was the comment of the Fairfield (South Carolina) Herald.[10] In the carpetbag constitutional convention of South Carolina (1868) 76 of the 124 delegates were colored, two-thirds of the Negroes being illiterates just emerging from slavery. These black members comported themselves in "bashful silence" while the whites attended to matters.[11] Of the whites one was put in jail for stealing his fellow members' belongings; others were accused of graver crimes; and in general it was remarked by the New York Times that hardly a white among the lot had a character that "would keep him out of the penitentiary."[12]

II

Supported by the Grant administration and fortified by military power, the Radical Republican state machines plunged the Southern commonwealths into an abyss of misgovernment. A congressional committee reported that one of the leading carpetbag governors made over $100,000 during his first year though his salary was $8000, while one of his appointees received fees exceeding $60,000 a year.[13] Another carpetbag governor was charged with stealing and selling the food of the Freedmen's Bureau intended for the relief of helpless and ragged ex-slaves. One of his associates was accused of falsely arresting Democratic members of the Florida state legislature in order to produce a carpetbag majority. F. J. Moses, scalawag, stated that he received $15,000 while governor of South Carolina for approving a large printing bill, $25,000 when speaker, and various other sums.[14]

Southern legislatures were composed largely, sometimes predominantly, of Negroes. J. S. Pike, in a passage that has become classic, described the dense Negro crowd which, amid clamor and disorder, did the debating, squabbling, and lawmaking in South Carolina. Speaker, clerk, doorkeepers, pages, and chaplain were black. No one talked more than five minutes, said Pike, without interruption. Their "bellowings and physical contortions" baffled description. It seemed to him barbarism overwhelming civilization with physical force; yet there was a curious earnestness about it all. In the confusion and uproar, with guffaws greeting the speaker as he rapped for order, the uncouth lawmakers were taking themselves seriously. "Seven years ago these men were raising corn and cotton under the whip of the overseer. Today they are raising points of order and questions of privilege. . . . It is easier and better paid. . . . It is their day of jubilee.[15]

Some of the justices put into office by the Radicals could not write. According to a report of conditions in Mississippi, where the Ames Republicans[16] controlled the Negro vote and used it "as a solid mass," the legislature contained Negroes who could neither read nor write, members of grand juries were "totally illiterate," and the Republicans

nominated as mayor of Vicksburg a man who was under indictment for twenty three offenses.[17] Taking a leaf out of the carpetbaggers' book, Negro members of the Florida legislature were said to have formed a caucus with a "smelling committee" to "ferret out all . . . money schemes." The arrangement broke down when it was found that the colored caucus chairman appropriated to himself the moneys intended to be distributed among members for the fixing of legislative votes.[18] A Negro leader in South Carolina, admitting the receipt of $5000 "in connection with" legislative matters, stated that he voted for the legislative measures because he thought they were right, and that by taking the money he was keeping it in the state! Refreshments supplied at public expense to South Carolina legislators included the finest wines, ales, whiskeys, and cigars; indeed the porter thought it impossible for men to drink so much whiskey and attend to any business.[19] State house "supplies" paid for out of public funds included many varieties of liquors, costly table delicacies, luxurious furniture in lavish amounts, horses, and carriages. For the one item of printing in South Carolina the cost per month under Republican rule was more than a hundred times that of the subsequent Hampton administration. In fifteen months under the Republican administration $835,000 was spent for printing as compared to $609,000 for seventy-eight years under the old régime.[20] In the matter of "state aid" to railroad building in Alabama, the notorious Stantons (John C. and Daniel N. of Boston) found their opportunity. Bringing no money into the state, they organized and promoted the Alabama and Chattanooga Railroad Company, obtained millions of state money from a bribed Radical legislature, built a hotel and opera house with some of the money, obtained fraudulent bond endorsements from the scalawag governor (William H. Smith), and left the state a wretched heritage of defaulted obligations.[21]

Huge debts were saddled upon the Southern states with the meagerest improvements to show for them. Millions in bonds in South Carolina were issued contrary to law, taxation being greatly increased, while the total assessed value of property in the state declined from $489,000,000 in 1860 to $90,000,000 in 1866.[22] Delicate women were reported selling provisions needed for their hungry children, in order to pay taxes; while for failure to pay taxes Southern whites were losing lands which were bought up by Negroes or Nothern speculators.[23] South Carolina newspapers were "full of reports of sheriff's sales," 74,000 acres being put under tax sales in a brief period in Darlington County, 86,000 acres in Williamsburg County, and more than two thousand pieces of real estate in Charleston.[24] Tax rates in Mississippi were fourteen times as great in 1874 as in 1869, the public debt being piled up annually at the rate of $664,000.[25] Grants under the scalawag Holden régime to railroad companies in North Carolina exceeded $27,000,000.[26]

One of the flagrant evils of misgovernment was seen in the militia of carpetbag times. White desperadoes from Missouri, enlisted as Arkansas militiamen, tore up and down the state smashing property, destroying crops, and committing murder.[27] Groups of Negro militia in the same state became murderous mobs, with defiance born of the belief "that crimes committed . . . as a mob . . . [would] not subject them to . . . punishment."[28] A Negro militia detachment of more than a hundred men dashed into an Arkansas town and galloped about, cursing, threatening, raiding a grocery store, and breaking into the jail.[29] Because of the terrorism practiced by the militia in North Carolina, Governor Holden was impeached and removed from office.[30] In South Carolina militia troubles developed into a war of races as outraged whites organized to protect their property and lives against armed Negro militiamen.[31] In this commonwealth the militia was almost entirely colored, and it was reported that at least two-thirds of the militia expenditures were a "huge fraud," the amount being in reality used for "political services."[32]

To use a modern phrase, government under Radical Republican rule in the South had become a kind of "racket." A parasitic organization had been grafted on to the government itself, so that the agencies of rule and authority were manipulated for private and partisan ends. Often in the reconstructed states government bore a bogus quality: that which called itself government was an artificial fabrication. Where the chance of plunder was so alluring it was no wonder that rival factions would clash for control of the spoils, nor that outraged citizens, seeking to recover the government for the people, should resort to irregular and abnormal methods. At times this clash of factions created the demoralizing spectacle of dual or rival governments. In Louisiana the Warmoth-McEnery faction battled furiously with the Kellogg-Casey faction.[33] In South Carolina "was seen the . . . spectacle of two speakers and two Houses conducting deliberations in the same hall. Motions, . . . [etc.] were heard by the respective speakers; neither speaker, however, recognized members of the other House."[34] In Arkansas similar conditions produced the cheap melodrama of the "Brooks-Baxter war," with rival "armies" facing each other in support of their "governments," resulting in some actual bloodshed, various arrests for treason, sundry impeachments, not a little *opéra bouffe* comedy, and general confusion.[35]

Such, in brief, was the nature of carpetbag rule in the South. The concept which the Radicals sought to disseminate was that the problems of restoration had all been neatly solved, the country saved, and the South "reconstructed" by 1868. That dignified publication known as *American Annual Cyclopedia* began its preface for the year 1868 with the following amazing statement: "This volume of the *Annual Cyclopedia*, for the year 1868, presents the complete restoration, as members of the Union, of all the Southern states except three [Virginia, Mississippi, Texas], and the final disappearance of all difficulties between the citizens of those States and the Federal Government." The fact of the matter was that this "complete restoration" was merely the beginning of the corrupt and abusive era of carpetbag rule by the forcible imposition of Radical governments upon an unwilling and protesting people. Before this imposition took place the Southern states already had satisfactory governments. It is a serious misconception to suppose that Johnson's efforts in the South had been altogether a "failure." On the contrary, in the years from 1865 to 1868, when Congress had not "reconstructed" a state except Tennessee, and when state governments in the South were imperatively needed for domestic purposes, such governments were set up by Johnson. It must not be forgotten that these were native white governments

genuinely supported and put into power by the Southern people, and that they functioned in the preservation of order and internal government in those important years that intervened between the surrenders and the establishment of carpetbag misrule by Congress. If one would seek to measure the importance of this, let him contemplate what would have been the result if these commonwealths had made no such adjustment and had waited several years for Congress to supply the pattern for state governments. Instead of saying that reconstruction had been solved by Congress in 1868, the truer generalization would be that the transition to normal polity in the South had been pretty well worked out by Johnson, that it was violently interrupted by the Radicals, and that only after the overthrow of the Radical régime (about 1877) did genuine political reconstruction get underway with any fair prospect for the future.

Another unfair conclusion is to attribute the excesses of the carpetbag period to the Negro. Though the Radicals used Negro voting and officeholding for their own ends, Republican governments in the South were not Negro governments. Even where Negroes served, the governments were under white control. It is the contention of Carter G. Woodson that "most of the local offices . . . were held by the white men, and [that] those Negroes who did attain some of the higher offices were . . . about as competent as the average whites thereto elected." He also argues that illiteracy among Negro officeholders has been exaggerated.[36] That the first phase of the Negro's experience of freedom after centuries of slavery should occur under the degrading conditions of these carpetbag years was not the fault of the Negro himself, but of the whites who exploited him. . . .

NOTES

1. W. L. Fleming, ed., *Documentary History of Reconstruction*, II, 44.
2. *Ibid.*, II, 81–82.
3. *Ibid.*, II, 83.
4. *Ibid.*, II, 85–86.
5. H. C. Warmoth, *War, Politics and Reconstruction: Stormy Days in Louisiana*, 225.
6. Simkins and Woody, *South Carolina during Reconstruction*, 75 n.
7. *Ibid.*, 79.
8. *Ibid.*, 80.
9. E. P. Oberholtzer, *Hist. of the U.S. since the Civil War*, II, 45.
10. Quoted in Simkins and Woody, 110.
11. *Ibid*, 91.
12. *Ibid*, 92–93.
13. Fleming, *Doc. Hist.*, II, 39.
14. *Ibid.*, II, 41. 15. J. S. Pike, *The Prostrate State*, 12 ff., quoted in Fleming, *Doc. Hist.*, II, 51 ff.
16. So named after General Adelbert Ames of Maine, who was provisional governor, United States senator, and then governor of Mississippi in the carpetbag period, and under whose Radi-cal rule there was violent opposition among the whites, leading to terrorism over the state and a serious race riot at Vicksburg on December 7, 1874.
17. Fleming, *Doc. Hist.*, II, 42-43.
18. *Ibid.*, II, 50-51.
19. *Ibid.*, II, 59.
20. *Ibid.*, II, 69.
21. A. B. Moore, "Railroad Building in Alabama During the Reconstruction Period," *Jour. of Southern Hist.*, I, 421-441 (Nov., 1935), especially 427-430.
22. Simkins and Woody, 175.
23. *Ibid.*, 178-179.
24. *Ibid.*, 180-181.
25. Fleming, *Doc. Hist.*, II, 71.
26. J. G. de R. Hamilton, *Reconstruction in North Carolina*, 448.
27. Fleming, *Doc. Hist.*, II, 73 ff.
28. *Ibid.*, II, 77.
29. *Ibid.*, II, 76.
30. *Ibid.*, II, 78.
31. Simkins and Woody, 485.
32. Fleming, *Doc. Hist.* II, 79.
33. See below (sec. vi of the present chapter); see also H. C. Warmoth, *War, Politics and Reconstruction . . . in Louisiana*, 233, and *passim*.
34. Simkins and Woody, 524.
35. J. M. Harrell, *The Brooks and Baxter War: A History of the Reconstruction Period in Arkansas*.
36. Carter G. Woodson, *The Negro in Our History*, 403 ff.

NO

Eric Foner

THE NEW VIEW OF RECONSTRUCTION

In the past twenty years, no period of American history has been the subject of a more thoroughgoing reevaluation than Reconstruction—the violent, dramatic, and still controversial era following the Civil War. Race relations, politics, social life, and economic change during Reconstruction have all been reinterpreted in the light of changed attitudes toward the place of blacks within American society. If historians have not yet forged a fully satisfying portrait of Reconstruction as a whole, the traditional interpretation that dominated historical writing for much of this century has irrevocably been laid to rest.

Anyone who attended high school before 1960 learned that Reconstruction was an era of unrelieved sordidness in American political and social life. The martyred Lincoln, according to this view, had planned a quick and painless readmission of the Southern states as equal members of the national family. President Andrew Johnson, his successor, attempted to carry out Lincoln's policies but was foiled by the Radical Republicans (also known as Vindictives or Jacobins). Motivated by an irrational hatred of Rebels or by ties with Northern capitalists out to plunder the South, the Radicals swept aside Johnson's lenient program and fastened black supremacy upon the defeated Confederacy. An orgy of corruption followed, presided over by unscrupulous carpetbaggers (Northerners who ventured south to reap the spoils of office), traitorous scalawags (Southern whites who cooperated with the new governments for personal gain), and the ignorant and childlike freedmen, who were incapable of properly exercising the political power that had been thrust upon them. After much needless suffering, the white community of the South banded together to overthrow these "black" governments and restore home rule (their euphemism for white supremacy). All told, Reconstruction was just about the darkest page in the American saga.

Originating in Anti-Reconstruction propaganda of Southern Democrats during the 1870s, this traditional interpretation achieved scholarly legitimacy around the turn of the century through the work of William Dunning and his

Reprinted from *American Heritage* 34 (October/November 1983). Copyright © 1983 by American Heritage, a division of Forbes Inc. Reprinted by permission.

students at Columbia University. It reached the larger public through films like *Birth of a Nation* and *Gone With the Wind* and that best-selling work of myth-making masquerading as history, *The Tragic Era* by Claude G. Bowers. In language as exaggerated as it was colorful, Bowers told how Andrew Johnson "fought the bravest battle for constitutional liberty and for the preservation of our institutions ever waged by an Executive" but was overwhelmed by the "poisonous propaganda" of the Radicals. Southern whites, as a result, "literally were put to the torture" by "emissaries of hate" who manipulated the "simple-minded" freedmen, "inflaming the negroes' egotism" and even inspiring "lustful assaults" by blacks upon white womanhood.

In a discipline that sometimes seems to pride itself on the rapid rise and fall of historical interpretations, this traditional portrait of Reconstruction enjoyed remarkable staying power. The long reign of the old interpretation is not difficult to explain. It presented a set of easily identifiable heroes and villains. It enjoyed the imprimatur of the nation's leading scholars. And it accorded with the political and social realities of the first half of the century. This image of Reconstruction helped freeze the mind of the white South in unalterable opposition to any movement for breaching the ascendancy of the Democratic party, eliminating segregation, or readmitting disfranchised blacks to the vote.

Nevertheless, the demise of the traditional interpretation was inevitable, for it ignored the testimony of the central participant in the drama of Reconstruction—the black freedman. Furthermore, it was grounded in the conviction that blacks were unfit to share in political power. As Dunning's Columbia colleague John W. Burgess put it, "A black skin means membership in a race of men which has never of itself succeeded in subjecting passion to reason, has never, therefore, created any civilization of any kind." Once objective scholarship and modern experience rendered that assumption untenable, the entire edifice was bound to fall.

The work of "revising" the history of Reconstruction began with the writings of a handful of survivors of the era, such as John R. Lynch, who had served as a black congressman from Mississippi after the Civil War. In the 1930s white scholars like Francis Simkins and Robert Woody carried the task forward. Then, in 1935, the black historian and activist W. E. B. Du Bois produced *Black Reconstruction in America*, a monumental reevaluation that closed with an irrefutable indictment of a historical profession that had sacrificed scholarly objectivity on the altar of racial bias. "One fact and one alone," he wrote, "explains the attitude of most recent writers toward Reconstruction; they cannot conceive of Negroes as men." Du Bois's work, however, was ignored by most historians.

It was not until the 1960s that the full force of the revisionist wave broke over the field. Then, in rapid succession, virtually every assumption of the traditional viewpoint was systematically dismantled. A drastically different portrait emerged to take its place. President Lincoln did not have a coherent "plan" for Reconstruction, but at the time of his assassination he had been cautiously contemplating black suffrage. Andrew Johnson was a stubborn, racist politician who lacked the ability to compromise. By isolating himself from the broad currents of public opinion that had nourished

Lincoln's career, Johnson created an impasse with Congress that Lincoln would certainly have avoided, thus throwing away his political power and destroying his own plans for reconstructing the South.

The Radicals in Congress were acquitted of both vindictive motives and the charge of serving as the stalking-horses of Northern capitalism. They emerged instead as idealists in the best nineteenth-century reform tradition. Radical leaders like Charles Sumner and Thaddeus Stevens had worked for the rights of blacks long before any conceivable political advantage flowed from such a commitment. Stevens refused to sign the Pennsylvania Constitution of 1838 because it disfranchised the state's black citizens; Sumner led a fight in the 1850s to integrate Boston's public schools. Their Reconstruction policies were based on principle, not petty political advantage, for the central issue dividing Johnson and these Radical Republicans was the civil rights of freedmen. Studies of congressional policy-making, such as Eric L. McKitrick's *Andrew Johnson and Reconstruction*, also revealed that Reconstruction legislation, ranging from the Civil Rights Act of 1866 to the Fourteenth and Fifteenth Amendments, enjoyed broad support from moderate and conservative Republicans. It was not simply the work of a narrow radical faction.

Even more startling was the revised portrait of Reconstruction in the South itself. Imbued with the spirit of the civil rights movement and rejecting entirely the racial assumptions that had underpinned the traditional interpretation, these historians evaluated Reconstruction from the black point of view. Works like Joel Williamson's *After Slavery* portrayed the period as a time of extraordin-

ary political, social, and economic progress for blacks. The establishment of public school systems, the granting of equal citizenship to blacks, the effort to restore the devastated Southern economy, the attempt to construct an interracial political democracy from the ashes of slavery, all these were commendable achievements, not the elements of Bower's "tragic era."

Unlike earlier writers, the revisionists stressed the active role of the freedmen in shaping Reconstruction. Black initiative established as many schools as did Northern religious societies and the Freedmen's Bureau. The right to vote was not simply thrust upon them by meddling outsiders, since blacks began agitating for the suffrage as soon as they were freed. In 1865 black conventions throughout the South issued eloquent, though unheeded, appeals for equal civil and political rights.

With the advent of Radical Reconstruction in 1867, the freedmen did enjoy a real measure of political power. But black supremacy never existed. In most states blacks held only a small fraction of political offices, and even in South Carolina, where they comprised a majority of the state legislature's lower house, effective power remained in white hands. As for corruption, moral standards in both government and private enterprise were at low ebb throughout the nation in the postwar years—the era of Boss Tweed, the Credit Mobilier scandal, and the Whiskey Ring. Southern corruption could hardly be blamed on former slaves.

Other actors in the Reconstruction drama also came in for reevaluation. Most carpetbaggers were former Union soldiers seeking economic opportunity in the postwar South, not unscrupulous adventurers. Their motives, a typically

American amalgam of humanitarianism and the pursuit of profit, were no more insidious than those of Western pioneers. Scalawags, previously seen as traitors to the white race, now emerged as "Old Line" Whig Unionists who had opposed secession in the first place or as poor whites who had long resented planters' domination of Southern life and who saw in Reconstruction a chance to recast Southern society along more democratic lines. Strongholds of Southern white Republicanism like east Tennessee and western North Carolina had been the scene of resistance to Confederate rule throughout the Civil War; now, as one scalawag newspaper put it, the choice was "between salvation at the hand of the Negro or destruction at the hand of the rebels."

At the same time, the Ku Klux Klan and kindred groups, whose campaign of violence against black and white Republicans had been minimized or excused in older writings, were portrayed as they really were. Earlier scholars had conveyed the impression that the Klan intimidated blacks mainly by dressing as ghosts and playing on the freedmen's superstitions. In fact, black fears were all too real: the Klan was a terrorist organization that beat and killed its political opponents to deprive blacks of their newly won rights. The complicity of the Democratic party and the silence of prominent whites in the face of such outrages stood as an indictment of the moral code the South had inherited from the days of slavery.

By the end of the 1960s, then, the old interpretation had been completely reversed. Southern freedmen were the heroes, the "Redeemers" who overthrew Reconstruction were the villains, and if the era was "tragic," it was because

change did not go far enough. Reconstruction had been a time of real progress and its failure a lost opportunity for the South and the nation. But the legacy of Reconstruction—the Fourteenth and Fifteenth Amendments—endured to inspire future efforts for civil rights. As Kenneth Stampp wrote in *The Era of Reconstruction*, a superb summary of revisionist findings published in 1965, "If it was worth four years of civil war to save the Union, it was worth a few years of radical reconstruction to give the American Negro the ultimate promise of equal civil and political rights."

As Stampp's statement suggests, the reevaluation of the first Reconstruction was inspired in large measure by the impact of the second—the modern civil rights movement. And with the waning of that movement in recent years, writing on Reconstruction has undergone still another transformation. Instead of seeing the Civil War and its aftermath as a second American Revolution (as Charles Beard had), a regression into barbarism (as Bowers argued), or a golden opportunity squandered (as the revisionists saw it), recent writers argue that Radical Reconstruction was not really very radical. Since land was not distributed to the former slaves, they remained economically dependent upon their former owners. The planter class survived both the war and Reconstruction with its property (apart from slaves) and prestige more or less intact.

Not only changing times but also the changing concerns of historians have contributed to this latest reassessment of Reconstruction. The hallmark of the past decade's historical writing has been an emphasis upon "social history"—the evocation of the past lives of ordinary Americans—and the downplaying of strictly political events. When applied to Reconstruction, this concern with the "social" suggested that black suffrage and officeholding, once seen as the most radical departures of the Reconstruction era, were relatively insignificant.

Recent historians have focused their investigations not upon the politics of Reconstruction but upon the social and economic aspects of the transition from slavery to freedom. Herbert Gutman's influential study of the black family during and after slavery found little change in family structure or relations between men and women resulting from emancipation. Under slavery most blacks had lived in nuclear family units, although they faced the constant threat of separation from loved ones by sale. Reconstruction provided the opportunity for blacks to solidify their preexisting family ties. Conflicts over whether black women should work in the cotton fields (planters said yes, many black families said no) and over white attempts to "apprentice" black children revealed that the autonomy of family life was a major preoccupation of the freedmen. Indeed, whether manifested in their withdrawal from churches controlled by whites, in the blossoming of black fraternal, benevolent, and self-improvement organizations, or in the demise of the slave quarters and their replacement by small tenant farms occupied by individual families, the quest for independence from white authority and control over their own day-to-day lives shaped the black response to emancipation.

In the post-Civil War South the surest guarantee of economic autonomy, blacks believed, was land. To the freedmen the justice of a claim to land based on their years of unrequited labor appeared self-evident. As an Alabama black conven-

tion put it, "The property which they [the planters] hold was nearly all earned by the sweat of our brows." As Leon Litwack showed in Been in the Storm So Long, a Pulitzer-Prize-winning account of the black response to emancipation, many freedmen in 1865 and 1866 refused to sign labor contracts, expecting the federal government to give them land. In some localities, as one Alabama overseer reported, they "set up claims to the plantation and all on it."

In the end, of course, the vast majority of Southern blacks remained propertyless and poor. But exactly why the South, and especially its black population, suffered from dire poverty and economic retardation in the decades following the Civil War is a matter of much dispute. In One Kind of Freedom, economists Roger Ransom and Richard Sutch indicted country merchants for monopolizing credit and charging usurious interest rates, forcing black tenants into debt and locking the South into a dependence on cotton production that impoverished the entire region. But Jonathan Wiener, in his study of postwar Alabama, argued that planters used their political power to compel blacks to remain on the plantations. Planters succeeded in stabilizing the plantation system, but only by blocking the growth of alternative enterprises, like factories, that might draw off black laborers, thus locking the region into a pattern of economic backwardness.

If the thrust of recent writing has emphasized the social and economic aspects of Reconstruction, politics has not been entirely neglected. But political studies have also reflected the postrevisionist mood summarized by C. Vann Woodward when he observed "how essentially nonrevolutionary and conservative Reconstruction really was." Recent writers, unlike their revisionist predecessors, have found little to praise in federal policy toward the emancipated blacks.

A new sensitivity to the strength of prejudice and laissez-faire ideas in the nineteenth-century North has led many historians to doubt whether the Republican party ever made a genuine commitment to racial justice in the South. The granting of black suffrage was an alternative to a long-term federal responsibility for protecting the rights of the former slaves. Once enfranchised, blacks could be left to fend for themselves. With the exception of a few Radicals like Thaddeus Stevens, nearly all Northern policymakers and educators are criticized today for assuming that, so long as the unfettered operations of the marketplace afforded blacks the opportunity to advance through diligent labor, federal efforts to assist them in acquiring land were unnecessary.

Probably the most innovative recent writing on Reconstruction politics has centered on a broad reassessment of black Republicanism, largely undertaken by a new generation of black historians. Scholars like Thomas Holt and Nell Painter insist that Reconstruction was not simply a matter of black and white. Conflicts within the black community, no less than divisions among whites, shaped Reconstruction politics. Where revisionist scholars, both black and white, had celebrated the accomplishments of black political leaders, Holt, Painter, and others charge that they failed to address the economic plight of the black masses. Painter criticized "representative colored men," as national black leaders were called, for failing to provide ordinary freedmen with effective political leadership. Holt found that black officeholders in South Carolina

mostly emerged from the old free mulatto class of Charleston, which shared many assumptions with prominent whites. "Basically bourgeois in their origins and orientation," he wrote, they "failed to act in the interest of black peasants."

In emphasizing the persistence from slavery of divisions between free blacks and slaves, these writers reflect the increasing concern with continuity and conservatism in Reconstruction. Their work reflects a startling extension of revisionist premises. If, as has been argued for the past twenty years, blacks were active agents rather than mere victims of manipulation, then they could not be absolved of blame for the ultimate failure of Reconstruction.

Despite the excellence of recent writing and the continual expansion of our knowledge of the period, historians of Reconstruction today face a unique dilemma. An old interpretation has been overthrown, but a coherent new synthesis has yet to take its place. The revisionists of the 1960s effectively established a series of negative points: the Reconstruction governments were not as bad as had been portrayed, black supremacy was a myth, the Radicals were not cynical manipulators of the freedmen. Yet no convincing overall portrait of the quality of political and social life emerged from their writings. More recent historians have rightly pointed to elements of continuity that spanned the nineteenth-century Southern experience, especially the survival, in modified form, of the plantation system. Nevertheless, by denying the real changes that did occur, they have failed to provide a convincing portrait of an era characterized above all by drama, turmoil, and social change.

Building upon the findings of the past twenty years of scholarship, a new portrait of Reconstruction ought to begin by viewing it not as a specific time period, bounded by the years 1865 and 1877, but as an episode in a prolonged historical process—American society's adjustment to the consequences of the Civil War and emancipation. The Civil War, of course, raised the decisive questions of America's national existence: the relations between local and national authority, the definition of citizenship, the balance between force and consent in generating obedience to authority. The war and Reconstruction, as Allan Nevins observed over fifty years ago, marked the "emergence of modern America." This was the era of the completion of the national railroad network, the creation of the modern steel industry, the conquest of the West and final subduing of the Indians, and the expansion of the mining frontier. Lincoln's America—the world of the small farm and artisan shop—gave way to a rapidly industrializing economy. The issues that galvanized postwar Northern politics—from the question of the greenback currency to the mode of paying holders of the national debt— arose from the economic changes unleashed by the Civil War.

Above all, the war irrevocably abolished slavery. Since 1619, when "twenty negars" disembarked from a Dutch ship in Virginia, racial injustice had haunted American life, mocking its professed ideals even as tobacco and cotton, the products of slave labor, helped finance the nation's economic development. Now the implications of the black presence could no longer be ignored. The Civil War resolved the problem of slavery but, as the Philadelphia diarist Sydney George Fisher observed in June 1865, it opened an even more intractable problem: "What shall we do with the Negro?" Indeed, he went on, this was a problem *"incapable* of any solution that will satisfy both North and South."

As Fisher realized, the focal point of Reconstruction was the social revolution known as emancipation. Plantation slavery was simultaneously a system of labor, a form of racial domination, and the foundation upon which arose a distinctive ruling class within the South. Its demise threw open the most fundamental questions of economy, society, and politics. A new system of labor, social, racial, and political relations had to be created to replace slavery.

The United States was not the only nation to experience emancipation in the nineteenth century. Neither plantation slavery nor abolition were unique to the United States. But Reconstruction was. In a comparative perspective Radical Reconstruction stands as a remarkable experiment, the only effort of a society experiencing abolition to bring the former slaves within the umbrella of equal citizenship. Because the Radicals did not achieve everything they wanted, historians have lately tended to play down the stunning departure represented by black suffrage and officeholding. Former slaves, most fewer than two years removed from bondage, debated the fundamental questions of the polity: What is a republican form of government? Should the state provide equal education for all? How could political equality be reconciled with a society in which property was so unequally distributed? There was something inspiring in the way such men met the challenge of Reconstruction. "I knew nothing more than to obey my master," James K. Greene, an Alabama black politician later recalled. "But the tocsin of freedom sounded and knocked at the door and we walked out like free men and we met the exigencies as they grew up, and shouldered the responsibilities."

"You never saw a people more excited on the subject of politics than are the negroes of the South," one planter observed in 1867. And there were more than a few Southern whites as well who in these years shook off the prejudices of the past to embrace the vision of a new South dedicated to the principles of equal citizenship and social justice. One ordinary South Carolinian expressed the new sense of possibility in 1868 to the Republican governor of the state: "I am sorry that I cannot write an elegant stiled letter to your excellency. But I rejoice to think that God almighty has given to the poor of S.C. a Gov. to hear to feel to protect the humble poor without distinction to race or color. . . . I am a native borned S.C. a poor man never owned a Negro in my life nor my father before me. . . . Remember the true and loyal are the poor of the whites and blacks outside of these you can find none loyal."

Few modern scholars believe the Reconstruction governments established in the South in 1867 and 1868 fulfilled the aspirations of their humble constituents. While their achievements in such realms as education, civil rights, and the economic rebuilding of the South are now widely appreciated, historians today believe they failed to affect either the economic plight of the emancipated slave or the ongoing transformation of independent white farmers into cotton tenants. Yet their opponents did perceive the Reconstruction governments in precisely this way—as representatives of a revolution that had put the bottom rail, both racial and economic, on top. This percep-

tion helps explain the ferocity of the attacks leveled against them and the pervasiveness of violence in the postemancipation South.

The spectacle of black men voting and holding office was anathema to large numbers of Southern whites. Even more disturbing, at least in the view of those who still controlled the plantation regions of the South, was the emergence of local officials, black and white, who sympathized with the plight of the black laborer. Alabama's vagrancy law was a "dead letter" in 1870, "because those who are charged with its enforcement are indebted to the vagrant vote for their offices and emoluments." Political debates over the level and incidence of taxation, the control of crops, and the resolution of contract disputes revealed that a primary issue of Reconstruction was the role of government in a plantation society. During presidential Reconstruction, and after "Redemption," with planters and their allies in control of politics, the law emerged as a means of stabilizing and promoting the plantation system. If Radical Reconstruction failed to redistribute the land of the South, the ouster of the planter class from control of politics at least ensured that the sanctions of the criminal law would not be employed to discipline the black labor force.

An understanding of this fundamental conflict over the relation between government and society helps explain the pervasive complaints concerning corruption and "extravagance" during Radical Reconstruction. Corruption there was aplenty; tax rates did rise sharply. More significant than the rate of taxation, however, was the change in its incidence. For the first time, planters and white farmers had to pay a significant portion of their income to the government, while propertyless blacks often escaped scot-free. Several states, moreover, enacted heavy taxes on uncultivated land to discourage land speculation and force land onto the market, benefiting, it was hoped, the freedmen.

As time passed, complaints about the "extravagance" and corruption of Southern governments found a sympathetic audience among influential Northerners. The Democratic charge that universal suffrage in the South was responsible for high taxes and governmental extravagance coincided with a rising conviction among the urban middle classes of the North that city government had to be taken out of the hands of the immigrant poor and returned to the "best men"—the educated, professional, financially independent citizens unable to exert much political influence at a time of mass parties and machine politics. Increasingly the "respectable" middle classes began to retreat from the very notion of universal suffrage. The poor were no longer perceived as honest producers, the backbone of the social order; now they became the "dangerous classes," the "mob." As the historian Francis Parkman put it, too much power rested with "masses of imported ignorance and hereditary ineptitude." To Parkman the Irish of the Northern cities and the blacks of the South were equally incapable of utilizing the ballot: "Witness the municipal corruptions of New York, and the monstrosities of Negro rule in South Carolina." Such attitudes helped to justify Northern inaction as, one by one, the Reconstruction regimes of the South were overthrown by political violence.

In the end, then, neither the abolition of slavery nor Reconstruction succeeded in resolving the debate over the meaning of freedom in American life. Twenty years before the American Civil War, writing about the prospect of abolition in France's colonies, Alexis de Tocqueville had written, "If the Negroes have the right to become free, the [planters] have the incontestable right not to be ruined by the Negroes' freedom." And in the United States, as in nearly every plantation society that experienced the end of slavery, a rigid social and political dichotomy between former master and former slave, an ideology of racism, and a dependent labor force with limited economic opportunities all survived abolition. Unless one means by freedom the simple fact of not being a slave, emancipation thrust blacks into a kind of no-man's land, a partial freedom that made a mockery of the American ideal of equal citizenship.

Yet by the same token the ultimate outcome underscores the uniqueness of Reconstruction itself. Alone among the societies that abolished slavery in the nineteenth century, the United States, for a moment, offered the freedmen a measure of political control over their own destinies. However brief its sway, Reconstruction allowed scope for a remarkable political and social mobilization of the black community. It opened doors of opportunity that could never be completely closed. Reconstruction transformed the lives of Southern blacks in ways unmeasurable by statistics and unreachable by law. It raised their expectations and aspirations, redefined their status in relation to the larger society, and allowed space for the creation of institutions that enabled them to survive the repression that followed. And it established constitutional principles of civil and political equality that, while flagrantly violated after Redemption, planted the seeds of future struggle.

Certainly, in terms of the sense of possibility with which it opened, Reconstruction failed. But as Du Bois observed, it was a "splendid failure." For its animating vision—a society in which social advancement would be open to all on the basis of individual merit, not inherited caste distinctions—is as old as America itself and remains relevant to a nation still grappling with the unresolved legacy of emancipation.

POSTSCRIPT

Was Reconstruction a Total Failure?

Both the traditional and revisionist writers of Reconstruction history have treated blacks in a passive manner. Traditionalists like Randall, who assumed the intellectual inferiority of Negroes to whites, argued that black politicians were the junior partners of the white carpetbaggers and scalawags in looting the Reconstruction governments. Revisionists like Kenneth M. Stampp, who believed in the biological equality of all human races, maintained that the black politicians did not constitute a majority in the Reconstruction government, were not totally corrupt, and did not want to disenfranchise whites but only desired their political and social constitutional rights. Writing at the peak of the civil rights movement in 1965, it appears that Stampp was trying to assure his readers that blacks only wanted to become good Americans and obtain (in this second Reconstruction Era) what had been denied them a century ago.

Professor Foner's essay makes it clear that the Reconstruction Era is in search of a new synthesis. One area that deserves further investigation is the role of the era's ex-slaves. In recent years, slavery has been reinterpreted from the point of view of the slaves rather than the slave owners. Post-revisionist writers must look at the newly freed blacks as actively struggling to achieve their rights and to assume their new responsibilities in the post–Civil War society.

Recent writers of this period have taken two different approaches—local history and comparative history. Thomas Holt's *Black Over White* (Illinois, 1977) is a sophisticated study of Negro political leadership in South Carolina during Reconstruction. Combining traditional sources like old letters, military service records, and newspapers with sophisticated quantitative analyses of voting records, Holt gives a complex picture of that reconstructed state. Reconstruction failed in South Carolina, says Holt, not because of corruption but because Negro leaders failed to develop a clear and unifying ideology to challenge whites who wanted to restore white supremacy.

Clearly, Holt is arguing from a "pessimistic" viewpoint which believes that Reconstruction accomplished very little because the federal government did not break up "the planter class" and give every former slave "forty acres and a mule." More hopeful about the achievements of the Reconstruction Era is Professor Eric Foner. In a series of essays published in 1984 by the Louisiana State University Press, Foner's *Nothing But Freedom: Emancipation and Its Legacy* compares American ex-slaves with those newly emancipated in Haiti and the British West Indies. Only in America were the freed men given voting and economic rights. Though these rights had been taken away from the majority of blacks by 1900, Reconstruction had, nevertheless, created a legacy of freedom which inspired succeeding generations of blacks.

Foner has provided us with the most recent summary of *Reconstruction: America's Unfinished Revolution, 1863–1867* (Harper & Row, 1988), a masterful treatment which should be compared with older works such as William Archibald Dunning's older, biased classic on *Reconstruction: Political and Economic* (Harper & Row, 1907) and E. Merton Coulter, *The South During Reconstruction, 1865–1877* (LSU Press, 1947), the last major work on the era written from the Dunning viewpoint. Before tackling Foner, students should read Kenneth M. Stampp's *The Era of Reconstruction, 1865–1877* (Knopf, 1965) and Michael Perman's *Emancipation and Reconstruction, 1862–1879* (Harlan Davidson, 1987). Finally, Staughton Lloyd has edited one of the best collections on *Reconstruction* (Harper & Row, 1967), which surveys the main viewpoints on the era.

CONTRIBUTORS
TO THIS VOLUME

EDITORS

JAMES SORELLE, a native Texan, received a Bachelor of Arts (1972) and a Master of Arts (1974) degree from the University of Houston and a Ph.D. from Kent State University (1980). He has taught at Ball State University and currently is an assistant professor of history at Baylor University. In addition to introductory courses in Western Civilization and American history, he teaches upper-level sections in Afro-American, urban, and late nineteenth- and twentieth-century United States history. His scholarly articles have appeared in the *Houston Review, Southwestern Historical Quarterly*, and a forthcoming anthology, *Black Dixie: Essays in Afro-Texan History in Houston*. He also has contributed entries to *The Handbook of Texas*.

LARRY MADARAS was born in Bayonne, New Jersey, in 1937. He attended Xavier High School in New York City and received his Bachelor's degree from Holy Cross College in 1959, an M.A. from New York University in 1961, and a Ph.D. from New York University in 1964. He has taught at Spring Hill College, the University of South Alabama, and the University of Maryland at College Park. He is currently teaching history and political science full-time at Howard Community College in Columbia, Maryland. He has been a Fulbright Fellow and has held two fellowships from the National Endowment for the Humanities. He is the author of dozens of journal articles and book reviews.

STAFF

Marguerite L. Egan   Program Manager
Brenda S. Filley   Production Manager
Whit Vye   Designer
Libra Ann Cusack   Typesetting Coordinator
Julie Arbo   Typesetter
Jean Bailey   Graphics Coordinator
Shawn Callahan   Graphics
Diane Barker   Editorial Assistant

AUTHORS

IRVING H. BARTLETT is a professor of American Studies at the University of Massachusetts in Boston, Massachusetts.

M. E. BRADFORD is a professor of English literature at the University of Dallas in Texas.

JON BUTLER is a professor of religious studies and American studies at Yale University.

LOIS GREEN CARR is an adjunct professor at the University of Maryland, College Park, and is also associated with the St. Mary's City Historic Commission.

HENRY STEELE COMMAGER has taught history for more than sixty years at New York University and Columbia University, among others, and is currently professor emeritus at Amherst University.

The late **AVERY CRAVEN** was professor emeritus of history at the University of Chicago.

CARL N. DEGLER is professor of history at Stanford University and a Pulitzer Prize-winning author whose social history text, *Out of the Past*, is now in its third edition.

ROBERT HUGH FERRELL is professor of diplomatic history at the University of Indiana and the author of numerous books, including *Woodrow Wilson and World War I: 1917–1921* (Harper & Row, 1982).

ERIC FONER is professor of history at Columbia University and the author of the major synthesis on *Reconstruction: America's Unfinished Business, 1863–1877* (Harper & Row, 1987).

EUGENE D. GENOVESE is professor of history at the University of Rochester and author of the major synthesis on slavery entitled *Roll Jordan Roll*.

The late **CARLTON J. H. HAYES** taught European history at Columbia University from 1910 to 1950, served as United States ambassador to Spain from 1942 to 1945, and was elected president of the American Historical Association in 1946.

The late **RICHARD HOFSTADTER** was professor of history at Columbia University and the greatest historian of the post–World War II generation. His books *The American Political Tradition* and *The Age of Reform* are considered classics.

RICHARD R. JOHNSON is associate professor of history at the University of Washington.

MICHAEL B. KATZ is a professor of history at the University of Pennsylvania in Philadelphia.

LYLE KOEHLER received a Ph.D. from the University of Cincinnati and works there in an administrative position.

ALLAN KULIKOFF is professor of history at Northern Illinois University in DeKalb.

JEAN BUTENHOFF LEE is an associate professor of history at the University of Wisconsin, Madison.

GERDA LERNER is Robinson-Edwards Professor of History at the University of Wisconsin, Madison.

RICHARD P. McCORMICK is professor of history at Rutgers University and author of numerous works on nineteenth-century politics, including *The Presidential Game: The Origins of American Presidential Politics* (Oxford University Press).

FORREST McDONALD is professor of history at the University of Alabama. In 1987 he was appointed by the National Endowment for the Humanities as the sixteenth Jefferson Lecturer in the Humanities.

WILLIAM G. McLOUGHLIN is a professor of history at Brown University in Rhode Island.

RICHARD B. MORRIS is the Governor Morris Professor of History Emeritus at Columbia University in New York City. Author of numerous publications on early American history, Morris's most recent work is *The Forging of the Union, 1781–1789.*

GARY B. NASH is a professor of history at UCLA and has written *Red, White, and Black*, which has changed our conception of the colonial period.

STEPHEN B. OATES is a professor of history at the University of Massachusetts, Amherst, and has written biographies of Nat Turner, John Brown, Abraham Lincoln, and Martin Luther King, Jr.

LESLIE HOWARD OWENS is a professor of history in the Afro-American program at the State University of New York at Stony Brook.

MICHAEL PARENTI received his Ph.D. from Yale University and has taught courses in political science at various colleges and universities. His most recent books are *Inventing Reality: The Politics of the Mass Media* and *The Sword and the Dollar: Imperialism, Revolution, and the Cold War.*

EDWARD PESSEN is a professor of history at Baruch College at the City Univeristy of New York and has written several important works on Jacksonian democracy.

The late **J. G. RANDALL** was the author of the standard textbook *The Civil War and Reconstruction* as well as a four-volume biography of Abraham Lincoln.

ROBERT V. REMINI is professor of history at the University of Illinois at Chicago Circle and is the author of six books about Andrew Jackson.

RAMON EDUARDO RUIZ is professor of history at the University of California, San Diego.

KENNETH STAMPP is Morrison Professor of History Emeritus at the University of California, Berkeley.

The late **ALICE FELT TYLER** was a professor of history at the University of Minnesota.

ALDEN T. VAUGHAN is professor of history at Columbia University.

LORENA S. WALSH is a fellow with the Colonial Williamsburg Foundation and has written several key articles on seventeenth-century Maryland.

NANCY WOLOCH has taught at several universities and has been a fellow of the National Endowment for the Humanities.

INDEX